Rosamond Jacob Diary Ms33,582, NLI.

ROSAMOND JACOB

THIRD PERSON SINGULAR

Leeann Lane

UNIVERSITY COLLEGE DUBLIN PRESS

PREAS CHOLÁISTE OLLSCOILE BHAILE ÁTHA CLIATH

2010

First published 2010
by University College Dublin Press
Newman House
86 St Stephen's Green
Dublin 2
Ireland
www.ucdpress.ie

© Leeann Lane 2010

ISBN 978-1-906359-54-6

CIP data available from the British Library

*The right of Leeann Lane to be identified as the
author of this work has been asserted by her*

Typeset in Scotland in Adobe Caslon and
Bodoni Oldstyle by Ryan Shiels
Printed in England on acid-free paper by
CPI Antony Rowe, Chippenham, Wilts.

Contents

—

Acknowledgements

—

In writing this book I have accrued numerous debts of gratitude. I would like to thank Irish Studies in Boston College for awarding me the summer fellowship in 2007 which allowed this work to develop. Thank you to my colleagues in Mater Dei Institute of Education (DCU).

I would like to acknowledge the help of the staff of the National Library of Ireland, the National Archives of Ireland and the society of friends libraries in Dublin and Waterford. I would like to thank and acknowledge the professionalism and patience of Barbara Mennell and Noelle Moran of UCD Press. They were a pleasure to work with.

Professor Maria Luddy encouraged this biography from the beginning and kept me motivated during periods in which my resolve flagged. To her and Professor Gerardine Meaney thanks are due for many interesting conversations on the importance of Jacob's diaries.

Catriona Crowe has fully supported this project and her enthusiasm and encouragement were unfailing and much appreciated.

Thank you to Derek Speirs for his expert help in reproducing images for the book.

Thank you also to Rachel Granville, Kevin Hickey, Dr Sinéad Kennedy, Dr Mary McAuliffe, Dr William Murphy and Dr Angela Veale. And to Dr Catherine Cox, a special thank you for stimulating discussions on history and writing, and for much support.

Finally thank you to my parents, Renée Lane and Dr Pat Lane, for their unfailing encouragement, and to my sister, Niamh.

LEEANN LANE
Irish Studies
Mater Dei Institute of Education
Dublin City University
October, 2010

Abbreviations

—

AE	George Russell
AOH	Ancient Order of Hibernians
BMH	Bureau of Military History
CID	Criminal Investigation Department
CND	Campaign for Nuclear Disarmament
GAA	Gaelic Athletic Association
GPO	General Post Office
IAOS	Irish Agricultural Organisation Society
IAVS	Irish Anti-Vivisection Society
IAW	International Alliance of Women
ICA	Irish Countrywomen's Association/Irish Citizen Army
IHA	The Irish Housewives Association
IHC	Irish Housewives Committee
IIL	Irish International League
IPP	Irish Parliamentary Party
IRB	Irish Republican Brotherhood
IV	Irish Volunteers
IVDF	Irish Volunteer Dependants' Fund
IWCA	Irish Women's Citizens and Local Government Association
IWFL	Irish Women's Franchise League
IWRL	Irish Women's Reform League
IWSF	Irish Women's Suffrage Federation
IWSLGA	Irish Women's Suffrage and Local Government Association
IWWU	Irish Women's Workers' Union
MWFL	Munster Women's Franchise League
NAA	Irish National Aid Association
NAI	National Archives Ireland
NATO	North Atlantic Treaty Organization
NAVDF	National Aid and Volunteer Dependants' Fund
RIC	Royal Irish Constabulary
RJD	Rosamond Jacob Diary
RJP	Rosamond Jacob Papers
SPCA	Society for the Prevention of Cruelty to Animals
SSP	Sheehy Skeffington Papers

UCD	University College Dublin
UI	United Irishmen
WILPF	Irish Women's International League for Peace and Freedom
WPDL	Women Prisoners' Defence League
WS	Witness Statement
WSPL	Women's Social and Political League
WSPU	Women's Social and Political Union
YMCA	Youth Men's Christian Association

Louis Jacob, Rosamond's father, 1897 Ms33,135, NLI.

Frank Ryan Graduation from UCD with a BA in Celtic Studies, 1925 Ms33,131, NLI.

ONE

INTRODUCTION(S)

—

A study of an individual life can illuminate social, economic, political and cultural patterns of change within society. Recent biographies of key figures in Irish republican and nationalist history have adopted this approach. Richard English's biography of Ernie O'Malley sees a study of the life as a means of closely investigating 'key themes in modern Irish experience'.[1] Likewise, one of the merits in a biographical study of Rosamond Jacob (1888–1960) was her involvement in so many of the diverse and intersecting campaigns of the revolutionary and Free State periods. What aids the historian in reconstructing her life is the large archive she bequeathed to posterity. The Jacob papers include a number of historically interesting unpublished novels. Of particular interest, however, is her daily diary maintained from 1897 until her death in 1960.[2]

In keeping with the chronological structure of most biographies, Jacob's life cycle is the spine running through this study. This first chapter acts as an introduction, setting the family background, the lapsed Quaker faith of the Jacobs and their commitment to nationalist and humanitarian politics. This introduction also establishes the themes that transcend the chronological spine of the work. The study begins by examining Jacob's involvement in suffrage and nationalist politics in the early twentieth century. Jacob's accounts of how local branches of organisations such as the Gaelic League, Sinn Féin and Cumann na mBan operated in Waterford allows the lens to be placed outside the metropolitan, the traditional focus of historians working in the areas of cultural nationalism and the suffrage campaign. Viewed from the position of historical hindsight, Jacob's activism up to 1922 coincided with the period when she was most optimistic, politically and personally. She was young, Dublin was lively and life beckoned. For radical women such as Jacob, active in the national and suffrage cause and the politics of cultural revival prior to 1922, the advent of Irish independence proved a disillusioning experience. This sense of disillusionment was mirrored in Jacob's personal life. She failed to

1   Richard English, *Ernie O'Malley: IRA Intellectual* (Oxford: Oxford University Press, 1998), p. vii.
2   The Jacob papers are held in the National Library of Ireland. Hereafter NLI. Rosamond Jacob Diary Ms 32,582 (1–171), NLI. Hereafter RJD and specific volume number.

establish herself as a successful writer and, unmarried, became increasingly lonely. By the mid 1930s her relationship with IRA activist and republican socialist, Frank Ryan, was over. By this time the excitement of first-wave feminism had become history and the subject of radio talks.[3] Commemoration was a feature of Jacob's life more than activism from this point. Jacob, as an increasingly isolated, single woman found social outlet and community in the organisations of female activism and self worth in philanthropic activities. Her diary entries are also noteworthy for the insight they offer into the later lives of women who were active in the nationalist cause or women who lost relatives in the service of the revolutionary struggle. Jacob records how many of these women perceived themselves as forgotten by a State which they believed owed them recognition and material recompense for their participation, or the involvement of their close relatives, in the national struggle. Notable examples are Jacob's descriptions of the later lives of Meg Connery, active in Cumann na mBan, and Mrs Mellows whose son Liam died during the Irish Civil War.[4]

A LIFE MORE ORDINARY

Amongst historians and literary critics Rosamond Jacob, if she registers at all, is a lesser-known novelist. She is labelled a feminist for her involvement in the suffrage cause and the campaigns for female equality in the Free State and she is the woman who had the 'affair' with the darling of republican Dublin in the 1920s and early 1930s – Frank Ryan. Historians are always constrained by the exigencies of what sources survive and it is noteworthy that Jacob's archive is so much richer in terms of actual physical sources when compared to more prominent female activists of the period, notably Dorothy Macardle, author of the first full scale account of the revolutionary period, *The Irish Republic*.[5] Indeed, Nadia Smith, in her recent biography of Macardle, notes that it was Jacob's 'extraordinary diary, which made the reconstruction of Dorothy's life

3   17 Aug. 1937, RJD Ms (82).
4   Meg Connery was a member of the Irish Women's Franchise League and Cumann na mBan and was active in many of the campaigns for female equality in the Free State period. She travelled to the Soviet Union with Jacob in 1931 as part of the deputation of the Irish Friends of Soviet Russia. Liam Mellows began his nationalist career as a member of the Fianna, becoming a member of the secret IRB in 1912. He was a founding member of the Irish Volunteers. Mellows was arrested as a member of the anti-Treaty side in September 1922 having been involved in the siege of the Four Courts in June. He was executed by the Free State Government on 8 December 1922. R. F. Foster, *Modern Ireland 1600–1972* (London: Penguin, 1989), p. 511.
5   Dorothy Macardle, *The Irish Republic* (London: Victor Gollancz, 1937).

possible'.[6] This diary falls under the category of what Philippe Lejeune describes as an 'all-purpose diary, written to accompany a life for as long as possible'.[7] The question arises as to how this archival material should be used. Jacob's archive is rich; her diary offers very detailed accounts of Irish politics and society, obviously from her particular perspective. To date, historians and literary critics have used Jacob's diaries as a source to plunder. Because she recorded in some detail most of the major debates and campaigns of Irish politics and culture of the first half of the twentieth century, historians have plucked sections often with no contextualisation of the diary or Jacob.[8] And as Cynthia Huff states in her consideration of manuscript diaries written by women: 'they remain archived: important enough to be preserved, but not important enough to be duplicated and publicly disseminated'.[9]

The ease with which the diary has been divorced from its writer and allowed to stand apart as a text providing colour and context for work on the revolutionary period and the years of internecine strife and bitterness after 1922 has much to do with Jacob's lack of the apparent exceptionality which merits biographical or critical study.[10] Unlike most subjects of Irish biography Jacob was not a prominent figure in Irish history, rather she was a fringe activist. Her fictional writings, although interesting to an historian, have limited aesthetic value. Jacob was in many cases a crowd member rather than a leader in the campaigns in which she participated – the turn of the century language revival, the suffrage campaign, the campaigns of the revolutionary period. She adopted an anti-Treaty stance in the 1920s moving towards a fringe involvement in the activities of socialist republicanism in the early 1930s while continuing to vote Fianna Fáil. Her commitment to feminist concerns

6   Nadia Clare Smith, *Dorothy Macardle: A Life* (Dublin: Woodfield Press, 2007), p. 1.

7   Philippe Lejeune, 'How do diaries end?', *Biography* 24: 1 (2001), p. 101.

8   Jacob's diary has been used as a source in Fearghal McGarry, *Frank Ryan*, 2nd edn (Dublin: UCD Press, 2010); Adrian Hoar, *In Green and Red: The Lives of Frank Ryan* (Dingle: Brandon, 2004); Smith, *Dorothy Macardle*.

9   Cynthia Anne Huff, 'Reading as re-vision: approaches to reading manuscript diaries', *Biography* 23: 3 (2000), p. 509. At the time of writing Professor Maria Luddy and Professor Gerardine Meaney are engaged in work to publish Jacob's diaries.

10 For an exception see Gerardine Meaney, 'Regendering modernism: the woman artist in Irish women's fiction', *Women: A Cultural Review* 15: 1 (2004). Both Meaney and Damian Doyle use Jacob's diary as a means of critiquing Kate O'Brien and Elizabeth Bowen. Gerardine Meaney, 'Women and writing, 1700–1960' in Angela Bourke et al. (eds), *The Field Day Anthology of Irish Writing*, vol. v (Cork: Cork University Press, 2002); Damian Doyle, 'A bio-critical study of Rosamond Jacob and her contemporaries', unpublished PhD thesis, University of Colorado, 2000. Although Meaney notably cites the importance of Jacob's novel *The Troubled House* in *The Field Day Anthology*, there is still no work which foregrounds Jacob.

was life long but at no point did she take or was capable of a leadership role. However, it was Jacob's failure to carve out a strong place in history as an activist which makes her interesting as a subject for biography. Her 'ordinariness' offers an alternative lens on the biographical project.[11] By failing to marry, by her inability to find meaningful paid work, by her countless refusals from publishers, by the limited sales of what work was published, Jacob offers a key into lives more ordinary within the urban middle classes of her time, and suggests a new perspective on female lives. Jacob's life, galvanised at all times by political and feminist debate, offers a means of exploring how the central issues which shaped Irish politics and society in the first half of the twentieth century were experienced and digested by those outside the leadership cadre. The history of the independence struggle and its aftermath is as much the history of men and women such as Jacob as it is of de Valera and Frank Ryan. Robert Fothergill in his study of English diaries discusses how the form permits an alternative perspective on 'the substance of history', turning it 'inside out'. Where one habitually thought of 'ordinary lives; forming a vast background to historical "events" now one's vision is of the great events passing behind the immediate realities that comprise an individual's experience . . . In the foreground is the individual consciousness, absolutely resisting the insistence of future historians that it should experience itself as peripheral'.[12]

One of the central themes that transcends the chronological spine of the biography is the position of single, heterosexual, women in the Free State. Katherine Holden states that 'marital status is a vital but largely unexamined analytical category for historians'.

The unmarried state is generally viewed as a stage or stages in the lifecycle preceding or following marriage, with never-married people seen as exceptions to the norm. Thus, while scholars have paid attention to power relations surrounding

11   The notion of 'investigating the torpor of an ordinary existence' was taken to a new level by the French historian, Alain Corbin, in his attempt to rediscover the world of the unknown and unexceptional nineteenth-century French clog maker, Louis-François Pinagot. Corbin writes that the history of 'the people' is based on a study of those 'who, by the mere fact of taking up their pens, excluded themselves from the milieus they described . . . On the basis of their writings we have been treated to any number of studies of "working-class language", "women's language", and the "literature of the excluded"'. Jacob, of course, was no Pinagot but her position outside the leadership cadre of feminist and nationalist activism offers a new perspective. Alain Corbin, *The Life of an Unknown: The Rediscovered World of a Clog Maker in Nineteenth-Century France* (New York: Columbia University Press, 2001), p. vii.
12   Robert A. Fothergill, *Private Chronicles: A Study of English Diaries* (London: Oxford University Press, 1974), p. 9.

workers, women, homosexuals, colonial people and people of colour, few similar analyses have been made of marital status from the perspective of single people.[13]

The ideology of domesticity and separate spheres that was pervasive in Free State Ireland permeates Jacob's diary; like so many of her generation of females, as a single woman with limited formal education, she was forced increasingly to live on the fringes of society. This sense of personal elision in Irish society was compounded by her increasing hostility to the dominant Catholic ethos of the new State. It was not just her gender coupled with her unmarried status that relegated Jacob to a fringe position in Irish society. From a middle-class Quaker background she did not fit neatly a Free State Ireland; the specifically Catholic middle-class values on which the ideologies of the new State were premised did not accord her a sense of belonging. English discusses the manner in which the Irish Revolution was a Catholic Revolution resulting in a very specific Republican 'definition of the national community' that 'rested on a series of interconnected foundations: religious, cultural, historical, and political'.[14] In many respects Jacob's concern with issues of mixed marriage within her own family in the 1940s indicates that her experience of the new State mirrored that recorded of, and by, many Irish Anglicans.[15]

Jacob's affair has always been discussed from the perspective of Ryan, notably in McGarry's and Hoar's biographical studies. Both historians have mined Jacob's diaries for what they can add to Ryan's politics. Yet the affair throws up more interesting concerns in relation to Jacob's own life and the position of single women in Irish society in the period. The wider perceptions and ramifications of the affair are interesting for what they say about women who did not fit neatly into the dominant domestic paradigm of wife and mother. This biography foregrounds the affair, not just because it was a defining experience from Jacob's perspective, but also to make a number of wider points to counter very stratified thinking about women's roles in Irish society in the period. Ryan and Jacob's affair was one in which he controlled when and where they met; he refused to acknowledge the relationship in public. One of the main questions that should be asked then is to what extent

13   Katherine Holden, *The Shadow of Marriage: Singleness in England 1914–60* (Manchester: Manchester University Press, 2007), p. 1.

14   English, *Ernie O'Malley*, p. 89.

15   F. S. L. Lyons discusses how Anglican minority in the Free State fluctuated between 'moods of almost total alienation and periods of relative tranquillity'. F. S. L. Lyons, 'The minority problem in the 26 counties' in Francis MacManus (ed.), *The Years of the Great Test* (Dublin: Mercier, 1967), p. 92. See also essays by Hubert Butler, for example, 'Boycott village' in Hubert Butler, *The Sub-Prefect Should Have Held his Tongue, and Other Essays* (London: Allen Lane, 1990).

is it valuable to foreground this secretive affair given Jacob's feminist leanings. The affair, in fact, allows an interrogation of certain terms or assumptions which are used in writing about female activism and which tend to simplify the reality of lived experiences. In particular, there is the assumption that women such as Jacob who were concerned with gender equality did not want to marry or form heterosexual relationships, and thus had no interest in the private sphere.

Any biographer is faced with the question of how far their subject is *sui generis*. Certainly, one has to take into account issues of personality. Jacob was a difficult individual, quick to take offence and lacking good social skills. A strong-faced woman who wore her hair in a simple bob, Jacob might be described as plain. Without doubt she had little confidence in her power to attract men, believing she lacked the requisite feminine charms and looks. Her contemporaries viewed her as an awkward individual. Jacob was aware of her shortcomings and the manner in which they influenced people's perceptions of her. Her description of Mary Pearse, sister of Patrick, who she met in 1916, offers an interesting insight into Jacob's self-knowledge:

> Miss Pearse & I came home together; she is very interesting & queer. She never seems to have tried to adapt herself to anyone a bit, & has never been thrown with other people, & so finds them all silly & troublesome – like an exaggerated copy of me.[16]

All this Jacob wrote into the character of Constance in her unpublished novel, 'Third person singular', written in the 1930s.[17] However notwithstanding personality quirks, Jacob's experience as a single woman in the first half of the twentieth century offers an insight into female lives outside the dominant domestic paradigm of the period, worthy of further exploration.

KEEPING A DIARY

In considering the interpretation of Jacob's diary a number of questions emerge. The motivation for why a person writes a diary needs to be addressed and the intended audience must be considered. In Oscar Wilde's *The Importance of Being Earnest* Cecily Cardew keeps a diary, describing it as 'simply a young girl's record of her own thoughts and impressions, and consequently meant for publication'.[18] Bloom discusses how 'truly private diaries

16   15 Dec. 1916, RJD Ms (30).
17   Rosamond Jacob, 'Third person singular', Rosamond Jacob papers, Ms 33,113(2), NLI. Hereafter RJP.
18   Oscar Wilde, *The Importance of Being Earnest* (London: A & C Black, 2004), p. 102.

are those bare-bones works' that record details of expenditure, the weather, visits to neighbours, etc. These types of 'bare-bones works' are 'so terse they seem coded; no reader outside the author's immediate society or household could understand them without extra-textual information'.[19] That Jacob's is not such a terse text, a line-a-day diary, is evidenced by the ease with which it has been mined for information about the political campaigns of the early Free State period. Yet Jacob did not intend her diary for publication; it is not in that sense a public diary as defined by Bloom.[20] Nevertheless she preserved it and continued to keep it into old age without any reference to its destruction. Moreover the diary is a layered text. There are 170 'ordinary' volumes of the diary dated 1897–1960. The final volume can be described as a type of 'secret diary'.[21] The 'secret' or 'second layer diary', which was written sporadically and spanned the major incidents in her life, was much more frank about her affair with Ryan and other relationships than the 'ordinary' or 'first layer' diary.[22] A diary in itself conjures up connotations of secrecy and privacy; Jacob then had a diary within a diary; her account of her life was layered. Within the 'first layer' diary there are, indeed, further layers. At the end of each calendar year Jacob engaged in an act of closure, summarising in hindsight the year's key events and concerns.[23]

In considering Jacob's increasing sense of existence at the fringes of an Irish society premised on motherhood and family, it is necessary to continue to interrogate the diary as a source, not just for what one reads in it but also for the question of the motivation for keeping it. Even if the writer does not intend his or her diary for public consumption, the very act of writing changes the events referred to. There is a degree of construction involved. Events are ordered, shaped, a certain view of self is put forward. How and why Jacob's view of self was shaped by the social, economic and political circumstances of her existence at various points in her life cycle is the concern of this biography. Lejeune notes how the all-purpose lifelong diary is rare. Many diary writers use the diary as an activity during periods of crisis. An adolescent diary often

19   Lynn Z. Bloom, "'I write for myself and strangers": private diaries as public documents' in Suzanne L. Bunkers and Cynthia A. Huff (eds), *Inscribing the Daily: Critical Essays on Women's Diaries* (Amherst: University of Massachusetts Press, 1996), p. 25.

20   Ibid., pp. 28–35.

21   RJD Ms (171).

22   The 'first layer' diary is very similar to certain Irish Quaker diaries that transcended the 'journal of conscience' genre. The famous example is Mary Leadbeater's diary of life and local politics in Ballitore, County Kildare in the late eighteenth and early nineteenth centuries. The diary spans the years 1769–1826. Ms 9292–346, NLI.

23   Lejeune, 'How do diaries end?', pp. 101–2.

ends on the brink of a great love affair. By contrast, there are examples of
diaries which end as life is overtaken by crisis, illness of family members, etc.[24]
Jacob's increasingly peripheral position in society meant that she did not
experience any of the factors which in many cases caused other diarists to
bring their text to an end. Her affair with Ryan did not come to any abrupt
end or point of crisis but rather fizzled out. A diary can, Lejeune argues, 'give
life the consistency and continuity it lacks'. In many respects keeping a diary is
an 'acceptance of life'. In Lejeune's words 'by writing today, you prepare your-
self to be able to live tomorrow, and to piece together, in a predetermined
framework of writing, the story of what you will have lived'.[25] Bloom's
comment on the self-focus in diaries is applicable to Jacob: 'through the act of
writing, the author not only composes her own character, she moves that
character to centre stage, becoming the principal actor in the drama of her
own story – whether in real life she was a major figure *or a bit player in a cast of
hundreds or thousands*' (my italics).[26] Jacob's use of her diary to impose order
and consistency on her life can be seen in her sometimes obsessive need to
ensure as complete a record as possible. Jacob's habits of composition mirrored
those of many diarists. Like the seventeenth-century Pepys, she did not always
enter events daily. At times she constructed the diary in stages, writing rough
notes which she then transcribed into the official volumes; she was forced
occasionally to return to old letters, spending a degree of time searching for
information to fill gaps in her memory. In 1924 she recorded that she spent an
evening in Waterford searching through letters she had sent to her Aunt
Hannah; there was, she wrote, 'a hole in my diary then, and I wanted them'. [27]
Her trip to the Soviet Union in 1931 was initially recorded in a travel journal
and later re-recorded in the official diary.[28] Her diary then was not a spontaneous production; there was an element of constructing and ordering a life.
Lifelong diaries, such as Pepys's, Fothergill argues, act as 'the book-that-
might-be'.[29] Certainly, Jacob's diary gave her life a shape and a means of
reflecting on and organising her existence. Her diary also fulfilled a 'compen-
satory function'. At times of intense isolation and feeling herself misunderstood
by family and friends, notably in the growing antagonism with her sister-in-
law, Dorothea, and her repeated altercations with those whom she shared living

24   Ibid., p. 105, p.106. See also Fothergill, *Private Chronicles*, p. 14.
25   Lejeune, 'How do diaries end?', p.107, p. 110, p. 100.
26   Bloom, 'I write for myself and strangers', p. 32.
27   12 Jan. 1924, RJD Ms (47).
28   See RJP Ms 33,129 (1).
29   Fothergill, *Private Chronicles*, p. 43.

quarters, Jacob used the diary to explain her position.[30] The diary in this capacity took on the form of a confidant, allowing her the space to put her own position forward. The early twentieth-century diarist, W. N. P. Barbellion, wrote in the context of his own need to keep a journal that 'what cannot be expressed one way must be expressed in another'. The journal 'serves to relieve ... pain caused by the pressure of the unexpressed self. It becomes a surrogate existence into which he projects all that he values of himself'.[31] Jacob may not have used her diary to this extent to project her true and most valued self but it clearly acted as a forum whereby she could articulate positions she failed to make clear to those with whom she interacted. In this way the diary entries represented, from her perspective, her 'real' self. She unburdened herself and the diary was then the 'secret listener'.[32]

Jacob may not have been behind the barricades of Irish political and feminist activism but her lifelong interest and involvement in many of the radical issues of the period draws attention to a broader-angle definition of what constitutes activism. Despite limited official activism, Jacob continued to educate herself in the ideologies and beliefs of the feminist campaign and, very importantly, her close observation of the different political, cultural and feminist campaigns that variously intersected and converged throughout the first five decades of the twentieth century provided the raw material for her novels. In many respects Jacob can be seen in the role of unofficial journalist of the period; that this role constitutes a hitherto under-explored form of activism should be recognised. The manner in which keeping a diary acts as a form of engagement in the body politic has been noted in work on nineteenth-century British diaries written by women. Huff discusses Marianne Estcourt's detailed description of her brother's death in the Crimea. By including newspaper accounts of the battles he fought and official letters on his death her text pushes the personal space of the diary into the public realm of military history and the history of empire. As Huff writes, 'even though Marianne could not fulfil the role of soldier, she could become part of the body politic by acting as its self-appointed chronicler'.[33] Jacob acted as a reporter. Educating herself in the issues of nationalism and suffrage through reading and attendance at meetings, she in turn domesticated contemporary political topics for friends and family through debate and discussion. The first stage comprised

30   In 1916 Jacob's brother, Tom, married Dorothea Farrington who was from a Cork Quaker family.
31   Barbellion published his text under the title *The Journal of a Disappointed Man* in 1919. Quoted in Fothergill, *Private Chronicles*, p. 85.
32   The novelist and playwright Fanny Burney (1752–1840) used the term 'secret listener' to describe one of the functions of her diary. Fothergill, *Private Chronicles*, p. 88.
33   Huff, 'Reading as re-vision', p. 519.

transcribing and analysing the events, issues and tensions in diary form. These
diary entries, and thereby Jacob's own lived experience of the period, can be
viewed as a form of journalistic fieldwork for her fictional and other writings.
One can find many of the diary entries reproduced almost verbatim in her
fictional writing or alternatively her own perspectives were grafted onto her
fictional characters.

    Callaghan, more so than Jacob's later Irish novel, *The Troubled House*, does
not operate successfully as a literary text; it does not transcend the social,
cultural and political context of its production.[34] Its characters are ciphers who
allow Jacob to negotiate her thoughts on issues around nationalism – republican and constitutional – and suffrage. As such, and given the manner in
which her diary entries acted as a first draft or inspiration, it operates more on
the level of journalistic coverage thinly veiled under the veneer of a fictional
text. In his biography of Kate O'Brien Eibhear Walshe uses O'Brien's novels
to write the life.[35] Jacob did not have the same ability as a writer as Kate
O'Brien to take her ideas beyond that of reportage, which goes some way to
explain the limited success of her published novels. But this 'journalism', both
in diary and fictional form, allows the historian to find an alternative perspective on many of the campaigns and cultural and social events of the period.
The manner in which the diary operated as a means of political and cultural
reporting is highlighted by the fact that Jacob's personal feelings are not
always recorded. While not making a comparison between the two diaries one
could use Fothergill's description of Pepys as tending 'to represent himself as
living very much on the surface' to describe the presence of Jacob at times
within her own life text.[36] Key events such as the death of family members are
noted but her personal feelings are not always evident. In July 1907 her father
died from TB; from 1906 he spent various periods at sanatoriums at Altadore
and Christchurch. Finally, on 28 June 1907 word came by telegram as to his
impending death; Jacob records no personal response and proceeds to detail
instead a walk up the Tramore road.[37] The same pattern was replicated on her
mother's death in 1919, and, much later on that of her brother, Tom, in 1959.
This lack of personal emotion should not be overstated. She did record her
own fear of isolation and loneliness during Tom's protracted illness; her sense
of loneliness as a single woman increasingly permeated the diary from the

34   *Callaghan* was published under a pseudonym. F. Winthrop, *Callaghan* (Dublin: Martin Lester,
      n.d. [1920]); Rosamond Jacob, *The Troubled House: A Novel of Dublin in the 'Twenties* (Dublin: Browne
      & Nolan, 1938).

35   Eibhear Walshe, *Kate O'Brien: A Writing Life* (Dublin: Irish Academic Press, 2006).

36   Fothergill, *Private Chronicles*, p. 13.

37   21 Dec. 1906, RJD Ms (13); 28 June 1907, RJD Ms (15).

1930s and her feelings for Frank Ryan are manifestly evident. The point, however, is that when personal feelings do intrude they are muted, and the diary holds a structure predominantly premised on political, social and cultural narration.

Rosamond Jacob was born in Waterford city on 13 October 1888, the third child of Louis Jacob (1841–1907) and Henrietta Jacob (*née* Harvey; 1849–1919). Tom Jacob, the oldest surviving child, was three years Rosamond's[38] senior. Louis and Henrietta's first-born child, Elizabeth Hannah, or Betty as she was called, died of scarlet fever at the age of five.[39] Louis Jacob was brought before the Magistrates in 1881 for failure to vaccinate the baby. Fined 5/-, he mused on how often he might expect to be prosecuted, not having 'the least idea of having it done'.[40] Despite her sister's death, Rosamond would continue to uphold an anti-inoculation position throughout her life. Indeed, both sides of her family supported this position. In 1911 her maternal uncle, Edmund Harvey, penned a letter to the *Waterford Standard* entitled 'Vaccination and doctors' and declared: 'We must not blindly accept all the views held by doctors in medical matters, but must use our own judgement first before accepting them'.[41] However, the death of Betty was likely to have had an influence on Rosamond's upbringing. A sickly child, she was treated with caution; ill health led to her being home schooled at various intervals between attendance at Newtown, the Waterford Quaker school, and the Protestant girls' school where she learned French and German between 1902 and 1906. From October 1899 she had a governess for two hours every day and on 19 February 1900 she recorded her return to school 'after nearly 4 months absence'; this was a common diary entry during her adolescence.[42] Her attendance at the Protestant

---

38 For the purposes of clarity I shall use refer to her by her first name in this section on family background. In all other places I will refer to her by surname.

39 Elizabeth Hannah, born 30 October 1879, died 10 November 1884. Jacob Pedigree, no. 21, Society of Friends Library, Dublin; Doyle, 'A bio-critical study of Rosamond Jacob', p. 17.

40 Letter from Louis Jacob to 'Hanney', 4 May 1881, RJP Ms 33,133 (2). Compulsory vaccination for smallpox was introduced in Ireland in 1863. See Deborah Brunton, 'The problems of implementation: the failure and success of public vaccination against smallpox in Ireland, 1840–1873' in Greta Jones and Elizabeth Malcolm (eds), *Medicine, Disease and the State in Ireland, 1650–1940* (Cork: Cork University Press, 1999), p. 139.

41 *Waterford Standard*, 24 June 1911.

42 13 Oct. 1899; 19 Feb. 1900, RJD Ms (2).

school came to an end shortly after her 16th birthday in 1904 for financial reasons: 'To school in morning, French and music. I am going to leave this half, except for music, because the fees have been raised, and Poppa says his pocket won't stand it.'[43] At this point the Jacobs lived in Newtown Road and the 1901 Census returns show that they were in a financial position to have one servant, Margaret Sinnott, a native of County Wexford. In 1911 they still employed one servant, Mary Josephine Bowe, aged 33.[44] While such references to money matters in the family were few, health was clearly an issue growing up; at the end of 1901 she recorded her state of health for each month of the year.[45] Even in times of good health, wet mornings kept her at home as her parents feared the onset of colds and chills.[46] Such periods of isolation possibly contributed to Rosamond's lack of fully developed social skills. Throughout her life numerous friends, acquaintances and family members commented on her awkward manner, her inability to read a social situation and her ability to generate discord. While Rosamond's outspoken manner, notably her refusal to hide her views on issues such as female rights and nationalism, might be seen as the hallmark of a principled activist, one must also recognise that this was a personality trait which afforded her much personal unhappiness in her dealings with others. Tact and compromise were never skills Jacob mastered.

Louis Jacob came from a Quaker family in Clonmel, meeting his wife, Henrietta, whom he married in 1878, through his sister Huldah; Huldah was married to Henrietta's brother, Thomas Harvey.[47] Louis, an aspiring artist, worked in his father-in-law's house-agent and stockbroking firm in Waterford; his son Tom would later go into this business.[48] Louis Jacob was a self-confessed agnostic, writing in May 1881: 'I can not believe just because there are penalties for not believing any more than I can feel hungry if I desire to'.[49] Before marriage he spent a period working in London and in Newcastle-on-Tyne in England, employed in the latter city by the engineering firm, Stephensons, which produced parts for locomotive engines. He noted how

43   28 Nov. 1904, RJD Ms (7).

44   http://www.census.nationalarchives.ie/reels/nai003500225

45   31 Dec. 1901, RJD Ms (3).

46   Doyle, 'A bio-critical study of Rosamond Jacob', p. 18.

47   Jacob Pedigree, no. 11; Doyle, 'A bio-critical study of Rosamond Jacob', p. 18.

48   Harvey & Son, 12 Little George's Street. This firm had before 1886 been Harvey & Smith, Stockbrokers and Insurance Agents. Circular letter describing the takeover of 'Harvey and Smith', 21 Apr. 1886, RJP Ms 33,136. When Rosamond was a child Thomas Newenham Harvey, her uncle, managed this business. Thomas, however, died childless following two marriages: first on 15 December 1870 to Louis's sister Huldah and second on 4 Feb. 1895 to Anne Poole. This allowed control of the business to pass to Tom Jacob. Harvey Pedigree, no. 36, Quaker Library, Dublin.

49   Letter from Louis Jacob to Hanney, 4 May 1881, RJP Ms 33,233 (2).

fortunate he was in Newcastle in the availability of libraries and reading rooms, commenting how he was reading, amongst other works, Ruskin's *The Elements of Drawing*.[50] He had not yet attended the 'first rate' theatre in the city continuing: 'I really hardly know what prevents me as I have a great curiosity to see a play & I have no scruple of conscience about it or any other influence to prevent my going'.[51] Louis's intellectual curiosity and appreciation of artistic endeavour would ensure that his children were brought up as full participants in the cultural life of Waterford in the early twentieth century. In her early diaries Rosamond regularly recorded her attendance at theatre and art exhibitions. As well as painting Louis tried his hand at writing fiction.[52] A lover of theatre against the strictures of Quakerism, similarly Louis's religious background did not preclude him from enjoying alcohol. This indulgence was also despite his daughter's objections which were to galvanise into a lifelong hatred of drink: 'I want to tell you', he wrote to her in 1894, 'because you have such a hatred of whiskey – I did not drink a single drop of what I brought with me until today – was I not a very good man'.[53] In London before marriage it is clear that Louis drank and enjoyed the experience. He wrote in 1878: 'By and bye [*sic*] I was in a pleasantly buzzy state as I got a large quantity of liquor supplied to me'.[54] Reading between the lines of some of Rosamond's diary asides a picture can be constructed of Louis as free spirited and not always constrained by family responsibilities. In 1878 he recorded how in London he received a letter that on first glance he believed to be from his future wife:

> The first sight of the letter disappointed me – it did not seem to be from the person I thought . . . Then I got frightened – Is there anything the matter with her. The other thought that filled my mind at the same time was a fear that perhaps her Puritan friends had found out something about my life which had shocked them & that she has not written in consequence.[55]

50 Letter from Louis Jacob to Edmund Harvey, 1 Nov. 1861, RJP Ms 33,233 (2); John Ruskin, *The Elements of Drawing* (London: Smith, Elder & Co., 1857).

51 Letter from Louis Jacob to Edmund Harvey, 1 Nov. 1861, RJP Ms 33,233 (2). While Quakers tended to be well versed in history and biblical studies, fiction and fanciful tales were disapproved of. This embargo on certain types of literature would explain Louis Jacob's comment on his attendance at the theatre. Maurice J. Wigham, *The Irish Quakers: A Short History of the Religious Society of Friends in Ireland* (Dublin: Historical Committee of the Religious Society of Friends in Ireland, 1992), p. 48.

52 For examples of this unpublished work see RJP Ms 33,137.

53 Letter from Louis Jacob to Rosamond Jacob, 6 June 1894, RJP Ms 33,233 (5).

54 RJP Ms 33,137 (7). The contents of Ms 33,137 comprise a set of notebooks containing stories written by Louis Jacob. Volume 7 contains some diary entries between stories.

55 RJP Ms 33,137 (7).

As a married man with a family, Louis regularly went by himself to Dublin; his daughter recorded the trips as visits to the National Gallery. In 1905 Rosamond noted how they received a telegram from him to 'say he has missed the train & won't be back till Friday. Just like him'. That same year she noted how he had twice gone to London during the year 'which seems extravagant'.[56] There is little, if any, reference to the state of her parents' marriage. In 1902 she briefly notes how her mother was 'melancholy', the line 'I wish she wouldn't be melancholy', suggesting that this may have been a regular occurrence.[57]

All Irish Jacobs of Quaker persuasion were descendants of Richard Jacob who, persecuted in England for his faith, left Lampford and settled in Cork around 1674 becoming a cutler.[58] Louis Jacob was very much within this family and wider Quaker tradition of dissent. Politically he championed the rights of oppressed nations and despised manifestations of conservative and imperialist politics, railing against British intervention in Afghanistan and elsewhere. Earl Cairns, he wrote in 1881, 'is considered to be a strong Evangelical Christian . . . And this man's religion is so little good to him that he thinks it a shameful thing for the government to give back self government to the Boers'.[59] The family, including the young Rosamond, would later watch avidly for signs of English defeat during the Boer War of 1899–1902. As an 11-year-old in 1900, Rosamond recorded that a 'very pretty thing happened in the Cape. Two battalions of Suffolk men, who were fighting the Boers there were given orders by the enemy (the Boers) to retire, and 3/4 of them immediately did so!'[60] Later she wrote:

> I went to town before dinner and did messages. It would make any right-minded cow ill to go into Croker's Shop! there are rows of British Generals (photos), and

56   28 Jan. 1903, RJD Ms (5); 3 May 1905, RJD Ms (8); 15 Sept. 1905, RJD Ms (9).

57   12 Mar. 1902, RJD Ms (3).

58   Handwritten account of the persecution of Richard Jacob attached to Jacob Pedigree; W. J. Jacob, 'The Dublin family of Jacob', *Dublin Historical Record* 11: 4 (June–Aug. 1940), p. 134.

59   Letter from Louis Jacob to 'Hanney', 4 May 1881, RJP Ms 33,233 (2). In 1877 Britain annexed the Afrikaner republic of the Transvaal. Hugh McClamont Cairns, first Earl Cairns and Lord Chancellor under Disraeli from February to December 1868 and from 1874 to 1880, was a descendant of seventeenth-century Scottish planters in Ulster. Cairns was a 'devout low-church man, whose evangelical piety . . . ruled his personal life'. He denounced the Treaty that recognised the Transvaal's effective independence after the Battle of Majuba in 1881. Richard Shannon, *The Age of Disraeli 1868–1881: The Rise of Tory Democracy* (London: Longman, 1992), p. 349; David Steel, 'Cairns, Hugh McCalmont, first Earl Cairns (1819–1885), lord chancellor', *Oxford Dictionary of National Biography* (Oxford; Oxford University Press, 2004' online edn, May 2006).

60   8 Jan. 1900, RJD Ms (2).

an uglier set of men you could never see. A big picture of Cronje's surrender, and war literature (from a British point of view, of course) enough inside to stack a library with.[61]

Louis Jacob's political affiliations were not always without contradiction. In the American Civil War (1861–5) he aligned himself with the Southern States who fought against the abolition of slavery; in the interests of peace, he was opposed to abolitionists inciting violent resistance. The possibility of slaves rising, he wrote, would lead to the committal of 'horrible cruelties . . . on masters & their families'.[62] Although having abandoned his faith, Louis Jacob was still culturally a member of the Society of Friends, committed to one of their core principles – the notion of peace. Like her father, Rosamond would also be strongly influenced by many of the core tenets of the Society of Friends while jettisoning any notion of religious belief. Like Louis also, Rosamond held strong political opinions, aligning herself against imperialism. Of course, this anti-imperialist perspective was not surprising; a belief in equality was fundamental to the Quakers and the radical nature of the politics of the Society of Friends in Ireland in the context of, for example, the 1798 Rebellion has been analysed.[63] Yet, like those of her father, Rosamond's political affiliations were often contradictory, most notable in her, often simultaneous, support for republicanism and her commitment to pacifism. Her affair with Frank Ryan in the late 1920s and early 1930s brought her into personal and political contact with a man who believed in the gun in politics. While this did not quite involve 'sleeping with the enemy' given her own commitment to the militant republican tradition and her anti-Treaty stance, during these years Rosamond still maintained an ideological attachment to the pacifism advanced by the Women's International League for Peace and Freedom established in 1915 to counter the patriarchal militarism which, its founders believed, had led to the outbreak of the First World War.[64]

Although she wrote in her autobiography that her was father was 'largely responsible for my being what I am. He was the most independent and self-supporting soul I ever knew', Rosamond was not just influenced by Louis

---

61 10 Apr. 1900, RJD Ms (2). Croker's shop was a book and stationery shop. George Day Croker is listed in the 1911 Census as a bookseller and stationer. http://www.census.nationalarchives.ie/reels/nai00350o103

62 Letter from Louis Jacob to Edmund Harvey, 6 July 1862, RJP Ms 33,233 (2).

63 Kevin O'Neill, 'Mary Shackleton Leadbeater: peaceful rebel' in Dáire Keogh and Nicholas Furlong (eds), *The Women of 1798* (Dublin: Four Courts, 1998), p. 142.

64 Rosemary Cullen Owens, 'Women and pacifism in Ireland, 1915–1932' in Maryann Valiulis and Mary O'Dowd (eds), *Women and Irish History* (Dublin: Wolfhound, 1997), p. 223.

Jacob's beliefs and political passions.[65] No less than her father, Rosamond's mother's family were involved and interested in the radical political issues of their time. In London in 1884 her mother attended the House of Commons writing that they were in 'great luck to come in for the Women's Suffrage debate', sharing the Ladies Gallery with women such as Isabella Tod.[66] Interestingly, as Rosamond would on so many occasions, Henrietta moved from abstract politics to commentary on the physical appearance of the main male protagonists. 'Parnell,' Henrietta noted, 'has grown his hair too long, and I like him much better without his beard'.[67]

The maternal side of Rosamond's family also offers evidence of a commitment to the values of education for both sexes. An extant letter to her maternal grandmother, Elizabeth Harvey, from a Quaker friend in Cork suggests that the letter writer views her as standing outside the expected role and aspirations of women in the mid nineteenth century. Mary Wollstonecraft's strictures in 1792 against women who, devoid of education and thereby equality, must snare husbands through artifice and artificiality are echoed in the following letter:

> I have no taste for most women. If they would only be natural & hearty I should like them well enough but so many are all hoops & conventionalities! they are so stiff & idea-less – so poor & mean in mind – so affected & self conscious – that – pah! – I always liked you & Maria – Thank goodness I always did! & H. E. W. & all other people of our sex who are human beings as well as women . . . In Cork our women are expected to be silent & stupid spectators . . . Blue stockingism is disapproved of here.[68]

Rosamond's was a home where ideas circulated and where she was encouraged to think and dispute; there was no sense within her immediate family that intellectual thought and endeavour was inappropriate for females.

65   Quoted in Doyle, 'A bio-critical study of Rosamond Jacob', p. 19. This author has not been able to locate the autobiography referred to which is allegedly in private family hands.

66   Isabella Tod (1836–96) was active in the broad based campaigns of the early suffrage movement in Ireland, notably the campaigns for equal educational opportunities and the campaign for the repeal of the Contagious Diseases Acts of 1864, 1866 and 1869.

67   Letter from HLH [Henrietta Harvey] to her mother, 13 June 1884, RJP Ms 33,233 (2).

68   Letter from Lizzie A[ddey] to Elizabeth [Harvey], 12 Jan. 1864, RJP Ms 33,233 (1). Wollstonecraft wrote on the need for women to dissimulate, stating, for example: 'It is vain to expect virtue of women till they are in some degree, independent of men'. She described such women as offering a 'fawning fondness of spaniel-like affection' to men to ensure they got married and survived once married. Mary Wollstonecraft, *A Vindication of the Rights of Women* (London: Longman, 2006), p. 172.

Her parents engaged with many of the key intellectual and political arguments of their time, more often than not from an anti-establishment perspective. In 1901, on St Patrick's Day, a holiday she always noted, Rosamond recorded the following family entertainment:

> Uncle N called before dinner . . . Two debates in the afternoon, one on the fitness or rather the unfitness of Englishman's wearing shamrock on St Patrick's Day, the other on whether missionary work is justifiable or otherwise. We decided that Englishmen should be forbidden to wear shamrocks, and that missionaries have no business to go converting people that don't want to be converted.[69]

Her home milieu created for Rosamond a sense that to debate and engage orally with the issues of the time was the norm and this became the manner with which she interacted with those she met outside the home. Beginning art classes in September 1902, by the end of the month she was discussing with her teacher the merits of all things Irish over all things English:

> I went to drawing class at Miss Smith's, and had quite an interesting argument with her about the ancient Irish and the Irish language. She considers the former just as barbarous a race as the Ancient Britons, I believe, and says there were no great or famous men among them.[70]

To a large degree interaction through debate became Jacob's default means of engaging with her peers, a trait that was to remain with her throughout her life and which was to cause her to be considered awkward and querulous even by many of those who knew her well.

From an early age Rosamond read voraciously; details of books read each year were recorded after the 31 December entry in her diary. Although her taste in literature and reading material was wide ranging, many of the books she records were products of the burgeoning Irish cultural revival of the period. In May 1901 she immersed herself in Standish O'Grady, reading *The Chain of Gold* and *The Flight of the Eagle*.[71] In August 1903 she was reading poems by William Rooney but comparing them unfavourably with those of

---

69 17 Mar. 1901, RJD Ms (2).

70 27 Sept. 1902, RJD Ms (4).

71 8 May 1901; 10 May 1901, RJD Ms (2). Standish O'Grady, *The Chain of Gold: A Tale of Adventure on the West Coast of Ireland* (London: T. F. Unwin, 1895); *The Flight of the Eagle* (London: Lawrence & Bullen, 1897).

Ethna Carbery.[72] Her lifelong interest in the heroes of the 1798 and 1803 republican period began at this time. In September 1903 the family had the first volume of Wolfe Tone's diary from the Free Library, while earlier in August she visited, with Tom, sights associated with the United Irishmen in Dublin, moving from the birthplace of Napper Tandy to the site on Thomas Street where Emmet was executed.[73] The family subscribed to magazines that promoted the values of Irish culture and history such as *The Irish Packet* and *The Irish Emerald*, Rosamond enjoying the serialised story on Robert Emmet and Sarah Curran in the former in October 1903.[74] Immersed in debate and literature from an early age, Rosamond would experience similar censure to that depicted in the above letter to her grandmother. While this criticism was not quite a disapproval of blue stockingism and was often in part the result of an antipathy to her strident manner rather than her views per se, nevertheless one can point to occasions where Rosamond was considered to have inappropriately strayed out of the private or women's sphere by engaging in political or intellectual debate. This certainly would have been the view of her sister-in-law, Dorothea, with whom she maintained a relationship increasingly fraught with tension and misunderstandings until the latter's death in 1957.

The Jacob family's agnosticism has been taken as a *sine-qua-non*. However, the isolation that ensued as they disengaged from the Quaker community in Waterford is over stated by Damian Doyle. Rosamond claimed in her unpublished autobiography that the family lived in 'a kind of isolation' as they did not attend Quaker religious ceremonies and, thus, were considered 'eccentric and blameworthy'.[75] Yet, her diary records her attendance at many of the wider cultural and social events of the Quaker community. This was a small community; in 1900 the Waterford Monthly Meetings had 160 Friends. By

72 13 Aug. 1903, RJD Ms (6). William Rooney (1873–1901) was an Irish language activist and a prolific writer for the Sinn Féin paper, *United Irishman*. P. J. Mathews, *Revival: The Abbey Theatre, Sinn Féin, The Gaelic League and the Co-operative Movement* (Cork: Cork University Press, 2003), pp. 98–9. Ethna Carbery was the pseudonym of Anna Johnston (1866–1902). Born in Ballymena, County Antrim, Johnston was co-founder with Alice Milligan of the *Northern Patriot*, which produced three monthly issues, and the *Shan Van Vocht*, published between January 1896 and March 1899. She was a contributor to the *United Irishman*. As Ethna Carbery, Johnston published popular verse and stories, *The Four Winds of Erinn* (1902) being an example of the former. Bourke et al.(eds), *Field Day Anthology*, vol. v, p. 922.

73 11 Sept. 1903; 28 Aug. 1903, RJD Ms (6).

74 8 Oct. 1903, RJD Ms (6). The *Irish Emerald* was a weekly Young Ireland publication which merged with *the Irish Shamrock* in 1912. The latter contained strongly nationalistic and patriotic material, much of it of a fictional nature. Tom Clyde, *Irish Literary Magazines: An Outline History and Descriptive Bibliography* (Dublin: Irish Academic Press, 2003), pp. 131–2.

75 Quoted in Doyle, 'A bio-critical study of Rosamond Jacob', p. 19.

1911 the Tipperary Monthly Meeting was amalgamated with that of Waterford, an indication of declining numbers.[76] On 4 March 1902 Rosamond recorded her mother's attendance at an essay meeting on artists at the Quaker meeting house.[77] On 14 October 1902 she noted the attendance of Tom and her mother at the General Meeting although she did record how, arriving later than the other two, she 'had not the cheek to go in alone, especially as I didn't know where to go'.[78] On 10 October 1905 she attended, with her mother and Hannah, the General Meeting at Newtown.[79] Indeed, Rosamond was present by herself at Quaker religious meetings in early adulthood and went into some detail as to how her decision to abandon attendance brought concern to those within her community; as late as April 1912 she testified to a belief 'in a life after death'.[80] On 5 December 1905 she was berated for the manner in which she and Tom had cut themselves off from the Waterford Friends. She agreed to attend a 'party of young friends' commenting, 'I daresay we are wrong but we don't exactly know how to avoid it'.[81] Rosamond's isolation was not then as extreme as she might have liked to portray it in later life, a construct that has been accepted unquestioningly by those who have written on her life and work.[82] Throughout her life Rosamond would continue to maintain ties to her Quaker background, although not on a religious level. Her diary entries until she left Waterford to move fully to Dublin in late 1919, in fact, show her to be immersed within the social and cultural world of the Quaker community. In October 1912, for example, she was Secretary of the Friends Literary Society Committee.[83] Her concern at the conversion of her niece and one of her nephews through marriage to Catholic spouses in the 1940s also testifies to her cultural links to Quakerism. Cultural Quakerism allowed Jacob to posit a counter-cultural belief system to facilitate a decrial of, as she perceived it, the repressive Catholic homogeneity of the new Irish State. Despite her move to Dublin in 1919 Waterford would always remain important in Rosamond's life – the place of holidays, family ties and her Quaker heritage. Links to her brother, Tom, and his children, Louis, Margie and Christy, became ever more important for Rosamond in later years as she did not marry and establish a family of her own.

---

76 Wigham, *The Irish Quakers*, p. 110, p. 114.

77 4 Mar. 1902, RJD Ms (3).

78 14 Oct. 1902, RJD Ms (4).

79 10 Oct. 1905, RJD Ms (10).

80 16 Apr. 1912, RJD Ms (23).

81 5 Dec. 1905, RJD Ms (10).

82 Doyle, 'A bio-critical study of Rosamond Jacob', p. 19.

83 17 Oct. 1912, RJD Ms (24).

THE ROLE OF WOMEN IN IRISH SOCIETY

Class issues do not figure overtly in Jacob's discourses. Yet class concepts are implicit in her life experience and in many respects received notions of class and gender conspired to frustrate her opportunities. Jacob lived at a point of transition in the lives of Irish middle-class women. The mid nineteenth-century campaign for increased female educational opportunities saw women enter third level institutions; Trinity College, Dublin, being the last of the Irish universities to open its doors to women in 1904. Yet it was only a minority of women who were in a position, both financially and psychologically, to avail of such opportunities. Despite Isabella Tod's declaration in favour of education for middle-class women in 1874,[84] most Irish women of Jacob's class expected to get married and educational advancement and a career were not held out as normative aspirations. Jacob was a generation too early in many respects. Caitríona Clear notes that Maura Laverty's[85] work as a journalist and radio broadcaster placed her in the 'first generation of women professionals in Ireland. These women were seen as a novelty in Ireland, as elsewhere, in the 1930s'.[86] Later generations of single women would find themselves with greater options than the limited few available to Jacob. While in no way as pathetic as the Brennan sisters in George Moore's 1886 novel, *A Drama in Muslin*, who, as unmarried women, were forced to live out their 'uneventful life . . . in maiden idleness; neither hope nor despair . . . [breaking] the cruel triviality of their days',[87] Jacob as a single woman with limited formal education and consequently no opportunities for meaningful employment found herself less than a whole person in the Free State; the dominant discourse of wife and mother worked, according to Jacob's testimony and life experience, to infantilise the single adult woman. Jacob exemplified Tod's concern that not all women could expect to get married and that education was necessary to prepare them for an alternative lifestyle.[88] The tragedy for Jacob was that she could see alternatives, her generation of women was a transitional one between those who adhered to the Victorian middle-class ideology of separate spheres

---

84   Isabella Tod, Extract from *On the Education of Girls of the Middle Classes* in Maria Luddy (ed.), *Women in Ireland 1800–1918: A Documentary History* (Cork: Cork University Press, 1995), pp. 108–10.

85   Laverty wrote successfully in a variety of genres, publishing as both an adult and children's novelist. She was also a playwright, a journalist and a writer of popular cookbooks. Bourke et al. (eds) *Field Day Anthology*, vol. iv, p. 1,037.

86   Caitríona Clear, '"I can talk about it, can't I?": The Ireland Maura Laverty desired, 1942–46', *Women's Studies* 30: 6 (2001), p. 821.

87   George Moore, *A Drama in Muslin* (Gerrards Cross: Colin Smythe, 1981), p. 58.

88   Tod, Extract from *On the Education of Girls of the Middle Classes*, p. 109.

and the next generation, who although forced to negotiate the identification of women and home enshrined in the 1937 Constitution, was still increasingly able to make counter-cultural choices. Jacob clung to a belief in herself as a writer even when she faced years of repeated rejections of her work by publishers, testimony perhaps to a need to define herself in terms of occupation and to give meaning and structure to her sense of self. It is noteworthy that so many female activists of the suffrage and revolutionary period became novelists in later life. Patricia Lynch,[89] Maura Laverty and Dorothy Macardle[90] were all activists in various ways who became writers in the Free State period. The difference was that, unlike Jacob, these women were able to carve out successful careers in this area. Jacob's sense of isolation and failure was then further compounded at meetings of the Women's Writers' Club[91] as these and other women discoursed on publishers and successful works.

Jacob's need to give meaning to her life explains in large part her membership of almost every left-wing, counter-cultural and feminist organisation in Irish society from the early twentieth century until her death. By her own witness she suffered from loneliness in later life. So many of her evenings were spent moving from committee meeting to committee meeting almost in an attempt to stave off facing her sense of isolation and provide her life with purpose. The historiography of Irish women has tended to adopt the Whig interpretative approach decried by the historians Moody and Edwards in the context of Irish nationalist history writing in the late 1930s.[92] While in no way

89   Like Jacob, Patricia Lynch's involvement in the feminist and republican activism was peripheral but, unlike Jacob, Lynch went on to carve out a successful career as one of Ireland's foremost children's authors of the Free State period and beyond, receiving amongst other plaudits a Tailteann Literary Award in 1932 for *The Cobbler's Apprentice* published by the Talbot Press the previous year. Prior to 1916 Lynch was a member of the Gaelic League in London and travelled to Dublin to report on the Rising for the *Workers' Dreadnought*, the organ of Sylvia Pankhurst's Workers' Suffrage Federation. Phil Young, *Patricia Lynch, Storyteller* (Dublin: Liberties Press, 2005), p. 88, p. 58, pp. 63–4; Leeann Lane, "'In my mind I build a house": the quest for family in the children's fiction of Patricia Lynch', *Éire–Ireland* 44: 1 & 2 (2009).

90   A member of Cumann na mBan and Sinn Féin, Macardle was arrested during the Civil War. During her year of imprisonment she took part in a Republican hunger strike. While her most famous work is *The Irish Republic*, she wrote both adult and children's fiction and plays, a number of the latter being staged at the Abbey Theatre. Bourke et al.(eds), *Field Day Anthology*, vol. v, pp. 174–5.

91   The Irish Women Writers' Club was founded in 1933 by Dorothy Macardle and Blanaid Salkeld. Members gathered for social events at which works in progress were read and discussed. The Club also facilitated the discussion of wider social and political matters. Smith, *Dorothy Macardle*, p. 68.

92   Ciaran Brady, "'Constructive and instrumental": the dilemma of Ireland's first "New Historians"' in Ciaran Brady (ed.), *Interpreting Irish History: The Debate on Historical Revisionism 1938–1994* (Dublin: Irish Academic Press, 1994), p. 17.

suggesting that the battle has been won, Irish women's history tends to focus on milestones in the struggle for equality. There is a reductive tendency to this approach. The Irish Housewives Association's[93] importance, for example, has been attributed to the manner in which the organisation 'provided an element of continuity for the women's movement, forming an important bridge between the more public and political female activism of the twenties and the sixties'. This interpretation of the association as a bridge linking first wave and second-wave feminism owes much to the title of the history of the organisation published by one of the founding members, Hilda Tweedy, in 1992 – *A Link in the Chain*.[94] The focus of Irish women's history is, thus, mostly focused on important or seminal periods or organisations in the struggle for gender equality. Exceptional women are those who are generally included in the survey texts and who are the subject for biographies which tend to be political in focus. However, a biographical study of a lesser female activist such as Jacob permits the historian to move away from a linear and positivist approach to the history of Irish women, and to shift the emphasis from female political activism towards a more holistic account of women's lives in the early independent Irish State.

While biographies on key figures in the canon of female activism have included some details of the private and the domestic,[95] the focus has yet primarily been on the political activities of such women. Similarly, what women's organisations did to advance the position of women in the Irish State has been given a degree of attention. However, the contemporary social and cultural role of such organisations as opposed to their work in advancing the cause of women in Irish society needs to be further considered. To examine the life of a woman like Rosamond Jacob allows emphasis to be placed on lived cultural and social experience. In many respects Jacob found solace, social outlet and community in such organisations as the Women's Social and Political League,[96] the Irish Women's Citizens and Local Government Association[97] and the Irish

---

93   The Irish Housewives Committee was formed in 1942 in the context of rising food prices and consumer rights during the Emergency. In 1946 it became the Irish Housewives Association.

94   Myrtle Hill, *Women in Ireland: A Century of Change* (Belfast: Blackstaff, 2003), p. 120; Hilda Tweedy, *A Link in the Chain: The Story of the Irish Housewives Association, 1942–1992* (Dublin: Attic Press, 1992).

95   See, for example, Margaret Ward's biography of Hanna Sheehy Skeffington which includes some detail on her domestic life, most notably her relationship with her son, Owen. *Hanna Sheehy Skeffington: A Life* (Cork: Attic Press, 1997).

96   Formed in 1937 to counter the political discrimination of women.

97   With the passing of the Representation of People Act in 1918 the Irish Women's Suffrage and Local Government Association became the IWCA concerned to monitor the progress of gender equality in Irish society.

Housewives Association. These associations provided a cultural and social space in the public sphere, which was particularly valuable for single women in an Ireland premised on notions of motherhood and family. Membership of various cultural and political organisations, feminist and otherwise, allowed Jacob to construct a psychological scaffold of value and meaning around her life. Many other female activists were variously members of the different organisations that comprised the structural framework of female activism in the period up to the 1960s. These women have been applauded for their energy and commitment to gender equality but it is necessary to adopt a more critical, nuanced approach to the issue of activism. We need to consider how such memberships and involvement might have contributed more to the individual than to the cause of female equality viewed in a linear manner from the position of hindsight. In many instances Jacob recorded apathy at WSPL meetings, increasingly less radical in the 1950s, becoming more of a talking shop than an organisation committed to activism. Many meetings she attended lacked a quorum. Yet, from a different perspective, these were important social gatherings where gossip was exchanged and a public, communal female space provided.

It is important, however, not to allow the disappointments and loneliness of Jacob's later years to retrospectively invade or shape an analysis of her early life. Jacob's was a childhood and adolescence full of intellectual curiosity and creativity. The family wrote and told stories, held salons at which they showed their art work and discoursed endlessly on national, international and feminist politics. Jacob entered into adulthood in the revolutionary period as a politically conscious and independently minded woman with a strong belief in activism, and a certainty that political, cultural and gender change was in the offing in Irish society.

TWO

SUFFRAGE AND NATIONALISM
1904–15

—

Jacob's early involvement in the cultural and nationalist organisations of the late 1890s and early 1900s testifies to her developing sense of self identity as an Irish nationalist and her growing feminist consciousness. The early years of the twentieth century saw her move from a family-based support for constitutional nationalism to growing interest in the more advanced nationalist discourse circulating in the period.[1] In many respects the shift was logical for Jacob reared as she had been on the staples of literary nationalism – the Irish papers and other forms of Irish cultural reading material of her adolescence.[2] Laffan discusses how the cultural nationalism of the Irish-Ireland movement was one force in a broad 'coalition of interests opposed to the cause of home rule'; a separate state would best foster the unique cultural identity of the Irish people.[3] Ella Young[4] wrote:

> The sagas, the tales of gods and heroes, the poems well-hammered and riveted with assonance and rhyme[,] these that belong to us . . . Padraic Pearse's determination that Ireland shall be worthy of them – these are building up our nationhood: these and the Gaelic language.[5]

1   Leslie Price (Mrs Tom Barry), member of the Cumann na mBan executive between 1920–4, described a similar political trajectory: 'My first recollections of nationality came through my mother's keen Parnellism and her and my father's pro-Boerism in the British attack on the Afrikaners.' Mrs Tom Barry, Bureau of Military History Witness Statement 1754, p. 1, NAI. Hereafter BMH WS and specific number.

2   Richard English, *Ernie O'Malley: IRA Intellectual* (Oxford: Oxford University Press, 1998), p. 6, p. 8.

3   Michael Laffan, *The Resurrection of Ireland: The Sinn Féin Party 1916–1923* (Cambridge: Cambridge University Press, 1999), p. 9.

4   Ella Young (1857–1956) was an artist, feminist and nationalist activist being involved in Inghinidhe na hÉireann established by Maud Gonne in 1900.

5   Ella Young, *Flowering Dusk: Things Remembered Accurately and Inaccurately* (New York: Longmans, Green, 1945), p. 66.

Throughout these early decades of the twentieth century Jacob was an inter-mittent member of a circle of women based in Dublin, women committed to suffrage, nationalism and the cultural activities of the Gaelic League, women who imbibed and lived in the exhilarating atmosphere of the turn of the century cultural revival. From 1909 Jacob made frequent and extended visits to Dublin, presenting such forays as an escape from the confines of her small Quaker community. Interaction with Dublin feminists, nationalists of various hues and cultural activists allowed Jacob's nascent political and feminist awareness to mature. Throughout the first two decades of the twentieth century Jacob continued to live at home in Waterford, despite her increasing cultural and political focus on the capital city. Her father's death on 10 July 1907 increased her obligations to her mother. Her mother's deteriorating health and her consequent family commitments prevented Jacob from leaving Waterford and setting up residence in Dublin, although clearly she craved more sustained interaction with her new social circle.

INTERSECTIONS: THE CAMPAIGNS OF CULTURE, POLITICS AND GENDER

Jacob's involvement in political and cultural activities in twentieth-century Waterford and Dublin point to the links between the cultural revival, nation-alist politics and the feminist programme. Historians and literary critics have placed a new focus on understanding the multiplicity of intersections which informed the discourse of the Irish renaissance. P. J. Mathews's *Revival* examines the 'commonality of purpose' between such 'self-help' groups as the Gaelic League, the Irish Agricultural Organisation Society and Sinn Féin.[6] Mathews argues that the tensions in Irish nationalism in the early twentieth century should not be interpreted as a struggle between clearly outlined cultural and political forms. It should instead, he argues, be seen as a 'battle between a newly emerging self-help consensus and old-style parliamentary politics'.[7] It is artificial to examine the campaign for suffrage and the wider women's rights based initiatives as a distinct movement divorced from the dominant discourse of revival in the early twentieth century.[8] Women such as Jacob did not neatly

6   P. J. Mathews, *Revival: The Abbey Theatre, Sinn Féin, The Gaelic League and the Co-operative Movement* (Cork: Cork University Press, 2003). See also essays on the revival in the special issue of the *Irish University Review* 33: 1 (2003).

7   Mathews, *Revival*, pp. 7–8.

8   Cliona Murphy rightly places the Irish Women's Franchise League (IWFL) within the context of the Irish cultural revival at the turn of the century. Cliona Murphy, *The Women's Suffrage Movement and Irish Society in the Early Twentieth Century* (New York: Harvester, 1989), p. 90.

compartmentalise the various campaigns in which they participated; the actual lived experience indicates the holistic approach many activists took in considering Irish political, cultural and feminist advancement in the period. Tension is a very different concept to division: tensions can be resolved or circumvented, division implies a much more unqualified breach and ignores complexity. Instead of absolute division between apparently binary oppositions, notably suffrage and nationalism, various stratagems were utilised by women such as Jacob to resolve the strains which participation in more than one form of political activism made manifest. Moving in the same small circles, female activists and women involved in the nationalist campaign were forced to establish a *modus vivendi*; the necessities of day-to-day interaction worked in many instances to transcend or shelve dissension. Helena Molony[9] wrote: 'Of course on the principle of Equal Rights we were all united, and we worked in the most friendly way with the Irish "Suffragettes".'[10] Jacob's daily diary testifies to intersections rather than divisions in feminist and nationalist politics. Her novel, *Callaghan*, is dotted with references to the GAA and the Gaelic League. Andy Callaghan's love of the Irish landscape is described in terms which echo many of the theosophically based nature writings of George Russell (AE), one of the key literary figures of the period.[11] Looking at the fir trees and wild wasteland surrounding his house Callaghan concluded that he 'seemed to be in the presence of a consciousness . . . loving and welcoming him like a transcendent mother'.[12] Danae O'Regan cites republicanism as the major theme in *Callaghan*. Although she discusses Frances Morrin's suffrage activities and offers an interesting analysis of Jacob's refusal to present a one-dimensional and uncritical portrayal of republicanism, obliging her 'readers to consider whether perhaps everything was not perfect even in a republican world', O'Regan fails to fully transcend a purely nationalist reading of the text.[13] As a

9   Helena Molony (1883–1967) was editor of *Bean na hÉireann* the journal of Inghinidhe na hÉireann. She fought in 1916 as a member of the Irish Citizen Army and spent time in jail as a result. She was a member of various left wing organisations in the Free State, notably the Irish Friends of Soviet Russia. In 1936 she became president of the Irish Congress of Trade Unions. Angela Bourke et al. (eds), *The Field Day Anthology of Irish Writing*, vol. v (Cork: Cork University Press, 2001), p. 119.

10   Helena Molony, letter to Sean O'Faolain relating to his biography of Markievicz, 6 Sept. 1934, enclosed as part of BMH WS 391.

11   See Nicolas Allen, *George Russell (AE) and the New Ireland, 1905–30* (Dublin: Four Courts Press, 1993); Leeann Lane, '"It is in the cottages and farmers' houses that the nation is born": AE's *Irish Homestead* and the cultural revival', *Irish University Review* 33: 1 (2003).

12   F. Winthrop, *Callaghan* (Dublin: Martin Lester, n.d [1920]), p. 128.

13   Danae O'Regan, 'Representations and attitudes of republican women in the novels of Annie M. P. Smithson (1873–1948) and Rosamond Jacob (1888–1960)' in Louise Ryan and Margaret Ward (eds), *Irish Women and Nationalism: Soldiers, New Women and Wicked Hags* (Dublin: Irish Academic Press, 2004), p. 82, p. 86, p. 95.

map of pre-1916 activism, *Callaghan* signals junctions and connections; the marriage between republican activist Andy Callaghan and suffrage campaigner Frances Morrin can be read as a paradigm for Jacob's view of the centrality and importance of feminist ideals within the nationalist campaign. This is not to suggest that the suffrage-nationalism 'marriage' was uncomplicated for Jacob but rather to argue that her focus was connection rather than disconnection.

The focus on division in the historiography of Irish female politicisation may be a consequence of the type of literature examined in considering the suffrage campaign. Attention has focused on polemical and journalistic speeches or retrospective autobiographical accounts rather than on the more immediate narratives of which Jacob's diary offers an example. Accordingly, sustained attention has been placed on the political conflicts that divided the suffrage campaign, notably the division between the militant campaign orchestrated from 1912 by the Irish Women's Franchise League and the struggle by suffragists to persuade the Irish Parliamentary Party MPs to include women's franchise in the third Home Rule Bill of 1912.[14] Historians also emphasise the opposition that developed towards women's suffrage in Ireland; this was a resistance similar to that which developed in other European countries. Women were not expected to play a role in politics because their place was deemed to be within the home. In Ireland there was strong opposition from the Catholic and Protestant churches to the idea of women's enfranchisement. The churches believed that women, domestically orientated, should not be encouraged to express political views in public.[15] From the perspective of the main political parties, there was uncertainty and fear at how a new female electorate would cast their votes.[16] Similarly, the tensions between nationalist women and women in the suffrage campaign are highlighted in the majority of works on the subject. Historians have reiterated that nationalist women felt strongly that the suffrage movement was an English cause and therefore antagonistic to the national struggle for independence. On the other hand, many suffragists such as Hanna Sheehy Skeffington felt that they could not support nationalist groups because of the subordinate position in which they placed their women members.[17] Work

14 See, for example, Rosemary Cullen Owens, *Smashing Times: A History of the Irish Women's Suffrage Movement 1899–1922* (Dublin: Attic Press, 1984).

15 See for example, Rev. Michael O'Kane, *Women's Place in the World* (Dublin: Gill & Son, 1913); David Barry, 'Female suffrage from a Catholic standpoint' (Sept. 1909) in Maria Luddy (ed.), *Women in Ireland 1800–1918: A Documentary History* (Cork: Cork University Press, 2003), pp. 280–3.

16 This concern about women voters mirrored the fears about the extension of the franchise to the poor and to the young.

17 See Margaret Ward, *Unmanageable Revolutionaries: Women and Irish Nationalism* (London: Pluto, 1995); Maria Luddy, *Hanna Sheehy Skeffington* (Dundalk: Dundalgan Press, 1995); Myrtle Hill, *Women in Ireland: A Century of Change* (Belfast: Blackstaff, 2003).

on unionist women has similarly placed the emphasis on division and tension within the women's movement; as the third Home Rule Bill was debated unionist suffragists were torn between either opposing the Home Rule Bill or fighting for the inclusion of women in any Home Rule settlement.[18]

While Jacob faced similar tensions to those experienced by nationalist feminists in a nationalist movement that declared a moratorium on all social, economic and political aspirations until independence had been won, her diary testifies to the manner in which female activists were centrally local within the revival ethos of the early twentieth century. The movements and activities of the cultural revival provided a common meeting ground for first-wave feminists of different political persuasions. Helena Molony's description of Ella Young illuminates the point: 'I was closely associated with her and she was very much with us [the Irish Citizen Army] but was more of an artist'.[19] What is noteworthy is how the female activists of Jacob's circle were able to express divergent viewpoints and still maintain and negotiate relationships within a female grouping which offered support networks and friendships independent of political persuasion. Often it was in the activities of the revival movements such as the Gaelic League that female activists were able to re-establish and reaffirm relationships damaged by political controversy. In March 1913, for example, Hanna Sheehy Skeffington persuaded Jacob to march with the suffragists in the St Patrick's Day Language Procession, stressing that it was not necessary to be part of any society. Later that night at the Gaelic League céilidhe Jacob was introduced to the suffragist Helen Laird.[20]

Jacob's visits to Dublin typically comprised theatre visits and language revival activities; in keeping with the revival's focus on the spirit world she attended séances and took a passing interest in Theosophy, distributing copies of Theosophical magazines in Waterford in August 1912.[21] Jacob became interested in the question of buying Irish goods and the revival of a national

---

18   See Diane Urquhart, (ed.), *The Minutes of the Ulster Women's Unionist Council and Executive Committee 1911–1940* (Dublin: Irish Manuscripts Commission, 2001); Diane Urquhart, *Women in Ulster Politics, 1890–1940: A History Not Yet Told* (Dublin: Irish Academic Press, 2000). Of course, as Ryan has argued, a close reading of the *Irish Citizen* shows that the paper acted as a forum for suffrage women of all political persuasions to negotiate and discuss political difference. Louise Ryan, *Irish Feminism and the Vote: An Anthology of the Irish Citizen Newspaper 1912–1920* (Dublin: Folens, 1996), p. 147.

19   Helena Molony, BMH, WS 391, p. 31.

20   15 Mar. 1913, RJD Ms (24). This may have been the American suffragist Helen Laird.

21   See for example, 7 February 1909 where she recorded her attendance at a private séance held by T. H. and Roger Webb at the Standard Hotel every Sunday. On 29 January 1911 she wrote: 'I went to the Harcourt St. séance in the morning, but nothing much happened except my Jacob grandfather saying he was glad to see me there'. 7 Feb. 1909, RJD Ms (21); 17 Aug. 1912, RJD Ms (23).

costume. In Dublin in early 1911 she went to Kellett's in Great George's Street and 'got a pattern of cream hopsack, intending to get myself a national costume'. Although Mary Colum[22] wrote that she suspected that the so called national costume worn by a number of revivalist women was essentially medieval European 'with a few fancy Celtic features attached', the material was of course Irish and the embroidery was based on, for example, the motifs in the Book of Kells and other Irish manuscripts or engravings on Irish monuments.[23] Jacob's nationalism was then multifocused in keeping with the prevailing revival discourse of early twentieth-century Irish society. For Jacob cultural and political expressions of nationality were not easily divisible; rather they intersected and combined, working as they did towards the one goal – a distinct Irish society and polity, and crucially one in which women were equal citizens. It was the latter priority that explains the description of Frances Morrin in her novel, *Callaghan*, as someone who was 'a suffragist ever since she was old enough to know what a vote was, but the fact had generally remained quiet and unobtrusive in the background of her mind'.[24] It is important to note how the evolving trajectory of Jacob's move towards separatist nationalism paralleled her growing involvement in all facets of cultural nationalism. Political and cultural nationalism both nourished and fed each other as her maturing political persona emerged during the revolutionary years.

NATIONALIST AND FEMINIST ACTIVISM
IN WATERFORD

In 1901 Jacob began a lifelong commitment to the Irish language, taking classes with her brother. In February 1906 the two were founding members of the Waterford Sinn Féin branch, referred to in her diary as the National Council.[25] Nationally Sinn Féin was established in November 1905, one more

22 Mary Colum (1884–1967), wife of the poet Padraic Colum, was involved in many of the organisations and activities of the cultural revival and became a novelist and literary critic.
23 Quoted in Nicola Gordon Bowe and Elizabeth Cummings, *The Arts and Crafts Movements in Dublin and Edinburgh 1885–1925* (Dublin: Irish Academic Press, 1998), p. 122. See also Janice Helland, 'Embroidered spectacle: Celtic revival as aristocratic display' in Betsey Taylor Fitzpatrick and James H. Murphy (eds), *The Irish Revival Reappraised* (Dublin: Four Courts Press, 2004).
24 Winthrop, *Callaghan*, p. 69.
25 She notes that she began to study Irish on 29 August 1901, RJD Ms (3); For the foundation of Sinn Féin in Waterford see 16 Feb. 1906, RJD Ms (11). For the complexities relating to the early nomenclature of the Sinn Féin Party see Kevin Rafter, *Sinn Féin 1905–2005: In the Shadow of Gunmen* (Dublin: Gill & Macmillan, 2005), pp. 44–5.

of the many political and cultural organisations of the later nineteenth and early twentieth centuries concerned to advance a broad-based nationalist revival.[26] Activities in the Waterford branch mostly consisted of talks on such topics as the land question or attempts to elect members to the Waterford Corporation. In this latter endeavour the success of Sinn Féin on the Dublin Corporation, where by 1908 12 out of 60 councillors supported the party, acted as an example.[27] To the RIC the branch appeared worthy of little comment. Up to late 1914 the monthly reports of the County Inspector only mentioned the existence of the branch when it became involved in 1911 anti-recruiting activities or in the protest against the visit of King George V.[28] After the split in the Volunteers in 1914 the monthly reports begin to posit a correlation between the local Sinn Féin branch and the Irish Volunteers.[29]

Jacob from an early age was someone who stood apart. Within her own community she was criticised for her refusal to conform to the mores of the Quaker meeting and for her lack of religious belief. This is highlighted in the following diary entry describing how fellow Quaker Annie

> had a go at me about religion, but much more tolerantly & sensibly than Charlotte or the Hills. She offered me a book In Relief of Doubt, & I said I wd read it but I thought when a person has no desire whatever to be a Christian, books wouldn't have much effect, which she did not deny.[30]

Her involvement in the Gaelic League and Sinn Féin marked her out as different among her peers at the Protestant School in Waterford. In one incident in 1906 she and Tom were taunted with being 'rrebels [*sic*] in a sort of a low growl' as they walked down Newtown Hill past a number of high school boys.[31] Indeed, anyone who supported the nascent advanced nationalist organisations was perceived as different in the period before 1916. Irish Volunteer member, Tom Kelleher, recalled how the Waterford Volunteers and members of Sinn Féin were, in the view of the Redmonites, 'all sorts of cranks, sore heads and dreamers.'[32] Robert Brennan testified to a similar

26   Rafter, *Sinn Féin*, p. 42.

27   See for example, 16 Nov. 1908; 24 Jan. 1909, RJD Ms (17); Rafter, *Sinn Féin*, p. 45.

28   See for examples, RIC County Inspector's Report for Waterford, June 1909, CO 904/78; May 1911 CO 904/84.

29   See for example, RIC County Inspector's Report for Waterford, Nov. 1914 CO 904/95.

30   16 Apr. 1912, RJD Ms (22). R. E. Welsh, *In Relief of Doubt* (Cincinnati: Jennings & Graham, 1907).

31   2 Dec. 1906, RJD Ms (13).

32   Tom Kelleher, BMH WS 758, p. 2.

perception of those involved in Sinn Féin in Wexford prior to 1916. Although some members were elected to Wexford Corporation, 'we were still,' he wrote, 'a very small minority of the general public, who seemed to think we were a little mad anyway.'[33] However, because she was a woman, a member of the Quaker community and a member of the middle classes, Jacob stood even further apart from the vast majority of those involved in advanced nationalist opposition throughout County Waterford in the period before and after 1916.[34] Hart discusses the dominant contemporary view of the Volunteers as 'idle and reckless men' belonging to the lower classes, mostly shop assistants and labourers.[35] In October 1914 the RIC County Inspector for Waterford dismissed the local Sinn Féin sympathisers stating that 'their class in life and influence is unimportant'.[36] The Bureau of Military History Witness Statements indicate a correlation between the lower and lower middle classes and a commitment to advanced nationalism and language activism in Waterford. Thomas Hallahan, Lieutenant of the Bonmahon Company 2nd Battalion, West Waterford Brigade, for example, was the son of a blacksmith and followed his father's trade after attending the local national school. [37] James Fraher, Captain, Dungarvan Company Irish Volunteers, Battalion Adjutant and later Brigade Adjutant, Waterford Brigade, was the son of a farmer, both parents being native speakers. His grandfather had been imprisoned in Waterford Jail in connection with the shooting of a land agent at Modeligo, County Waterford, during the Land War of 1879–82. Fraher was educated to second level and became an apprentice to Crotty's hardware stores in Dungarvan, County Waterford. A member of the Gaelic League, he went on to join the National Volunteers when formed in Dungarvan in 1914 and Sinn Féin when it was started in the town in 1918[38] William Keane, Vice-Commandant, East Waterford Brigade, 1920–1, was one of 12 children of farm labourers and received 'the ordinary National School Education'.[39] Jacob's growing support for advanced nationalism and her involvement in Sinn Féin and the Gaelic League caused her to move in circles outside those considered appropriate

33   Robert Brennan, *Allegiance* (Dublin: Browne & Nolan, 1950), pp. 8–9.

34   The majority of the Dublin Quaker community, controlling much of the commerce of the capital, were opposed to Home Rule as detrimental to the well being of the Irish economy. They were, Gaughan argues, also committed to the maintenance of the Protestant Ascendancy. J. A. Gaughan (ed.), *Memoirs of Senator James G. Douglas, 1887–1954: Concerned Citizen* (Dublin: UCD Press, 1998), p. 4.

35   Peter Hart, *The IRA and Its Enemies: Violence and Community in Cork 1916–1923* (Oxford: Clarendon Press, 1998), pp. 138–9.

36   RIC County Inspector's Report for Waterford, Oct. 1914, CO 904/95.

37   Thomas Hallahan, BMH WS 1128, p. 1.

38   James Fraher, BMH WS 1232, p. 1, p. 6.

39   William Keane, BMH WS 1023, p. 1.

both to her class and gender. Although women were participants in League activities and the evidence is that there was a Protestant interest in the language,[40] her diary suggests that her involvement in the wider nationalist movement as represented by Sinn Féin and her growing separatism were frowned upon, or at best not understood, by her wider family and by those within the Waterford Quaker community.

At this stage in her life Jacob did not overtly articulate any equation of Irishness and religious affiliation. In the nineteenth century, language, religion and later nationalism became inextricably combined. The link between Catholicism and nationalism was decisively forged in Daniel O'Connell's campaign in the 1820s for Catholic Emancipation and in his later campaign for the repeal of the Act of Union, both crusades bringing the Catholic priest into Irish politics. James Duffy's periodical, the *Irish Catholic*, appeared in February 1847 and was published monthly with 22 issues appearing in total. The article entitled 'a Catholic Literature for Ireland' in the first issue anticipated the blend of national and Catholic values that was to come to the fore in the later nineteenth century. [41] The equation of Irish cultural identity with Catholicism reached the zenith of expression during the cultural revival. Men such as D. P. Moran and Daniel Corkery distilled and honed sentiments expressed earlier by such as Duffy, producing a prescribed and narrow version of Irishness that designated Yeats, Synge and others of the Protestant Anglo-Irish caste as essentially un-Irish. O'Leary notes how many of the most influential writers of the language revival identified Irish literature as Catholic literature.[42] Considering Anglican women active in the early twentieth-century nationalist campaign, Walsh discusses the various stratagems through which they negotiated the essentialist view of Irishness as Catholic, rural and nationalist. With no Republic to support, even in theory, prior to 1916 and no

---

40   Timothy G. McMahon, '"All creeds and all classes?" Just who made up the Gaelic League?', *Éire–Ireland* (Fall/Winter, 2002), p. 135, p. 157.

41   W. J. Mc Cormack, 'The intellectual revival (1830–50)' in Seamus Deane (ed.), *The Field Day Anthology of Irish Literature*, vol. v (Derry: Field Day, 1991), p. 1,292. To counter alien influences Ireland needed, O' Duffy argued, a Catholic literature: 'A literature religious to the core, which should reflect the majesty and eternal truth of our Faith and its beauty and poetry as well; Irish, too, to the core – thrilling with our Celtic nature, and coloured by our wonderful history; such a literature, and its glorious associate, a high Catholic and national art'. James Duffy, 'A Catholic literature for Ireland' in Deane (ed.), *Field Day Anthology*, vol. i, p. 1,296.

42   Philip O'Leary, *The Prose Literature of the Gaelic Revival, 1881–1921: Ideology and Innovation* (Pennsylvania: Pennsylvania State University Press, 1994), p. 23. The view of Irishness as Catholic, rural and nationalist was to be enshrined, for example in Daniel Corkery, *Synge and Anglo-Irish Literature* (Cork: Cork University Press, 1913) and found weekly utterance in D. P. Moran's newspaper, *The Leader*, established in 1900.

legislative body prior to 1919, a sense of Irish identity 'depended upon a mixture of aspiration and actuality: that is, what the prime movers defined as Irish, and what the bulk of the population actually was'.[43] Jacob testified to no such need to accommodate herself to a view of Irishness and Catholicism as synonymous, although certain diary asides do suggest that at some level she had absorbed the equation. For instance, in January 1909 when a Miss Bowman wanted the YMCA to organise an anti-suffrage demonstration Jacob described her as 'more contemptible than any man'. Jacob continued her harangue in a manner which suggested certain notions of inevitability, notably the concept that all Catholics were automatically nationalists: 'I would class an anti-women's rights woman along with a loyal Irish Catholic and a Frenchman who sneers at Jeanne d'Arc ... on the very lowest scale of traitorous meanness, too low to hate and too wicked not to hate'.[44] Although such references to the essentialist nationalism of Catholics were few in her diary, it should be noted that Jacob aligned herself with a particularly Protestant nationalist tradition through her early and enduring interest in the events and personages of 1798. As Walsh states, noting the multitude of references to 1798 in *Bean na hÉireann*: these 'historical moments so identifiably Protestant, act as a means of substituting the author's right to participate in nationalist politics, as successors to that Protestant revolutionary heritage.'[45]

Jacob did betray a certain disdain for Catholicism at this time. Most tangibly Jacob's innate anti-Catholicism was, in this period, usually targeted at the large clerical presence within the Gaelic League. She was also conscious of the power of the Catholic Church in the wider society. In 1907 she noted the comments of the local Gaelic League secretary, Upton, while at tea in the Jacob house: 'Sinn Féin makes rather for free thought, which is rather unfortunate because if it goes any distance that way it will be up against the church, and that would be the end of it. I suppose he is right.'[46] Later that year, planning the local Gaelic League summer feis she intervened when one member suggested the recitation of *Salve Regina*, 'saying that there shouldn't be Catholic prayers in the competitions, the G. L. being non sectarian'.[47] However, Jacob's anti-clericalism was not just directed at the Catholic Church but was all embracing. Visiting relatives in Wexford in June 1908 she attended the local Quaker meeting, commenting disdainfully:

43 Oonagh Walsh, *Anglican Women in Dublin: Philanthropy, Politics and Education in the Early Twentieth Century* (Dublin: UCD Press, 2005), pp. 47–8.

44 22 Jan. 1909, RJD Ms (19).

45 Walsh, *Anglican Women in Dublin*, p. 44. *Bean na hÉireann* was the organ of Inghinidhe na hÉireann published between 1908 and 1911 with irregular publication in 1909.

46 9 Mar. 1907, RJD Ms (14).

47 21 Mar. 1907, RJD Ms (14).

When I went to mass at Ring I heard a sensible sermon about stealing & betting, & when T. went to church in gCorcaigh he heard a sensible sermon about prudence, but I don't believe anyone ever heard any sort of a Dissenter say a sensible, practical word . . . According to them . . . nothing is worthy . . . except perverting [the word converting crossed out] people.

Jacob believed 'that to do right for conscience's sake is a higher & better reason than to do right because otherwise God won't have you in heaven' and such was the motivation behind her involvement with fellow Friends in the distribution of poor relief in Waterford.[48] At one level Jacob rejected any manifestation of proselytising regardless of denomination and thus appeared to be as anti-Protestant as she was anti-Catholic. However, at a certain level Jacob's anti-Catholicism betrayed an inchoate sense of cultural and class superiority. Canon Sheehan's *My New Curate* drew the following invective from her pen:

They are the worst kind of priests, wanting to have the making of every pie in the parish, and to have the people obedient children to them . . . telling them they'll lose their souls if they do anything for their country, and praising the system of marrying off your daughters without consulting them, not telling them the name of their husband until a day or two before the wedding.[49]

As fellow students in the Protestant school looked with horror on Jacob's nationalism, Catholic acquaintances recoiled from some of her actions and beliefs, an instance being her subscription to the *Peasant*.

The peasant [*sic*] came to me at the college and when I was reading it in recess, a young priest . . . showed a sort of mute horror of it, as if he wouldn't touch it with a 10 foot pole. Afterwards when I was reading it at home, the elder Doyle remarked coldly 'The Peasant is an avowedly anti-clerical paper' as you would say 'the P. is an avowedly diabolical paper'.[50]

48   19 Aug. 1910, RJD Ms (20). For her work in the area of poor relief see, for example, 8 Dec. 1909; 22 Dec. 1909, RJD Ms (19).

49   2 Feb. 1908, RJD Ms (16). While she preferred *Lisheen* to *My New Curate* one of her further objections to Sheehan was, with the exception of *Glenanaar*, 'he can never draw a live woman'. 5 Feb. 1908, RJD Ms (16). *My New Curate* originally appeared as a serial in the *American Ecclesiastical Review*; the first edition came out in December 1899. *Glenanaar: A Story of Irish Life* was first published in 1904. *Lisheen* was published in 1907.

50   7 Aug. 1908, RJD Ms (16). The *Peasant* was the successor of the *Irish Peasant* established in 1903 by James McCann, MP. At the close of 1906 Cardinal Michael Logue threatened to denounce the

Jacob's unwillingness to hide her beliefs made her on many occasions a target of hostility. Her developing feminist consciousness manifested itself initially in her criticism of her female contemporaries in Waterford. She could not engage, as they did, in discussing the local High School boys.[51] Later that year, returning from a trip to the Druid's Glen while on holidays with her family in Wicklow, she castigated the weak nature of the women who 'screamed incessantly all the way' and who required a large amount of assistance in negotiating their retreat from the Glen.[52] On another occasion she noted with disdain the tendency of women to 'giggle' and was dismissive of frivolous flirting between the sexes.[53] Indeed, Jacob in some of her diary entries appears slightly prudish at this stage in her life by contrast with her frank and unashamed account of her secret, passionate affair with Ryan in the 1920s. Her prudish nature manifested itself in her attitude to new female fashions, particularly the tight skirts, of the early twentieth century.

I went to visit Lasairfhiona[54] in the afternoon and spent a good while there, watching people in their best clothes in the street and particularly the hobble skirts getting on the tram. Indeed Lasairfhiona's skirt was as tight as any of them, there didn't look to be more than 2 yards of stuff in it.[55]

In later life she was 'scandalised' by the very short, 1960s-style skirts of the visiting delegates from the International Alliance of Women.[56] For Jacob, 'sense and right principles, and even heroism,' were the qualities that should make a woman attractive and these were the characteristics with which she directed her life throughout this period and beyond.[57]

Irish Peasant unless the family closed it down. The paper, under the editorship of William Ryan, had displayed sympathy for Sinn Féin and Ryan, although a Catholic and more devout than the previous editor, P. D. Kenny, believed in 'progress through free debate by autonomous individuals rather than pronouncements by the hierarchy'. Ryan took over the title of the paper and re-established it as the *Peasant*. Patrick Maume, *The Long Gestation: Irish Nationalist Life 1891–1918* (Dublin: Gill & Macmillan, 1999), pp. 83–4.

51   3 July 1905, RJD Ms (9).

52   7 Aug. 1905, RJD Ms (9).

53   23 Nov. 1907, RJD Ms (15).

54   Lasairfhíona Somers was involved in Sinn Féin in Dublin since its inception in 1905. Jacob began a friendship with Somers during her visits to Dublin from 1909. Maume, *The Long Gestation*, p. 58.

55   19 May 1912, RJD Ms (23).

56   28–9 June 1960, RJD Ms (170).

57   14 July 1911, RJD Ms (22).

Jacob's budding feminist sensitivity has to be ascribed in part to her Quaker upbringing. The concept of equality was central to the Society of Friends. As early as 1789 the Friends had moved beyond the term fraternity, accepting its limitations in the area of gender, while five years later Women Friends had achieved the right to hold an independent Women's Yearly meeting.[58] Jacob's growing feminism also illuminates the manner in which the suffrage campaign developed out of a broad-based demand for women's rights amongst a small group of Irish women and men. Philippa Levine states: 'Few women were so engrossed by suffrage activity that they were not severally involved in other areas and in developing a more far-reaching feminist perspective which perhaps saw voting rights as symbolically central to full citizenship, but which never represented them as a total panacea'.[59] Jacob's feminist beliefs and demands were wide ranging from an early point in her life. Interested in such concerns as female education, she read the magazine produced by Alexandra College, the school founded in 1866 to offer an academic education to girls. At a local Sinn Féin meeting she reproved as 'nonsense' the speaker who declared that it wasn't to the benefit of the community that women should be too well educated.[60] Following her first sighting of Douglas Hyde at the Gaelic League events of 'Domhnach na nGaelige' on 20 September 1908 she described him as 'much uglier than his portrait' and noted how in his speech relating to the position of Irish in the National University 'he spoke as if all the students in it would of course be masculine'.[61] Jacob increasingly questioned the gender inequality that she perceived to operate at all levels of society. She observed the sexual double standard inherent in the response of the clerical element in the Waterford branch of the Gaelic League to the question of foreign dancing. She never heard, she declared, 'Fr Ormonde[62] talk so much nonsense in a given time before'. He 'cast aspersions on every decent woman that dances them (the men don't matter half so much of course)'.[63] The question of what constituted an Irish as opposed to a foreign dance – a raging debate in *An Claidheamh Soluis* in the early 1900s – was very much a feature of Jacob's account of many of the meetings of the Waterford branch of the League. The fact that the move towards an interest in dance

58   Kevin O'Neill, 'Mary Shackleton Leadbeater: peaceful rebel' in Dáire Keogh and Nicholas Furlong (eds), *The Women of 1798* (Dublin: Four Courts, 1998), p. 142, n. 10.
59   Philippa Levine, *Feminist Lives in Victorian England* (Oxford: Blackwell 1990), p. 125.
60   22 Nov. 1907, RJD Ms (15).
61   20 Sept. 1908, RJD Ms (17).
62   Father Ormonde was President of the Waterford Branch of the Gaelic League, 'St Patrick's day', *Waterford Standard*, 18 Mar. 1911.
63   13 May 1907, RJD Ms (14).

within the League originated in London exacerbated this issue with figure dances denounced as not Irish.[64] Noted League member Éinrí Ó Muireaghasa, also took a gendered approach to the issue. In a letter to *An Claidheamh Soluis* on 24 February 1906 he argued that for social reasons women should not be obliged to refuse an invitation to participate in a foreign dance. Men, however, should politely refuse on the basis of principle.[65] Visiting Mount Mellary during her visit to the Ring Gaeltacht in County Waterford in the summer of 1907, Jacob recorded the different treatment meted out to the men and women. As soon as the lay brother who received her group heard they were from Ring he dismissed them as vegetarians and gave them, along with some other visiting females, nothing to eat but bread and butter:

> Then he took us upstairs and showed us a view of the cemetery, full of little black crosses, from the windows. The boys had come long before, and had got a fine hot dinner, and had been shown all over the schools and the monastery, and had seen the library and the museum, but we, as women, might not see anything but the cemetery and the chapel. I will never go there again unless it is in a coat and trousers.[66]

Jacob would later use and highlight the gendered experience of this visit in 'Third person singular'. In the novel Hugh McNevin comes upon Mrs Ambrose weeping for the loss of her baby on the gallery in Mount Mellary. However, he is unable to help not knowing the cause of her sadness, or find out any more details and blames 'the monks for their troublesome habit of separating their male and female guests at meals.' Later in the day he sees the woman and her companion returning to the female hostel in a raging storm and is overcome with anger:

> a delicate wand-like thing at the mercy of the storm . . . The sight of her . . . reawakened his anger against the customs of the place. A woman like that must walk half a mile through the storm to her lodging, while he might sit at ease under the monastry [*sic*] roof!.[67]

Reading Emily Brontë's *Wuthering Heights* Jacob wrote of its hero, Heathcliff: 'One thing I like about him is that he did not have different standards for judging men & women'.[68]

64　Helen Brennan, *The Story of Irish Dance* (Dingle: Brandon, 1999), p. 31, p. 29.

65　Ibid., p. 35.

66　10 Aug. 1907, RJD Ms (15).

67　Rosamond Jacob, 'Third person singular', RJP Ms 33113 (2), NLI, pp. 22–4, p. 30, p. 34.

68　1 Jan. 1914, RJD Ms (26).

Jacob's diary records her growing sense that women were elided from the historical picture. In September 1907 on a family visit to Cork she paid a visit to the 1798 monument on the Grand Parade. While she found the list of names on the monument 'very instructive' she registered her disapproval of the absence of 1848 women and the manner in which Anne Devlin's name appeared at the bottom of all the 1803 men, 'the only woman there at all'.[69] She similarly criticised Stephen Gwynn's biography of Robert Emmet published in 1909 for 'not a word about Anne Devlin's sufferings in the cause'.[70] This concern with the erasure of women from the historical record was highlighted by other female activists; in 1846 'Mary of the Nation' indicated the necessity for a book on the 'Illustrious Women of Ireland' while the revival of women from nationalist history and mythology featured strongly in the agenda of Inghinidhe na hÉireann, members assuming the names of historical Irish women.[71]

Critical of a society which designated women as the weaker sex and ascribed meek and passive characteristics to them, Jacob's continuing involvement in her local Gaelic League branch was fraught with frustration. Eoin MacNeill and Douglas Hyde established the Gaelic League in 1893 to revive, what was at this point in time, an almost moribund language. In his 1892 lecture to the National Literary Society, 'The necessity for de-Anglicising Ireland', Hyde stated that 'within the last 90 years we have, with an unparalleled frivolity, deliberately thrown away our birthright and Anglicised ourselves. None of the children of those people of whom I have spoken know Irish, and the race will from henceforth be changed'.[72] The Waterford branch was established on 29 November 1900.[73] The RIC estimated the membership of the County Waterford League, with branches in Waterford City and Dungarvan, at 91 for the year ending December 1901.[74] By January 1916 the figure was 340.[75] The local League gave classes in Irish. Jacob worked from Father O'Growney's *Simple Lessons in Irish*, the foundation text for students beginning the language under the auspices of the League. She mastered the addressing of letters and

69   15 Sept. 1907, RJD Ms (15).

70   22 Nov. 1909, RJD Ms (19). Stephen Gwynn, *Robert Emmet* (London: Macmillan, 1909).

71   Antoinette Quinn, (ed.), 'Ireland/Herland: women and literary nationalism, 1845–1916' in Bourke et al. (eds), *Field Day Anthology*, vol. v, p. 899.

72   Douglas Hyde, 'The necessity for de-Anglicising Ireland' in Deane (ed.), *Field Day Anthology*, vol. ii, p. 532.

73   Gaelic League first list of branches with officers and annual subscriptions 1897–1906, Ms 11538, NLI.

74   McMahon, 'All creeds and all classes', p. 123.

75   RIC County Inspector's Report for Waterford, Jan. 1916, CO/904/99.

parcels in the language and participated in Irish dancing classes.[76] Jacob enjoyed the wider cultural debates at the meetings, particularly the castigation of all manifestations of English culture, the offshoot of many of the ideas in Douglas Hyde's 1892 speech:

> Seaghan Ua Floinn . . . makes a long lecture to us about the wickedness of Ireland in general and Waterford in particular, and the horrid English penny dreadfuls etc that people read instead of Irish books . . . very clever and sort of satisfying to listen to, and makes one approve of him very much.[77]

Further lectures involved 'the backwardness of Irish education, how children are never taught Irish history'.[78] Indeed, many of the meetings focused less on the language than on cultural harangues:

> at 9.30 he shut up the book . . . and gave us a short conversational lecture on the English people, their animalism, want of mind and love of food and drink; contrasting them very unfavourably with the French which was pleasant.[79]

From 1906 Jacob, following the norm amongst many aspiring language activists of the period, spent a time each year at a League summer school in the Ring Gaeltacht. From 1904 over a dozen summer colleges were established by those involved in the language revival. The agenda of these colleges was comprehensive with instruction not just in the mechanics of language learning but in history, Irish music, dance and literature.[80] Ring was one of three colleges established in 1905 following the establishment of the flagship school the previous year in Ballingeary, County Cork.[81] As a summer school student Jacob was able to point to the pedagogical impediments to mastery of the language due to the methods pursued by many early teachers in the cause:

76 For examples of these activities see, 19 Dec. 1904; 10 Feb. 1905, RJD Ms (7); McMahon, 'All creeds and all classes', p. 127.

77 23 Mar. 1905, RJD Ms (8).

78 17 Apr. 1905, RJD Ms (8).

79 29 May 1905, RJD Ms (8).

80 Timothy G. McMahon, '"To mould an important body of shepherds": the Gaelic summer colleges and the teaching of Irish history' in Lawrence W. McBride (ed.), *Reading Irish Histories: Texts, Contexts and Memory in Modern Ireland* (Dublin: Four Courts, 2003), p. 118.

81 Breandán S. Mac Aodha, 'Was this a social revolution?' in Seán Ó Tuama (ed.), *The Gaelic League Idea* (Cork: Mercier, 1972), p. 22.

came in for a composition lesson by Dr Henebry . . . His method is to read aloud a few sentences in English from a newspaper or such, and let everyone take them down, then translate them into Irish himself & let everyone copy it down. One of the things he gave us was a boy's letter to his father from Ring, that he invented himself . . . But he took all the spirit out of it when he put it into Irish.[82]

Indeed, this was an endemic problem with the summer programmes sponsored by the League as the organisation had no mechanism to control quality in what were essentially unofficial schools, although the establishment of the first school to systematically train Irish language teachers in Ballingeary was an attempt to introduce certain measurable educational standards.[83] From early 1908 Jacob began piping lessons and by July could play four tunes 'after a fashion', the 'Minstrel Boy', 'Balance the Straw', 'the Foggy Dew' and 'Maidrin Ruadh'. During this period she also attended a number of GAA fixtures, going to Dungarvan on 21 June 1908 to see the All Ireland hurling final between Cork and Kilkenny.[84]

Aside from her irritation with the bureaucracy of, and lack of dynamism in, the League, Jacob was increasingly perturbed by the lack of female representation at committee level. In 1905 she recorded her anger at the election of a local committee of six men with no female representation, despite the fact that the women attended meetings more frequently than the men. Natural justice should ensure, she believed, that both sexes should be represented on the committee and amongst the officers.[85] The lack of female representation at officer level in the Waterford Branch mirrored the profile of women within the wider League. An examination of the national executive committees for 1903–4 and 1913–14 showed both to be 'overwhelmingly male', despite the more regular attendance of women at meetings.[86] At the Feis run by the local branch of the Gaelic League in 1908 Jacob made it a point to sit on the platform 'for principle's sake, to show the women present that there were women in the League so that they shouldn't have that excuse for not coming'.[87] In Dublin in 1908 for Domhnach na nGaeilge, hosted by the Gaelic League, she described

---

82   3 Aug. 1906, RJD Ms (12). Richard Henebry was a native speaking Catholic priest of the diocese of Waterford and Lismore. Timothy G. McMahon, *Grand Opportunity: The Gaelic Revival and Irish Society, 1893–1910* (Syracuse: Syracuse University Press, 2008), p. 40.

83   McMahon, 'To mould an important body of shepherds', pp. 128–9.

84   18 Mar. 1908; 17 July 1908; 21 June 1908, RJD Ms (16).

85   16 Oct. 1905, RJD Ms (10).

86   McMahon, 'All creeds and all classes', p. 131.

87   14 May 1908, RJD Ms (16).

the procession and noted the lack of involvement by women.[88] Jacob became increasingly preoccupied with the lack of sustained cultural and political activity amongst women, particularly in the Gaelic League. The problem appeared to be the unwillingness of women to assume leadership roles. Jacob's description of the general meeting of the local Gaelic League in October 1912 recorded how 'there are never enough women to vote for'.[89] In July of 1913 the members of the local League discussed the problems at headquarters during which 'Miss Purcell & Miss Casey as usual were dumb & passive'.[90] Following the local meeting of 18 December 1913, Jacob recorded how she 'attacked' a fellow League member, Miss Doyle, for her lack of activity. Jacob castigated her unwillingness to work towards finding new and cheaper rooms for meetings and for 'her refusal to ever take the chair at committees'. Jacob continued: 'She put it all down to having no time, which doesn't apply to the latter accusation. It encourages men to think women don't want to come forward or do anything in the least public'.[91]

Jacob stood out in Waterford by her willingness to participate in such cultural activities as the Gaelic League and other revivalist organisations and by her growing feminist and political consciousness. At school she had to explain what hurling was.[92] In December 1905 she was the only woman for most of the time at a local Sinn Féin meeting, a fact which horrified her fellow school colleagues when she recounted it to them.[93] In November 1906 she was the only woman among 20 at the National Council meeting of the League.[94] An avid reader from an early age, despite limited formal education Jacob was intellectually precocious. She liked, by her own admission, people coming to her for her views 'and (outwardly at least) accepting what I tell them'.[95] Debates with her fellow students in the Protestant girls' school in Waterford and with members of the Waterford community ended invariably with Jacob's dismissal of opposing attitudes: 'Of course they are violently anti-women's rights and think it absurd nonsense for women to want to have any vote in the way they are governed. Those women there seem to despise politics as a frivolous pursuit entirely beneath them'.[96] Jacob dismissed Mina Orr, a close

88 20 Sept. 1908, RJD Ms (17).
89 19 Oct. 1912, RJD Ms (24).
90 11 July 1913, RJD Ms (25).
91 18 Dec. 1913, RJD Ms (26).
92 25 Mar. 1905, RJD Ms (8).
93 11 Dec. 1905, RJD Ms (10).
94 2 Nov. 1906, RJD Ms (13).
95 23 May 1913, RJD Ms (25).
96 7 May 1906, RJD Ms (11).

family friend and fellow Quaker, as someone who had no opinions on the subject of the suffrage campaign; Mina's father, by contrast, felt that the suffragettes were 'public nuisances' and that the home was the proper sphere for women, in direct contradistinction to Jacob's own belief that 'the suffragettes are some of the finest women that England ever produced'.[97] On 16 June 1906 she recorded how her fellow students 'talked a lot of nonsense about Miss Billington & the other suffragettes.[98] They make one think of that line in "Munster", "bloodless, white-souled, contented slaves"'.[99]

Within Waterford society Jacob's self image was that she was viewed as eccentric in her views generally and more specifically in her commitment to Irish nationalism and feminism. Her account of the Quaker essay meeting at which members read their work on a pre-arranged topic, which she attended on 14 December 1909, betrays an attitude of resentment to what she perceived as her outsider status:

> The lecture was Bertie Grubb on some old Friends . . . Edith Bell said how noble they were & what a pity there were no Irish friends fit to be classed with 'these English worthies', whereupon I was constrained to mention that these English worthies were mostly American, & one of them French; and on that everyone – even the Newtown boys – tittered as if I had said something absurd. I wish I could go somewhere where I wasn't known, & believed beforehand to be mad, so that my remarks might for a time at least be taken on their own merits and not discounted at once as the necessarily absurd talk of a lunatic.[100]

This sense of being perceived as different because of her views and her willingness to voice them would remain with Jacob throughout her life, becoming painful in later years when family members increasingly came to view her as different and, at times, difficult. At this point in time, however, Jacob's immediate family were tolerant of her political views although she does note

---

97   3 Nov. 1906, RJD Ms (13).

98   Teresa Billington-Greig (1877–1964) was a member of the Women's Social and Political Union (WSPU). In 1905 she became a full-time organiser for the cause of female suffrage from within the Independent Labour Party and in 1906 a paid organiser within the WSPU. Leaving the WSPU over differences with Emmeline Pankhurst's authoritarian-style leadership, Billington-Greig formed the Women's Freedom League in 1907 with Charlotte Despard. In later years her commitment to women's activism took the form of lecturing and writing. Elizabeth Crawford, *The Women's Suffrage Movement: A Reference Guide 1866–1928* (London: UCL Press, 1999), pp. 54–5.

99   16 June 1906, RJD Ms (12).

100 14 Dec. 1909, RJD Ms (19).

in passing in April 1905 that her mother refused to let herself and her brother attend the Gaelic League meeting that night: 'she seems to have quite a prejudice against it. It is very provoking.'[101] While Tom joined her at meetings of the local branches of the Gaelic League and Sinn Féin, her mother was a constitutional nationalist and a supporter of John Redmond.

Redmond, of course, was the Irish Parliamentary candidate for Waterford and Jacob went with her mother to the Town Hall to view his 'triumphant entry into the town' following the 30 January 1900 unification of the Irish Parliamentary Party under his leadership.[102] In the very early years of the twentieth century Jacob mirrored her mother's support for the Party, commenting on her attendance at, and enjoyment of, a lecture by Redmond almost a year later:

> Once he referred to a cartoon in some paper, in which 'I was depicted as a large surly tabby cat. My tail was spread before me on the floor and my bristles were all on end. Before me were Chamberlain and Balfour and Chamberlain said to Balfour "That is the cat that has been troubling us so in Parliament. We must cut a few inches off his tail". And Mr Balfour with more sense replied "We may cut his tail but we can never pare his claws"'. We nearly died laughing.[103]

A year later again Jacob was at the ceremony which gave Redmond the Freedom of the City of Waterford, describing him as looking 'more like a little cute owl than ever'. His speech was 'admirable and very cheerful' and after singing God save Ireland she was introduced to him and had 'the honour of shaking hands with him twice'.[104] Jacob, however, was no indiscriminate supporter of the Irish Parliamentary Party at this point in her political development. In 1904 she attended, with Tom, the Parnell anniversary procession in Dublin and while staying at her Aunt Nanny's house came across a work by Justin McCarthy, a series of biographical sketches and portraits of British politicians.[105] 'I don't like', she wrote:

---

101 6 Apr. 1905, RJD Ms (8).

102 22 Apr. 1900, RJD Ms (2). The IPP had been split since 1891 between Parnellites and anti-Parnellites in the wake of the revelations of Parnell's adulterous relationship with Katharine O'Shea The party was reunited on 30 January 1900 and a week later Redmond was elected as leader. Frank Callanan, *T. M. Healy* (Cork: Cork University Press, 1996), p. 437.

103 2 Sept. 1901, RJD Ms (3).

104 12 Sept. 1902, RJD Ms (4).

105 Justin McCarthy, *Modern Leaders: Being a Series of Biographical Sketches* (New York: Sheldon & Co., 1872).

J. Mac C., he treats Balfour etc too much like equals and decent people, whereas he ought to consider them as the dust under his feet. I don't approve of so-called Irish Nationalists that go a-whoring after English statesmen & edit 'Society papers' like him and T. P. O'Connor.[106]

T. P. O'Connor had close personal contacts with British Labour and Liberal activists and that made him 'a useful go-between' for the Irish Parliamentary Party but 'also encouraged charges of subservience by the Irish Party to British politicians', exactly what Jacob denounced.[107] By 1905 she was beginning to question some of Redmond's sentiments, particularly in the context of the relationship of a future Home Rule Ireland to the wider British Empire:

> [Redmond] said one or two things that I didn't exactly like, particularly one about how valuable a contented Ireland would be to 'the Empire', which is a horrible possibility that should not be talked about.[108]

Although there was tolerance for her political beliefs, within her wider family, particularly on the male side, Jacob was treated with 'authoritative sternness'.[109] Indeed, she led a very sheltered life in Waterford despite her political radicalism and during the first two decades of the twentieth century did not operate as a fully autonomous individual. This can be detected in commonplace asides in her diary. As late as 1915, when Jacob was 27, she recorded her desire to take her felt hat to Dublin for wet weather 'but wouldn't be let, & had to take only velvet & plush ones'.[110] During the height of the Irish militant suffrage campaign in 1914 Jacob received a letter from Hanna Sheehy Skeffington indicating her intention to travel to Waterford with other members of the IWFL to heckle Redmond and asking for her help with hospitality. Jacob noted: 'Hospitality certainly, unless Mamma objected violently, but as to going with them, I should probably not be let'; Jacob was in her mid twenties at this point.[111] Her reply to Sheehy Skeffington further exemplifies her lack of self rule at this age in her life: 'As for my joining in the protest, my mother is very much opposed to such an idea, that I'm afraid it is out of the question'.[112]

106 9 Oct. 1904, RJD Ms (7).
107 Maume, *The Long Gestation*, p. 238.
108 1 Dec. 1905, RJD Ms (10).
109 21 Nov. 1909, RJD Ms (18).
110 25 Feb. 1915, RJD Ms (28).
111 6 Jan. 1914, RJD Ms (26).
112 Jacob to Hanna Sheehy Skeffington, 7 Jan. 1914, Sheehy Skeffington papers Ms 33, 608 (9), NLI (hereafter SSP).

Given Jacob's consciousness of the lack of sexual equality in society from an early point in her life it was obvious that she would become interested in the suffrage campaign. What rendered the situation complex was that Jacob's commitment to the idea of female equality caused her to stand apart in the nationalist circles in which she moved. The discourse of language activism in Waterford constructed the woman of the Gaelic League as a counter to the image of the suffragette. This can be gleaned from newspaper accounts of local League activities. Repeatedly the women of the Gaelic League were commended for their catering skills at League céilithe. More overtly the domestic role of the women was countered to the 'screaming sisterhood' of the suffrage movement and the latter fringed or 'othered' in that way. The *Waterford News* reported on the language activities of 17 March 1911:

> The cailíní of the Gaelic League were much in evidence in the demonstration: about 60 or 70 girls participated. This reminds me of the arrangement in Irish social life. While we have hundreds of societies for the social well being of our young men, there is no provision whatever outside the Gaelic League for our young women. I think some of our militant suffragettes might agitate this question. Women's rights, I take it, means something more than marking X every five years after the name of some prospective Parliamentary noodle.[113]

While this passage is relatively benign the issue was expanded on after the next year's St Patrick's Day League celebrations:

> I noticed a number of prettily-attired cailíní under the Gaelic League banner: there was nothing fantastic or suffragette-looking about them, for the maidens of our race have a higher and more inspiring mission in the world than smashing windows or flinging brick-bats.[114]

Prettily attired, the women of the Gaelic League are normalised by contrast to the fantastic suffragette – an 'other' in Irish society. Thus one is talking about layers of tensions that Jacob was forced to negotiate. However, as will be shown, she did attempt to negotiate involvement in these apparently contradictory campaigns of suffrage and nationalism – cultural and political.

From 1905 onwards Jacob lost no opportunity to air her views in favour of the parliamentary vote for women and to question others as to their stance,

---

113 'Some aspects of the St Patrick's Day procession', *Waterford News*, 24 Mar. 1911.
114 Ibid., 22 Mar. 1912.

bringing the topic into such forums as the Gaelic League.[115] The commonality of intellectual space and discourse generated between the suffrage cause
and the revival needs to be noted. What stood out for her as a 'fine night' at the
League was one in which the local language activist, Mr Brett, spent an hour
discussing 'home life in ancient Ireland, & how the woman bossed everything
in the home'.[116] Many of the male Gaelic Leaguers in Waterford believed that
'a woman's right place is in the kitchen'.[117] Support for the female franchise,
where it existed, was often based on the manner in which women would use
the vote to enforce the values of the home on the wider public sphere. A
League committee meeting in November 1906 drew the following opinions:

> Then, via Mitchel, we got to slavery and the American War, and Fr O. said it would
> have been better not to free the slaves all at once, but gradually, and to have educated
> them a bit first, so I asked him was he in favour of women suffrage, and rather to my
> surprise he said he was, and that if women had votes there would be fewer pubs.[118]

Jacob worked through debate and through the example of her politically
conscious life to dissuade the male members of the League of many of these
gendered viewpoints. Reading a published work on the political dependence
of women in November 1907 she loaned it to fellow League member, Upton.[119]
While the League acted as a social outlet for women, many branches still
operated a gender divide, running separate male and female classes. In planning
League events, such as feiseanna, women were in many cases given an auxiliary
role providing badges and making decorations. The discourse of the League
was overtly modelled on the separate spheres ideology; women's role in language
activism was within the home educating children in the language and in Irish
values.[120] This perspective also permeated the local branch of Sinn Féin;
Jacob's voice here, as elsewhere, was raised in counter-cultural defence. At a
meeting in November 1907 her brother Tom gave a paper on primary education
in Ireland. Jacob noted its positive reception but also observed how the paper
gave rise to negative remarks on notions of co-education: One listener:

115   28 Nov. 1906, RJD Ms (13).

116   4 Dec. 1907, RJD Ms (15). Mr P. Brett was Vice-President of the Waterford Branch of the Gaelic
League, 'St Patrick's Day', *Waterford Standard*, 18 Mar. 1911.

117   20 Nov. 1907, RJD Ms (15).

118   28 Nov. 1906, RJD Ms (13).

119   20 Nov. 1907, RJD Ms (15).

120   McMahon, 'All creeds and all classes', p. 136. A notable example is the case of Mary Butler. See
Frank A. Biletz, 'Women and Irish-Ireland: the domestic nationalism of Mary Butler', *New Hibernia
Review* 6: 1 (2002), pp. 59–72.

didn't approve of co-education, said it made boys effeminate and girls mannish, and anyhow it wasn't for the good of the community that women should be too well educated, & he didn't approve of female suffrage . . . I spoke too . . . to reprove Bogaigh for his nonsense about women's education & to say I disagreed with the essay in thinking the language the most important thing to teach children in the schools, for Irish history is more important.[121]

In this latter comment Jacob touched on the manner in which early leaders of the cultural revival considered an understanding of Irish history to be an integral component to the study of the language. The League sponsored an understanding of Irish history through the running of lectures, writing competitions, publications and *tableaux vivants*.[122] One of Jacob's roles with the local Gaelic League was to conduct the history exams held at the summer feiseanna.[123] As Jacob worked to change the views of those within the League opposed to such issues as female equality, she also worked to educate her fellow Quakers towards an appreciation of Irish culture:

We had the club at Summerville in the afternoon . . . I had the choice of a subject for the next meeting and am going to try & remedy their education with a few classics such as Deirdre and Cúchulain, out of Joyce's Ancient Romances.[124]

Jacob's involvement in language activism in Waterford was the springboard which gave her access to a new world in Dublin that was to broaden and deepen her nascent but growing feminist and political awareness. In September 1908 she went to Dublin to attend a Language Procession, staying again with her Aunt Nanny. Increasingly from this date, Jacob was brought into the world of the Dublin cultural revival and she partook avidly in all opportunities to expand her political horizons through engagement and interaction with those involved in the various self help, cultural and political movements of the capital city. In a similar manner, the visits to Dublin prior to 1916 of the Wexford language, Sinn Féin and IRB activist, Robert Brennan, created a contrast between 'the home atmosphere' and the sense of political and cultural possibilities that permeated the pre-revolutionary capital.

---

121 22 Nov. 1907, RJD Ms (15).

122 McMahon, 'To mould an important body of shepherds', pp. 120–1.

123 See, for example, 23–4 June 1908, RJD Ms (18).

124 11 July 1910, RJD Ms (20). P. W. Joyce (tr.), *Old Celtic Romances* (London: C. Kegan Paul & Co., 1879).

A visit to Dublin in those dark days was like a tonic. Every person one met seemed to be a rebel of some sort and one felt it was only a matter of time until all Ireland would follow Dublin's lead. The stimulating atmosphere was not by any means confined to the political field. There were poets, essayists and artists galore and one met them everywhere.[125]

Jacob's diary is rich with the perception of Dublin as a place of cultural ferment and possibilities, a feature of so many of the memoirs and other textual accounts of the capital in the period. Mary Colum described how all the diverse national movements of the period, 'focused towards one end – a renaissance . . . were beginning to make the pulses of the young and eager beat faster and faster'.[126] Ella Young declared that the 'National Spirit has more than stirred; it has lifted its head and shouted. Everywhere little clubs are springing up for the study of the Irish language and Irish history'. Young noted that Inghinidhe na hÉireann 'are reviving everything at once'.[127] Jacob enjoyed sitting on the tram to Stephen's Green and overhearing four women, strangers to her, 'discussing ancient Irish female costume with deep interest'.[128]

SUFFRAGE

From early 1909 Jacob began to take a more active role in the women's rights movement; she attended the YMCA woman suffrage debate in Waterford on 22 January 1909, commenting approvingly on the speakers in favour and dismissing as 'rot' and 'nonsense' those who spoke against.[129] In that same month Jacob paid another visit to Dublin. She spent 30 January in the National Library reading Madden on 1798.[130] From this point Jacob developed a lifelong interest in the events surrounding 1798 which would culminate in her publication of *The Rise of the United Irishmen* in 1937 and her biography of Matilda Tone, *The Rebel's Wife*.[131] The next day she met Anna and Thomas Haslam for the first time, betraying in her description of the meeting her lack of clarity on the divisions within the suffrage cause; both the Haslams she described as

125 Brennan, *Allegiance*, p. 20, pp. 16–17.
126 Mary Colum, *Life and the Dream* (New York: Doubleday, 1947), p. 95, p. 109, p. 94.
127 Young, *Flowering Dusk*, p. 70, p. 71.
128 23 Nov. 1909, RJD Ms (19).
129 22 Jan. 1909, RJD Ms (17).
130 Richard Robert Madden, *The United Irishmen: Their Lives and Times*, 7 vols (1842–6).
131 Rosamond Jacob, *The Rise of the United Irishmen 1791–94* (London: Harrap, 1937); *The Rebel's Wife* (Tralee: *Kerryman*, 1957).

'ardent Suffragists, if not Suffragettes'.[132] Although passionately interested in concepts of gender equality and feminist consciousness raising, at this period in her life Jacob was obliged to educate and familiarise herself with the complexities of the suffrage campaign. Suffrage events in Waterford were organised under the auspices of the Irish Women's Suffrage and Local Government Association until September 1911 when a Waterford Branch of the Munster Women's Franchise League was established following a talk by Suzanne Day, co-founder of the Cork branch.[133] Dr Mary Strangman was vital in the organisation of Waterford suffrage activities.[134] An examination of the local press indicates that she was to the fore in organising the MWFL to press their case to government, particularly on occasions when the leader of the IPP, John Redmond, visited his Waterford constituency. On 23 February 1912 the following report appeared in the *Waterford News*

> A deputation from the Irish Women's Suffrage Societies was received by Mr Birrell at the Irish Office, Old Queen St, Westminster.
>
> Mary Strangman represented the affiliated societies in Belfast, Lisburn, Rostrever, Birr, Athlone, Mitchelestown, Cork, Skibbereen, Queenstown and Waterford.[135]

That one person represented all these different areas shows how thinly spread the personnel of the suffrage campaign were and how important individuals were in advancing the cause. In January 1910 Jacob attended Strangman's lecture on women's suffrage at the Waterford Town Hall. At the lecture, Jacob was acquainted with historical facts 'that were quite new to me', noting in her diary

---

132 31 Jan. 1909, RJD Ms (17). For Anna Haslam's oppositional attitude to the militant suffrage campaign conducted in England by the WSPU from 1903 and in Ireland from 1912 by the IWFL founded in 1908 see Carmel Quinlan, *Genteel Revolutionaries: Anna and Thomas Haslam and the Irish Women's Movement* (Cork: Cork University Press, 2002), pp. 150–90.

133 'Women's suffrage movement', *Waterford Standard*, 30 Sept. 1911. Suzanne Day (1890–1964) was a founding member of the Munster Women's Franchise League. She was elected a Poor Law Guardian for Cork Board of Guardians in 1911. At the outbreak of the First World War she left Ireland to help war victims in France.

134 Mary Strangman was a Protestant doctor and suffrage activist. In 1911 she lived alone with her servant. She did not fill out the census form herself and the enumerator included the following remark: 'Head of family is a Suffragette and states she did not sleep in house on 2nd April but in enumerator's opinion she did and probably was not enumerated elsewhere that night.' Her age was stated to be 'probably' 35. http://www.census.nationalarchives.ie/reels/nai003499390. The *British Medical Journal* on 27 Jan 1912 listed Strangman as honorary doctor to the Waterford Maternity Hospital and Burshall Asylum and notes her election as the first woman to Waterford Corporation in 1912.

135 'Women's suffrage – deputation to Mr Birrell, *Waterford News*, 23 Feb. 1912.

information on Romilly's Act of 1850 where the word person or man was taken
to mean both man and woman unless expressly stated to the contrary.[136] Jacob
records Strangman's discussion of the lack of custody rights for married
women and noted the general feeling among female activists that if women
gained the vote, inroads could be made against immorality and rescue work
enhanced.[137] As late as 1910, two years after the IWFL was founded, and seven
years after Emmeline Pankhurst and her daughters, Christabel and Sylvia,
established the militant Women's Social and Political Union (WSPU) in
England, Jacob did not recognise the female-only nature of these organisation.
Winston Churchill, she wrote in the context of the General Election of 1910,
'is much worried by Suffragettes, female and male'.[138]

During her visit to Dublin in early 1909 Jacob visited the Abbey Theatre to
see productions of the *The Man who Missed the Tide* by W. F. Casey and
Yeats's *Cathleen Ní Houlihan*. Three days later she attended a debate in the
Mansion House on a resolution demanding compulsory Irish in the National
University.[139] On the 10 February 1909 she first met Madeline ffrench Mullen,
whom she described 'as a very pleasant bright girl'; Madeline was to become a
close friend and visited Jacob in Waterford on a number of occasions.[140] At
this first meeting, Madeline asked Jacob to contribute to *Bean na hÉireann*,
published between 1909 and 1911 as the paper of Inghinidhe na hÉireann,
founded by Maud Gonne in 1900.[141] The aims of Inghinidhe na hÉireann
were both cultural and political. Their focus was an independent Ireland and
their support for such manifested itself in an active anti-recruitment campaign
against the Boer War. Although *Bean na hÉireann* facilitated debate between
suffragists and nationalists, it was committed to national independence rather
than any purely feminist agenda. Few members of Inghinidhe na hÉireann
joined the suffrage campaign, contending that looking for the vote from the
British parliament was a betrayal of the struggle for national independence.

136 Under the terms of this act, women claimed, unsuccessfully, the right to vote after the 1867
Franchise Extension Act.

137 14 Jan. 1910, RJD Ms (19).

138 9 Dec. 1910, RJD Ms (20).

139 5 Feb. 1909; 8 Feb. 1909, RJD Ms (17). For a discussion of the campaign for compulsory Irish in
the National University see McMahon, *Grand Opportunity*, pp. 73–81.

140 Madeline ffrench Mullen (1880–1944) fought in 1916 as a member of the Irish Citizen Army. A
close friend of Dr Kathleen Lynn with whom she lived from 1914, ffrench Mullen was active in the
setting up of St Ultan's Hospital for children in 1919. See Margaret Ó hÓgartaigh, *Kathleen Lynn:
Irishwoman, Patriot, Doctor* (Dublin: Irish Academic Press, 2006).

141 10 Feb. 1909 (17).

This was a stance which Jacob herself later adopted as she refused to join either the IWFL or the MWFL.

Returning to Waterford after her Dublin visit in 1909, Jacob worked distributing *Bean na hÉireann* newspapers, offering them on trial to Gety's shop and placing an advertising poster in the local Gaelic League rooms.[142] Throughout 1909–14 Jacob's active work on behalf of the suffrage cause was confined to collecting signatures. On 3 July 1912 she noted how on the way home from a Society for the Prevention of Cruelty to Animals (SPCA) meeting she called on a Mrs Dwyer 'and got her to sign a suffrage demand – not petition exactly'.[143] However, despite such limited activism, Jacob continued to educate herself in the ideologies and beliefs of the feminist campaign and, very importantly, her close observation of the different political, cultural and feminist campaigns which variously intersected and converged throughout the first two decades of the twentieth century provided the raw material for her first novel, *Callaghan*, set in 1912–14. It should be noted that Jacob's refusal to hide her views and her willingness to debate on the issue of female suffrage was a form of activism by stealth. Her discussions gradually normalised, for example, the debate on the vote for women for many family friends and those within her circle. She noted in her diary on 13 November 1909 'a heated Suffragette argument after tea' and commented how Mr Orr 'would give women votes the way he wd throw a bone to an importunate dog, and that is a good way for him to have got I think. He wouldn't have gone so far 3 years ago'.[144] The importance of this form of activism is reflected in *Callaghan* as Miss Doran, secretary to the IWFL, attempts to encourage members in the provinces to 'educate their friends and acquaintances and prepare the ground'.[145]

SUFFRAGE VERSUS NATIONALISM

At one level family commitments, in particular to her mother, prevented Jacob from taking a more active role in the suffrage campaign. On a number of occasions Jacob noted how she was unable to participate fully in Dublin activism because of her mother's ill health and increasing psychological dependence on her daughter. 'Whenever I go away anywhere', Jacob noted in 1913, 'I find M[other] worse when I come home'.[146] Henrietta Jacob's health

---

142 21 May 1909; 18 July 1909, RJD Ms (18).

143 3 July 1912, RJD Ms (23).

144 13 Nov. 1909, RJD Ms (18).

145 Winthrop, *Callaghan*, p. 73.

146 6 June 1913, RJD Ms (25).

suffered in the wake of her husband's death; in 1912 she was declared to be suffering from debility leading to 'neuritis'.[147] In the height of the anti-welcome campaign against the Royal visit in 1911 Jacob was asked to travel to Dublin to distribute leaflets but noted 'I can't for Mamma may be coming home then, & even if she's not coming till Monday I couldn't for I probably wouldn't be home by Monday evening'. [148] Later that year, in August 1911 she was obliged to cut her Dublin visit short because her mother 'has not been well since the thunderstorm & the heat of those few days'.[149] In March 1913 she was able to leave her mother and spend some time in Dublin because 'Miss Boyd is coming while I am away'.[150] Jacob, as a single woman, was throughout her life considered responsible for the care of older family members, women who did not have children being expected to adopt a caring role according to the dictates of the ideology of separate spheres.[151] The main reason, however, for Jacob's failure to take a more active and decisive role in the suffrage campaign was her growing commitment to advanced nationalism and her anti-English impulses. Many nationalist activists of the period testified to an inherent Anglophobia, formed early in life. Repeating tropes appear in many of the retrospective memoirs of activists in the proto republican cause of the period: a disdain for monarchy and revulsion towards all cultural and social manifestations of Englishness. Ernie O'Malley wrote how in youth he 'had the inborn hatred of things English, which I expect all Irishmen inherit'.[152] Maud Gonne stated that by the time she had 'reached the age of reason and was a free agent' she had determined that maintenance of the British Empire was not worth the price of 'famine in Ireland, opium in China, torture in India'.[153] Jacob's stance against the Boer War has been previously noted. Queen Victoria's death in January 1901 occurred on the same night as the death of the household cat, Pansy. 'And', Jacob wrote, 'we would all much rather go into mourning for her than for that hideous old woman'. It is notable that this is a diary entry written near to the moment rather than the construction of a retrospective trope to bolster the ideal of advanced nationalist commitment from an early age. Much of Jacob's unhappiness at the Protestant girls' school was the result of nationalism

147 5 Aug. 1912, RJD Ms (23).

148 7 July 1911, RJD Ms (22). Jacob's mother had been in Blarney, County Cork, with her sister Hannah, for a change of air.

149 7 Aug. 1911, RJD Ms (22).

150 5 Mar. 1913, RJD Ms (24)

151 6 June 1913, RJD Ms (25); 5 Aug. 1912, RJD Ms (23).

152 Quoted in English, *Ernie O'Malley*, p. 1.

153 A. Norman Jeffares and Anna MacBride White (eds), *The Autobiography of Maud Gonne: A Servant of the Queen* (Chicago: University of Chicago Press, 1998), p. 10.

expressed within her family. A fashion for wearing buttons of political figures saw Jacob aligned against her schoolmates when one:

> suddenly . . . snatched out of my dress the little button with portrait of Parnell, Wolfe Tone, and Emmet on it that I always wear, and ran away with it . . . We had a good deal of argument, they said the rebels never succeeded.[154]

Her fellow students wore buttons depicting 'Edwards or Alexandras or generals and talked a lot of nonsense.'[155] Reading a work on Finn McCoole was 'stigmatised as rum'.[156] The final school day at the Protestant school in 1903 was 'nice enough but sickeningly loyal'. Everyone but her family gave two renditions of 'God Save the King'.[157] In 1905, on her 17th birthday Jacob received a variety of texts that indicate the manner in which the family had immersed themselves in the cultural values of Irish-Ireland. Her father presented her with *Footprints of Emmet*, while she received *Gill's Irish Reciter, Aids to Irish Pronunciation* and *Songs of Erin*, from her mother and Tom respectively.[158]

During the period of debate on the third Home Rule Bill of 1912 the issue of suffrage versus the nationalist cause crystallised. In 1910 a cross party conciliation committee had been appointed to draft a women's suffrage bill that would find favour with all parties. The following year, the new Conciliation Bill came before the Parliament; 31 Irish Parliamentary Party MPs voted for the Bill on its first reading, but on the second reading in 1912 not one did. Home Rule was the priority and the actions of the Irish MPs can be explained in part in relation to fears of the fall of the government over the issue of women's suffrage.[159] In 1907 to be a suffragette was for Jacob the height of 'revolutionary opinions'. She described the language activist Upton, as 'something of a suffragette, so I don't see how he could have more revolutionary opinions'.[160] Increasingly, however, Jacob came to see the advanced nationalist cause as one that had to take precedence over suffragism. Her evolution towards advanced nationalist beliefs made it easier to prioritise the national issue over the suffrage cause. Unlike Hanna Sheehy Skeffington, Jacob was not willing to ask for the vote from an alien parliament and her move towards advanced nationalism allowed her to sidestep the perfidy of the Irish Parliamentary Party on the issue of the vote for women. Her thinking

154 9 May 1903, RJD Ms (5).

155 9 Dec. 1903, RJD Ms (7).

156 8 Oct. 1903, RJD Ms (6).

157 17 June 1903, RJD Ms (6).

158 13 Oct. 1905, RJD Ms (10).

159 See Rosemary Cullen Owens, *Louie Bennett* (Cork: Cork University Press, 2000), pp. 17–18.

160 9 Mar. 1907, RJD Ms (14).

was akin to that of Francis Sheehy Skeffington who created an analogy between the sacrifices of the suffragist and those of Irish republican heroes such as Emmet and Tone, declaring in the *Irish Citizen* in July 1912: 'There is a stronger and purer Nationalism in Mountjoy Prison at this moment than any Mr Redmond's followers can boast'.[161]

Jacob's anti-Englishness contributed to her unwillingness to formally join the IWFL. Her inability to commit formally to a suffrage organisation was based in part on her perception of the links between the English and Irish campaigns, although Hanna Sheehy Skeffington and Margaret Cousins were concerned to highlight that the IWFL and the WSPU ran separate and distinct operations. In 1912 when an English suffragette threw a hatchet in the carriage in which the English Prime Minister Asquith, and John Redmond were travelling, Jacob dismissed the hyperbole of the Press, but made very clear her attitude to the involvement of English suffragists in the Irish campaign.

> Emer [Helena Molony] says the hatchet . . . was only a toy hatchet, so they need not have made such a fuss about it. The way the papers talked you'd think it was a bomb. All the same I wish English suffragists would stay at home & carry on their campaign in their own country.[162]

In 1912 the *Waterford News* published the following letter from Jacob designed to ask the MWFL why the principal speaker was

> invariably a foreigner – English or otherwise . . . I have grown tired of hearing from a Waterford platform such phrases as 'Here in Great Britain', 'How we lost our colonies in America', 'This kingdom' (meaning England) and 'Magna Charta [*sic*], the foundation of your liberties.' And when the speakers do happen to remember that they are not addressing an English audience the result (generally an attempt at humour or flattery) is such as to wish that they had not remembered it. As long as Irish women's franchise societies depend largely on imported speakers they will find it difficult to repel the accusation of being merely offshoots and appendages of the English suffragist movement.[163]

Jacob was obliged to explain repeatedly why she did not join either the IWFL or the MWFL.[164] In October 1913 she explained to Mrs Hayden of the

---

161 Margaret Ward, 'Hanna Sheehy Skeffington (1877–1946)' in Mary Cullen and Maria Luddy (eds), *Female Activists: Irish Women and Change 1900–1960* (Dublin: Woodfield Press, 2001), pp. 92–3.

162 25 July 1912, RJD Ms (23).

163 *Waterford News*, 25 Oct. 1912.

164 13 Feb. 1914; 15 Dec. 1913 RJD Ms (26).

MWFL that she did not join 'partly because I was a Separatist & partly because they did nothing but import English speakers'.[165]

This issue of English speakers was obviously an ongoing concern for Jacob. She recorded in her diary how Mary Strangman asked her at a suffrage meeting in 1914 if she was now 'satisfied, having a meeting with only Irish speakers'. Jacob's retort highlights her extreme anti-English sentiments and the divergence of her views from many in the suffrage campaign: 'I said I thought Miss Day might have said more about sweated workers *here* & less about them in England, but I was informed that it was a worldwide move-ment etc etc.'[166] In Mrs Coates's house for tea on 10 March 1913 Jacob recorded details of a conversation on the merits and demerits of compulsory Irish. Her anti-English views were the strongest in the room and the diary entry highlights her abhorrence at the opinions, and lack of political radicalism, amongst the other guests:

> Mrs Coates deprecates the hatred of England which people are so apt to have when they are patriotic, nobody else talked quite such rot, but they did not definitely agree with me, that the more of that the better.[167]

For many female activists the suffrage campaign was, as Strangman had informed Jacob, an international one. Louie Bennett, Secretary of the Irish Women's Suffrage Federation (IWSF) from 1911–13, made clear the uniquely Irish nature of the organisation in May 1913 but emphasised the international nature of first-wave feminism: 'we suffragists are working for all women . . . we recognise the bond of sisterhood uniting women of every nationality without losing anything of the strong, free, Celtic spirit and passionate instinct for independence characteristic of that spirit'.[168] Indeed, for Bennett, the inter-national bonds created by the women's and labour movements were becoming so strong as to mitigate the forces of nationalism.[169] Later in life Jacob would increasingly embrace the international lens of female activism. In the period

---

165 17 Oct. 1913, RJD Ms (25).
166 24 Feb. 1914, RJD Ms (26).
167 10 Mar. 1913, RJD Ms (24).
168 Quoted in Cullen Owens, *Louie Bennett*, p. 21. Louie Bennett (1870–1956) was involved throughout her life in the twin causes of suffrage and labour. In 1911 she founded with Helen Chenevix the Irish Women's Suffrage Federation to link all Irish suffrage organisations. Two years later she founded the Irish Women's Reform League dedicated to both suffrage and labour issues. She became secretary of the Irish Women's Workers Union in 1916 and was involved in working for women's labour rights until 1955. Bourke et al. (eds), *Field Day Anthology*, vol. v, p. 565.
169 Cullen Owens, *Louie Bennett*, p. 23.

prior to 1916, however, political freedom was the ultimate achievement for Jacob, without which language revival or the attainment of female suffrage was of little or no value. Wales, she wrote:

> is a melancholy example of the state to which the Gaelic League without the help of politics, would bring Ireland. Nationality without a language is better than language without nationality.[170]

The ideal was a person 'who can combine a passion for the language with thorough good Fenian sentiments'.[171] She dismissed James Stephens's *The Crock of Gold*, published in 1912, for the way he 'carefully ignores politics & nationality & everything of that sort'. For Jacob nationality and political freedom were synonymous.[172] She truly embraced Helena Molony's sentiment expressed in *Bean na hÉireann* in July 1909 when she wrote that in themselves the study of the language, Irish history, Irish economics were of no value 'if there is not behind the great driving force . . . love of Ireland and of everything great and small that belongs to Ireland because it belongs to Ireland'.[173] Despite the plethora of suffrage organisations that existed by the early 1910s Jacob noted a central lacunae and wrote a letter to the *Irish Citizen* in March 1913 'on the desirability of a Nationalist women's franchise society'.[174] This letter indicates her prioritising of the national cause over suffrage but also indicates that this was an uneasy choice for her; the ideal was a forum where she could commit herself fully as a suffragist and as a nationalist. Jacob did not, therefore, eschew suffrage for nationalism but sought to establish a synergy of commitment at various intersecting levels.

    Despite her lack of official affiliation to a suffrage organisation, Jacob continued to attend suffrage activities in Waterford. On 13 February 1914 she attended a 'sort of suffragist at home' in a Miss Lowell's house at Lower Newtown. This was targeted at 'non-members, to get them interested'.[175] This testifies to the manner in which division could be circumvented. It was not always nationalism versus suffragism; the situation was more complex and fluid than it has often been represented. This suffrage 'at home' meeting high-

---

170 13 Jan. 1910, RJD Ms (19).

171 12 May 1911, RJD Ms (21).

172 29 Dec. 1912, RJD Ms (24).

173 Quoted in Nell Regan, 'Helena Molony' in Cullen and Luddy (eds), *Female Activists*, p. 143.

174 19 Mar. 1913, RJD Ms (24). By 1910 there were eighteen suffrage societies in Ireland, which made provision for various political and religious beliefs. Cullen Owens, *Louie Bennett*, p. 13.

175 13 Feb. 1914, RJD Ms (26).

lighted the manner in which women saw the vote as allowing them transform the existing social and economic system, through introducing reforms such as better housing, education and measures designed to lower infant mortality, as well as ending the exploitation of women in the work place. This approach stressed women's distinctive experiences as wives and mothers and how these could be used to humanise or civilise political activity. Those who attended the meeting listened to details about the white slave traffic and heard the story of a policeman who assaulted his sergeant's young daughter. What Maria Luddy describes as 'the picture of moral guardianship pioneered by women' in the nineteenth century was then very much a feature of the early twentieth-century suffrage meetings Jacob attended.[176] Strangman, who attended the meeting, was concerned to gather a party from within the MWFL to demand to be present at an impending infanticide trial.[177] Jacob, however, was opposed to the way in which women used their socially ascribed role as mothers to argue for the franchise; her approach to winning female suffrage was based on notions of equal rights for men and women. On 26 November 1913 Dr Strangman spoke at the Quaker meeting house on the subject of women's suffrage and Jacob's comments indicate the manner in which her claim to the vote was founded on such an equal rights approach:

> Edith Bell was saying how you had to blush for the doings of militants & that she thought someone said suffragists were against marriage, so I said that was the queerest thing said yet, in face of all the motherhood rot in the suffrage journals, (using more moderate language of course) & that women always seem to think it necessary to blush for what any women does, but men never take the crimes of other men on the shoulders of their sex that way.
> . . . She [Strangman] talked a good deal of morals & venereal disease, more than they liked, I think . . .[178]

176 Maria Luddy, *Women and Philanthropy in Nineteenth-Century Ireland* (Cork: Cork University Press, 1995), p. 145.

177 Ryan discusses the Watching the Court Committee established in May 1914 under the umbrella of the Irishwomen's Reform League. Between 10 and 20 members undertook to 'watch' cases at three of the Dublin Courts. However, it is clear from Jacob's diary entry that this activity was also carried on, albeit less formally, in areas outside Dublin. Louise Ryan, 'Publicising the private: suffragists' critique of sexual abuse and domestic violence', Louise Ryan and Margaret Ward (eds), *Irish Women and the Vote: Becoming Citizens* (Dublin: Irish Academic Press, 2007), p. 78.

178 26 Nov. 1913, RJD Ms (25).

NATIONALISM: THE ANTI-WELCOME CAMPAIGN

Jacob's early activism in the campaign for Irish independence was in the anti-welcome campaign, the response of Irish nationalists to the Royal visit of July 1911. As a tribute to the newly crowned George V and his wife, Mary, the authorities organised the signatures of as many 'Irish Marys' as possible. In response Inghinidhe na hÉireann set out to gather a counter set of signatures to act as a denunciation of monarchy and colonialism. This use of counter spectacle as a tool against manifestations of imperialism, of course, had been the impetus that had given birth to Inghinidhe na hÉireann in the first place when a nationalist alternative to the children's free treat in honour of Queen Victoria on 4 April 1900 was arranged.[179] In Waterford the loyal petition was organised by Mrs de la Poer and by May the *Waterford Standard* happily reported the collection of 5,591 signatures and the sum of £64 16s 6d.[180] Helena Molony, however, punctured any sense of achievement when she remarked on the 'smallness of the figure' in view of the number of women in the county.[181] In March 1911 Jacob's mother suggested the collection of anti-welcome signatures in Waterford. Jacob created a typewritten form and brought the matter to Mr Downey of the *Waterford News*, who agreed to keep the form in the office and put a notice in the paper informing people of the procedure. Jacob was to the forefront in collecting signatures for the 'disloyal protest', a task she found difficult: 'It is odious work taking it round'.[182]

Jacob's anti-Englishness solidified in this period. Those who refused to sign the petition were dismissed as English.[183] The unwillingness of some women to sign the protest rankled heavily with her and she attributed their actions to their lack of status under an oppressive patriarchal system: 'I went along Ballytruckle a bit, looking for names, but found everyone either impenetrably stupid or averse to do anything without asking their husbands'.[184] Feminist issues were always part of Jacob's desire for nationalist advancement. Indeed, in more than one campaign Jacob found the oppression of women under patriarchy a serious barrier to advancement. In June 1914 she was involved in collecting signatures for a petition to Waterford Corporation about humane slaughtering procedures. At Mrs Brabazon's house she found a note pinned to the door saying that she could not sign it due to her husband's

179 Ward, *Unmanageable Revolutionaries*, p. 48.
180 *Waterford Standard*, 20 May 1911.
181 *Waterford Standard*, 24 May 1911.
182 6–9 Mar. 1911 RJD Ms (21).
183 Ibid.
184 13 Mar. 1911, RJD Ms (21).

business-related objections to the family name appearing on the petition. 'Its [*sic*] hard,' Jacob wrote, 'to know which of them to despise more'.[185] Jacob's reference to why she believed women did not sign her anti-welcome protest mirrors the concern of nationalist activists to expose why women signed the loyal protest. Shop assistants and other such 'vulnerable' groups in society were represented as being forced to sign by employers who feared the approbation of upper-class customers.[186] The *Waterford Standard* reported the comments of Helena Molony at a meeting in the city in May:

> Mistresses in the shooneen district in Dublin . . . who keep three or four domestic servants, simply give these lists to the girls. They could not expect them to do anything else but sign. They were dependent on their place for a living, and if they refused to sign, it would mean the loss of their situation. This was how many hundreds of signatures were got.

Molony went on to claim that old age pensioners were similarly threatened with the loss of pensions in the workhouses.[187]

The anti-welcome campaign intensified for Jacob in April 1911 when Madeline ffrench Mullen came to stay with her in Waterford. ffrench Mullen enthused Jacob with details of how she and Helena Molony campaigned in Dublin, putting up notices for an anti-welcome meeting to be held in the capital and how they 'came near being arrested'. Jacob listened avidly to news of a successful women's anti-welcome meeting held earlier in April at 6 Harcourt Street in Dublin. ffrench Mullen galvanised Jacob into action with her plan to establish a Waterford women's anti-welcome meeting. Jacob was clearly enamoured by her multi-faceted nationalist commitment as ffrench Mullen examined all the Waterford shops to see if they sold Irish goods. Jacob revelled in the excitement of watching Madeline pin an anti-welcome ballad 'To the Marys of Ireland' on to the side of the carriage coming back from a trip to Tramore 'for the next comer to see'. 'Now I should never have thought of that', Jacob wrote.[188] What is noteworthy in Jacob's excitement at ffrench Mullen's activism is the gap between Jacob's intellectual radicalism and the actual extent of her involvement in feminist or nationalist campaigns. This would be a pattern throughout Jacob's life. This was in contrast with someone like Molony who was arrested for throwing stones at illuminations of the King and Queen on the corner of Grafton Street. Molony's account captured the

185 27 June 1914, RJD Ms (27).

186 Ward, *Unmanageable Revolutionaries*, pp. 76–7.

187 *Waterford Standard*, 24 May 1911.

188 7–8 Apr. 1911, RJD Ms (21).

radical nature of female involvement in such activities; that sense of breaking boundaries that Jacob desired but never experienced at this point other than on a cerebral level:

> At that time no well brought up girl would dream of throwing stones in public, for any purpose whatever. The Suffragettes had not yet gone into real action for their cause, and we all would have thought it undesirable – if we had paused to think at all.[189]

Throughout April and May 1911 Jacob helped to organise the Waterford women's anti-loyal meeting, which was to be held following a public meeting in opposition to the Royal visit. The local language activist Upton was a key figure orchestrating the public meeting.[190] In April 1911 a letter appeared in the *Waterford News* from the secretaries of the anti-welcome campaign in Dublin, addressed to the women in Waterford calling on them not to sign the loyal address.[191] A speaker was to be invited from Dublin, the choice being Helena Molony, with Jennie Wyse Power[192] as an alternative. A small committee was organised in the locality and time was spent 'hunting up names of people whom it wd be worth while to ask to the meeting.'[193] Jacob herself wrote circulars, which were copied by her brother Tom, asking women to attend the public meeting and noting the presence of Helena Molony as one of the invited speakers.[194] She encountered opposition to bringing the issue into the Gaelic League. In particular, the secretary of the branch objected to her attempt to have female Gaelic League members sign the disloyal petition as 'it was entirely a political matter'. She stated that he wrote, 'just as a loyalist would write'.[195] Similarly when a Miss B refused to attend the women's meeting on the same grounds Jacob launched a strident invective:

> She is one of the non-politicals, who deceive you into thinking they are good patriots with their Gaelic League & Industrial Revival activity, & then bust up

189 Helena Molony, BMH WS 391, pp. 15–16.

190 9 Apr. 1911, RJD Ms (21).

191 *Waterford News*, 28 Apr. 1911.

192 Jennie Wyse Power (1858–1941) began her nationalist career in the Ladies Land League of 1881. She was late involved in Inghinidhe na hÉireann, Cumann na mBan and the IWFL. After the rising she was involved through Sinn Féin in supporting the dependants of those imprisoned. A supporter of the Treaty she served as a senator, 1922–36. Sinead McCoole, *No Ordinary Women: Irish Female Activists in the Revolutionary Years* (Dublin: O'Brien, 2004), pp. 212–13.

193 9–22 Apr. 1911, RJD Ms (21).

194 17 May 1911, RJD Ms (21).

195 12 Mar. 1911, RJD Ms (21).

when its a question of coming out openly as Nationalists . . . People do make me wild when they prate about taking no part in politics, & not taking either side, as if such conduct showed their transcendent wisdom & virtue, instead of being plain cowardice & inertia.[196]

This issue of the non-political status of the League was becoming increasingly divisive by the second decade of the twentieth century, as evident in the 1913 Árd Fheis. Thomas Ashe reflected at leadership level the beliefs Jacob held as an ordinary member, agitating for the organisation to take a nationalist stance on political issues.[197]

The Waterford anti-loyal meeting held on 21 May 1911 was successful by Jacob's standards, although dismissed by the RIC County Inspector who commented that the 'meeting was not attended by any local persons of note and may be regarded as unimportant'.[198] The *Waterford Standard* belittled the meeting as unrepresentative despite the large attendance. The paper declared that the meeting had 'one object, that of making the promoters appear ludicrous in the eyes of the general public'. Councillor Owen Dawson chaired the meeting addressed by three Dublin speakers, Molony, Dr McCartan and the O'Rahilly.[199] Jacob was critical of comments by a number of the local male speakers who protested that they intended no disrespect to the King.[200] Local Councillor M. Quinlan proposed a resolution against the right of a public body 'to make a gesture of loyalty in view of the withholding of self-government'.[201] For this reason, Jacob accepted the O'Rahilly's speech as the best: 'he talked straight plain Fenianism all the time, with no pretence of respect or liking for George & Mary'.[202] In all this activity Jacob continued to link her efforts with the efforts of those in Dublin. One of the latter, a Miss Dowley, regaled her with details of the scheme to set fire to the Kingstown decorations in the middle of the night before George and Mary arrived. 'It would,' Jacob wrote,

196 8 Apr. 1911, RJD Ms (21).

197 McMahon, 'All creeds and all classes', p. 130. Thomas Ashe died on hunger strike in 1917 demanding political status as a Sinn Féin prisoner. His death followed an attempt by the government to force feed him.

198 RIC County Inspector's Report for Waterford May 1911, CO 904/84.

199 *Waterford Standard*, 24 May 1911. Dr Pat McCartan was a republican nationalist from County Tyrone. The O'Rahilly was a member of the central executive of the Gaelic League from 1912 and managing director of *An Claidheamh Soluis* from 1913. He wrote for *Sinn Féin* and was a co-founder of the Irish Volunteers. R. F. Foster, *Modern Ireland, 1600–1972* (London: Penguin, 1989), p. 473.

200 21 May 1911, RJD Ms (21).

201 *Waterford Standard*, 24 May 1911.

202 21 May 1911, RJD Ms (21).

'be splendid if it could be done & if they would burn properly'.[203] Despite her local activities during the anti-welcome campaign, Jacob still occupied a fringe role in the political scene in which she mixed. On 6 August 1911 Countess Markievicz and Helena Molony were arrested for assaulting a policemen at a meeting in Beresford Place. This meeting was held to honour both Molony herself and Mr McArdle for their activities in the anti-welcome campaign, activities that had led to their arrest and imprisonment.[204] Jacob was asked to fill in for Markievicz as the Queen of Ulster in the Oireachtas pageant entitled 'the Feis of Tara'; this episode shows how Jacob was not on the political cutting edge but instead filled a secondary role in the campaign.[205] This was to be a theme of Jacob's activism throughout her life.

Jacob's increasing focus on the female activist social circle in Dublin from 1909 did not go unnoticed by the Quaker community in which she lived. 'Charlotte came in this morning', she wrote, and 'was rather shocked to hear where I was going to stay'. In the midst of the IWFL plan to heckle Redmond during his visit to Waterford in 1914 Jacob sent a note to Hanna Sheehy Skeffington: 'I should think it likely that care will be taken to prevent any not well-known – to – be – respectable – women getting into the Town Hall at all – I am *not* thought very respectable'.[206] Jacob in all likelihood was not considered as a danger to the *status quo* in Waterford unlike the suffrage agitator described below in the *Waterford News*. What influenced the treatment of the suffrage cause in the Waterford press was the fact that Redmond held his seat for Waterford. Nicholas Whittle, in his Bureau witness statement noted that even in cases where there was a Fenian tradition among Waterford families support was often transferred to the Irish Parliamentary Party in the early twentieth century.[207] The *Waterford News*, while willing to report on suffrage meetings, was not willing to recognise or legitimise any attempt by suffragists, local or otherwise, to have their demands recognised by the Irish Parliamentary Party. In February 1913 Redmond was in Waterford to open a new bridge and the paper minimised, ridiculed and denounced the attempts by suffrage campaigners to protest his refusal to allow votes for women be included in the 1912 Home Rule Bill, making clear the lack of support for their demonstration:

203 18 May 1911, RJD Ms (21).

204 McArdle had been arrested during an incident where the police attempted to stop Markievicz burning a Union Jack; Molony had been arrested for throwing stones at the illuminations erected in honour of the royal visit. Molony refused to pay the fine and was sentenced to imprisonment for a month although she served only a few days. Anne Marreco, *The Rebel Countess* (London: Weidenfeld & Nicolson, 1967), pp. 141–2, p. 144.

205 7 Aug. 1911, RJD Ms (22). In the event Jacob was not needed for the pageant.

206 Jacob to Hanna Sheehy Skeffington, 20 Jan. 1914, SSP Ms 33,608 (9).

207 Nicholas Whittle, BMH WS 1105, pp. 13–14.

Waterford had its first experience of a militant Suffragette display on Monday but it was a very tame and unexciting affair indeed. The two ladies who traveled all the way from Dublin for the purpose of interrogating Mr Redmond might have saved themselves the time and trouble . . . One of the ladies – a Miss Hayes – asked Mr Redmond when he was going to open the bridge for the women of Ireland, and immediately she did there were cries of 'Suffragettes,' 'put them out,' 'kick 'em out,' etc. Mrs Poole who was standing close to the Suffragette told her to 'go away girl,' and a constable caught her by the shoulder and helped her away . . . the crowd was hostile.[208]

The use of the term 'the Suffragette' – in particular, the use of the definite article – works to establish an 'other' or even dehumanise the female activist. Indeed, her cause is arguably diminished as the report emphasises that the stable force in society – the married Mrs Poole – dismisses her as a girl. The female agitator is then outside Waterford politics and a destabilising element in society. However, according to the report the strength of feeling for Redmond and the cause of Home Rule – 'the crowd' – is sufficient to neutralise this element.

On a personal level one of the most favourable consequences of Jacob's political activity in response to the Royal visit was the standing invitation she received from Helena Molony to stay with herself and Markievicz when she travelled to Dublin; this, Jacob wrote, 'will be most valuable to me'.[209] These visits were an experience in bohemian living as she recorded her first cigarette taken in the company of Molony and John Brennan.[210] She noted how Molony, John Brennan and Madeline ffrench Mullen were 'very fond of smoking'.[211] Jacob did not easily shake off this sense of participating in an alternative life in Dublin. Nearly a year later the idea of smoking was still tinged with a perception of experiencing something illicit and daring; this was arguably a response to the restrictions she faced within her family and community in Waterford. Recording on a gathering she attended in the house of the poet, Blanaid Salkeld, in May 1912 she wrote how Mrs Salkeld 'produced cigarettes or I suppose I should say she passed around the smokes'.[212] Although captivated by the new milieu in which she found herself Jacob was not overawed and, inwardly at least,

---

208 *Waterford News*, 14 Feb. 1913.

209 22 May 1911, RJD (Ms 21).

210 John Brennan was the pseudonym of the suffragist and nationalist activist Sidney Gifford, who contributed to such papers as *Sinn Féin*, *Bean na hÉireann* and the *Irish Citizen*.

211 1 Aug. 1911, RJD Ms (21).

212 10 May 1912, RJD Ms (23). Blanaid Salkeld (1880–1959) was involved in the Gaelic League and the Abbey Theatre, writing a number of plays for the latter under the pseudonym Nell Byrne. Salkeld also wrote poetry. Bourke et al. (eds), *Field Day Anthology*, vol. v, p. 639.

was willing to criticise and evaluate those women with whom she mixed, many of them feminist leaders in Dublin in the period. She noted with equanimity Molony's sexual preferences and attitude to love and relationships:

> She seems to regard men, as men, more as the relaxation of an idle hour than in any more serious light, does not appear to believe much in the one love of a lifetime, but rather in one minor flame after another. She prefers women and Madame prefers men.[213]

Jacob was a woman of committed and passionate principles and her diary offers a good account of her unwillingness to accept unquestioningly any viewpoint that clashed with her own. Although she recorded that Hanna Sheehy Skeffington was the only friend she made in 1913, she was opposed to Hanna and Francis's attitudes, for example, to the anti-vivisection campaign: 'their idea . . . that it is mostly its uselessness that condemns it' was very different to Jacob's opposition on grounds of cruelty.[214] Indeed, Jacob's fervent anti-vivisectionist belief and commitment to animal rights added to her growing antagonism towards Markievicz; Jacob described her 'callous talk about shooting birds' and stated that 'Madame is a bloodthirsty sports-woman . . . and the [Fianna] boys seem the same in theory. Now if some humane person had charge of the Fianna, what a lot of good might be done'.[215] Jacob herself did not recognise the cultural clash inherent in such a statement. Markievicz, as a member of the Anglo-Irish, came from a tradition committed to hunting and shooting; Jacob's Quaker background ensured that she was immersed in a culture dedicated to the humane treatment of animals. Jacob's commitment to humane animal slaughtering and animal rights located her firmly within the values of her Waterford Quaker community at the same time as her radical political beliefs alienated her from many of them. In June 1911 she met Mr Green, Secretary of the Irish Anti-Vivisection Society, who she admired instantly as 'a Nationalist & a Gaelic Leaguer besides being an anti-vaccinationist, & apparently an anti- vivisectionist, and by no means a good Catholic'. At his request she wrote an anti-vaccination letter to the local press.[216] A combined Waterford and Wexford division of the Anti-Vivisection Society was inaugurated on 22 April 1911.[217] Many of Jacob's

213 4 Aug. 1911, RJD Ms (21).
214 25 Dec. 1913, RJD Ms (26); 19 Mar. 1913, RJD Ms (24).
215 30 July 1911, RJD Ms (22).
216 7 June 1911, RJD Ms (22).
217 *Irish Times*, 13 May 1911, p. 11. The issue of vivisection was strongly debated from the 1870s. See Rod Preece, 'Darwinism, Christianity and the great vivisection debate', *Journal of the History of Ideas* 64: 3 (July 2003), pp. 399–419.

friends and contemporaries would come to view Jacob's concern for animal welfare as bordering on obsessive. Even at this point her views were stronger than many within her community as the following diary extract on a proposed anti-vivisection meeting in Waterford in May 1911 shows:

> There is to be an anti-vivisection meeting at the town hall to-morrow, & Stephen Coleridge is to speak. Anna Bell says she will go, but she 'is far more interested in the prevention of cruelty to children' . . . Honestly I wish all vivisection would take to experimenting exclusively on children instead of on animals; then there would be a chance of something being done about it.[218]

In Dublin society she took issue with the three Gifford sisters, Sidney, Nellie[219] and Muriel,[220] who mocked her for bringing home a stray cat and told 'horrible stories of what fun they used to have tormenting cats . . . & evidently thinking it a ridiculous joke that anyone should bother about what happened to a cat'.[221] In Jacob's perception Catholics were particularly unconcerned with the suffering of animals. Because Helena Molony was, according to her, less religious than Lasairfhíona Somers 'she has more realisation of the rights of animals'. 'I do believe', Jacob wrote, 'that no pious Catholic can be found who has a conscience towards animals and what could anyone say worse of the Catholic religion?'[222]

While Jacob enjoyed the company of Molony on her visits to Dublin she could not say the same for Markievicz. 'Madame came back to dinner,' she wrote on 15 May 1912, 'I saw too much of her altogether'.[223] The following extract from Jacob's diary seems to suggest divergent political viewpoints between herself and Markievicz, and a belief that hers was the more radical stance. She describes Markievicz as clad

> in a filthy old painting apron . . . looking most disreputable. And talking worse, she revolted me altogether with the way she talked about politics . . . The way they both praise John Redmond is a constant puzzle and annoyance to me.[224]

218 7 May 1911, RJD Ms (21).

219 Nellie Gifford was involved in the Rising as a member of the Irish Citizen Army.

220 Unlike her sisters Sidney, Nellie and Grace, Muriel was not active in the politics of the period.

221 4 Aug. 1911, RJD Ms (22).

222 18 Sept. 1911, RJD Ms (22); 8 May 1911, RJD Ms (21).

223 15 May 1912, RJD Ms (23).

224 7 May 1912, RJD Ms (23).

Markievicz and Molony were at this time, 1912, living at 49B Surrey House, Leinster Road, a residence Seán O'Faolain described as 'untidy, unkempt and next to uncomfortable'; Markievicz herself he described as 'dishevelled', echoing Jacob's description of the Countess's personal appearance.[225] Although Jacob, like Markievicz, came to believe that national independence had to predate female suffrage, she was highly critical of the auxiliary role of women in the nationalist movement and the attitude of male nationalists to the issue of female equality; this may explain the above reference to Redmond. The Irish Parliamentary Party MPs, as noted, had been crucial to the defeat of the various women's suffrage Bills put forward by the Conciliation Committee in the period 1910–13. Of course, the radicalism of Markievicz was ultimately far in advance of Jacob's, participating in the 1916 Rising not as a member of Cumann na mBan but as an officered member of the Irish Citizen Army which was founded in 1913 to protect workers' rights during the 1913 Strike and Lock Out. By 1915 the socialist, James Connolly, had linked the Irish Citizen Army with the fortunes of the Irish Volunteers, believing that national independence was a necessary prerequisite to the successful reorganisation of Irish society on socialist lines or believing, in the words of Seán O'Casey, that the 'people of Ireland were not ripe enough to be shaken from the green tree of Nationalism into the wider basket of an Irish Labour Army'.[226] Jacob's attitude to the 1913 strike was interesting. The denunciation by the Catholic Church of the proposed plan to send the children of striking workers to England on the basis of the threat to their faith is an iconic image of the strike. The lines of division tend to be viewed as a Catholic bourgeois capitalist class, symbolised by William Martin Murphy, in opposition to the poor of Dublin city who were supported by a left wing, in many cases non-Catholic, intelligentsia. Jacob, despite her non-Catholic background and her sense of herself as a radical, was opposed to the economic actions of the Irish Trade Union and General Workers' Union particularly on the grounds of Larkin's Englishness. Jacob's hostility to Markievicz also seems to have been fuelled by the Countess's full-scale participation in this strike, providing sustenance to the families of workers locked out without pay. Jacob recorded visiting Molony on 11 December 1913, the latter staying at this point with Dr Kathleen Lynn, where the conversation moved onto the subject of the strike: 'we agreed most enthusiastically about the revolting unwholesome Englishness of Larkin

---

225 Seán O'Faolain, *Countess Markievicz* (3rd edn, London: Cresset Library, 1967), p. 97, p. 98. Marreco does note that Markievicz moved between two extremes in her personal appearance. When out of uniform or not dressed up for social events she was uncaring and shabby in the manner in which she presented herself. Marreco, *The Rebel Countess*, p. 237.
226 Seán O Casey, *The Story of the Irish Citizen Army* (Dublin: Maunsel, 1919), pp. 7–8.

& the strike & all, including Larkin's use of the word "kiddies", & she [Molony] said Madame had lost some of her sense, & follows . . . blindly'.[227] Molony herself wrote in her witness statement given to the Bureau of Military History in a similar fashion to Jacob: 'All the sympathy of the Irish-Ireland movement was with the strikers but not all of us were in sympathy with James Larkin, or his outlook, which was that of a British Socialist. He attacked the "Nationalist" outlook, which he dubbed "Capitalist"', Molony adding that there 'was some foundation' for the latter.[228] One of Markievicz's biographers presents a more benign, or indeed naïve, reading of Markievicz's support for James Larkin but still conveys that sense of blind devotion indicated by Jacob when she writes: 'The fact that Constance only had to read a newspaper item about Larkin to be filled with so much enthusiasm that she thereupon decided to bicycle into Dublin to attend a meeting planned in his honour shows that she was already thinking as a socialist'.[229] As late as 1925 Jacob still evinced a hostility to Larkin commenting on 'an inter-national organisation to help prisoners that has just been set on foot. But apparently Larkin is in it here'.[230] The tendency of a number of women to idealise the male nationalist politicians infuriated Jacob as was very evident in a diary entry earlier in 1913:

> D. [orothea] was pleased to find that I liked Mrs S. S. [Sheehy Skeffington] and she says she is losing her interest in Home Rule because of J. E. R. [Redmond] & his party's attitude to women. That's what it is to care for apparent patriots instead of for one's country.[231]

Yet, as will be shown, Jacob developed her own cult of nationalist politicians, infatuations or, what would be described today as 'crushes'; this was to be a shifting canon during her life.

NATIONALISM: CUMANN NA MBAN

From mid-1914 into 1915 Jacob's family commitments appear to have heightened. On 5 February 1915 she noted how her mother had come down to dinner for the first time in weeks.[232] From the summer of 1914 to the summer

227 11 Dec. 1913, RJD Ms (25).
228 Helena Molony, BMH WS 391, p. 17.
229 Marreco, *The Rebel Countess*, p. 136.
230 11 Feb. 1925, RJD Ms (47).
231 19 Mar. 1913, RJD Ms (24).
232 5 Feb. 1915, RJD Ms (28).

of 1915 she spent most of her time in Waterford, holidaying during both those summers in Tramore with family. In that time span she went to Dublin for one brief trip. Her political focus for the years 1914–16 was on the activities of Cumann na mBan. Cumann na mBan was formed in 1914 as an auxiliary to the Irish Volunteers; their function was to help in equipping men to defend Ireland. Attending the local Gaelic League meeting on 11 February 1914, Jacob was delighted to hear that 'they are at last starting a Volunteer branch here'.[233] The Waterford Volunteers were launched at a public meeting at the City Hall in March of that year.[234] On 1 April she arrived home to find Liam Mellows, talking with her mother; he informed her of 300 volunteers already signed up in Waterford.[235] Mellows visited Waterford frequently in the early 1910s and by 1912 had organised the Waterford branch of the Fianna – the Thomas Francis Meagher Slua.[236] Andy Callaghan, the hero of *Callaghan*, was partly modelled on Mellows. During that April visit to Waterford, Mellows dined with the Jacobs and he recalled his organisation of the anti-British Army demonstrations in Athlone the previous December:

> he . . . saw the military with a piper's band, playing national tunes, and people following them, & he decided this was going too far, & gathered the Fianna and the local Pipers' Club and made a banner, and brought off the demonstration with such success that the regiment – out for recruiting – left the town early the next morning.[237]

Jacob reproduced this scene in the novel. To oppose the attempt at army recruitment in the locality, Andy Callaghan organised the Kilmartin branch of the Fianna, which he himself had established, together with the local pipers' band who marched under a banner which read: 'No flag but this for Irishmen'.[238] Similar real-life nationalist disruptions against army recruitment took place in Waterford. Local Fianna member, Patrick Hearne, recalled how during the recruiting campaign in the height of the conscription issue in 1918 they 'had our band rebuilt and we specialised in upsetting most of their recruiting meetings by

233 11 Feb. 1914, RJD Ms (26).
234 Pat McCarthy, 'The Irish Volunteers in Waterford, part I, 1913–1916', *Decies* 60 (2004), p. 200.
235 1 Apr. 1914, RJD Ms (26).
236 James Nolan, BMH WS 1369, p. 3. Mellows's role as full-time organiser for the Fianna allowed him the necessary cover to carry out recruitment to the IRB. McCarthy, 'Irish Volunteers in Waterford', p. 199.
237 2 Apr. 1914, RJD Ms (26).
238 Winthrop, *Callaghan*, pp. 86–9.

arranging our parades and route marches so that we would clash with them'.[239] Jacob herself had earlier in June 1911 helped to distribute leaflets against recruitment to the RIC as part of her Sinn Féin activities.[240]

Much of Jacob's correspondence in the years immediately before the Rising appears to have been on the issue of Cumann na mBan activities. In May 1914 she noted a letter she received from Lasairfhíona Somers. The letter was 'all about Cumann na mBan in Áth Cliath, they seem to be booming'. Later that evening, at a Gaelic League meeting, Jacob discussed the possibility with Miss Doyle of starting a Waterford branch of the organisation. Once again, however, she considered the inert nature of the women with whom she was surrounded a serious obstacle to achieving such a goal.[241] Jacob appeared to see no paradox in her own limited involvement in the formal suffrage and nationalist organisations of the period and her criticism of the passive nature of Waterford women. Despite such censure it was not Jacob who established the Waterford branch of Cumann na mBan in August 1914 but Miss Alice Colfer.[242] Jacob's role, as secretary, was to inform the local press of the proposed plans and to issue reports to the press on meetings. Indeed, on hearing that Miss Colfer was leaving Waterford at the end of August and would not be in a position to direct the local branch Jacob declared: 'I'm not sure I'd have joined it if I had known that'.[243]

The tensions between nationalist and unionist women on the outbreak of the First World War were clearly seen in the attempts to set up the Cumann na mBan branch in Waterford. Many women believed Cumann na mBan to be an 'ambulance class' in view of the European war. At the meeting in the Waterford Town Hall on 10 August 1914 a number of women left when the constitution of Cumann na mBan was read aloud and on hearing Miss Colfer announce, in the words of Jacob, that 'we would only keep the Volunteers to defend Ireland *for* Ireland, not for England or any other country'.[244] Jacob, Miss Colfer and another woman then proceeded to take down names and addresses in relation to an affiliation fee. At this point Jacob's anti-Englishness

239 Patrick Hearne, BMH WS 1742, p. 6.

240 3 Mar. 1911, RJD Ms (21).

241 13 May 1914, RJD (26).

242 Alice Colfer had been elected Honorary Secretary of the Waterford Branch of the Gaelic League in Jan. 1914. A teacher, she had spent periods in the Irish speaking districts in County Waterford. *Waterford News*, 23 Jan. 1914.

243 10 Aug. 1914, RJD Ms (27).

244 9–10 Aug. 1914, RJD Ms (27). For a report of Miss Colfer's address see *Waterford News*, 14 Aug. 1914.

and separatist views drastically exacerbated the emerging split between nationalist and loyalist women at the meeting:

> a woman with an English accent got into an altercation with Miss C., in the course of which Miss C. seemed doubtful whether she wd approve of C. na mb. nursing English soldiers in case of war, & said she would far rather be nursing German ones, but she modified her previous remark on consideration, & said we would nurse anybody. Then I pointed out the English accent to her & she read out the rule about only Irishwomen being eligible as members and that hit the shoneen crowd . . . They said it was too narrow.

Jacob's comments here indicate her unrepentant anti-Englishness; her language bordered on bigoted as she diminished those who did not accord with her views, referring to the woman with the English accent on one occasion as 'the accent'. At the meeting on 10 August Miss Colfer was elected as president for the duration of her time in Waterford, Miss Hyland as vice-president, Miss M. Hannigan as treasurer, with Jacob as secretary.[245]

The meetings of the Waterford branch of Cumann na mBan were held in the local Gaelic League rooms. From the outset the branch was beset by a lack of members despite the 70 initial enrolments noted by the *Waterford News*.[246] When the RIC Inspector for Waterford began enumerating the membership of the various nationalist organisations in January 1916 Cumann na mBan had only eight members.[247] Discussions were held as to what activities the branch should engage in and Jacob collected about 20 names for a First Aid class.[248] The high point of the First Aid meetings organised under the auspices of Cumann na mBan was on 9 September 1914 when 17 attended, a figure that was to diminish steadily in the following weeks.[249] The branch clearly suffered from a lack of focus; no sustained objectives were established at any point. On 12 January 1915 a diminished meeting 'tried to think of something a small branch with no money could do. We thought of getting a dozen or two

245 10 Aug. 1914, RJD Ms (27). At the general meeting of the Waterford branch of Cumann na mBan on 17 September 1914 Miss K. Barron and Miss B. Murphy replaced Colfer and Hyland as president and vice president respectively. RJD Ms (27).
246 17 Aug. 1914, RJD Ms (27). *Waterford News*, 14 Aug. 1914. Although the presence of a branch of Cumann na mBan is listed in the RIC Inspector's August 1914 Report for Waterford no numbers are given. CO 904/94.
247 RIC Inspector's Report for Waterford, Jan. 1916, CO 904/99.
248 17 Aug. 1914, RJD Ms (27).
249 9 Sept. 1914; 16 Sept. 1914, RJD Ms (27).

Volunteers every week & selling them to people'.[250] It was little wonder then
that the branch folded on 19 January.[251] Maeve Cavanagh MacDowell recorded
a similar sense of frustration with the Harcourt Street Branch of Cumann na
mBan in the lead up to the Rising. She preferred the route marches and other
activities of the Irish Citizen Army as Cumann na mBan were 'only collecting
money and such like activities'.[252] Indeed, such a lack of focus was not just a
feature of some branches of Cumann na mBan prior to 1916 but was a problem
for the manifold forms of nationalist organisations in the period. Robert
Brennan noted the problems in sustaining Sinn Féin activity in Wexford:

> in the absence of any programme of work in Sinn Féin to which the individual
> could devote himself, branches were continually falling off, so that by the time the
> Home Rule Bill of 1912 was introduced we seemed to be going backward as rapidly
> as the Redmondite Party stung into activity by our opposition was going forward.[253]

Jacob's comments when the Waterford branch of Cumann na mBan fell into
abeyance indicate her relief which forces one to return to question her ability
or willingness to lead and direct activism rather than merely participate and
observe with a writer's eye:

> Kathleen Hicks and May New came up in the afternoon to tell me that the
> meeting on Tuesday evening was a complete fiasco, no one there but the Brennans
> and Miss Keane, who all withdrew at the notion of being political and anti-
> Redmond. That settles it, as ten members is the minimum for a branch, and in
> some ways it is rather a relief.[254]

By contrast with Jacob's lack of overt activism, Kathleen Hicks was described
by Irish Volunteer, Tomas O'Cleirigh, as 'one of our best workers' and he
described how she was involved in a fracas when the RIC and Redmondites

250 12 Jan. 1915, RJD Ms (28). *The Volunteer* was the organ of the Irish Volunteers. It was edited by
Eoin MacNeill from late 1914 to April 1916.

251 The RIC Inspector's Report for Waterford still continued to list one branch of Cumann na mBan
in Waterford throughout 1915. For months at beginning of 1915 see CO 904/96.

252 Maeve MacDowell, BMH WS 258. Maeve Cavanagh was a poet published in *The Irish Worker*,
The Irish Peasant and the *Catholic Bulletin*. Her role in 1916 was in the Irish Citizen Army as messenger.

253 Brennan, *Allegiance*, p. 12.

254 19 Jan. 1915, RJD Ms (28). Probably Kathleen Hicks, living in number 32 South Parade, Waterford,
who was 15 at the time of the 1911 census and had both English and Irish. http://www.census.
nationalarchives.ie/reels/nai003500656. Probably May New, living in 24 Barrack Street, Waterford,
who was 13 in 1911. http://www.census.nationalarchives.ie/reels/nai003506084.

fought against Sinn Féin supporters during the Waterford by-election in 1918.[255] The remaining members of the Waterford branch became members of the central branch of Cumann na mBan.[256]

Shortly after the dissolution of the Waterford branch of Cumann na mBan in early 1915 Jacob went to Dublin for the first time in nearly eight months. She visited the Cumann na mBan headquarters at Kildare Street, having earlier sent them an account, which did not reach them, of the failure of the Waterford branch.[257] Encouraged by Hanna Sheehy Skeffington, Jacob sold copies of the *Irish Citizen* during the anti-recruiting meetings held by her husband, Francis, on 7 March 1915. Later that week she attempted on a number of days to attract sales on Grafton Street, on one such occasion sharing the job with Miss Walsh, one of the suffragettes imprisoned in Tullamore in 1913.[258] The Sheehy Skeffingtons were shocked to discover that Jacob was not intending to go to Sylvia Pankhurst's meeting in O'Connell Street on 19 March and seem to have been influential in encouraging her to change her mind.[259] In the event Sylvia Pankhurst did not attend due to the Liberal Government's decision under the terms of the Munitions of War Act, 1915, to allow women to do work designated male to enable men to enlist. Jacob reported how Meg Connery and Francis Sheehy Skeffington spoke 'excellently, also Miss Bennett, not so well, J. Connolly & various people out of the audience'.[260]

Returning to Waterford, Jacob left again quickly to spend Easter in Cork with her relatives. Jacob was back at home once more in late April and her correspondence and the arrival of a number of visitors kept her in touch with escalating political events. Although Jacob was prepared to put her nationalist sentiments ahead of an official commitment to feminism, she was critical of the auxiliary role of women in such nationalist organisations as Cumann na mBan. This is noteworthy since historians tend to delineate a clear cut division between women such as Sheehy Skeffington who refused to consider that female rights

255 Tomas O Cleirigh, BMH WS 972, p. 16.

256 This might explain the failure of the RIC Inspector to note the cessation of activities in Waterford Cumann na mBan at this point in January 1915.

257 16 Mar. 1915, RJD Ms (26).

258 7 Mar. 1915; 9 Mar. 1915; 12 Mar. 1915, RJD Ms (28). Annie Walsh was one of three suffragettes who smashed the fanlight over the door of the United Irish League's Office in Dublin and windows in the home of Irish Parliamentary Party MP, John Dillon. William Murphy, 'Suffragettes and the transformation of political imprisonment in Ireland, 1912–1914' in Louise Ryan and Margaret Ward (eds), *Irish Women and the Vote: Becoming Citizens* (Dublin: Irish Academic Press, 2007), p. 125.

259 17 Mar. 1915, RJD Ms (28).

260 19 Mar. 1915, RJD Ms (28).

would organically follow independence and women like Mary MacSwiney who were content to fulfil a subordinate female role in the interests of the greater good of the national campaign.[261] At the end of April 1915 Eilís Nic Chárthaigh, a travelling Cumann na mBan organiser, visited Waterford. Originally from Dungarvan, Nic Chárthaigh's role was to visit local branches and organise drilling competitions for feiseanna; Jacob loved that she brought a series of detectives in her wake. More importantly, Jacob's censure of Nic Chárthaigh's attitude to the status of the organisation testifies to her own refusal to accept uncritically all aspects of the nationalist programme and power structures.

> She . . . seemed to me to look on Cumann na mBan too much as an auxiliary to the Volunteers, but it would be strange if she did not, finding all the provincial branches almost entirely dependent on the kindness and encouragement of the local Volunteers. Miss Brodar agreed with me in blaming the women's uselessness on their upbringing, and in thinking that C. na mB. should be more independent of the I. V. I think she must be something like a suffragist.[262]

This is an interesting use of the label suffragist embedded in a conversation on Cumann na mBan, and thereby within the wider discourse of nationalism. Nationalist women, according to Jacob's use of the term suffragist, were either desirous of autonomous organisation in the service of the cause or were content, as Nic Chárthaigh and MacSwiney, to accept auxiliary status. Jacob had met Mary MacSwiney as the Waterford Branch of Cumann na mBan was established in 1914. She became increasingly interested in MacSwiney's prioritising of the nationalist campaign over suffrage. But Jacob was not unquestioning of MacSwiney priorities, indicating her own more complex negotiation of the tension. On 17 July 1914 she recorded details of a letter from MacSwiney. By this date Redmond, in an attempt to overcome deadlock on the 1912 third Home Rule Bill, had agreed to the temporary exclusion of the six north-eastern counties.[263] Where MacSwiney focused on the issue of the betrayal of the nationalist cause involved in Redmond's gesture, Jacob was concerned to probe the issue of the status of Cumann na mBan vis-à-vis the Volunteers: 'Redmond catastrophe, very interesting but ignoring the question about C. na mb. being represented on the Provisional Committee. I answered her mostly about that point.'[264]

261 See, for example, Ward, *Unmanageable Revolutionaries*.
262 23 Apr. 1915, RJD Ms (28).
263 See Maume, *The Long Gestation*, pp. 143–4; Callanan, *T. M. Healy*, pp. 491–505.
264 17 July 1914, RJD Ms (27).

Shortly after Nic Chárthaigh's visit in April 1915 Jacob heard from fellow Waterford activist, Upton, how Nic Chárthaigh had been arrested but released again due to lack of evidence against her; with such entries her diary recorded her growing sense of the escalation of political events during 1914 and 1915.[265] She embraced the news of the Howth gun running on behalf of the Volunteers in June 1914: 'Great news except for the people killed and their friends'.[266] *Callaghan* was written after 1916 but it does reflect Jacob's sense of political expectation during 1915–16. At the end of the novel, the suffragist Frances Morrin marries the local Volunteer leader, Callaghan, knowing that the Volunteers 'may have to come out fairly soon now'. Frances and Callaghan determine to enjoy life in the meantime, 'and then, if all goes to all, we'll have the champagne and chocolate creams to finish up the burst. After that we can settle down to ordinary life, or if we don't manage to survive it – well, we'll have had our chew off the sugarstick'.[267] During this period and despite her criticism of their secondary role in the struggle for freedom, Jacob continued to communicate with Cumann na mBan members and headquarters, receiving their new leaflet, 'Why Ireland is poor', on 20 May 1915.[268]

The outbreak of the First World War in 1914 heightened Jacob's anti-English sentiments. Whereas many activists for women's rights, notably Francis Sheehy Skeffington and Louie Bennett, were opposed to war, seeing it as the product of patriarchal militarism and as such a threat to feminism, Jacob's opposition came from a trenchantly nationalist standpoint.[269] Her response to the war showed little of her later pacifist leanings.[270] For Jacob the war was an English war and Irishmen who enlisted were traitors to Ireland and the national cause. She wrote that she took pleasure in imparting these views to two girls who called collecting money 'to send luxuries to Waterford traitors now prisoners in Germany'.[271] Jacob's hostility to Redmond's commitment of the Volunteers to guard Ireland to permit the withdrawal of British troops for the war effort was frenzied with rage in many passages in her diary.[272]

265 28 Apr. 1915, RJD Ms (28).

266 27 June 1914, RJD Ms (27).

267 Winthrop, *Callaghan*, pp. 234–5.

268 20 May 1915, RJD Ms (28).

269 Cullen Owens, *Louie Bennett*, p. 22.

270 She did tell ffrench Mullen about what she described as a 'neutrality league' in October 1914. 10 Oct. 1914, RJD Ms (27).

271 23 Apr., 1915, RJD Ms (28).

272 In a speech at Woodenbridge, County Wicklow on 20 September 1914, Redmond formally committed the Irish Volunteers to the war in the service of the Empire, believing that this would hasten the granting of Home Rule by a grateful British government. This gesture caused a split in the Volunteers: those who did not follow Redmond maintaining the nomenclature Irish Volunteers, the other group becoming the National Volunteers.

Redmond committed his crowning act of treason, offering the Volunteers, as if he was a king & a general combined, to the British government to defend this unfortunate country for the empire against the Germans if Asquith wd withdraw all the British troops from here.[273]

Jacob's anti-Englishness shaded into a nascent pro-German stance on a number of occasions but this should not be over emphasised. Jacob was not alone in moving towards a rhetoric that was less a manifestation of deep or well thought out pro-German sentiments but rather a forceful expression of anti-Englishness. This nuance was lost on the RIC Inspector for Waterford who commented on more than one occasion on the pro-German sympathies amongst the local Sinn Féin adherents.[274] Molony lamented in *Bean na hÉireann* in 1910, in the context of growing tensions between England and Germany, that nationalist Ireland had, with the exception of the Fianna, no armed force to 'offer Germany in return for her help'.[275] Molony's focus was less pro-German than anti-English. The English were concerned at the possibility of a German invasion; this represented an opportunity for nationalist Ireland in the context of the Irish-English dialectic. Similarly, Jacob recorded Mrs Pearse & Mrs Clarke in November 1916 'agreeing that they would gladly put up with German tyranny here for the sake of seeing it in England'.[276] At a concert in Liberty Hall in November 1916 the audience were treated to a rendition of 'Sinn Féiners, pro-Germans, alive alive oh' described by Jacob as 'a grand song'.[277] However, one should note Jacob's uncertain views on Germany in the extract below:

> Miss O Shea from Rinn [Ring] came to see me . . . She is more pro-German than I am; has lived in Germany and seems to like them greatly, and thinks if they came here we should receive them civilly. I suppose we should – certainly it would be the expedient course, for our own sakes.[278]

273 4 Aug. 1914, RJD Ms (27).

274 Indeed, the July 1915 report, for example, recorded how the words 'Up Germany. Remember 98' were found by the police printed from the inside on the parcels office of the Great Southern & Western Railway Company in Waterford. A local Sinn Féin activist and railway clerk, W. J. Redmond, was suspected of being the responsible party but no proof was forthcoming. CO 904/97.

275 Regan, 'Helena Molony', p. 144.

276 25 Nov. 1916, RJD Ms (30). Kathleen Clarke (1878–1972) was a founding member of Cumann na mBan. She was jailed for participation in republican activities after the Rising. She set up the Irish Volunteer Dependants' Fund immediately after 1916. She was a Sinn Féin councillor for Dublin corporation in 1919. In later life she was a Fianna Fáil senate member from 1927–36 and was first female Lord Mayor of Dublin from 1939–41. Bourke et al. (eds), *Field Day Anthology*, vol. v, p. 175.

277 27 Nov. 1916, RJD Ms (30).

278 3 Sept. 1914, RJD Ms (27).

More centrally located within the parameters of anti-English rather than pro-German nationalist activities, Jacob became involved in the anti-recruiting activities in which Francis Sheehy Skeffington was to the fore. In Kilkenny on 10 October 1914 to meet Madeline ffrench Mullen for the day, she left an *Irish Citizen* in the women's waiting room and a couple of anti-enlisting leaflets in the men's.[279]

Jacob did not restrict her censure of the responses to the war to sections of the nationalist community; various feminist organisations were also criticised for their willingness to suspend the suffrage campaign and partake in war work. Many feminists in both England and Ireland suspended suffrage activities for the duration of the war although June Purvis's 2002 biography of Emmeline Pankhurst offers a more complex reading of the situation. Purvis argues that Emmeline's support for the British Government during the war must be seen as a form of 'patriotic feminism' rather than an 'abrupt about turn'.[280] Of course, for Jacob, as for so many Irish female activists, there could be no transformation into patriotic feminists; Jacob was adamant that England's war was not that of Ireland also. Indeed, this reflected the view of the local Gaelic League who declared in its *Waterford News* column: 'We . . . have nothing to say to the justice or injustice of the war but our own war against Seoininism must be continued with increased vigour'.[281] The MWFL's metamorphosis under the guidance of Edith Somerville[282] and Suzanne Day, 'into a sort of ambulance corps, at the service of the local Volunteers' drew caustic comment from her, as did the fact that Dorothea Farrington, her future sister-in-law, 'is working for it harder than she ever did when it was a suffrage society, as far as one can judge by letters'.[283] One of these letters informed Jacob how Mary MacSwiney had resigned her membership of the MWFL in a dramatic row at a 'Suffrage At Home' during which the war was referred to 'in orthodox British style' and 'awful war pieces – Bravo Kitchener kind of business' were recited.[284]

279 10 Oct. 1914, RJD Ms (27).
280 June Purvis, *Emmeline Pankhurst* (London: Routledge, 2002), pp. 268–9.
281 *Waterford News*, 27 Nov. 1914.
282 Part of the writing duo Somerville and Ross, the Anglo-Irish Edith Somerville was a key member of the MWFL.
283 28 Aug. 1914; 9 Sept. 1914, RJD Ms (27).
284 13 Oct. 1914, RJD Ms (27).

'CALLAGHAN': A SUFFRAGE-NATIONALIST MARRIAGE

The legacy of Jacob's involvement in the multifaceted feminist and nationalist campaigns of the early twentieth century is the novel *Callaghan*. This represents one of the very few examples of Irish suffrage fiction in contrast with the literature of the English suffrage campaign which has received a degree of attention.[285] For most Irish women writers their relationship to the political creeds of unionism or nationalism was more important than feminism. Certainly Gerardine Meaney's analysis of the subversive potential of female political writing has to be acknowledged; late nineteenth-century nationalist women writing in defence of the nation could claim the right of women to participate in the political life of a newly independent Irish State.[286] Jacob herself reflected the view that female participation in the national cause was simultaneously feminist activism in the statement by Bridie Quinlan in *Callaghan*: 'Do you think women are going to kill themselves collecting money and burying guns and learning first aid for you, and then let themselves be barred out of parliament. Nice fools they'd be'.[287] However, the novel is much more overt in its desire to unite female participation in both the suffrage and nationalist campaigns.

In many respects *Callaghan* fits the paradigm of English suffrage literature. *Callaghan* conforms to the type of dialogic texts produced by English writers involved in the suffrage campaign. Norquay describes the latter as 'full of discussion and debate; the novels packed with reported speech, the poetry full of declamation. . . . the clash and clamour of many voices is inescapable.'[288] *Callaghan* situates itself within a series of interlocking dialogues. Jacob subscribes to the form of English suffrage fiction but her novel presents a different context given its Irish focus. The tension between form and context may explain its lack of commercial success. Unlike English suffrage fiction there was no readership for a novel set in Ireland attempting to negotiate a space for feminism within a nationalist novel; anti-colonial cultural nationalism has been described as 'traditionally inhospitable to gender politics'.[289] *Callaghan* offers a unique example of an attempt to incorporate issues of gender within

285 Glenda Norquay, *Voices and Votes: A Literary Anthology of the Women's Suffrage Campaign* (Manchester: Manchester University Press, 1995), pp. 2–3. See Leeann Lane, 'Rosamond Jacob: nationalism and suffrage' in Ryan and Ward (eds), *Irish Women and the Vote*, pp. 171–88.

286 Gerardine Meaney, 'Women and writing, 1700–1960' in Bourke et al. (eds), *Field Day Anthology*, vol. v, p. 766, p. 769.

287 Winthrop, *Callaghan*, p. 224.

288 Norquay, *Voices and Votes*, p. 9.

289 Antoinette Quinn, (ed.), 'Ireland/Herland: women and literary nationalism, 1845–1916' in Bourke et al. (eds), *Field Day Anthology*, vol. v, p. 896.

the parameters of a polemical text premised on the principles of cultural and political nationalism. O'Regan suggests that Jacob's unwillingness to present an uncritical portrayal of republicanism, in particular her willingness to critically analyse the escalation of republican violence exemplified in the violent proclivities of Andy Callaghan, may explain why it took her ten years to find a publisher for her next novel, *The Troubled House*.[290] Jacob's refusal to adhere to the principles of 'successful popular indoctrination' by relying on the repetitive nationalist imagery and plot demanded of political fiction may also explain why *Callaghan* was such a publishing flop, and the consequent difficulties she had in bringing out her later work.[291] In many respects *Callaghan* was the fictional equivalent of *Bean na hÉireann* with its dual focused slogan: 'Freedom for our Nation and the complete removal of all disabilities to our sex'.[292]

Frances Morrin challenges representations and expectations of early twentieth-century femininity. A single woman at the beginning of the novel, she lives with her married brother and his family in rural Ireland. Frances is criticised by other members of the community for her refusal to adhere to the role expected of women in society. In this Frances is very much modelled on Jacob's sense how of she was perceived by others. Notably Frances shocks the rector's wife by her attendance at a Sunday hurling match.[293] Frances objects to the way in which she and her sister-in-law are referred to in the neighbourhood as Dr Morrin's sister and Dr Morrin's wife, never by their own names. Like Jacob, Frances becomes enmeshed in the suffrage campaign as she moves between rural Kilmartin and Dublin. However, unlike Jacob, Frances is willing to become an active member of the IWFL.[294] No attention has been paid to how this tension between women in the suffrage campaign and nationalist women manifested itself in literature beyond the level the polemical debates conducted in papers such as *Bean na hEireann* and the *Irish Citizen*. *Callaghan* shows Jacob attempting to reconcile her commitment to female equality and her support for the national campaign. In her refusal to prioritise suffrage over the national cause Jacob is represented in the novel by Una. This debate, arguably modelled on the debate between MacSwiney and Sheehy Skeffington, is one of the chief instances of Jacob's reliance on the dialogic approach of English suffrage novels.[295]

---

290 O'Regan, 'Representations and attitudes of republican women', p. 85, p. 87.

291 Quinn, 'Ireland/Herland', p. 896. On 29 May 1922 Jacob noted how only 330 copies had been sold in total and only 70 in the past year. RJD Ms 32,582(41).

292 Quinn, 'Ireland/Herland', p. 898.

293 Winthrop, *Callaghan*, p. 29, p. 11, pp. 16–17.

294 Ibid., pp. 69–70.

295 For examples of the debate between nationalist women and women in the suffrage campaign see Luddy (ed.), *Women in Ireland*, pp. 301–4.

Frances attends her first suffrage meeting in the company of Una to hear Mrs Wall, newly released from prison, speak on the life and work of Josephine Butler, the founder of the Ladies National Association for the Repeal of the Contagious Diseases Acts. Jacob rehearses many of the arguments used by female activists in their demand for the vote, utilising the form of question and answer at the end of Mrs Wall's speech. This would have been the form of the suffrage meetings she herself attended throughout the period in Waterford and on her visits to Dublin. The moral argument in favour of women's suffrage is highlighted in Mrs Wall's talk, as was the commonly held recognition that the vote was not a panacea for all manifestations of gender equality. Enfranchised women would, however, Mrs Wall argued, be in a position to tackle the economic causes of prostitution.[296] To this point Jacob's suffrage text subscribed to the English model. However, the crucial issue of campaigning for the vote from an English parliament causes her text to diverge and become peculiarly Irish. Una decries Mrs Wall as speaking 'as an Englishwoman throughout'. Una offers her reasons for not joining the IWFL, the following discourse rehearsing the arguments for and against the suffrage campaign in Ireland from the perspective of nationalism:

'. . . I'm a prejudiced, narrowminded Separatist, and I don't want a vote for the British Parliament, and I couldn't make friends with British suffrage societies or belong to any political organisation that recognises this country as part of the United Kingdom, and mixes itself up in British politics, the way all Irish suffrage societies do . . .'

'Well, I'm an extreme Nationalist myself,' said Miss MacDermot, 'but that doesn't prevent me working as a suffragist too. I want a vote for whatever Parliament is governing me.'

This was almost how Jacob herself excused her non-membership of the IWFL to Hanna Sheehy Skeffington in 1913:

I don't think, with my political views, I could conscientiously join any suffragist society, as long as we are governed by the British Parliament. A suffrage society must occupy itself chiefly with trying to get the parliamentary franchise from the British parliament; I don't want the British parliamentary franchise – at least I would rather not have it than ask the British parliament for it. A suffrage society must send deputations to British Cabinet ministers, and deal with the viceroy as if it recognised his right to be there – in fact it must accept the powers that be, and as

296 Winthrop, *Callaghan*, pp. 72–3.

it seems to me, it must practically admit the right of Great Britain to govern Ireland. Every organisation whose object is to get new laws made must of necessity do this. Of course the Gaelic League comes under this heading to some extent, but its whole tendency is towards a separate Irish nation.[297]

Una's description of herself as a separatist and Jacob's reference to a separate Irish nation are important to note. Jacob did not join a formal suffrage society fearing that the issue of votes for women would jeopardise a Home Rule settlement but on the basis of wider, increasingly separatist, concerns around national integrity and identity that she had formulated by the time she wrote to Hanna in late 1913. Una believes that earlier campaigns directed at the British parliament, such as the Catholic Emancipation campaign of the 1820s, merely acknowledged the right of the British to rule the Irish and introduced the disabling concept of parliamentarianism; Una proudly accepts the title Sinn Féiner, indicating her commitment to Arthur Griffith's concept of withdrawal from Westminster. Yet, Una was willing to sell suffrage papers with Frances on Grafton Street and attend in her company a Suffrage At Home.[298] Frances spends eight months in Dublin, filling her time as a backup worker very much as Jacob did. Frances worked

> as assistant secretary to a suffrage society and unofficial helper to other revolutionary organisations. . . . to cook soup by the gallon for locked-out workers and their children, . . . to do propaganda work among poor women . . . to heckle speakers at public meetings, and to make speeches herself. She had come to be on intimate terms with almost every suffragist in Dublin . . . and she had made a creditable name for herself among them. They spoke of her as a thoroughly dependable woman, who could be trusted always to fill a gap and never to make one, who never lost control of herself, and who was pleasant to everyone.

Although the work was mundane Frances enjoyed the excitement of moving beyond the expected role of women in society and of living 'an independent life, full of incident and interest'.[299]

Attracted to the republican activist, Andy Callaghan, Frances is, however, repeatedly brought into conflict with him over his attitude to women. On the level of aesthetics he disapproves of women smoking as it yellows their hands. He believes that the O'Meagher family who built his house died out when the

297 Jacob to Hanna Sheehy Skeffington, 24 Nov. 1913, SSP Ms 33,608 (9), NLI.
298 Winthrop, *Callaghan*, pp. 73–4.
299 Ibid., pp. 119–20.

last son was killed during the Cromwellian period despite surviving daughters: it 'was evident that the daughters did not matter'.[300] On the engagement of Frances and Andy, Jacob utilises one of the reiterant plot forms identified by Joannau – 'conflicting desire to be loved and the desire to be active and independent'. 'When presented with a choice between the claims of her male admirer and the claims of political commitment, the suffragette usually opts for love . . . But sometimes she is able to dispense with an unsympathetic man's services . . . or else to convert a seemingly intractable opponent of women's suffrage to the suffragette cause'.[301] Callaghan is opposed to Frances returning to her suffrage work following their engagement; he had difficulty in 'trying to assimilate the idea that a woman might have public duties which seemed to her so important as a man's . . . It was too difficult'.[302] Earlier Callaghan had prevented Frances protesting against Redmond's refusal to consider the issue of female suffrage. Crucially Callaghan used his superior strength to constrain Frances. Callaghan's fear of violence being directed against Frances by Redmond's supporters was no barrier to his belief that he had the right to restrain her; Jacob highlights the fundamental nature of male power over women in a scene with suggestions of sexual assault. Arguably this scene was designed to make a wider point about the manner in which male power and superior strength was utilised as a weapon against the suffragettes; the controversial and topical issue of forcible feeding must have been in Jacob's mind in constructing this scene.

> Callaghan . . . stood up and caught her abruptly in his arms, holding her with his left arm round her waist, and, with his right hand on the back of her head, pressing her face against his breast, to keep her from screaming in her sudden terror, until she could neither speak nor breathe.
> 'Be quiet!' he said roughly, as Frances made a desperate attempt to free herself and did her best to cry out.

Frances, despite herself, is physically attracted to Callaghan at this point. He is conscious of her 'soft form' as he restrains her; afterwards he falls 'limply' to a chair. Almost in post-coital mode, he lights his pipe in a 'half-conscious craving for consolation'. Again, Jacob utilises many of the devices of English suffrage fiction to make points about the nature of patriarchal power: 'she

300 Ibid., p. 3, p. 50.
301 Maroula Joannou, 'Suffragette fiction and the fictions of suffrage' in Maroula Joannou and June Purvis (eds), *The Women's Suffrage Movement: New Feminist Perspectives* (Manchester: Manchester University Press, 1998), pp. 111–12.
302 Winthrop, *Callaghan*, p. 174.

could not feel just then that it mattered much what his motives had been; what mattered was that he had thwarted her by means of physical force, and that she could not defend herself or retaliate'. Callaghan, the physical match for any man, cannot understand 'the sense of utter helplessness that he had aroused in Frances'. Before Frances could go to bed she had to wash her hands and face 'severely' and hang her dress out the window to 'purify' it. Frances is only able to restore her sense of equanimity and re-establish a relationship with Callaghan as she gains an insight into his physical vulnerability when, following a car accident, he lay 'helpless and senseless in the hands of others'.[303] Jacob's description of male physical power captured much of what suffrage campaigners experienced. For Hanna Sheehy Skeffington the scene 'reminded her of assaults by policemen in the suffrage agitation' and she was 'disgusted' at the attraction Frances felt for Callaghan at this point.[304]

The violence of the later suffrage campaign was felt at the level of local Waterford politics. By the second decade of the twentieth century there was growing recognition in Waterford society of the idea of female suffrage. Suffrage meetings were publicised or reported on as a matter of course. Similarly, the RIC County Inspector for Waterford did not consider suffrage meetings worth noting. In his report for April 1911 he declared 'There is nothing of special interest to report', proceeding then to give a brief précis of the suffrage meeting held at the Town Hall on 20 April. He concluded by stating: 'About 200 persons attended but there was no demonstration hostile or otherwise.'[305] There was, however, outrage at the idea of female militancy in pursuit of the vote. When the Dean of Waterford agreed to chair a talk by Miss Margaret Ashton, Chairwoman of the Lancashire and Cheshire Union of the Women's Liberal Federation, on 20 April 1911, he did so having been 'assured that Miss Ashton was a non-militant Suffragette'.[306] Even at this he felt the need to issue a denunciation of the recent census strike by suffrage activists. The census, he declared,

> was for the good of the whole community, for the good of the State . . . avoiding of the census was unworthy of a good citizen. If he might put the matter in a nutshell it was simply this – women claim that they should have their full rights as citizens. Here they had at all events one right as citizens.[307]

303 Ibid., pp. 137–9, p. 143.
304 19 Dec. 1920, RJD Ms (38).
305 RIC County Inspector's Report for Waterford, Apr. 1911, CO 904.
306 Of course, the Dean showed his complete lack of understanding of the suffrage campaign as a suffragette was by definition a believer in militant tactics. Non militants were known as suffragists.
307 *Waterford Standard*, 22 Apr. 1911.

The Waterford press records a sort of grudging surface acceptance by men of the more visible presence of women in public life in the early twentieth century consequent on expanding educational opportunities and the opening up of the local government franchises. By 1911 Irish women had received the right to sit on and vote for County Councils. A year later Waterford Corporation had two women councillors, Strangman and Mrs Lily Poole.[308] However, at various pressure points the acceptance of the greater presence of women in Waterford public life was shown to be superficial. And, crucially, the violence of the suffragettes was turned back as a weapon against women who sought to leave the private sphere. Poole, elected a month after Strangman, in February 1912, declared that 'now she had got in, she would do all in her power to show that a woman would be equal to a man.'[309] This was easier said than done as a very interesting argument at a Corporation meeting in August of that year signified. In a debate over the right of a woman to apply for the position of secretary to the City Insurance Committee, the incident of the hatchet thrown into the carriage in which Redmond and Asquith were travelling in July 1912 by the WSPU activists made its presence felt in the council chambers. Councillor Hackett stated, with a highly resentful tone: 'I agree with you women are quite capable of doing everything a man can do nowadays'. To which Mrs Poole replied: 'So you will find eventually', prompting a knee jerk reaction from the Mayor who declared: 'I promise you I won't vote for a woman'. At this point the latent discomfort of some male councillors at shifting gender roles in Waterford society came to the fore, a discomfort similar to that Jacob described through the character of Andy Callaghan:

> Mr Feely said a woman could be secretary as well as a man, and Dr Strangman said that should be made clear.
>
> 'Take care any of them (the women) don't have a hatchet,' said Mr Hackett.
>
> . . . Mr Hackett . . . said he did not agree with Dr Strangman at all that a woman ought to get this position. He thought that women ought to be kept out of such places.
>
> . . . the gentleman went on to say that Dr Strangman always availed of every opportunity she got to put in a word for the women. He had no objection to her doing so, but at the present time women were unfortunately trying to drive men out of positions by accepting a lower wage and he thought that the men of

308 Lily Poole, a Catholic, was married to the Church of Ireland photographer Arthur Poole. At the time of the 1911 census Lily Poole was 43 and described as a photographer's assistant. The couple had four children. http://www.census.nationalarchives.ie/reels/nai003501324.

309 *Waterford Standard*, 24 Feb. 1912.

Waterford should take up the cudgels and keep Dr Mary Strangman from getting in a woman to the position. Dr Mary Strangman never lost an opportunity of putting in a word for the women. He did not object to that at all; in fact he gave her credit for it; but as a man he was there to say that a woman ought not to take a man's place at all.

This passage is an interesting example of gender rage at the dissolving or shifting parameters of separate spheres. One can sense Hackett's frustration as he begins to repeat himself. And more interesting is the reference to men taking up the cudgels against women. Women with hatchets are strenuously denounced. But Hackett, albeit probably unconsciously, employs the language and imagery of violence in an attempt to re-establish a gender hierarchy at the level of local politics and local jobs, as Callaghan used force to counter Frances.[310]

Opposed to Frances's independent political protest in the cause of suffrage as unbefitting to her sex and her duties to him as her future husband, Callaghan has less of a problem with her involvement in a dangerous arms smuggling incident in which he rushes a police barrier and kills an officer. Attempting to dissuade her, the struggle manifests itself as a half-hearted verbal argument rather than the physical assault prompted by her feminist politics.[311] Her writing reveals that for Jacob male objection to female political involvement is masked behind notions of respectability and inherent gender characteristics; in reality the issue was a concern with female independence from the constraints of patriarchy. Callaghan had no sustained objection to Frances's activism when it was under his tutelage and in the service of a campaign that underscored the gender hierarchy reflected in the division between the Irish Volunteers and Cumann na mBan so abhorred by Jacob. This was exactly Hanna Sheehy Skeffington's point when she wrote in July 1912 equating suffrage militancy with the tradition in Ireland of national militancy against colonial oppression. What had distinguished women's militancy for the vote was that it was militancy in support of their own rights: 'This element of unwomanly selfishness was repellent to the average man, who only applaud the stone thrower as long as the missile is flung for them and not at them'.[312]

Received notions of masculinity and femininity are exposed in *Callaghan*. Andy is opposed to Frances's activism but he believes that she could only despise him as a man if he did not take the risks necessary in defence of his political principles. For example, he intends to break up a recruiting meeting

310 *Waterford News*, 2 Aug. 1912.
311 Winthrop, *Callaghan*, p. 190.
312 Quoted in Ward, 'Hanna Sheehy Skeffington', pp. 94–5.

despite the certain jail sentence if apprehended. Notably, despite Frances's objections she is aware that she cannot restrain him by force as he did her.[313] When the two get married at the close of the novel, Jacob appears once again to depend on a reiterant suffrage plot form. When Frances announces her engagement her brother's response is typical; her suffrage activities will, he assumes, as a matter of course come to an end. Again issues of power, both physical and otherwise, are to the fore as he remarks, albeit teasingly, 'You'll have someone to keep you in jolly good order now, Fanny'. Callaghan himself is subject to a violent start when Frances signals her intention to return to suffrage work following her engagement. Yet Jacob does not portray Callaghan as completely anti-suffrage; he admired Frances's commitment and the 'regal air' she was prone to adopt in defence of her principles. His fundamental problem was his inability to 'assimilate the idea that a woman might have public duties which seemed to her so important as a man's'.[314] In this Jacob testifies to the manner in which entrenched patriarchal attitudes would be far more difficult to eradicate than the opposition to the vote itself. And in many respects this scenario plays true in her novel; the gender hierarchy is re-established with the closing marriage and nationalism is prioritised over suffragism. While the latter reflects Jacob's own inability to formally join the suffrage cause, the re-establishment of gender power structures is more problematic and arguably reflects the manner in which Jacob's novel mirrors the forms of English suffrage literature: Frances opts for love rather than continued activism. Although she insists on paying half the registry office fee there is a sense that Callaghan's priorities subsume hers. As they attend their wedding breakfast Callaghan's house is raided; the concerns of nationalism are to the fore then at the close of the novel. Earlier Frances had realised that 'nothing else in the world counted for half as much with her' as Callaghan.[315] She vehemently denies Dr Morrin's assertion that her feminist activism will cease on marriage. Yet when she and Callaghan appear in Jacob's next novel, *The Troubled House*, she occupies the domestic role of wife and mother. She is described, not as a feminist, in this novel, but as a pacifist.[316] While Frances's brother informs Callaghan that he cannot continue to engage in reckless politically motivated actions after his marriage it is clear that this is just rhetoric; Callaghan in *The Troubled House* is still fully implicated in the intrigue and danger of the national struggle.

313 Winthrop, *Callaghan*, p. 200.

314 Ibid., p. 156, p. 170, p. 171, p. 174.

315 Ibid., p. 145.

316 Jacob, *The Troubled House: A Novel of Dublin in the 'Twenties* (Dublin: Browne & Nolan, 1938), p. 91.

The elision of feminist politics from Frances's life post marriage to Callaghan can be read on a number of levels. Arguably Jacob herself prioritised nationalism over suffrage but the situation is not as simple as that. The structuring element of *Callaghan* like so many English suffrage novels is romance ending in marriage; in these novels the concept of choice is crucial to the plot. Norquay cites the novel *A Fair Suffragette* as an example of a choice amenable to the dominant ideologies of the day, notably the importance of marriage as one of the key institutions on which the future of the English race is predicated. In this novel by Mollwo the heroine continues her activism in a limited sphere, however, crucially giving up the campaign for the vote. She thus submits to patriarchal authority. 'For a writer to place the cause in opposition to marriage meant playing upon such anxieties, whereas a reconciliation of personal and political commitments was infinitely more reassuring.'[317]

The ending of Jacob's text has to be read in the context of the representation of various life roles for women in her next novel, *The Troubled House*. The characterisations of Frances Morrin, Maggie Cullen and the artist, Nix, need to be considered together. Here the characters indicate that Jacob believed society to have reached a point where alternative female existence was possible. In *The Troubled House* Maggie is a mother and wife but it must be strongly noted that she is decentred from her family by her long absence from the country due to the illness of her sister. When she returns she does not neatly fit her ascribed social role as submissive wife and her radical politics place her in opposition to her husband, a supporter of the Irish Parliamentary Party. Thus Maggie offers a counter image to that of Frances; both women are still, however, located within the institution of marriage and the societal expectations of wife and mother. Nonetheless, Maggie's character does suggest that Jacob believed that women could be equal if not dominant within the marriage relationship. Again, we must return to the fact that, despite her feminist beliefs, Jacob at no point jettisoned the idea of marriage. The portrayal of Nix, a bisexual female artist, indicates Jacob's perception that other lives were opening for women in the period. This reveals Jacob's growing sense of fluidity as an individual in this second decade of the twentieth century; with exposure to varied lived examples, she increasingly believed that choices existed for her as a woman as she prepared to leave Waterford and immerse herself fully in the cultural and political world of Dublin radicalism.

---

317 Norquay, *Voices and Votes*, pp. 31–2.

THREE

REVOLUTIONARY YEARS: WATERFORD
1915–19

The rising on Easter Monday 1916 passed unnoticed by Jacob. Her diary entry for 24 April reads: 'Wet day, nothing doing.'[1] The following morning news of the events in Dublin began to trickle down to Waterford. Before the confusion sparked by Eoin MacNeill's countermanding order, the intention was that local outbreaks were to occur simultaneously with the insurrection in Dublin on Easter Sunday.[2] Cumann na mBan activists, Maeve Cavanagh McDowell and Marie Perolz, independently recorded how they were sent to Waterford during the week before Easter Monday to inform local Volunteer Seán Matthews of the plan to rise.[3] Later in the week Matthews received word from J. J. O'Connell that Eoin MacNeill had called off the Rising.[4] It was decided that Waterford activist, Liam Walsh, who was to attend the Annual GAA Congress in Dublin, would attempt to find out further information and communicate back.[5] Walsh made contact with Eoin MacNeill and confirmed his orders to the Waterford Volunteers. The resulting confusion is evident in the Bureau of Military History witness statements. According to Cavanagh McDowell she took the counter order of the Military Council of the IRB to rise on Monday to Waterford.[6] Another witness claimed that the Waterford

1 24 Apr. 1916, RJD Ms (29).

2 R. F. Foster, *Modern Ireland, 1600–1972* (London: Penguin, 1989), p. 481.

3 Maeve Cavanagh McDowell, BMH WS 258; Marie Perolz, BMH WS 246. Mary Perolz (1874–c.1950) was a member of many of the key feminist and nationalist organisations of the revolutionary period: Inghinidhe na hÉireann, Cumann na mBan, the Irish Women Workers' Union and the Irish Citizen Army. Sinead McCoole, *No Ordinary Women: Irish Female Activists in the Revolutionary Years* (Dublin: O'Brien, 2004), pp. 198–9.

4 John Jeremiah (Ginger) O'Connell (1887–1944) was a Volunteer organiser and lecturer on military tactics to the Volunteers and the Fianna. He would adopt a pro-Treaty stance and had a number of posts in the Irish Army through 1922 to his death. Marie Coleman, 'O'Connell, Jeremiah Joseph ('J. J.', 'Ginger'). *Dictionary of Irish Biography.*

5 Pat McCarthy, 'The Irish Volunteers in Waterford, 1913–1916, part I', *Decies* 60 (2004), p. 212.

6 Maeve Cavanagh McDowell, BMH WS 258.

Branch of the Irish Volunteers received word on Easter Monday 'that our services were not required at present but to continue the important work and get more young men into the ranks'.[7] A further member recalled that no military action was taken due to lack of arms and ammunition. The British Army takeover of the General Post Office on the Quay at Waterford precluded the destruction of telephone wires in the building, a strategy allegedly planned in 1915 between the local branch of the Volunteers and Patrick Pearse, member of the Irish Republican Brotherhood Supreme Council and Secret Military Council. One witness recalled that a gunboat was stationed at the port, a military guard was placed on the Waterford General Post Office and Customs House and a semi-armed train arrived at Waterford Station.[8] Some arrests of local men were made, amongst whom were Seán Matthews, Liam Walsh and P. Brazil.[9] The rest of the week was, Jacob noted, 'a period of suspense & wild rumours.'[10] Jacob made little or no reference to any possibility that the local Volunteers had plans to join in what was intended as a nationwide rebellion against the British presence in Ireland; the focus of her diary entries were almost entirely on events in Dublin. Throughout the next few weeks Jacob recorded the second-hand information she received, often days after the event. On the 3 May she noted that 'this was the day Pearse, Clarke and MacDonagh were shot, at about 4.30 in the morning I believe, though it wasn't known till Thursday.'[11] Jacob herself did not travel to Dublin until 13 May, staying only two days, returning to Waterford on the afternoon of the 15 May. She recorded the ruined state of city centre and visited friends to check on their well being and to hear their stories of participation in the events of the Rising. Family commitments still forced Jacob to remain in Waterford; she continued her pattern of making short forays to the capital to refresh her political enthusiasms until her mother died in 1919.

REVOLUTIONARY ACTIVISM

The months leading up to Easter 1916 were fairly inactive ones for Jacob. She was involved in little political activity or campaigning and her diary records the day-to-day events of family life, interspersed with visits from Upton,

7   Tomas O Cleirigh, BMH WS 972, p. 6.
8   Michael F. Ryan, BMH WS 1709, p. 6.
9   Seán Matthews, BMH WS 1022, p. 6; Patrick Hearne, BMH WS 1742, p. 6.
10 25 Apr. 1916, RJD Ms (29).
11 3 May 1916, RJD Ms (29).

bearing news from Dublin. On 3 August 1915 he brought 'a great account' of the Jeremiah O'Donovan Rossa funeral in Dublin on the 1st of the month. This was a large funeral that brought together in the public space thousands of citizens, uniformed Volunteers and members of the Irish Citizen Army to pay tribute to the dead Fenian who had been accused of fomenting rebellion in 1865 and sentenced to penal servitude, living out the end of his life in the United States. This was an emotive affair and a testimony to the growing visibility of a newly emergent national community. Pearse's funeral oration was designed to aid in the construction of this community; collective mourning for a national martyr was harnessed to political ends.[12] Jacob took pleasure from the fact that the 'Redmondite element was kept very much in the background' during proceedings.[13] Even at a remove from the iconic events of 1 August Jacob still acted as part of this emerging national community. The imagined community, of which Jacob considered herself to be within, represented a generational shift not necessarily solely in terms of age profile but also in terms of aspiration and national ambition. If the Gaelic League disseminated, in the words of McMahon, a 'teleological interpretation of the nation-in-formation',[14] stalwart members such as Jacob represented citizens-in-waiting. Seton Watson defined a nation as existing 'when a significant number of people in a community consider themselves to form a nation or behave as if they formed one'.[15] By the early twentieth century a new more holistically minded generation of Irish nationalists reared, as Jacob had been, on the cultural signifiers of the Irish-Ireland movement had sloughed off the dead skin of commitment to a jaded and outmoded Irish Parliamentary Party. Laffan discusses how supporters of Sinn Féin and the Volunteers tended to be young by contrast with the Irish Parliamentary Party support base.[16] James Connolly described the IPP MPs in September 1915 as having spent 'forty years babbling in the wilderness at Westminster'. All the alleged successes of the Party, notably the successful solution to the land question, he attributed to the struggle of the people, to 'a fight fought and won outside Parliament'. The

12 Paige Reynolds, 'Modernist martydom: the funerals of Terence MacSwiney', *Modernism/Modernity* 9: 4 (2002), p. 535.

13 3 Aug. 1915, RJD Ms (29).

14 Timothy G. McMahon, '"To mould an important body of shepherds": the Gaelic summer colleges and the teaching of Irish history' in Lawrence W. McBride (ed.), *Reading Irish Histories: Texts, Contexts and Memory in Modern Ireland* (Dublin: Four Courts, 2003), p. 118.

15 Quoted in Benedict Anderson, *Imagined Communities: Reflections on the Origin and Spread of Nationalism* (rev. edn, London: Verso, 1991), p. 6, n. 9.

16 Michael Laffan, *The Resurrection of Ireland: The Sinn Féin Party 1916–1923* (Cambridge: Cambridge University Press, 1999), p. 191.

third Home Rule Bill, excluding as it did the six north-eastern counties, and its suspension for the duration of the war, he described as a 'pitiful abortion'.[17]

Jacob's participation in the events leading up to 1916 continued to be at one remove as she relied on news from local activists who moved between the capital and the various nationalist outposts. On 13 November 1915 Upton's report of how 'Bridie Dalton is learning to shoot with a pistol, and Miss MacCarthy too' both indicated the expectation of rebellion and the consequent expanding political opportunities for women.[18] While the majority of those women who would participate in the Rising engaged in supportive roles by cooking, caring for the wounded and carrying dispatches, the greater part of women in the ICA and a number in Cumann na mBan were trained in the use of weapons.[19] Molony, a member of the ICA, recalled how she 'always carried a revolver. About 1910 shortly after the Fianna started Madame had taught me to shoot'.[20] Margaret Skinnider, who also fought with the ICA was proud of how, disguised as a boy within the Fianna at target practice, she 'hit the bull's-eye oftener than any of them', adding that Markievicz had 'accustomed them [the Fianna] to expect good marksmanship in a woman'.[21] Jacob recorded the sense of political expectation while also documenting her own more mundane activities on behalf of the Society for the Prevention of Cruelty to Animals and the Poor Relief Committee, her attendance at the Friends essay meetings and the state of the Waterford Gaelic League which was completely deficient in dynamism during 1915 and the first half of 1916 as the following entry testifies:

> I went to a committee . . . mostly feis bills and the question of what answer to make to the suggestion of the Coisde Gnótha that we should have the Oireachtas here next year. It would need a great deal of work, more than we have people for.[22]

A 'so called general meeting' on 3 November had only nine members present despite the fact that according to the figures of the RIC County Inspector two months later the membership was 340.[23]

Waterford Nationalist Society reflected on a microcosmic level the patterns and trends within Irish society, although the fact that Redmond was

---

17   James Connolly, 'The party versus the people', *Worker's Republic*, 4 Sept. 1915.

18   13 Nov. 1915, RJD Ms (29).

19   Lisa Weihman, 'Doing my bit for Ireland: transgressing gender in the Easter Rising', *Éire–Ireland* 39: 3/4 (2004), p. 229.

20   Helena Molony, BMH WS 391, p. 26.

21   Margaret Skinnider, *Doing My Bit For Ireland* (New York: Century, 1917), p. 27.

22   20 Oct. 1915, RJD Ms (29).

23   3 Nov. 1915, RJD Ms (29); RIC County Inspector's Report for Waterford, Jan. 1916, CO 904/99.

the Irish Parliamentary Party MP for the city heightened tensions. One member of the Irish Volunteers described Waterford as 'the greatest Imperialist City outside Belfast'.[24] Outside of Ulster, Waterford was the city that was most heavily dependent on the army and munitions industries, resulting in a wartime economic boom.[25] As Waterford was a port, there were recruits to the merchant service.[26] Denis Madden, Intelligence Officer, Waterford Brigade, who came to Waterford from Cork in 1906, recalled how he was 'disappointed' in the city. Growing up in Cork city he was educated in the history of nationalist Ireland; he learned Irish after school, played hurling, and did step dancing. As a clerk in a solicitor's firm in Fermoy, County Cork, he attended Gaelic League meetings and read Griffith's *United Irishman*, later *Sinn Féin*. Even in Fermoy, a 'stronghold' of the British Army, 'we were asking questions'. By contrast, he found Waterford a 'right seóinín town. The ascendancy class seemed to dominate everything . . . The Corporation were a flunkey lot, mostly. Redmond was our "incomparable leader" according to . . . the *Waterford News*'.[27] In considering why Waterford city and hinterland did not do more in the War of Independence, IRA activist Michael Ryan noted the lack of a 'continuous tradition favouring a militant nationalist outlook in the city'. He cites the lack of a 1798 or Fenian tradition in the city although refers to the Young Ireland tradition in the Ballybricken district where Thomas Francis Meagher had supporters. Ryan notes how the loyalist element in Waterford gained in strength with the outbreak of the war and guessed that there were not more than 200 Sinn Féin supporters.[28] Irish Volunteer Thomas Brennan recalled how 'the political set up in Waterford was a most peculiar one'. He described three 'anti-national elements' opposed to 'anything appertaining to republicanism': Unionists, 'the 'Ballybricken pig buyers', an element 'which was entirely pro-Redmond and pro-British', and those with connections to the British Army. As a result of the unique political configuration of the city key republican figures from elsewhere in the country would later descend on Waterford during the two crucial 1918 elections which saw the decimation at national level of the Irish Parliamentary Party and the rise of Sinn Féin as the beneficiary of the Rising.[29] Attempts were made to educate the public on the opinions and aims of Sinn Féin by holding public meetings at every point in the city with sufficient road space to hold a crowd. Previously public meetings

24 Tomas O Cleirigh, BMH WS 972, p. 35, p. 16.
25 Laffan, *The Resurrection of Ireland*, p. 125.
26 Michael F. Ryan, BMH WS 1709, p. 4.
27 Denis F. Madden, BMH WS 1103, pp. 1–3, p. 4.
28 Michael F. Ryan, BMH WS 1709, pp. 31–2.
29 Thomas Brennan, BMH, WS 1104, pp. 2–3.

had traditionally been held at Ballybricken Hill and the Mall.[30] Madden, who left Waterford for Tralee in early 1914, returned to the city in August 1917 describing it as,

> seething with pro-British flunkeyism. The separation money, and all the relatives at home, and the overall influence of Redmond and his AOH bosses. Drink was cheap and was flowing day and night. The Peelers gave the blind eye to all the aggressions of the Party rabble. Degeneracy reached its crescendo during the General Election 1918. Money was spent on drink and the mobs were inspired to throw bottles and stones. 'Bottle for bottle and stone for stone' said Peter O'Connor off a Redmondite platform. Our men were perfectly orderly and there was no blackguardism from our side. It took all the efforts of imported Volunteers to get any kind of fair play for the voters.[31]

The language and tone of the statements are interesting in presenting the Sinn Féin element as on the defensive and as innocent victims of a hostile mob. Whittle summed up the attitude of the republican element in the Waterford Volunteers: 'they would strike back if they were struck at, but the question of they themselves taking the initiative to crush once and for all a group who were a menace to national progress was beyond them'.[32] One member of the Irish Volunteers later recalled how 'Life as a republican in Waterford was very hard and rough. The Redmondites, who by the way were more British than the British themselves, were ever attacking our members'.[33] Another volunteer noted, in the context of the First World War, the popularity of Redmond in Waterford 'so that what he said about such matters, that is, public statements of policy, were accepted without question by practically everyone in the constituency'. Consequently, when Redmond called on the Irish Volunteers to support the war 'I conceived it to be my duty to join the British Army in obedience to the appeals of the Irish Party leaders'.[34] Even before Redmond's appeal, on the outbreak of war in August 1914, walls and hoardings in the city 'were covered with eye-catching posters showing ruined homes and shrines in Belgium and asking Irishmen to come to the aid of the gallant little ally. Cardinal Mercier's appeal and pictures of helpless Belgian mothers and children were on every dead wall'.[35]

---

30 Thomas Brennan, BMH, WS 1104, pp. 2–3; Nicholas Whittle, BMH, WS 1105, p. 37.
31 Denis F. Madden, BMH, WS 1103, p. 18.
32 Nicholas Whittle, BMH, WS 1105, p. 3.
33 Tomas O Cleirigh, BMH WS 972, p. 35, p. 16.
34 Lieutenant Colonel P. J. Paul, BMH WS 877, p. 2.
35 Michael F. Ryan, BMH WS 1709, p. 3.

Many of the Bureau of Military History witness statements testify to the synergy of interest and personnel between the Gaelic League, Sinn Féin and the Irish Volunteers throughout County Waterford both before and after the Rising. Tom Kelleher from Cappoquin recalled how 'weekly parades continued during 1918 and we had the usual Sinn Féin and Gaelic League activities in conjunction with the Volunteers'. These he described as 'kindred organisations'.[36] Indeed when Cumann na mBan was established in August 1914 the Gaelic League Notes in the *Waterford News* declared: 'We hope that the lady Volunteers will give a lead to the men in the matter of speaking Irish. The majority of the members have a fair knowledge of Irish'.[37] Thomas Hallahan, Volunteer member in Bonmahon, County Waterford, organised a Sinn Féin Club in 1917 which held meetings, gave lectures and 'staged some Irish-Ireland concerts . . . to stir up enthusiasm'.[38] In Waterford City the weekly ceílithe held in the Volunteer Hall were the 'rallying front' for the Volunteers.[39]

Much of the focus of the Irish Volunteers in Waterford was directed at protecting the Sinn Féin side during the elections of 1918.[40] Extra Volunteers were drafted in from the neighbouring areas, it being the perception that Redmondite violence was perpetrated 'with the connivance of the alleged custodians of law and order, the RIC, with the help of British military forces stationed in Waterford'.[41] Waterford City was a garrison town and had two British Army barracks and five RIC barracks.[42] One volunteer involved recalled how 'a man from a flying column said to me years afterwards, he had tougher fighting in Waterford during these elections than he had with the "column"'.[43] According to one witness lack of arms meant that the main weapon of defence was a stick or hurley.[44] During the 1918 by-election the National Flag hanging from the upper window of the Volunteer Hall was burned and street violence led to injuries on polling night.[45] Nicholas Whittle recalled polling day during the General Election of 1918 in the election rooms where 'Patrick W. Kenny, the election agent, was sitting near me, a large

36 Tom Kelleher, BMH WS 758, pp. 2–3. See also Sean Toibin, BMH WS 757, p. 3. Again the word kindred is used.

37 *Waterford News*, 14 Aug. 1914.

38 Thomas Hallahan, BMH WS 1128, p. 1.

39 Nicholas Whittle, BMH WS 1105, p. 5.

40 Lieutenant Colonel P. J. Paul, BMH WS 877, pp. 5–6. The RIC County Inspector estimated that 400 Volunteers were imported into Waterford during the March by-election. CO 904/105.

41 George C. Kiely, BMH WS 1182, p. 3.

42 Patrick Hearne, BMH WS 1742, p. 1.

43 William Keane, BMH WS 1023, p. 6.

44 James Mansfield, BMH WS 1229, p. 2.

45 Nicholas Whittle, BMH WS 1105, pp. 15–16.

sticking-plaster on his forehead. Dr Vincent White, the Sinn Féin candidate sat next to him, similarly bandaged'.[46] The 1918 elections marked a high point in nationalist activity in Waterford during the revolutionary period. IRA activism did continue in the area during the Anglo-Irish War 1919–21, local members carrying out training routines, hampered by a lack of arms.[47] Raids for arms were carried out by Waterford IRA companies in 1920 on houses of individuals 'unsympathetic' to the republican cause; Thomas Brennan cites raids in the Killoteran district, one mile west of the city, in the Grace Dieu area to the north and in the Butlerstown area three miles to the west.[48] A number of later recollections testify as to how the membership of the Waterford IRA rose during the conscription threat of 1918 only to diminish once the threat had passed.[49] This mirrored Jacob's account of the peaks and troughs in the nationalist organisations she was involved in during the period, in particular, she noted how the galvanising effect of 1916 quickly tampered off in associations such as the local branch of the Gaelic League.

Despite her participation in republican and language organisations Jacob was at a remove from the violence and class discourse that permeated political activism in Waterford in the period 1915–21. Jacob's commentary offers no class-based analysis as is acutely evident in the witness statements cited. Her involvement in nationalist politics was sheltered and more abstract than participatory. In contrast, repeatedly the Bureau of Military History witness statements make reference to the Ballybricken pig buyers as a central spoke in the caucus of Redmondite support in Waterford. One witness stated that these families had ancestors involved in the Young Irelanders and were later supporters of Parnell during the split. Their violent opposition to Sinn Féin he attributed to their intense loyalty to Parnell and Redmond and that they 'could see no merit in any organisation or party which had anti-Parnellites . . . as members or supporters'.[50] However, the constant reference to this group as pig buyers is noteworthy. Edmund Downey noted that up to 1897 Ballybricken was the 'most thriving part of Waterford', the centre of the city's important

---

46   Ibid., p. 48.

47   Seán Matthews, BMH WS 1022, pp. 10–11.

48   Thomas Brennan, BMH WS 1104, p. 8.

49   Ibid., p. 7; Seán Matthews, BMH WS 1022, p. 8. In April 1918 the Military Services Bill was passed extending conscription to Ireland, the British needing manpower following heavy losses in France. Due to public opposition in Ireland, backed by the Catholic Church, the Government was not able to enforce the legislation. Patrick Maume, *The Long Gestation: Irish Nationalist Life, 1891–1918* (Dublin: Gill & Macmillan, 1999), pp. 205–6; Laffan, *The Resurrection of Ireland*, pp. 138–42.

50   Michael F. Ryan, BMH WS 1709, p. 12.

livestock and bacon-curing industries.[51] Issues of class permeated Waterford politics as can be seen in so many of these Bureau of Military History witness statements. Michael Ryan stated that his first involvement in a nationalist organisation was as a member of the youth group established by the Ancient Order of Hibernians in Waterford. These 'Hibernian Scots' he recalled did not survive long and were replaced by the Fianna. However, he wrote, it 'is not to be inferred that all or indeed any of the Hibernians joined the Fianna – there was a little social snobbery – and anyway the Fianna was a little advanced in outlook for Nationalists of that day'.[52] Whittle shows interest in the 'historical background to the Ballybricken pig buyer, as they appeared different generally to the ordinary run of Waterford citizens, and paraphrases the conclusions of Canon Patrick Power, who noted that there was

> no historical background to the peculiar characteristics of the Waterford pig buyers. In common with men who make their living by dealing with livestock, they acquired a love of things garish. They resembled the gypsy by the love of show, of shined brasses in the homes and their ignorant outward show generally.

Whittle himself continues offering a class-based analysis redolent of much of the invective of George Russell and W. B. Yeats against the vulgarity of the rising middle classes in Irish society in the late nineteenth, early twentieth centuries. Russell's diatribes focused on the lack of culture and nefarious influence of the gombeenman was a regular feature of his editorship of the *Irish Homestead* between 1905 and 1923. Russell posited a direct link between the gombeenman and the Irish Parliamentary Party. Whittle's analysis of the Ballybricken pig buyers similarly laid emphasis on vulgarity and lack of culture:

> My personal recollection of all the Waterford pig buyers was that they were an absolutely illiterate class, without a knowledge or respect for learning. They came out of a period when the pig buyer and cattle dealer literally bludgeoned the small farmer when the latter came to offer his stock for sale at a fair. An organised system of what I should term 'blackmail' existed amongst them in the method of buying. Behind the front line of buyers was second line, known as tanglers, the latter making the running for the former. Through the two groups, a technique was evolved whereby each buyer would select freely his own victim at a fair and none of

51 Edmund Downey, *Waterford: An Illustrated Guide and Tourists' Handbook* (Waterford: Waterford News, n.d. [c.1931]), p. 31. After 1897, Downey argued, local changes in the pig-buying and bacon industries diminished the trade.
52 Michael F. Ryan, BMH 1709, pp. 1–2.

his competing buyers would interfere. In fact, farmers who set out to break this
discreditable technique were frequently beaten up at fairs. These same pig buyers
were the moulders of the blackguardly election methods which were typical of the
Redmonite Party in the Waterford elections.[53]

By contrast, Whittle identified those who 'broke the back of Redmondite
rowdyism in Waterford' as 'largely belonging to one class. I refer to the
children and grandchildren of evicted farmers who lost their homes during the
Land League agitation and prior to it. A large number of these came into
Waterford city to work … Also in this group were sons and grandsons of men
who had been evicted from their farms in South Kilkenny'.[54]

During the months leading up to the Rising Jacob maintained her connection to the wider political world not only through word of mouth accounts
from local activists but also through her reading, regularly taking the *Spark*, the
Workers' Republic founded by James Connolly in 1898 and the *Fianna*, the
monthly organ of Fianna Éireann, amongst other papers. She interested herself
in the debate over Connolly's *Labour in Irish History*, published in 1910, as to
whether Larkin or Connolly was 'keener on socialism compared to nationality'.[55] The *Spark*, was a paper brought out weekly from December 1914 by Seán
Doyle with contributors from amongst 'the more intransigent separatists'.
Indeed, one can see the attraction of the paper for Jacob in Maume's description
of it as a 'virulent scandal-sheet … attributing moral corruption to the Irish
Party, AOH, Dublin Corporation, British Army, Government and British
people generally'.[56] In Waterford Jacob would have been able to buy such
republican papers in a number of premises. One witness wrote how there

> were a number of shops which catered for the new minority group – Ned Cannon's
> in O'Connell Street – Mrs Clancy's, Colbeck Street and Mrs O'Reilly's Parnell
> Street. In these shops one could obtain copies of 'Nationality', 'Young Ireland' and
> the other papers which had long or short lives before being banned by the British.
> One could get photographs of the 1916 leaders, patriotic greeting cards, songs,
> badges, etc. in these shops.[57]

---

53   Nicholas Whittle, BMH WS 1105, pp. 50–1.
54   Ibid., p. 55.
55   See, for example, 16 Aug. 1915; 28 Dec. 1915, RJD Ms (29). The *Fianna* was published between
     February 1915 and the time of the Rising, J. Anthony Gaughan, *Scouting in Ireland* (Dublin: Kingdom
     Books, 2006), p. 45.
56   Maume, *The Long Gestation*, pp. 162–3.
57   Michael F. Ryan, BMH WS 1709, p. 47.

The RIC Inspector General viewed these journals as offering support to Sinn Féin, helping to spread 'sedition' and exercising 'a deterrent effect on recruitment'. Moreover, he believed that subscription rates indicated that such papers could not be run on business lines and must therefore be funded from Germany.[58] The subscription figures for Waterford certainly indicate low subscription rates: '*Irish Volunteer* (24) *Nationality* (14) *the Spark* (2) *Hibernian* (3) & *Fianna* (3)'.[59] Jacob's crude and simplistic anti-British comment on a sightseeing trip with the Dwyers of Waterford placed her firmly in the virulent camp that was the readership of the *Spark*: 'They had a Union Jack on their car, which cast a slur over us too and made us ashamed to be seen with them'.[60] In part, such unsophisticated anti-British sentiments were Jacob's response to her sense of political impotence; as she became more involved, albeit in a fringe capacity, in the political activities centred on Dublin from 1916 to 1922 she toned down her anti-British comments. That such sentiments became more nuanced testifies to Jacob's evolving political persona.

Jacob was quietly beginning her career as a writer at this period; commissions were gradually coming her way for review work.[61] Culturally, she continued to attend local nationalist concerts and speeches and to record any events she considered notable from a republican political perspective. She went to the Manchester Martyrs' Concert held in the Town Hall in Waterford on 23 November 1915 describing how Pim[62] spoke of the attempt to rescue the Fenian prisoners, Thomas Kelly and Timothy Deasy, from Manchester Jail on 18 September 1867.[63] Pim's talk followed earlier renditions of anti-recruiting poems and songs. The next day Pim was involved in an attempt to form a branch of the Irish Volunteers in Waterford.[64] He was present for tea at the Jacob house that night where he continued his account of the Manchester Martyrs.[65]

Jacob was on a family visit in Cork when Terence MacSwiney was arrested and jailed for seditious speech making in January 1916; she records meeting

58   RIC Inspector's Report for Waterford, Feb. 1916, CO 904/99.

59   Ibid.

60   9 Sept. 1915, RJD Ms (29).

61   See for example, 31 Jan. 1916, RJD Ms (29): 'May New paid me a visit a.d. . . . She said Eamonn Ó Duibhir wanted me to write a review of Rossa's recollections for the Gaodhal.'

62   Herbert Moore Pim had been an Ulster Unionist before his conversion to both radical nationalism and Catholicism. He directed Sinn Féin Party's business between his release from jail in August 1916 and Griffith's release in December 1916. Laffan, *The Resurrection of Ireland*, p. 70.

63   The attempt resulted in the death of a policeman and the death of William Philip Allen, Michael Larkin and William O'Brien by execution although both Kelly and Deasy escaped custody.

64   RIC County Inspector's Report for Waterford, Nov. 1915, CO 904/98.

65   23–4 Nov. 1915, RJD Ms (29).

'Miss MacSwiney jr'.[66] On 10 February 1916 Jacob attended Pearse's lecture on nationality with her brother Tom, describing it as 'very good, about the definition of nationality not being . . . found in the statute book of the nation's enemy but in the writings of the fathers of the nation, Tone, Davis, Lalor and Mitchel, each developing & expanding what the last said.' Pearse's pamphlets and speeches in the years immediately before the Rising all elaborated on his thinkings on these four 'evangelists' or 'fathers of the nationalist religion'.[67] However, Jacob was no passive listener; Pearse 'talked a good deal about the national character, & praised it as I thought much more than it deserved.' Despite such criticism Jacob developed her own cult of Pearse, one of her many 'crushes' directed at revolutionary or political leaders of the national cause. Pearse was in her mind at this point in time, 'plain & simple & un-self-conscious & modest'. Although not very good looking, he had an 'interesting & attractive face, and there's a great charm about his voice too'.[68] Jacob was not unique in developing a form of hero worship for the leaders of the Rising. Richard English notes how 'public veneration became a standard feature of Irish nationalist politics in the post-1916 years'.[69] However, some interesting points can be made in distinguishing the male tendency from the female tendency in the period, Jacob's experiences offering some salient examples.

PERSONAL ISSUES

As with the events leading up to the event, Jacob's knowledge of the Rising was at one remove: 'I think it was on Sunday we heard of Madame getting a life-sentence, and somewhere at this time Major MacBride and Eamonn Ceannt were shot.'[70] A newspaper report was the source from which Jacob learned of Francis Sheehy Skeffington's death as he attempted to stop the public engaging in looting. He was shot, she wrote, 'for being himself, I

66   14 Jan. 1916, RJD Ms (29). MacSwiney was arrested and charged with having incited young men to join the Volunteers rather than the British army at Ballynoe, County Cork. The crown prosecutor argued that he had publicly suggested that Redmond should be shot for his support of Irishmen fighting for England while he focused on MacSwiney's criticism of the British government for conniving at the armed status of Ulster Unionists. Francis J. Costello, *Enduring The Most: The Life and Death of Terence MacSwiney* (Dingle: Brandon, 1995), pp. 58–60.

67   Ruth Dudley Edwards, *Patrick Pearse: The Triumph of Failure* (Dublin: Irish Academic Press, 2006), pp. 253–60.

68   10 Feb. 1916, RJD Ms (29).

69   Richard English, *Ernie O'Malley: IRA Intellectual* (Oxford: Oxford University Press, 1998), p. 9.

70   8 May 1916, RJD Ms (29).

suppose'.[71] Jacob attempted to assuage feelings of being outside the fulcrum of activities and knowledge through reading Pearse's poetry and surrounding herself with fellow-Pearse devotees. A cult of Pearse developed quickly in the immediate aftermath of the rebellion. Celia Shaw, a student in University College Dublin at the time of the Rising, noted how many households displayed a picture of Pearse next to that of Christ.[72] In Waterford picture postcards of the rebel leaders were 'freely sold'.[73] Jacob was *'awfully* glad' of Kitty Power's company that week. 'This evening she suddenly remarked that she was going to change her historical character in the favourite book to Pearse.'[74] For single women such as Jacob male nationalist activists almost took on the role of potential lover or partner. Sometime around 1915 she developed feelings for Tony Farrington, brother of Tom's future wife, Dorothea, who spent time at the Jacob home during the summer months of that year. It does not appear that she at any stage expressed these feelings or that they were reciprocated or even recognised by the object of her affection. Her feelings were not recorded in her daily diary but rather in the second layer or secret text where they appear as much stronger than any feeling she evinced for Tony's brother Ben. On 7 July 1915 she confided to this text: 'all the afternoon & evening I have been ravished with his beauty'; her rather turgid poem, 'Bun Machain', expressed the unrequited nature of her feelings:

> So in the rain, among the furze and heather
> We climbed and played above that leaden sea.
> It was the last of all our days together
> And I loved you, but you cared nought for me.[75]

Jacob continued to place all her affections on Tony throughout 1916 writing at the close of the year.

> 1916 wasn't exactly worse than 1915, but of course it was much duller. It would have been worse than 1915 but for Tony's letters. But it is awful getting no good of these years for want of him, presently I won't be young any more, and I will still be waiting years for fortnights as I am doing now. I can enjoy things at the time, but I'm glad when each month is over, & the time behind looks grey and unregrettable.[76]

71 9 May 1916, RJD Ms (29).
72 Diary of Celia Shaw, Ms 23409, NLI.
73 RIC County Inspector's Report for Waterford, June 1916, CO 904/100.
74 4–5 May 1916, RJD Ms (29).
75 RJD Ms (171).
76 Ibid. Many of these extracts do not follow the conventional diary format as they are random musings with limited dates and there appear to be gaps in time between entries.

Service and interest in the nationalist cause allowed her to escape her unreturned feelings for Tony. She desperately needed a purpose, to feel part of something at this point in her life and she was haunted by feelings of inadequacy in the area of relationships.

> It was a very bad thing for me that Upton didn't let me write regular articles for the Harp; it would have been a great help to me, but it seems as if nothing wanted anything I write; every paper has as much stuff as it wants. I can't think of things to write about my head is so haunted with Tony, & even if it wasn't I couldn't. I wonder what age shall I stop caring that men don't like me or that I can't do anything I want to do. If I cd once succeed in doing something I wouldn't mind dying.[77]

The manner in which the last line above is redolent of Pearse's famous motto culled from Cúchulainn – 'I care not though I were to live but one day and one night provided my fame and deeds live after me' – is hardly surprising given Jacob's close attention to the works of Pearse in this period.[78] And if one was to reduce Jacob's life in future years to the form of a paradigm it is expressed in the diary extract above. She desired a relationship and although she never wrote of a desire to get married, neither did she ever express any negative attitude towards the institution. Jacob expected to form a meaningful, lifelong relationship and have children. At the end of 1917 the second-layer diary includes the following statement of frustration: 'What sort of a year was 1917? Not much of a one, nothing good happened of a personal nature except getting taught jewelry at the Tech; no baby, no Tony, no nothing. I'm still waiting years for fortnights'.[79] Jacob became increasingly haunted by a sense that she did not have the attributes men looked for in a woman. Her awkward personality and lack of social skills were impacting negatively on her sense of herself and the possibilities that life held out for her at this crucial stage. What compounded her sense of failure with men was the fact that she had no other outlet. It must be remembered that at the time of the Rising Jacob was 28, still living at home and having had no intimate male relationship despite her desire for such. Untrained for any career, taking care of an increasingly invalided mother, her outlets for her emotional and sexual needs were few. And all around her society and politics were in flux, and everyone she knew seemed to be a part of the exciting political march to change. The desire for a love object,

---

77   Ibid.

78   Quoted in Sean Farrell Moran, *Patrick Pearse and the Politics of Redemption: The Mind of the Easter Rising, 1916* (Washington, DC: Catholic University of America Press, 1994), p. 160.

79   RJD Ms (171). This extract is dated 2 Jan. 1918.

the pent up emotions around her feelings for Tony Farrington, together with her wish to be involved in the nationalist movement, found outlet in her adoration of the martyrs of 1916, particularly Pearse. She displaced feelings for Tony Farrington onto Pearse, writing for example:

> Sometimes when I'm copying out How does she Stand I can think of nothing but Pearse – or if I hear something fresh about him. I believe he would have been less certain not to care for me than Tony. He [Pearse] has a tremendous power over me, I mean the thought of hearing his voice again is marvellous.[80]

The manner in which this form of hero worship was an outlet for emotional needs in Jacob would be evident also throughout the years of the War of Independence and the post-Treaty period. In many respects her relationship with Frank Ryan was the consummation of one of these cerebral relationships of an earlier period. Ryan had all the perceived qualities she associated with the nationalist heroes that she venerated during this time. Ryan was most notably an activist in the national cause and thereby the real life replica of unattainable nationalist figures such as the dead Pearse.

When Jacob finally did travel to the capital on 13 May 1916 she was still at one remove from the political core of revolutionary Dublin. All those she visited had been active participants and were still fully implicated in the political fallout from the events of Easter week. Her purpose in travelling to Dublin was 'to see people instead of trying to write to them'. Arriving by the 9.40 a.m. train she travelled into Dublin by tram, passing the Four Courts, 'a testimonial to the bad shooting of the British army'. She described in full detail the effect of British tank bombardment of the rebel stronghold:

> The block between O'Connell St & Beresford Place is smashed to bits, a few back walls left standing, but the fronts gone, & all up O'Connell St the same sort of thing was visible . . . walked up O'Connell St – which is practically destroyed on both sides from the bridge to the Pillar, only a few houses on the left corner of the quays left – & viewed the post office, just the bare walls left, no roof, floors or windows. There were little curls of smoke out of some of the heaps of ruins still, & bits of wall about 40 feet and 8 wide standing up here and there among them. The front of the Imperial hotel is left but nothing whatever behind it. The post office

80 29 Mar. [1916] RJD Ms (171). P. H. Pearse, 'How does she stand? Three addresses' (The Bodenstown series no. 1) (Dublin: Irish Freedom Press, 1915). This was a collection of earlier speeches: two orations on Emmet delivered in New York on 1 and 8 March 1914 and a Tone commemoration speech given in June 1913 at his grave. Dudley Edwards, *Patrick Pearse*, p. 230.

especially was an appalling sight, heaps of stones inside & long crooked pieces of burnt metal and huge empty window holes and piles of stone and rubbish all along the pavement before it.[81]

Patricia Lynch's more contemporary account of the state of Dublin also testified to how 'dense clouds of smoke obscured the ruins'.[82] A similar scene of ruin met Jacob the next day on her way to visit the Somers in Delgany: 'the dispensary near Ball's Bridge all over bullet marks & broken windows and another house or two nearly as bad'.[83]

In Dublin, Jacob saw the ffrench Mullens, hearing news from Mrs ffrench Mullen[84] of how their house in Moyne Road was searched by soldiers following the incarceration of her son, Douglas, in Richmond Barracks and Madeline in Mountjoy. Madeline was arrested for her involvement with the Citizen Army in Stephen's Green and the College of Surgeons; Douglas had fought at the South Dublin Union under Eamonn Ceannt. Jacob arranged to visit Madeline with her mother on the following Monday. At Delgany she heard of Lasairfhíona's arrest during the Rising near Jacob's factory. Lasairfhíona told her the story of how she and a Miss Keogh from Gorey were searched in Trinity College, the soldiers believing the latter to be Countess Markievicz. Lasairfhíona's brother, Charlie, was also arrested and although released after a few days had still to report to the police every day.[85] On 15 May Jacob called on Hanna Sheehy Skeffington in Grosvenor Place and from there attempted to see Madeline in Mountjoy but had to leave before she gained entry. In the waiting room she met Miss O'Rahilly, Mrs Sean Connolly, Mrs Sean McGarry and Mrs Ashe.[86]

In the descriptions of her three days in Dublin, Jacob was very clearly an onlooker. She listened to how siblings were active jointly in the experience, which exacerbated her sense of exclusion and inaction. She moved rapidly

---

81   13 May 1916, RJD Ms (29).

82   Patricia Lynch, extract from *Workers Dreadnought*, 13 May 1916 in Angela Bourke et al. (eds), *The Field Day Anthology of Irish Writing*, vol. v (Cork: Cork University Press, 2002), p. 113.

83   14 May 1916, RJD Ms (29).

84   McCoole incorrectly states that both Madeline's parents were dead at the time of the Rising. McCoole, *No Ordinary Women*, p. 161.

85   13–14 May 1916, RJD Ms (29).

86   15 May 1916, RJD Ms (29). Miss O'Rahilly was Anna Rahilly, sister of Michael Rahilly who changed his name to The O'Rahilly. She was active in the language revival and worked after the Rising with the National Aid Employment Agency and the Prisoners Dependants and in the service of Sinn Féin during the 1918 election. McCoole, *No Ordinary Women*, pp. 173–4. Mrs Sean Connolly's husband, killed in the General Post Office, was the first casualty of 1916. Mrs Mairead Ashe was the widow of Thomas Ashe.

between different families who played key parts in the Rising noting their grief, concerned for their well-being and always herself on the fringes of suffering and therefore involvement. Jacob was deeply conscious and highly resentful of her place as an outsider. Although her animosity to Markievicz was already established it was heightened during the post-1916 period by the latter's exclusion of Jacob as someone of no importance when she came to Waterford in November 1917 to lecture on her experiences during the Rising.[87] During this time fellow nationalist, Mrs Murphy, invited Jacob to travel with the Countess and spend the night in Carrick-on-Suir. Jacob duly telephoned Markievicz to enquire if room could be made for her in the car: 'she said she'd let me know if there was a seat vacant, but I never heard any more till days afterward when I found there were 2 or 3 cars went, full of joy riders, & the Countess never asked if room could be made for me at all'.[88] Summing up the year at the end of 1916 she offered a rare insight into her deeper feelings. In that year her brother Tom married Dorothea Farrington. Although their house, St Declan's, was within easy range of the Jacob family home, she confessed to being lonely without him. Jacob had an increasingly uneasy relationship with Dorothea. Although the tensions between the two were not fully articulated until the later 1920s there were a number of instances of hostility during this period which clearly added to Jacob's sense of isolation. In 1915 Jacob wrote: what 'would I do if Mamma was not willing to criticise Dorothea sometimes? I would be 10 times more oppressed than I am by her charms & virtues & the general adoration that surrounds her'.[89] Dorothea considered her outspoken opinions and growing feminism as unsuitable. A dispute about men's clothes in September 1916 drew the following fractious comment from Jacob: 'Dorothea objecting to my views & thinking them very wrongheaded & narrow, as usual, because I *had* views'.[90] More interestingly she admits to how, despite enjoying her second trip to Dublin in July 1916, she

> was all the time suffering from envy & jealousy of the people I met who had been out in the Rising. It seems as if I was destined to be an outsider & a looker-on in everything all my life; *never* to be in it. The people in Dublin are very nice to me, but I'm outside all the time, because I don't live there.[91]

87 Markievicz toured around Ireland in the months following her release from Aylesbury prison on 17 June 1917 speaking of her prison experiences and in support of Sinn Féin. Anne Marreco, *The Rebel Countess* (London: Weidenfeld & Nicolson, 1967), pp. 236–8.

88 3 Nov. 1917, RJD Ms (32).

89 Sept. 1915, RJD Ms (171).

90 11 Sept. 1916, RJD Ms (30).

91 31 Dec. 1916, RJD Ms (30).

Reading stories of her father while ill and confined to bed in March 1917 she reflected wistfully on 'what a fearfully uneventful life I have had compared to what he had had at my age'.[92] It never crossed Jacob's mind to consider that as a woman an eventful life was not considered appropriate. Indeed, why should it have when she had the counter examples of Madeline french Mullen and Lasairfhíona Somers, amongst other women, who had been involved in 1916 and who, from Jacob's perspective, embraced life in all its exciting and active possibilities. Traditionally in periods of flux and transition in history a space was created whereby gender relations could be scrutinised and a desire for change articulated. The most famous example is that of the French Revolution; Olympe de Gouges argued for women's political rights, publishing her 'Declaration of the Rights of Women and the Female Citizen' in 1791. During the early years women were empowered to take to the streets and form political clubs but as the revolution evolved or became institutionalised the builders of the new order had the power to close down those clubs and call women back to their homes. As the revolution progressed there was an increasing stress on women's role as mothers of citizens in the new order; this was a public function but one carried out within the private sphere.[93] In Ireland alternative roles were overtly articulated and practiced by women during the years 1913–22. At a lecture delivered to the Students National Literary Society in Dublin Markievicz stated that the 'old idea that a woman can only serve her nation through her home is gone . . . you must make the world look upon you as citizens first, as women after'.[94] This was one of the core principles by which Jacob desired to live her life.

Although Jacob had set out to become a writer she suffered from laziness, probably fuelled by self-doubt. At the end of 1916 she admitted that she was too idle to take advantage of the free time she had since Tom's marriage to write in the mornings, she lists the work she has done up to 1916 but is conscious that she has not written anything saleable, for her the mark of success.[95]

---

92 17 Mar. 1917, RJD Ms (31).

93 For women in the French Revolution see, for example, Dominique Godineau, 'Daughters of liberty and revolutionary citizens' and Elisabeth G. Sledziewski, 'The French revolution as the turning point' in Georges Duby and Michelle Perrot (eds), *A History of Women: Emerging Feminism from Revolution to World War* (London: Belknap, 1993), pp. 15–32; pp. 33–47; Olwen Hufton, 'Women in revolution 1789–1796', *Past and Present* 53 (1971), pp. 90–108.

94 Countess Markievicz, 'A call to the women of Ireland being a lecture delivered to the students' National Literary Society, Dublin, under the title of "Women, ideals and the nation"' (Dublin: Fergus O'Connor, 1918), p. 12, RJP Ms 33,127 (2).

95 31 Dec. 1916, RJD Ms (30).

Many of her Dublin friends did try to spur her activity. Hanna Sheehy Skeffington believed she should be able to write children's books while Lasairfhíona Somers urged her to write more.[96] A few years later in 1918 Jacob entered and won the prize competition offered at the Sinn Féin Convention for an essay on 'Ireland's case for independence'; this entry was the result of Hanna's influence who made her 'feel it was pure laziness if I did not'.[97]

Jacob's sense of isolation within her family and from the political events she considered formative in the nation's struggle for independence was enhanced by her desire for male friendship. Again this desire was made clear in her frank summing up of the year 1916. As was usual when she summed up a year Jacob mused on acquaintances and friends made during the year with a unique addendum: 'I don't seem to have made any new friends this year, unless I could count the Pearses ... I *should* like to have a few masculine friends, but that doesn't seem to be the will of God'.[98] At tea with the Gaelic League activist, Miss Scarlett in 1918, a fellow guest, Miss Fleming, 'as usual made me die of envy talking of her various young male friends – the sort of friend that wants a long talk in a lonely place when he's starting for war'.[99] The romanticised notion of love and relationships contained in this notion of intense liaison in the context of war should be noted. With no real experience Jacob's view of male-female relationships was based, almost like the fictional Isabel Sleaford in Mary Elizabeth Braddon's *The Doctor's Wife* (1862), on notions of romance gleaned from reading and this in part could explain her tendency to hero worship those within the growing nationalist pantheon of the period.[100] A potential lover had to be heroic, active and willing to sacrifice his personal happiness in the service of his country.

Jacob's notion of equality between the sexes even extended to her ideas on love and her refusal to accept the conventional notion of a passive feminine role as central to male-female relationships may also explain, in some way, her lack of success in attracting men at this stage in her life. Her views on such topics emerged in family discussion, often with Dorothea present, and arguably fueled the tensions between the two women. In many cases, as the following example illustrates, these discussions were innocuous, but they do indicate Jacob's alternative viewpoints by comparison with the other members of her family:

96 17 June 1916, RJD Ms (30); 14 Aug. 1917, RJD Ms (31).
97 2 Nov. 1918, RJD Ms (35).
98 31 Dec. 1916, RJD Ms (30).
99 19 Aug. 1918, RJD Ms (34).
100 Mary Elizabeth Braddon, *The Doctor's Wife* (Oxford: Oxford University Press, 2008).

D. & T. to dinner . . . we were discussing why women don't write lovesongs as
much as men do. Mamma & D. consider that they don't want to, not feeling the
same need for self-expression as men do, which seems a pity . . . I don't see why
not. I don't understand the feminine idea of love.[101]

Similarly, Jacob had no understanding of anyone who would agree to the idea
of a woman promising to obey a man in the marriage service and was horrified
at family members who saw the wording as only a form which should not be
spoiled with alterations: 'I wish I could understand that sort of mind; it is
an absolute sealed book to me'.[102] Jacob was constantly perplexed by gender-
specific attitudes to love and sex. Discovering that Ned Stephens, a family
friend in Dublin, never kissed his male children she mused to herself: Is kissing
purely sexual to men, then?[103] Yet, despite her views on the equality of men
and women in relationships, Jacob betrayed a certain desperateness to form a
sexual relationship or to have, at the very least, a close male friendship. In late
1917 she noted a letter from Dorothea making reference to a communication
she had from Charlie Murphy telling of his desire 'of going to a ceilidh with
Rose' in Dublin – 'but he was too busy & I was too busy (I certainly wasn't, but
I believe the ceilidh didn't happen till I was gone). I'm sure I should have been
extremely glad to go'.[104] In March of 1918 she notes how the same Charlie
Murphy had come to tea and commented admiringly: 'I do think his hair is a
trifle long, but it's beautiful'.[105] Jacob was never shy in noting, where she saw
it, the physical beauty of men but believed that she was different to other
women in this.

When I talked about how the beautiful lines in a man's figure are hidden & hardly
ever shown by some of the thick loose clothes they wear, Mamma said she didn't
want lovely lines in a man, & Tash said she had never observed male beauty.
Neither have most women, and practically every woman wd think lovely an
unsuitable word to use about a man.[106]

During the raid on Hanna Sheehy Skeffington's house in October 1920 she
described the policeman who entered with ten privates and an officer 'as a very

101 13 May 1917, RJD Ms (31).
102 29 Sept. 1919, RJD Ms (36).
103 6 Dec. 1920, RJD Ms (38).
104 30 Dec. 1917, RJD Ms (33).
105 17 Mar. 1918, RJD Ms (33).
106 2 June [?1917], RJD Ms (171).

fine, tall, handsome young man'.[107] The male model at her life drawing class in the Metropolitan Art School which she attended on moving to Dublin drew her admiration: 'practically naked, & he certainly was lovely'. She was dismayed when at the next sitting he was fully clothed: 'the model had trousers on, confound him. What hideous things they are after bare legs'.[108] Jacob even imagined Rochester in Charlotte Brontë's *Jane Eyre* in a physical manner. Enjoying the book on a second reading while in jail for anti-Treaty activities in early 1923 Jacob was once more impressed by the 'strong impression' of love offered by Brontë, a love Jacob admired as 'individual, keen, refreshing . . . but I can't escape the conviction that he [Rochester] was hairy all over'.[109]

Jacob's attitudes to men and relationships in many ways indicate the paradoxes she faced as a single woman and a feminist in a society gradually evolving alternative female roles to the domestic ones which prevailed throughout the nineteenth and early twentieth centuries. In many respects Hanna Sheehy Skeffington's comments on Jacob's attitudes were highly perceptive:

> I had some conversation with Hanna on sex at dinner; she said she was glad to be through with sex & regarded it as rather a nuisance & a hindrance in life. There is a kind of coldness & asceticism about her. She said she had imagined a romance about me & Ben, but also that she had imagined me like Dr Lynn & Madeline, having no use at all for men.[110]

What Hanna touched upon was the problem for many women like Jacob, a problem that is reflected in the often stratified thinking of many practitioners of women's history in Ireland. Ward notes how Madeline ffrench Mullen and Kathleen Lynn lived two doors down from Hanna, commenting: 'It was a predominantly woman-centred existence, one dedicated to humanitarian service and political causes'.[111] It should be remembered that in some instances a number of the women with whom Jacob interacted in these years were committed to the intimacy of same-sex relationships or were like Sheehy Skeffington and Margaret Cousins in marriages where companionship rather than sex took precedence even in the early years. Jacob recorded how Hanna told her that she and Frances had separate bedrooms: 'she thinks that the most civilised way; never liked sleeping with anyone. She is very ascetic.'[112] While in

107 4 Oct. 1920, RJD Ms (37).
108 24 Jan. 1921; 14 Feb. 1921, RJD Ms (39).
109 21 Jan. 1923, RJD Ms (43).
110 22 Oct. 1919, RJD Ms (36).
111 Margaret Ward, *Hanna Sheehy Skeffington: A Life* (Cork: Attic Press, 1997), p. 223.
112 10 Nov. 1919, RJD Ms (36). For Margaret Cousins's revulsion at the concept of sexual intercourse see J. H. Cousins and M. E. Cousins, *We Two Together* (India: Ganesh & Co. Ltd, 1950), pp. 108–9.

many respects Ward's description of a woman-centred existence around Hanna Sheehy Skeffington in the period is apposite, it may simultaneously be consider-ed reductive in its designation of a notion of collectivity to women's experiences and aspirations. As Jacob believed in and pronounced on gender equality and the ability of women to live independent lives, and as she surrounded herself with many apparently like-minded women, she was perceived to be, if not anti-men, as having in some way transcended the need for a traditional heterosexual relationship based on intimacy and children. Recognition of this tendency to reduction allows a very different reading of Jacob's life to an analysis based on an automatic equation of strong feminist beliefs with lesbianism or nonconformity by heterosexual women in terms of desire for marriage and children; the historian must be careful to avoid embedded and false binaries which work to counter the complexity of the lived experience.

Jacob's failure to establish any meaningful male relationships during this period in her life does, as noted, explain her tendency to develop crushes on various male figures to the fore in the national cause. This tendency was presumably exacerbated by the failure of her family to permit her to operate as a fully independent adult. The tendency of the family to accord Jacob a child-like status even in her 20s and early 30s is a reflection of the status accorded to single women in Irish society: 'Pouring rain,' she wrote in November 1918, 'and Mamma wd not let me out after tea'.[113] Staying with her aunts in Dublin shortly after her mother's death in early 1919 they considered that her arrival home 'was terrible late'; she had been handing out leaflets about children kidnapped by, in the words of Arthur Griffith speaking in the Dáil, 'English militarist forces'.[114] Establishing herself permanently in Dublin in late 1919 she was forced to acquaint herself with the rudiments of budget management and basic account holding, 'it's dreadful', she wrote, 'to be so ignorant about banking'.[115] Jacob's admiration for the politics of certain male leaders was bound up with her own sense of what type of a man she desired and indicates her craving for adventure and an almost storybook like heroism. When Cathal Brugha, described by one historian as 'the most strenuous opponent of the 1921 Treaty', was shot in the second week of the Civil War she declared: 'I do like a man who *cannot* surrender'.[116] Jacob clearly craved excitement as is

---

113 30 Nov. 1918, RJD Ms (35).

114 Foster, *Modern Ireland*, p. 508; 8 Apr. 1919, RJD Ms (35). Three children were kidnapped, one being released after a period of almost five hours. *Dáil Éireann Debates*, vol. 1, 10 Apr. 1919.

115 22 Oct. 1920, RJD Ms (37).

116 5 July 1922, RJD Ms (41).

evident in her account of her midnight motorcycle ride in March 1922 after a visit to Margot Trench:[117]

> after talking with her a good while . . . a plain young man called Henry Connor –
> came in. He was a hot anti-democrat, ostensibly . . . but he was the kind of pleasant
> creature you can fight with without being serious. They were both pro Treaty . . .
> When I started to go at 11, Connor offered to run me home on the back of a motor
> bike, & I jumped at it. They made me sit astride, in somebody's old trench coat,
> and he went like the devil, and it was just the lovely sensation I knew it wd be. I was
> so excited I had to wake up J. W. to tell her about it.[118]

Jacob's deification of Pearse after the events of 1916 gave way to a brief idolisation of Arthur Griffith during 1917 and 1918; Griffith's stature rose when she compared him with Eamon de Valera. In November 1917 both men spoke in Waterford, Jacob preferring Griffith's address.[119] Her 30th birthday saw her receive a picture of de Valera as a present.[120] This present is an interesting comment on the material culture of Jacob's nationalist world. Jacob regularly wore a republican badge after the Rising, marking her as a member of the nationalist community: 'my republican badge got me into conversation with an official at the station, who said he had not thought there were any Sinn Féiners in Bray'.[121] Attending art classes in the technical school in Waterford before her move to Dublin she made, amongst other items, Sinn Féin rings. A Christmas present to Jacob from Lasairfhíona Somers in 1919 included, along with a number of handkerchiefs, a republican pincushion.[122] The RIC County Inspector's Report for Waterford in June 1916 stated that 'picture postcards and sheets of portraits of rebel leaders were freely sold'.[123] Laffan writes how 'mourning badges . . . became talismans, and . . . were central to the iconography of the Irish revolution.'[124]

---

117 Margot Trench was the granddaughter of the Protestant Archbishop Trench of Dublin. She was a member of both the Gaelic League and Cumann na mBan. Nicola Gordon Bowe and Elizabeth Cummings, *The Arts and Crafts Movements in Dublin and Edinburgh, 1885–1925* (Dublin: Irish Academic Press, 1998), p. 197.

118 18 Mar. 1922, RJD Ms (40).

119 11 Nov. 1917, RJD Ms (32).

120 13 Oct. 1918, RJD Ms (34).

121 28 July 1916, RJD Ms (30).

122 Ibid.; 18 Dec. 1918, RJD Ms (35); 31 Dec. 1919, RJD Ms (36).

123 RIC County Inspector's Report for Waterford June 1916, CO904/100.

124 Laffan, *The Resurrection of Ireland*, p. 55.

By contrast to Jacob's hero worship of many of the prominent male nationalist figures of the period, her admiration of Hanna Sheehy Skeffington was genuine and increasingly based on intimate knowledge. After 1916 Jacob's relationship with Hanna, and indeed Owen Sheehy Skeffington, developed and it was Hanna's house in Belgrave Square where she first boarded when she finally left Waterford on 7 October 1919.[125] By early 1921 Jacob could declare of Hanna: 'I don't think I know anyone whose presence & conversation *always* is so exhilarating to me'.[126] Hanna's response to *Callaghan* was carefully documented in Jacob's diary, as one whose opinion counted more than any other.[127] In many ways Jacob modelled herself politically on Hanna. It was Hanna's opinion she sought out and recorded on the Treaty split, allowing it to become her own. On 10 December 1921 she went over to Belgrave Road 'to hear Hanna's opinion of the crisis. She is against the Treaty & she & Dr Lynn & Madeline were writing to Dáil members'. She visited the following day to find Hanna and Lynn going through the list of Dáil deputies 'sorting out "Mickites & Devites"'. This type of entry in the style of reportage suggests that she herself was not sufficiently knowledgeable about the events and issues to come to a self-appointed stance. On 14 December she had Hanna to dinner and the talk revolved around the day's happenings in the Dáil. Again Jacob was on the fringes of political developments, forced, as she had been during 1916, to learn details second hand and unable to gain admittance to what she described as the 'secret' session of the Dáil on 14 December despite the fact that 'many strangers . . . got in simply by influence.[128] A week later, on a visit to Belgrave Road, she heard news of the Dáil sittings, recording Hanna's perception of a press bias against republicans.[129] During the tragedies of the Civil War Jacob described Hanna as 'a great blessing to me all this time, a kind of support & exhilaration to my mind, though less a pacifist than I am'.[130] The use of the word exhilaration on more than one occasion by Jacob indicates the galvanising role Hanna played in her life. Her relationship with Hanna generated a sense of purpose in Jacob. When she considered boarding with Hanna she

---

125 8 Apr. 1919, RJD Ms (35). This was the date on which Jacob asked Hanna if she would consider her as a boarder.

126 2 Feb. 1921, RJD Ms (40).

127 19 Dec. 1920, RJD Ms (38).

128 On the 14 December at the morning sitting of the Dáil it was decided to discuss the 'genesis of the proposed treaty' and the disagreement over the powers of the Plenipotentiaries who negotiated and signed the Treaty. *Dáil Éireann Debates*, vol. 3, 14 Dec. 1921.

129 10–11 Dec. 1921; 14 Dec. 1920; 21 Dec. 1920, RJD Ms (40).

130 17 July 1922, RJD Ms (41).

wrote: 'I think I could be useful in some ways'.[131] Her comparison of their
relative commitment to pacifism also indicates how Jacob modelled herself on
Hanna; she was the touchstone against which Jacob formulated or weighed
her own political and feminist ideas. In the context of pacifism referred to by
Jacob, Sheehy Skeffington distinguished between militancy and militarism.
Opposed to the latter as the institutional response of those in authority to
power challenges, she believed that militancy was a legitimate response of the
oppressed to the oppressor. She linked suffrage militancy with the militancy
of the colonial oppressed in Ireland and elsewhere. This was in contrast to
Louie Bennett, for example, who was opposed to all forms of violence.[132]
Jacob's attitude to violence fell somewhere between these two positions, and
arguably she never clarified her position even to herself. Her Quaker upbringing
led her to identify strongly with the pacifist approach. Clearly her support for
republican nationalism, her later anti-Treaty position, her willingness in the
later 1920s and early 1930s to support Frank Ryan in hiding weapons and on an
emotional level, subverted her avowed commitment to pacifism. However,
she did make a distinction between violence as a premeditated act as opposed
to that carried out on impulse, writing in August 1912 when suffrage violence
was high in both Ireland and England:

> J. Upton came & paid us a visit . . . We were talking about the Suffragettes, and I
> said I didn't think isolated acts of violence done in cold blood for the sake of
> violence, were the wisest method to adopt; that I thought as for riot & bloodshed,
> they would be justified in going to almost to any lengths, but it should be done in
> crowds, & in hot blood, to be effective – the way Nottingham Castle & Hyde Park
> railings that they talk so much of, were done.[133]

Yet despite this condemnation of premeditated violence, Jacob believed
in political assassination to the horror of the Quaker, Josephine Webb:
'Josephine was shocked at Mrs P. & me for defending political assassination.
Mrs P. had mentioned the Phoenix Park murders with approval, & we went
on from there'.[134]

131 8 Apr. 1919, RJD Ms (35).

132 Ward, 'Hanna Sheehy Skeffington', pp. 94–5.

133 8 Aug. 1912, RJD Ms (23). In 1866 the Hyde Park railings were torn down as a spontaneous action
during a protest organised by the Reform League, established in 1865 to agitate for universal suffrage.

134 22 Sept. 1916, RJD Ms (30).

THE GAELIC LEAGUE

Back in Waterford on the 15 May after her first visit to Dublin in 1916, Jacob continued her hero worship of Pearse, reading 'Íosagán', refusing to censure the piety of the story; 'if you must have piety', she declared contrary to her usual views on religiosity, 'it's a nice sort of piety, & exquisitely told'.[135] Her veneration of Pearse extended for a time to Mrs Pearse and her daughters, whom Jacob met on her second visit to Dublin in 1916. On that occasion Mrs Pearse lent her a copy of Pearse's pamphlet, 'How does she stand', which Jacob copied on return to Waterford.[136] In December of that year Jacob was employed crocheting a jacket for Mrs Pearse. Such activity confined Jacob to a very traditional female role in the service of the national cause; earlier in November of 1916 she testified to knitting with her mother and Dorothea for Frongoch Prison Camp in Wales, where many of those involved in 1916 were sent.[137] Of course, many other women more radical than Jacob performed similar duties. Dr Kathleen Lynn testified to making 'great preparations for sending parcels to Frongoch' that same Christmas.[138]

Jacob was initially galvanised by the Rising and, in particular, by her trip to Dublin. Indeed, the local political arena was for a time, according to her testimony, transformed in the wake of the events of Easter week. The almost moribund Waterford branch of the Gaelic League was revitalised; notwithstanding the fact that the meetings continued to discuss the same concerns relating to the Oireachtas and issues around instruction, all the members, except for Father Dowley and P. de Brett, had, she wrote, 'twice the Sinn Féin spirit they used to have, except those who were always all right'.[139] In October 1916 the RIC County Inspector noted the increased hold of Sinn Féin over the committee of the local Gaelic League: 'now quite half are pronounced Sinn Féiners & there are some more of Sinn Féin Tendencies.'[140] Sinn Féin candidate in the 1918 elections, Dr Vincent White, wrote how the functions of the Waterford Gaelic League 'meant much to me; they showed the new Ireland which had emerged out of the 1916 Rising.'[141] However, soon again apathy and petty squabbling came to the fore. This experience of lassitude within the Waterford League reflected the general pattern of growth and decline within

135   24 May 1916, RJD Ms (29).
136   31 Oct. 1916, RJD Ms (30).
137   27 Dec. 1916; 5 Nov. 1916, RJD Ms (30).
138   Dr Kathleen Lynn, BMH WS 357, p. 8.
139   26 May 1916, RJD Ms (29).
140   RIC County Inspector's Report for Waterford Oct. 1916, CO904/101.
141   Dr Vincent White, BMH WS 1764, p. 13.

the wider organisation. The League had expanded fivefold by 1902, continuing to grow at a lesser rate until 1908, by which date it contracted until the
Anglo-Irish War brought about a new phase of dynamism. The lack of solidity
within the League resulted in a pattern where branches tended to go through
cycles of failure and revival or re-establishment. One factor to cause a falling off
in members was the shift within branches from 'propagandist lectures or
dances to classroom work, numbers dwindled because most people were drawn
into the league for the *craic* associated with it'.[142] Certainly Jacob's account of
indifference and internecine feuding suggests that there was little or no 'craic'
to be had in the Waterford branch in the period after the post-1916 enthusiasm
had waned. Father Dowley's lack of progress in organising the local feis forced
the branch to forgo the event, opting to hold a concert or an aeridheacht in
September instead and appointing a sub-committee to that end. Jacob was
highly critical of Father Dowley's lack of work; given her repeated negative
comments on the high level of clerical participation in the League it is safe to
assume that her frustration was heightened by Dowley's profession.[143]

Earlier in the year, at a meeting to make arrangements about flag selling
for the Gaelic League on St Patrick's Day 1916 Jacob noted the crowds of
'noisy and chattering' girls in attendance and betrayed her anti-clericalism and
indeed anti-Catholicism in the line: 'It seemed to be all Fr Dowley's doing; he
went round to the schools and told them all to send kids. Just the Catholic
style.' At the Pearse lecture on that same day she revelled in the disrespect
accorded to the priests in attendance: 'We sat in the front row . . . & presently
Fr Dowley wanted us to move & leave the front row for priests, but we
wouldn't so he & others brought in cushioned forms from the council chamber
& planted them in front of us, but anyone sat in them, including Matt Keating
MP'.[144] Although Jacob tended to be quite strident in her dislike of aspects of
Irish Catholicism[145] her anti-clericalism continued to encompass the Church
of Ireland. Attending a lecture by Strangeman in Waterford on 'Women in
Industry' at the Protestant Hall, in February 1918, she noted the Dean's
presence in the chair surrounded by two other members of the Protestant
clergy noting how 'Protestants can be fairly priest ridden too'.[146] Jacob's consciousness of both the Catholic and Protestant clerical presence at such events

142 Timothy G. McMahon, '"All creeds and all classes"': Just who made up the Gaelic League?' *Eire-
Ireland* (Fall/Winter 2002), p. 122, pp. 124–5, p. 126.

143 11 Aug. 1916, RJD Ms (30).

144 10 Feb. 1916, RJD Ms (29).

145 Jacob described Charlotte Despard in pejorative terms as seeming to be 'a great Catholic' when
she spoke at the IWFL. 22 Jan. 1921, RJD Ms (39).

146 11 Feb. 1918, RJD Ms (33).

was quite likely heightened by the lack of clergy in the Society of Friends. It was also heightened by her personal lack of religious faith. Her anti-Catholicism, most particularly, was exacerbated by the triumphalist Catholicism that was an increasing feature of Irish society in this period. Historians have viewed such exultant Catholicism as one of the salient features of the Free State established in 1922; Jacob's diary testifies to an increasingly visible Catholicism during this earlier period, almost grooming itself to take its central place in the new State. Already at this period, Jacob, as a non-Catholic and a non-believer, represented an Irish tradition that was in the process of marginalisation. In March 1921 six men were hanged in Mountjoy for terrorist activities during the Anglo-Irish War. Visiting with Ella Young and Estella Solomons[147] during that month, the conversation revolved around the role of the Catholic Church, in Jacob's words, 'in relation to the religious orgies that go on outside Mountjoy during executions'. Jacob was in the minority; all other visitors:

> think them all right, & a sign of strong spiritual life, and E. Y. thinks they strengthen the national will & do a lot of good. I'm not psychic enough to feel that, & my idea is that their only justification is the comfort they seem to give the victims. E. Y. told me I was a Pharisee. People seem to find me very arid & materialistic where religion comes in.[148]

Reynolds notes how the Catholic Church during the Anglo-Irish War had the ability to 'channel political energy into the passive ritual of prayer', in this way 'disciplining the Irish public'.[149]

Despite the initial spurt of enthusiasm in the Waterford branch of the Gaelic League post 1916, local jealousies soon re-emerged. Arrangements and planning for the aeridheacht were fraught with trivial tensions:

> I went to a G. L. committee after tea & they spent a lot of time trying to make Connolly be see [*sic*] to the aeridheacht which he wouldn't do, out of pique at being deprived of the secretaryship years ago. There were only Kearns & Coffey & Miss Doyle there besides me, and there were very severe things said of Fr Dowley.[150]

147 Estella Solomons was the wife of the poet Seamus O'Sullivan and herself a supporter of the nationalist cause.
148 16 Mar. 1921, RJD Ms (39).
149 Reynolds, 'Modernist martyrdom', pp. 551–2.
150 18 Aug. 1916, RJD Ms (30).

The recurring argument as to equality of representation between the sexes at committee level still reigned in the branch, clearly fomented by Jacob's own attitudes: 'P. Woods said our rule was no more & no less than 4 women, & I said women & men should be equally eligible without distinction of numbers & proposed a resolution to that effect which was carried.'[151] At an Oireachtas committee meeting on 16 July 1917 it was decided that all the female members of the branch would take responsibility for the Industrial Exhibition to be held at the Technical School in Waterford. This tendency within the League to treat women as an undifferentiated mass was, Jacob believed, representative of 'the Irish passion for segregating the sexes'.[152] Jacob believed that men and women should integrate fully, commenting on the attitudes of family friend, Ned Stephens: 'He considers its very wrong for men & women to live separate lives without plenty of intercourse with each other, wherein I entirely agree with him.[153] The concern to segregate men and women was also a criticism she had of Sinn Féin; she bemoaned the fact that all the sellers for the flag day in November 1917 were girls and noted scathingly the lack of female political ambition and drive: 'Its marvellous the activity of women in collecting money, the horriblest of all forms of political work, & the one they seem to take to most.'[154] Jacob herself loathed any form of collecting but seemed powerless to insinuate herself into more meaningful roles.

The most endemic problem faced by the Waterford branch of the Gaelic League was the lack of committed members. Repeatedly Jacob testified to meetings that could not be held due to the lack of a quorum. On the evening of 22 February 1917 she attended an Oireachtas committee 'but there weren't enough present & we only talked'.[155] Jacob was, moreover, critical of the lack of direction in the League at national level. People, she wrote, 'are *always* discussing that [what the League should do to save the language], & the League *never* seems to do the right thing.' [156] The conservative, reactionary attitudes of a number of League members also drew comment from her. At the Ard Fhéis in Dublin in 1919 she noted 'a resolution to take measures against immoral literature, which was supported in several hot & silly speeches, but was quashed by a few cool sentences from Griffith'.[157] O'Leary notes in his study of the prose literature of the Gaelic revival that the core issue was 'what

151 17 Oct. 1916, RJD Ms (30).
152 16 July 1917, RJD Ms (31).
153 2 Jan. 1918, RJD Ms (33).
154 9–10 Nov. 1917, RJD Ms (32).
155 22 Feb. 1917, RJD Ms (31).
156 7 Aug. 1917, RJD Ms (31).
157 8 Apr. 1919, RJD Ms (35).

kind of books in Irish a Gael would welcome or tolerate'; nativists within the League viewed the language as a bulwark against the immoral and corrupting values of English literature.[158] This idea would reach its zenith in the Censorship of Publications Act, 1929. In December 1913 the Gaelic League columnist in the *Waterford News* spoke glowingly of the *Catholic Bulletin* 'doing excellent constructive work to cultivate a taste for wholesome literature, and every Irish man and women who is anxious to help the campaign for the suppression of dirty English publications should push the sale'.[159] Despite consciousness of the failings of the League both at national and at local level, Jacob continued to attend classes and worked at improving her language skills. In November 1917 she was reading Father Peadar Ó Laoghaire's *Séadna*, described as the first major prose work in the language of the Revival.[160] At the Waterford Féis in 1918 she once again judged the junior history competition.[161] For Jacob membership of the League was a political statement and she refused to accept Hyde's emphasis on the pre-eminence of cultural revival over political activism; she highly approved of de Valera's speech at the Waterford Town Hall during the Waterford Oireachtas in August 1917, despite her other reservations about the man and her annoyance at the lack of women on the platform:

> He opposed the idea that the League could be non political in the national sense; said if he were an Imperialist it wd be his duty to try & discourage the language because it stands in the way of absolute union between this country & England; it tends towards separation rather, its only in the sense of not siding with one party that the League can really be non-political. This was highly applauded.[162]

CUMANN NA MBAN

Following the Rising Jacob began drilling classes and talk commenced on revitalising the local branch of Cumann na mBan.[163] However, as much as with the local Gaelic League, such attempts failed to progress much beyond the level of talk. Efforts to have meetings at the local Volunteer Hall were protracted, not due to any apparent hostility on the part of the Volunteers but

---

158 Philip O'Leary, *The Prose Literature of the Gaelic Revival, 1881–1921: Ideology and Innovation* (Pennsylvania: Penn State University Press, 1994), p. 14, pp. 31–4.

159 *Waterford News*, 12 Dec. 1913.

160 O'Leary, *The Prose Literature of the Gaelic Revival*, p. 11.

161 9 July 1918, RJD Ms (33).

162 7 Aug. 1917, RJD Ms (31).

163 11 July 1916; 8 Aug. 1916, RJD Ms (30).

as a result of the failure of Cumann na mBan members to talk to the relevant men.[164] Having finally arranged for permission to drill at the Volunteer Hall in Thomas Street, a new problem manifested itself as meetings clashed with those of the local Fianna who were also using the hall: 'They had drilling & a warpipes & we couldn't do much with the noise'.[165] What is often elided from the historical picture in a teleological treatment of the national struggle in the period 1913–21 is everyday experience for participants at ground level. The mundane nature of involvement and the petty squabbles are often forgotten in a concentration on core female and male activists. Jacob's diary testifies to how often little was achieved at nationalist and feminist meetings in Waterford. She records repeatedly the debilitating effects of internecine squabbles within such nationalist groups as the Gaelic League and Cumann nBan. This theme is reflected in Joe Kelly's remark in *Callaghan* on Redmond assuming the Presidency of the Volunteers in 1914: 'I had serious thoughts of chucking it myself . . . but I decided not to – 'twould be too like the people Bridie tells me about in the Gaelic League, that claim to be as keen as anyone but drop the whole business if a thing is done that they object to'.[166] A Cumann na mBan meeting in Waterford on 15 August 1916 'didn't do much, except arrange to try to get up a hurling club, at E. Robinson's suggestion.' At this meeting Jacob's love of instructing came once again to the fore; she read aloud part of the *Cork Free Press* on Casement to the assembled group.[167]

Jacob's tendency to take and maintain dislikes against people, as had earlier been evident with Countess Markievicz,[168] was also was apparent in her Cumann na mBan activity during these years. On the way home from the meeting in September 1916 'K. H. [Kathleen Hicks] & I had a lot of talk . . . she says the Volunteers have something against Mrs Roche, but she doesn't

164 29 Aug. 1916, RJD Ms (30).

165 12 Sept. 1916, RJD Ms (30). By 1913 the Waterford Fianna was up and running, although one member recalled the difficulty of organising a nationalist youth organisation in a city with a strong branch of the Baden Powell Boy Scouts and a general public which 'frowned on any organisation which did not flaunt the "Union Jack" at its head'. Patrick Hearne, BMH WS 1742, pp. 1–2; James Nolan, BMH WS 1369, p. 2.

166 F. Winthrop, *Callaghan* (Dublin: Martin Lester, n.d. [1920]), p. 130.

167 15 Aug. 1916, RJD Ms (30). The *Cork Free Press* was the paper edited by William O'Brien from 1910–16. O'Brien founded the All-For-Ireland League in 1910, a dissident group from the Irish Parliamentary Party.

168 Markievicz was not the only prominent member within the Dublin circles of activism and intellectualism to which Jacob took a dislike. Estella Solmons was also subject to censure in Jacob's diary as in the entry for 25 May 1921 when she described a visit to Ella Young: 'Estella Solmons & her velveteen friend the poet came in, but didn't say much, & what E. S. did say wd have been better left out'. 25 May 1921, RJD Ms (39).

know what; & that her presence keeps a lot out of it. Damn her, I wish she
would meet with a fatal accident, & damn them too, that stay out of it because
of her & leave me alone with her.' Six days later Jacob went to Dungarvan to
fund raise at a Tipperary–Limerick hurling match, arranging to go only because
she heard that Mrs Roche was not, '& then she did after all, to my great
disgust'.[169] Indeed, Jacob's hostility to Mrs Roche, the reasons for which she
never specified, took precedence over her commitment to Cumann na mBan.
In November 1916 she explained to fellow member Maudie Walsh over tea 'the
propriety of letting C. na mb. drop as long as Mrs Roche makes no sign. There
are practically no members left, & Mrs R. would prevent its ever coming to
good while she's in it'.[170] It is noteworthy that Jacob preferred to let the local
wing of the organisation fall into abeyance rather than challenge Mrs Roche to
impose her own direction on the meetings. Despite what she would have
considered as Mrs Roche's politically correct anti-Redmond stance and her
interruption of the politician when he spoke in Waterford in October 1917, her
personal antagonism directed her comments: 'she admired herself so much &
talked so much about it that you would prefer a person who had not the courage
to lift a finger'. Jacob herself, it should be noted, had merely booed Redmond
as he passed close to her after the speech and had made no attempt to interrupt
the meeting.[171] Mrs Roche, by contrast, according to the testimony of one local
Volunteer 'was the first person I saw displaying the present National flag in
Waterford' and was 'evicted from premises in Parnell Street'.[172]

The Waterford branch of Cumann an mBan was somewhat reconstructed
when Jacob received a card from Seán Matthews, Company Adjutant and
later Captain of the 'B' Company, 4th Battalion, then Battalion O/C, inviting
her to a meeting at the Volunteer Hall on 31 January 1917 about starting a
'ladies auxiliary'. Debate ranged around the concept of an auxiliary female
political organisation. Matthews himself stated that the women could 'be
Cumann na mban or a ladies' auxiliary whichever we liked'. This may seem a
strange request given the presence of the former in Waterford. However,
Laffan notes the confusion over the role of women in Sinn Féin in the post-
1916 period; as late as 1919 the belief was still widely held that Cumann na
mBan was an auxiliary to Sinn Féin. Matthews recommended the establishment of Cumann na mBan in Waterford

169 5 Sept. 1916; 11 Sept. 1916, RJD Ms (30).
170 7 Nov. 1916, RJD Ms (30).
171 6–7 Oct. 1916, RJD Ms (30).
172 Michael F. Ryan, BMH WS 1709, p. 7.

as we cd make out our own program then, whereas if we were an auxiliary 'you'd have to take your program from us, & we might often have no work to give you, & then dry rot would set in.' I advocated the same choice on different grounds & it was agreed on.

Jacob's objection was to the very idea of 'being anything auxiliary'.[173] However, the auxiliary nature of Cumann na mBan itself was not remarked on, possibly a reflection of the internal changes in the organisation post 1916; at its 1917 Convention the organisation demanded equality with the Volunteers. Many of the meetings of this newly formed group in Waterford were informative and educational rather than sites of activism. On 28 February the group read some of *Ghosts*, Pearse's 1915 treatise on the moral corruption of Redmondism and the manner in which it represented a deviation from an unbroken nationalist tradition.[174] Members attended first aid classes and drilling, a comment on the changed nature of the organisation since it was conceived in 1914, Pearse declaring at that time that he 'would not like the idea of women drilling and marching in the ordinary way'.[175] At no point, however, did there appear to be any sense of a purpose to such drilling activities among the members of Waterford Cumann na mBan. Jacob records no sense of any charged political context to their activities. She does note the occasions on which the premises in Thomas Street were searched by the authorities but in a highly matter of fact way.[176] Activism comprised getting signatures for a Cumann na mBan protest.[177] Again, not unlike the Waterford branch of the Gaelic League, the organisation appeared to wax and wane following the initial enthusiasm immediately after 1916. The RIC monthly report records an increase in membership from 10 in June 1917 to 30 the following month, the figure dropping once more to 10 in October. During the conscription crisis of 1918 the Inspector noted: 'The branches of Cuman na Mban increased from 35 to 80 during the Month and many of these Women's Sinn Féin Clubs are now learning first-aid and ambulance work'. In June 1918 a branch was formed in Dungarvan.[178] On 23 April 1918 Jacob remarked: 'There was a Cumann na

173   31 Jan. 1917, RJD Ms (31).

174   28 Feb. 1917, RJD Ms (31); Maume, *The Long Gestation*, p. 164.

175   See for example, 30 Apr. 1917, Ms (31); 10 Nov. 1917, Ms (32); Quoted in Rosemary Cullen Owens, *Smashing Times: A History of the Irish Women's Suffrage Movement, 1899–1922* (Dublin, Attic Press, 1984), p. 109.

176   17 Oct. RJD, 1916, RJD Ms (30).

177   1 Mar. 1917, RJD Ms (31).

178   RIC County Inspector's Report for Waterford, June 1917, July 1917, Oct. 1917, May 1918, June 1918, CO 904/103; CO 904/104; CO 904/106.

mBan branch being started at the Volunteer Hall, with Mrs Power & Miss Doyle at the head of it'.[179] This appeared to be yet another new attempt at re-organisation for the branch.

Jacob herself travelled as an invited speaker to other Cumann na mBan branches, addressing the branch which was to be formed in Carraig on 5 May 1918. She read out the Constitution and commented on the activities of members during 1916, noting that this 'frightened some women out of joining'. She was, however, at pains to point out that members could be active in the organisation 'without taking a share in bloodshed'.[180] The Waterford branch of the organisation gave the impression of greater activity in early 1919 although Jacob herself was certainly not a central player as is evident from her use of the word 'they' in the following entry of 24 January: 'I went to a Cumann na mban gen. meeting in the evening. They are going to have a big sort of bazaar at Easter, to get money for the election fund and for themselves'.[181] In February she attended a meeting, open to non-members, in the committee rooms of the Waterford Town Hall to hear Countess Plunkett speak.[182] In June 1919 she was 'overjoyed' to discover that the branch had requested from the central authority a dispensation from involvement in the flag day on the grounds that 'it would inflame the Redmondites & cause violence & injure our chances at the next election, & anyhow only 6 were willing to sell'. Jacob felt that aside from the last reason, these were poor grounds on which to base the request. She herself, however, 'was just as glad' despite the fact that she supposed the Waterford branch 'will be despised for ever'.[183] Jacob's involvement continued in such a fringe capacity. She noted how she was received at a meeting in January 1920 'more kindly than I deserved'.[184] This may have been a reference to her inability to get on with other members such as Mrs Roche. Other testimonies highlight the lack of focus in the Waterford branch of Cumann na mBan. Lieutenant Colonel P. J. Paul, Commanding Officer, East Waterford Brigade, 1919–21, paid tribute to the organisation for their assistance in the years up to the Truce but noted how

> as an organised body [it] might not have seemed of much consequence. It was as individuals that the members assisted the wounded, prisoners and their depen-

179 23 Apr. 1918, RJD Ms (33).

180 5 May 1918, RJD Ms (33).

181 24 Jan. 1919, RJD Ms (35).

182 3 Feb. 1919, RJD Ms (35). Countess Plunkett was the mother of Joseph Mary Plunkett executed as one of the 1916 rebels.

183 10 June 1919; 17 June 1919, RJD Ms (35).

184 18 Jan. 1920, RJD Ms (36).

dents. It was hard to get them to work under their own officers. Consequently their services were more availed of as individuals and it was only shortly before the Truce that a definite attempt was made to organise this women's auxiliary organisation on a proper military basis. Máire Comerford[185] came down from Dublin as GHQ organiser some time before the Truce and she did succeed to some extent in putting the organisation on some sort of basis but this did not improve the work or the services rendered by these women who still worked better as individuals under the direct instructions of various Volunteer officers.

Jacob's name does not appear on the list of women he mentions.[186]

Jacob's peripheral position within Cumann na mBan during the post 1916 years can be attributed to a number of factors. Clearly, personality clashes aside, Jacob was unimpressed by the lack of dynamism and direction within the branch, yet her own character traits did not equip her to command leadership and effect change. Jacob was always much more comfortable involved in organisations with a strong leadership. Allied to this was her inherent sense of opposition to female only and auxiliary organisations. On her first visit to Dublin following the Rising Jacob records her interest in the Irish Citizen Army, noting Madeline ffrench Mullen's comments on gender equality within its ranks.[187] Helena Molony recorded in later life how on Easter Monday at 'the last minute, when we were going off at 12 o'clock, Connolly gave out revolvers to our girls, saying: "Don't use them except in the last resort".'[188] Indeed, Jacob was opposed to the manner in which the gender hierarchy within nationalist politics, outside the unique example of the Irish Citizen Army, played out in the private sphere. Meeting Mrs Ceannt, widow of Eamonn Ceannt, signatory to the proclamation, in Scoil Éanna in July 1916, Jacob expressed her distaste for the manner in which she never knew anything of her husband's political plans and the subservient, domestic role she played around him in the home. She:

> told us about her last interview with her husband, & how she used have the other leaders to tea with him, & lay the table & then go off & leave them alone all the

185 Máire Comerford became a Cumann na mBan activist after 1916. During the War of Independence she was involved with the White Cross and as a courier for Michael Collins. A staunch opponent of the Treaty she refused to follow de Valera into parliamentary politics in 1926. Her commitment to Sinn Féin continued into the 1970s when in 1974 she was arrested at a meeting in Dublin. McCoole, *No Ordinary Women*, pp. 150–1.
186 Lieutenant Colonel P. J. Paul, BMH WS 877, pp. 60–1.
187 20 June 1916, RJD Ms (30).
188 Helena Molony, BMH WS 391, p. 33.

evening and never know anything about their plans. It seems to me that would be an intolerable way to live.[189]

FIANNA GIRLS

The necessity for Waterford members of Cumann na mBan to share premises with the Fianna resulted in a considerable overlap between the meetings of the two groups, joint gatherings often concluding in shared cultural activities, such as dancing and singing; all joined in a rendition of 'Soldiers Are We' on 21 September 1916.[190] Indeed, the RIC County Inspector was dismissive of republican activism in the city noting in October 1916 that although the Fianna met regularly and the Irish Volunteers met every night 'most of the time is spent in card playing & dancing, this is the means by which the leaders get their followers to attend, & probably accounts for their having got a few recruits'.[191] Jacob was troubled at the militarism of the Fianna. When Markievicz spoke in Waterford on her role in the Rising Jacob described her as speaking 'very well' but added the caveat: 'a little too bloodyminded. I don't think boys under 16 ought to be let use arms at all; it can't but be bad for them'.[192] Although Jacob's statement may have been influenced by her visceral antagonism to Markievicz it is noteworthy, as will be discussed, that Jacob elaborated on the sentiment in Maggie Cullen's response to her youngest son Roddy's role in carrying ammunition and messages for his brother Liam during the Anglo-Irish War in *The Troubled House*. The military nature of the Fianna was overt. Its constitution allowed for members to be court martialled if they failed to obey orders. In *Bean na hÉireann* the members were described as the recruits for the army of the new Ireland.[193] In the introduction to the Fianna handbook of 1914, written by Markievicz, she laid emphasis on danger and fear: 'It will take the best and noblest of Ireland's children to win Freedom, for the price of Freedom is suffering and pain. It is only when the suffering is deep enough and the pain almost beyond bearing that Freedom is won'. She talked of 'martial music and the rattle of arms'.[194]

Jacob took on a degree of responsibility for the Fianna girls in early 1918. She became honorary president, chairing their meetings. On investigation she

189 22 July 1916, RJD Ms (30).

190 21 Sept. 1916, RJD Ms (30).

191 RIC County Inspector's Report for Waterford Oct. 1916, CO 904/101.

192 1 Nov. 1917, RJD Ms (32).

193 J. Anthony Gaughan, *Scouting in Ireland* (Dublin: Kingdom Books, 2006), p. 36, p. 35.

194 *Fianna Handbook* (Dublin: Patrick Mahon, 1914), p. 7.

found 'that the Fianna council governs girls as well as boys, without the girls having any representation on it – they let themselves be called a ladies auxiliary, so what can they expect'. Fianna member, Moses Roche, recalled sometime in 1917–18 that 'there was a ladies auxiliary branch called a "sluagh" attached to the Fianna in Waterford, and it was principally from members of that sluagh we got our first aid'.[195] Jacob wrote to Markievicz 'to ask how the girls in Dublin manage their affairs, but God knows if I'll ever get an answer'.[196] No reply appears to have been received but in February 1918 'the girls informed me they had news from Dublin that they shd not be in the Fianna at all, but in the Clan na Gael Girl Guides so apparently they must set this up for themselves somewhere, and I don't know how the classes are to be managed'.[197] Despite this uncertainty she instructed the girls in Irish history, offering lessons on, for example, the Nine Years War and the Flight of the Earls.[198] Molony recorded that Inghinidhe na hÉireann, 'hard pressed to cope with everything', abandoned boy's classes, having found them 'hard to manage'. When Markievicz formed the Fianna, Molony continued, she 'did not start anything for girls. She did not like girls, and there were, of course, those classes in the Inghinidhe for them.'[199] Membership of the Fianna was open 'to all boys who endorse its Constitution and make the Declaration of the Fianna'. And the *Fianna Handbook* of 1914 makes no reference to girls.[200] However, it appears that branches calling themselves Fianna Girls did exist both before and after the Rising. In Dublin in August 1918 Jacob called to Michael Chadwick who worked with the Dublin Girl Scouts and with whom she had been communicating regarding organisational instructions. He showed her the Fianna handbook, which was difficult to obtain, and promised to send her a couple of copies. She lamented to him 'as to the touchiness & tale bearing of the girls' and took heart that he seemed 'to know very well what it is'.[201] Jacob's lament to Chadwick was not an isolated example of irritability with the demeanour and attitudes of the girls' section of the Waterford Fianna. The lack of seriousness of purpose of the girls was the cause of their being excluded from the premises except on Thursdays and Sundays. This incident saw many of Jacob's perennial complaints about gender equality, male attitudes to women and the

195 Moses Roche, BMH WS 1129, p. 2.
196 11 Jan. 1918; 16 Jan. 1918, RJD Ms (33).
197 27 Feb. 1918, RJD Ms (33).
198 9 May 1918, RJD Ms (33).
199 Helena Molony, BMH WS 391, p. 55, pp. 58–9.
200 *Fianna Handbook*, p. 167.
201 23 Aug. 1918, RJD Ms (34).

lack of assertiveness amongst women in nationalist organisations coalesce. The ban on the girls attending the republican meeting place in Waterford with the exception of two designated nights of the week was:

> the conclusion to which their own frivolous ways & the men's passion for card-playing & instinct for having everything for themselves & the meekness of the leading women have brought things.

Jacob, of the four women who were appointed to make rules for the girls, was the only one who spoke up for their rights, 'though Miss Skeffington would fight if the girls were sufficiently working members to make it possible to stand out for real equality for them'.[202] Jacob objected on more than one occasion to women who refused to take seriously the issues she considered important and who instead acted in what she would have considered a demeaning way, flirting and betraying an interest in the less serious pursuits of life. She was particularly vehement against women who flirted and conducted relationships with soldiers during the Anglo-Irish War. Nothing bothered her as much during this period as observing girls walking with soldiers.[203] This concern had been core to Inghinidhe na hÉireann. Molony recorded how anti-recruiting leaflets were 'in all cases addressed to Irish girls appealing to them not to consort with the armed and uniformed enemies of their country'.[204] This subject was a source of controversy between Jacob and close friend, Helen McGinley, during the Anglo-Irish War, Jacob highly censorious of how she 'practically flirts with them [the Black and Tans] while they search her'.[205] Of course, Jacob's knowledge and experience of this matter of the social interaction between women and the British armed forces was relatively abstract. She was removed from the more brutal manifestations of its consequences as she would only have read about women who were punished for company keeping. Louise Ryan documents incidents where young girls had their hair cut off for consorting with policemen; this had its mirror image in similar incidents against women by the Black and Tans during the Anglo-Irish War.[206]

202 26 Jan. 1919, RJD Ms (35).

203 31 Dec. 1921 [notes on the year], RJD Ms (40).

204 Helena Molony, BMH WS 391, pp. 2–3.

205 16 Dec. 1920, RJD Ms (38).

206 Louise Ryan "'Drunken Tans": Representations of sex and violence in the Anglo-Irish War (1919–21)', *Feminist Review* 66 (Autumn 2000), pp. 82–3.

SINN FÉIN

Jacob's most committed political involvement was in the newly reconstituted post-1916 Sinn Féin. The Rising, dubbed by the British as a Sinn Féin instigated insurrection, witnessed the decimation of the Irish Parliamentary Party, although it was a number of months before it was clear that the Sinn Féin Party could respond to the challenge of its 'new-found national prominence'.[207] The Sinn Féin party that emerged as the parliamentary victor in the 1918 election was radically different to its predecessor, representing 'advanced nationalism in many spheres, including the women's movement'.[208] Jacob's desire for immediate involvement in the post-1916 local branch of Sinn Féin drew negative comment and she should wait, she was told, until they chose to 'invite the ladies'. It is noteworthy that Dr Vincent White, in discussing the reconstituted Sinn Féin branch in Waterford, mentioned how the organisation included 'about 12 men who had been members of Sinn Féin since its foundation'; no mention is made of Jacob's involvement from the outset. Another list of those prominent in 1918 includes a H. Jacob.[209] Local activist, Nicholas Whittle's language is significant when he describes how on the day of the 1918 General Election he 'found himself alone in the election rooms with a couple of girl helpers'.[210] This suggests an inherent gendered approach to politics amongst members of the Waterford Sinn Féin executive; women were invisible and clearly not seen on equal terms. In commenting on the violence of Redmondite supporters at the General Election of 1918 Whittle wrote how this would have an effect in 'retarding a certain type of our supporters in casting their votes. I refer to women, particularly the aged'.[211] White notes how, by 1917, attendance at Waterford Sinn Féin meetings had grown 'so much' that a permanent premises was established at Colbeck Street.[212] In 1917 a courier team of cyclists comprising both men and women was organised. This was intended to act as a link with similar organisations throughout the County and was used to keep lines of communication open in the event of conscription.[213] The growth of Waterford Sinn Féin was paralleled throughout the country. By October 1917 there was something in the range of 1,200 clubs with around 250,000 members, the Party growing by 1918 to reach a similar

207 Rafter, *Sinn Féin*, pp. 48–9.
208 Foster, *Modern Ireland*, p. 488.
209 Dr Vincent White, BMH, WS 1764, p. 12.
210 Nicholas Whittle, BMH, WS 1105, p. 29.
211 Nicholas Whittle, BMH, WS 1105, p. 44.
212 Dr Vincent White, BMH, WS 1764, p. 1, p. 2.
213 Nicholas Whittle, BMH, WS 1105, p. 7.

position to that held by the Irish Parliamentary Party under Parnell in the 1880s.[214] The Party, in the words of Rafter, 'came to represent the new confident calls for political change'.[215]

Criticism of Jacob's attempt to be to the fore in Sinn Féin activities in Waterford did not impact on her and she attended the meeting on 12 July 1917 which concerned itself mainly with revising the parliamentary register in advance of a possible election. A procession was held in honour of the Sinn Féin success at the East Clare by election on 10 July 1917 at which de Valera achieved a landslide victory, defeating the Irish Parliamentary Party candidate, Patrick Lynch, KC, by 5,010 votes to 2,035.[216] The procession in Waterford comprised male members of Sinn Féin, the Volunteers, the Fianna and Cumann na mBan, all led by the local piper's band named in honour of Thomas Francis Meagher.[217] Jacob took a fairly active role in Sinn Féin election activity. On 19 July 1917 she, together with other local members, travelled to Kilkenny to participate in an election rally, having become 'infected' by the enthusiasm of other members for the expedition at the meeting the previous night. Speakers included the Sinn Féin candidate, William T. Cosgrave, de Valera and Markievicz, the latter who 'talked sickening stuff about having been supported in jail by love coming over the western waves'. Jacob considered that she improved greatly once she moved on to pay a tribute to the women in the College of Surgeons during the Rising. Jacob clearly enjoyed the sense of comradeship and the feeling of partici-   pation in an increasingly triumphant cause; on the train journey back to Waterford that night 'most of the people in the corridor sang the Soldier's Song & other things, & coming out of the station in Waterford the whole crowd seemed to be singing it'.[218]

Notwithstanding criticism from some quarters of Jacob's refusal to adopt a subservient political position becoming her gender, she was made Vice-President in September 1917 partly, according to her testimony, because she was the only survivor of the old National Council branch.[219] From this date until she finally left Waterford in late 1919, Jacob's visits to Dublin were organised around her participation as a Waterford delegate at the yearly Sinn Féin conventions. On 24 October 1917 she left Waterford, staying with Mrs ffrench Mullen, Madeline at this point was living with Kathleen Lynn. At this

214 Foster, *Modern Ireland*, p. 488.

215 Rafter, *Sinn Féin*, p. 49.

216 Brian M. Walker (ed.), *Parliamentary Election Results in Ireland, 1801–1922* (Dublin: Royal Irish Academy, 1978), p. 184.

217 12 July 1917, RJD Ms (31).

218 18–19 July 1917, RJD Ms (31).

219 4 Sept. 1917, RJD Ms (31).

Convention Jacob adopted the role of feminist watchdog. This was a crucial time for women to have their voices heard as 'party strategists . . . sought to clarify what exactly Sinn Féin stood for'.[220] The central fault line was between those who – represented in 1917 by Plunkett – wanted commitment to republicanism through the Liberty League and those – represented by Griffith – who still clung to the notion of a dual Monarchy and the concept of passive resistance. At a Convention convened by Plunkett in April 1917 a split was averted, both groups maintaining their separate identities but linking with the new central Mansion House Committee. One interesting reference in Jacob's diary, made as an aside, was that the newly reconstituted organisation in Waterford was 'a Liberty League, which doesn't seem to me such a good name'.[221] The latter remark suggests that at the level of ground membership there was not always recognition of the fissures dividing the movement at the national level in the post-1916 period. Initially no women were elected to the Mansion House Committee but Molony and Countess Plunkett were last minute additions when opposition was raised.[222] To rectify such inequality at future conventions and to ensure the continued advance of women within Irish political life the female delegates established the League of Women Delegates, meeting one month after the April Convention. This organisation comprised women delegates to all Irish republican conferences.[223] Events between the April and October Conventions of 1917 showed that women were going to have to fight to realise the guarantee of gender equality enshrined in the 1916 Proclamation. De Valera replaced Griffith as President and the Party was dedicated to achieving a republic.[224] Female activists were highly conscious of the need to assert the position of women within Sinn Féin at this transitional point as the Party's ideology became institutionalised and overtly stated. Up to this point the Party had been 'less of a formalised political organisation and more of a group of like-minded individuals doing their best without any real agreement about their intended end-objective'.[225] At the October Convention 1917, however, the 'inchoate movement' had achieved a united

220 Rafter, *Sinn Féin*, p. 54.

221 1 June 1917, RJD Ms (31); The RIC Inspector's Report for Waterford in May 1917 estimated membership of Waterford Sinn Féin at between forty and fifty but added 'as this does not exceed the nominal membership of the old Irish Volunteers it is obvious that the cause is not making rapid strides'. CO 904/103.

222 Margaret Ward, *Unmanageable Revolutionaries: Women and Irish Nationalism* (London: Pluto, 1995), pp. 123–4.

223 Cullen Owens, *Smashing Times*, pp. 117–18; Margaret Ward, 'The League of Women Delegates and Sinn Féin', *History Ireland* 4: 3 (1996), p. 38.

224 Laffan, *The Resurrection of Ireland*, p. 118.

225 Rafter, *Sinn Féin*, p. 51. See also Laffan, *The Resurrection of Ireland*, p. 84.

front.[226] Women such as Molony and ffrench Mullen spoke to Jacob of the necessity that the Convention 'should declare unmistakably for a republic, and the danger of Griffith's non-republicanism & autocratic spirit'.[227] Jacob worked behind the scenes to raise both the number of women members in the movement and the profile of existing female members. She brought leaflets on the importance of women joining Sinn Féin to an IWFL meeting in Dublin.[228] Jacob recorded a conversation between ffrench Mullen and Molony on the difficulties 'they had in forcing 6 women onto the Sinn Féin executive against the will of Griffith & Milroy etc'. This attempt had been ongoing since the meeting of the League of Women Delegates on 30 July.[229] In reality only four women were co-opted to the executive, Áine Ceannt, Jennie Wyse Power, Miss Plunkett and Molony, Ceannt then standing down in favour of Lynn.[230] On the opening day of the Convention, in response to a note passed to her by Lynn, Jacob asked on what franchise would a future independent Constituent Assembly be elected, noting how the English parliamentary franchise would exclude women. Griffith's response was to state 'that whatever the franchise was, it would include them, which is the straightest statement he has ever made on the point'.[231] Jacob's initial enthusiasm following Griffith's comments was reiterated in the *Irish Citizen* in the wider context of the adoption of the principle of equality within Sinn Féin. The paper offered:

> our hearty congratulations to the promoters and spokesmen of the Sinn Féin Convention for the broad statesmanship and the public spirit they have displayed in endorsing and embodying in their new constitution, in the most unequivocal terms, the democratic principle of the complete equality of men and women in Ireland.

The writer noted Jacob's question relating to the franchise, after commenting on the 'fine spirited' speech of Dr Lynn in support of the motion of female equality. Concern was, however, expressed at the paucity of female delegates.[232]

Jacob attended the reception of the League of Women Delegates in Countess Plunkett's house on 26 October travelling to the reception by car with Dr Lynn and Madeline ffrench Mullen. In keeping with the multifaceted

226 Laffan, *The Resurrection of Ireland*, p. 117.

227 1 Oct. 1917, RJD Ms (32).

228 29 Sept. 1917, RJD Ms (31).

229 1 Oct. 1917, RJD Ms (32); Ward, 'The League of Women Delegates and Sinn Féin', pp. 39–40.

230 Cullen Owens, *Smashing Times*, p. 116; Ward, 'The League of Women Delegates and Sinn Féin', p. 40.

231 25 Oct. 1917, RJD Ms (32).

232 *Irish Citizen*, 4: 52 (Nov. 1917).

approach adopted by many to issues of nationalism and national identity, Jacob noted how Kathleen Lynn wore a dark blue and white national costume; at this reception the name of the League was Gaelicised.[233] In her diary Jacob delineated the role of Cumann na dTeachtaire, stressing the organisation's desire to galvanise and educate women to political involvement. A wide-ranging approach to political activity was adopted; Cumann na dTeachtaire aimed to 'link up other women's organisations too & encourage all to do Feminist work together'. Meetings were open to any country delegate who was in Dublin. Jacob, however, believed that the delegates at the October 1917 meeting were naïve about female membership in the Sinn Féin clubs in the country as they 'seemed to think all that was needed was for them to join the clubs & then they wd work just like men'.[234] Jacob's own first-hand experience of female apathy and diffidence in the face of male authority belied the confidence and expectations of the women delegates, although it is likely that such confidence on the part of the other delegates was a front. Noting the difficulties women had in securing four representatives to the executive Ward states how 'different reality was from appearance'. The desire to extend the League outside Dublin was frustrated by the fact that only 12 female delegates had been selected by clubs around the country to attend the October Convention.[235] Jacob's scepticism was borne out the following month when Markievicz visited Waterford, a visit the RIC County Inspector dismissed declaring, 'I do not think she roused any enduring enthusiasm except among possibly the Boy Scouts'.[236] The prominent members of the local Sinn Féin had a carriage waiting into which Markievicz was placed together with three men while all the women who had come out to greet her, Jacob declared, 'followed in the mud'.[237] Indeed, Jacob found herself playing a secondary position to the male members when on the evening of the 8 November she attended a general meeting in Waterford to hear delegates' accounts of the October Convention. When she arrived, O'Connor was offering his account, leaving little for her to add except for a 'few more general sort of impressions'.[238] Although she chaired the meeting when de Valera spoke on the 'Theological innocence of rebellion against unlawful activity, & the attitude of Sinn Féin to labour', she continued to lament the ingrained discriminatory attitudes to female members. She was, however, allowed to attend a rifle class

233 26 Oct. 1917, RJD Ms (32); Ward, 'The League of Women Delegates and Sinn Féin', p. 41.
234 26 Oct. 1917, RJD Ms (32).
235 Ward, 'The League of Women Delegates and Sinn Féin', p. 40.
236 RIC County Inspector's Report for Waterford, Nov. 1917, CO 904/104.
237 1 Nov. 1917, RJD Ms (32).
238 8 Nov. 1917, RJD Ms (32).

where she 'learned that an oak is the best tree to shelter from bullets behind, being hardest for them to get through, & how a cartridge is made'.[239]

The Waterford branch of Sinn Féin appeared to follow the pattern of the Waterford divisions of Cumann na mBan and the Gaelic League. For all these organisations a period of anticlimax set in once the post-1916 enthusiasms waned. Jacob noted the comments of Seán Matthews at a general meeting of Sinn Féin on 7 February 1918 to the effect that the club was 'decaying'. Thus Waterford Sinn Féin had began to decline before Dublin Castle's arrest of leading Sinn Féiners on trumped up allegations of links with Germany (the 'German Plot') or before the War of Independence triggered the nation-wide weakening Hanna Sheehy Skeffington noted as Director of Organisation in 1920:

> For obvious reasons, which there is no need stating here, the organisation has suffered grievously during recent months, our organisers one after another being imprisoned or otherwise put out of action the local Clubs left leaderless, their funds and literature seized, their halls burnt, their social and other activities banned, their members marked, so that there was no possibility of their functioning or even meeting.[240]

When Jacob returned to Waterford in November 1919, the Carstand Powers family 'could tell me nothing of the Club except that it is sinking to a low level, & in common with Sinn Féin everywhere else has sold its soul to Labour without getting any adequate return. An anti-Redmond song at a Labour concert here lately was hissed off the stage, they say.'[241] A discussion was held in February 1918 on how to circumvent decline. Despite Jacob's active participation in the matter, supporting the suggestion to hold lectures with visiting speakers from Dublin, she was left feeling sidelined as a woman. One member, Wheeler, she noted, 'always speaks . . . as if women had no existence'.[242] This, of course, was not a perception peculiar to Jacob as the concerns of female activists to gain representation on the Sinn Féin executive indicated, nor was the lack of equality accorded to female members a problem peculiar to Waterford. Rather, as Jacob was fully aware, this was endemic within national political life. She castigated de Valera's speech in Waterford[243]

239 30 Jan. 1918, RJD Ms (33).

240 Report on Sinn Féin by Hanna Sheehy Skeffington, c.1920, Director of Organisation, SSP Ms 33,621 (6).

241 29 Nov. 1919, RJD Ms (36).

242 7 Feb. 1918, RJD Ms (33).

243 This meeting was proclaimed and had to be held three miles outside the city with an attendance of about a thousand. RIC County Inspector's Report for Waterford, Nov. 1917, CO 904/104.

in November 1917 writing: 'He had the usual way of saying men & every man etc, as if there were no women in the country'. Later in the evening following that speech she had tea with de Valera and Griffith at Power's Hotel. During this meeting de Valera was told of her objections, responding that 'he wished he always had someone to prompt him on that point when he was going to speak. I said I didn't think he should require prompting at this time of the day'.[244]

Jacob's sense of the lethargy endemic in the Waterford branch of Sinn Féin was not confined to a criticism of the female members. The rank and file of the wing she decried as meek, content to be led unquestioningly by a few dominant and domineering types at the helm. Of course, election losses in the early part of 1918 in South Armagh, East Tyrone and Waterford itself had a dampening effect nationally on the enthusiasms generated by the flush of victories at by-elections in 1917.[245] In September 1918, local Waterford activist, Wheeler, brought forward his idea of imposing a parliamentary type structure on the branch, where members took responsibility for certain departments, for example, membership, social life, representatives. According to Jacob's report of the meeting the ordinary members 'submitted with their usual meakness'; she herself, added representatives of Labour and Cumann na mBan and somebody to look after the reading room and the organisation of lectures.[246] Again, internal bickering stymied purposeful activity. Squabbling and antagonisms were, indeed, endemic within the Party at national level. Laffan notes how in 1917 personal 'dislikes soon proved as damaging to the unity of the Sinn Féin movement as were ... differences of principle'. Many of these dislikes were centred on Count Plunkett, who as the leading figure in 1917 lacked the political acumen demanded by his position and, unlike Griffith, was unable to compromise.[247] The squabbling in Waterford is clear in the debate at local level about the relationship between the Labour Party, established in 1912, and Sinn Féin. No general election pledge was hammered out between Sinn Féin and Labour; Sinn Féin decided in August 1918 to run candidates in every constituency but with a willingness to modify as the situation necessitated. In the event in November, Labour decided not to contest the election. However, it is clear from Jacob's account that at local level there were discussions between Labour and Sinn Féin to attempt to arrange a compromise to avoid splitting the vote, members of Sinn Féin often being members of trade unions.[248] At a

244 11 Nov. 1917, RJD Ms (32).

245 Rafter, *Sinn Féin*, pp. 54–5.

246 5 Sept. 1918, RJD Ms (34). See also 12 Sept. 1918, RJD Ms (34).

247 Laffan, *The Resurrection of Ireland*, pp. 86–9.

248 Laffan notes how, in the context of the South Kilkenny seat, the Thomastown branch of Sinn Féin asked its members who belonged to the Transport Union to vote for 'genuine' Sinn Féiners first. Ibid., p. 159.

meeting on 9 October 1918 John Gallagher told of an offer made by the Labour Party through another Sinn Féin representative, a Mr Coates, on the matter of dividing up constituencies between the two parties in the next election: 'they wd not fight 3 neighbouring constituencies if we wd leave them the city'. Gallagher failed to call a committee and instead informally consulted one or two members and sent a message to headquarters informing them that Waterford Sinn Féin did not wish to adhere to the election pact, much to the annoyance of other members who felt that consultation was in order. Jacob's report of the Sinn Féin Convention of October 1918 was filled with details of the debate over the election relationship between the Party and Labour, common shibboleths about socialism emerging:

> Headquarters had drawn up a pledge, promising that you were out for a Republic & wd resign if Labour asked you to go to Westminster, which was the price they demanded for giving a Labour candidate a clear field. Even this did not satisfy everyone; one man said the Labour candidate in his division believed in Karl Marx's doctrines, & how cd he vote for him? Fr O'Flanagan pointed out that you must vote for the Republican candidate whatever his minor sins; even if he disagrees with you in religion or social questions, he is the lesser of 2 evils.

Jacob did note that at the 1918 Convention there were more women delegates than there had been the previous year.[249]

Beyond attendance at local meetings, Jacob did plebiscite work for Sinn Féin throughout February 1918. Under the Representation of People Act 1918 women over the age of 30 who were householders or who were married to householders or who were graduates were granted the vote. On 11 February Jacob targeted the monastic institutions in the locality and was surprised to receive a favourable reception at the Good Shepherd Convent.[250] In early March she visited a number of old women's institutions. [251] Although Jacob found such work frustrating and menial it was crucial to the success of Sinn Féin in the December elections of that year. The Party was ground breaking in its electioneering tactics, organising, as Jacob did, the voter registers, ensuring that agents were placed at polling booths to deter impersonation of voters and ensuring that both the local and national sections of the Party shared the workload.[252] Margaret Brady, a member of Cumann na mBan in Leitrim

249 30 Oct. 1918, RJD Ms (35).
250 11 Feb. 1918, RJD Ms (33).
251 2 Mar. 1918, RJD Ms (33).
252 Rafter, *Sinn Féin*, p. 52.

noted the importance of women in the new centralised election work orchestrated by Sinn Féin and added a twist to the issue of voter impersonation:

> Our Branch had been organised for some time prior to the 1918 General Election, and we made a large amount of emblems and flags and such things for the campaign. On the day of the voting we took over a vacant house in the town of Cloone where we cooked and supplied meals to the Volunteers on duty that day ... We enjoyed ourselves very much that day personating voters. We voted for dead and absentee voters and also for people whom we knew would be hostile to Sinn Féin.[253]

Jacob's election work did not stop at such work to update the electoral register. Despite her accounts of endemic apathy within the local branch of Sinn Féin, Vincent White recorded a 'sense of purpose' following the death of Redmond on 6 March 1918: 'life took on a quick tempo in Waterford city'.[254] White was nominated Sinn Féin candidate in the by election which followed on 22 March and certainly Jacob herself was stimulated to a rare display of activism becoming embroiled in an incident with a contingent of Irish Parliamentary Party supporters. The IPP held a procession on 12 March during which she hung a flag out of the drawing room window inciting their anger and in the process mildly injuring herself:

> a lot of them came in and hurled themselves against the door, & yelled & shouted, and put up a torch to burn the flag, I pulled it in just in time & they threw the torch in after it, but it went out as soon as it fell. My face & blouse were drenched with paraffin & the drawing room smelt of it for days. They also threw a stone through the fanlight.[255]

Local Volunteers mobilised during the campaign 'to safeguard speakers at Sinn Féin meetings and to give protection to all those who were working for the success of the Sinn Féin candidate'.[256] According to the Sinn Féin Director of Elections, Nicholas Whittle, the election had large-scale consequences for the future of Irish independence and he quoted Griffith as saying that if the IPP won the election then the government would be in position to introduce conscription.[257] This was a particularly violent election with assaults

253 Mrs Margaret Brady (*née* Sweeny), BMH WS 1,267, p. 2.
254 Dr Vincent White, BMH WS 1764, p. 1, p. 2.
255 12 Mar. 1918, RJD Ms (33).
256 Thomas Brennan, BMH WS 1104, p. 2.
257 Nicholas Whittle, BMH WS 1105, p. 9.

on Sinn Féin supporters and prominent opposition from the local 'separation women' who benefited from war allowances.[258] Notwithstanding the IPP success in the election when William Redmond received 1,242 votes to White's 745,[259] Waterford Sinn Féin quickly began to make preparations for the next election. Jacob was appointed sub director of Finance, much to her horror, claiming she 'knew nothing about money'. She was obliged to sign orders and detail expenditure. Ward committees were also formed to make a list of 'everyone in each street who *ought* to have votes, so as to compare these with the list of claims to be published shortly'.[260] The Sinn Féin candidate, White, later wrote:

> Looking back on it all now, the public affronts which I so often received at the hands of the ignorant shoneens of Waterford, pale into insignificance before the recollection of the magnificent spirit of the supporters who stood four square behind me.

White claimed that Waterford Sinn Féin recognised that their support base had grown appreciably in the interval between the March and December 1918 elections, the conscription crisis reversing the downward trajectory of the Party nationally following its three election defeats in early 1918.[261]

Jacob's diary testifies to the acceleration of political events in May 1918. On the morning of the 18 May news of the arrests in Dublin of prominent leaders of Sinn Féin the previous night reached Waterford. Arrests had been made on the basis of alleged contacts between Sinn Féin and Germany dubbed the 'German Plot'.[262] The British Government, forced to concede that conscription could not be introduced to Ireland without severe violence, chose to move against 'groups which they blamed for their humiliation'.[263] Public opposition to conscription and the arrests further radicalised the political climate. Support for Sinn Féin grew, Griffith being elected in East Cavan in June despite being detained in prison.[264] With the arrest of many male leaders, female activists found themselves in political demand where previously, according to Jacob's

258 Laffan, *The Resurrection of Ireland*, p. 126.

259 Walker, *Parliamentary Election Results in Ireland*, p. 185.

260 13 May 1918, RJD Ms (33).

261 Dr Vincent White, BMH WS 1764, p. 10, p. 11. However, Waterford was one of the two contested seats won by the Irish Parliamentary Party in December 1918, the other being the Falls seat in Belfast. Laffan, *The Resurrection of Ireland*, p. 164, p. 128.

262 Maume, *The Long Gestation*, p. 207.

263 Laffan, *The Resurrection of Ireland*, p. 142.

264 Rafter, *Sinn Féin*, p. 56.

testimony, they had been merely tolerated. This necessity to court women was compounded by the granting of the franchise to certain women under the January 1918 Act. 'They will, Jacob wrote, 'be much more respectful to women from this out'.[265] A Sinn Féin election committee in Waterford held on 20 May 1918 considered suitable women to direct Party operations in case conscription was introduced before the election. Again, Jacob recorded her sense of the lack of commitment among women members, claiming that half the women wouldn't accept the posts.[266] In this respect she was not exaggerating. Attempting to organise women to speak during the election campaign in November 1918 she was only able to find two to travel in the wagonette and not one who would speak.[267] On 4 July Jacob documented the Lord Lieutenant's declaration of Sinn Féin, the Gaelic League, Cumann na mBan and the Volunteers as dangerous societies; the next day all public meetings were proclaimed.[268] A year later, Jacob was still fully immersed in this caucus of revolutionary groupings, but now, from a Dublin perspective.

265 15 Nov. 1918, RJD Ms (35).
266 20 May 1918, RJD Ms (33).
267 16 Nov. 1918, RJD Ms (35).
268 4–5 July 1918, RJD Ms (33).

FOUR

REVOLUTIONARY YEARS: A DUBLIN FOCUS

1916–21

———

From late 1916 Jacob set about trying to integrate herself into the activism of Dublin; it is evident that she was concerned to prepare a meaningful foundation on which she could build a life in the city once family commitments permitted her to do so. On 16 November 1916 she received the communication she had been awaiting for from Mrs Pearse, informing her that she could share a room at Scoil Éanna with Miss Bulfin, a daughter of William Bulfin.[1] Jacob wrote glowingly of the Pearses. Although she described Margaret Pearse as plain, she admired her abruptness as not of the disagreeable kind.[2] Later, she was to describe her as '*very* attractive, very abrupt & straight & natural & interesting'. She admired her capacity for work, which probably said more about Jacob's own desire for meaningful employment in the national/feminist cause than any real knowledge of Margaret Pearse's life.[3] The Dublin of Jacob's diary in this period was one of fierce activity and a sharp sense of expectation. All movements and cultural activities seemed to be pointing in the same direction – towards freedom, at this point for both men and women. One gets a wonderful glimpse of the intertwinings of the different campaigns of the time as the intellectual discourse of freedom and equality permeated all aspects of Dublin activism. Events would reveal, of course, just how much of this enthusiasm and expectation was naïve, particularly on the question of women's freedoms and equality.

One of the key components of female activism after the Rising was to see to the welfare of the families of those incarcerated or killed. Kathleen Clarke used

1   Catalina Bulfin's brother Eamonn had attended St Enda's. Catalina was arrested while working for the anti-Treatyite Austin Stack. She would later marry Seán MacBride. Sinead McCoole, *No Ordinary Women: Irish Female Activists in the Revolutionary Years* (Dublin: O'Brien, 2004), p. 144.
2   31 Oct. 1916; 20 Nov. 1916, RJD Ms (30).
3   23 Nov. 1916, RJD Ms (30).

the £3,100 remaining from IRB funds left to her by her husband for this purpose. The Irish Volunteer Dependants' Fund (IVDF) was established with Clarke as President and Áine Ceannt in the role of second in command. Parallel to the establishment of this Fund was the formation of the Irish National Aid Association (NAA). The NAA, according to Kathleen Clarke, was established under the auspices of the Irish Parliamentary Party; the two organisations eventually merged to become the National Aid and Volunteer Dependants' Fund (NAVDF), the influence of the IPP being removed. On 20 June 1916 Jacob delivered £11.10.0 collected in Waterford for the IVDF to Miss McMahon at 1 College Street who 'talked about the NAA, but it seems they don't misuse the money, & it's only the personnel of the committee that is so objectionable'.[4] In September Jacob attended a meeting of the NAA Society in Waterford Town Hall, 'thinking that as the 2 societies were united we had a right to go, & J. D. Walsh whom we met outside, saw no objection, but Alderman Power, being in the chair, & his daughter very much at the head of affairs, turned us out'.[5] Kathleen Clarke saw the Fund not just as a means of alleviating misery but also as a vehicle for carrying on the revolutionary struggle, the Rising merely being 'the first blow'. In February 1917, Michael Collins, newly released from jail took over the position of Secretary of the NAVDF.[6] Female activists held meetings to demand the release of prisoners and worked to disseminate propaganda on behalf of the Republic.[7] In the immediate weeks following the executions Cumann na mBan had Mass said every Sunday in St Mary of the Angel's Church, Church Street, Dublin, for those who died in the Rising. Protest meetings against the executions and imprisonments followed the service; this augmented the pattern whereby nationalist politicians harnessed death and mourning for a political ends.[8] Collective commemoration in religious form aimed to revitalise the national spirit and to galvanise to further action those released from jail.[9]

---

4   20 June 1916, RJD Ms (30).

5   1 Sept. 1916, RJD Ms (30).

6   Kathleen Clarke, *Revolutionary Woman* (Dublin: O'Brien, 1991), p. 130, p. 138; Ward, *Unmanageable Revolutionaries*, pp. 119–20.

7   Margaret Ward, *Unmanageable Revolutionaries: Women and Irish Nationalism* (London: Pluto, 1995), pp. 119–20.

8   Clarke, *Revolutionary Woman*, p. 127.

9   Margaret Ward, 'The League of Women Delegates and Sinn Féin', *History Ireland* 4: 3 (1996), p. 38.

ERRAND GIRL

Jacob's first visit during her November 1916 Dublin sojourn was to Madeline
ffrench Mullen. Madeline was to find Jacob work 'but she talked so much I
got no light on the subject'. Madeline did agree to take Jacob to the shirt
factory at Liberty Hall. Helena Molony describes the foundation of this
factory during the 1913 strike, the description highlighting the link between
socialist and nationalist politics in the period between 1913 and 1916:

> A small co-operative store had been established in Liberty Hall by Miss Delia
> Larkin during the strike . . . There was a little shirt-making factory as well as the
> shop. It specialised in a workman's shirt, the 'Red Hand', which retailed at 2/6d.
> The concern gave employment to 8–10 girls, none of whom could get employment
> as they were 'marked men' on account of their strike activities. Eventually they all
> fought in the Rebellion.[10]

The clothing co-operative and shirt factory cloaked the manufacture, under
the direction of Molony, of uniforms and other items in preparation for the
imminent uprising.[11] Jacob did find work of a sort, filling in for ffrench Mullen
when she went to hospital for an operation on her throat to relieve hoarseness
and swelling. Jacob was to attend to the correspondence relating to the shirt
factory and to keep an eye on the workrooms. ffrench Mullen also spoke of
research work relating to a possible coal deposit under the Parliament buildings that Jacob might conduct in the National Library. Two days later Madeline
was to take her to the Library but Jacob waited for her to no avail. Calling at
Dr Lynn's later that evening she was informed that one of the shirt makers at
Liberty Hall had a child sick with diphtheria and all other matters were
forgotten in the crisis.[12] While Jacob accepted this as a reasonable explanation,
Madeline's failure to remember their appointment followed a pattern that
heightened Jacob's sense of exclusion from the core of Dublin activism. She
knew few, she wrote, worse at keeping appointments than Madeline.[13] It is
clear from Jacob's diary that there were a number of key activists who were
centrally and viscerally involved; these women surrounded themselves with
participants who played much more fringe and desultory roles, who could be
used for ground work yet who were dispensable. Such was Jacob's role in

10   Helena Molony, BMH WS 391, p. 20.
11   Nell Regan, 'Helena Molony' in Mary Cullen and Maria Luddy (eds), *Female Activists: Irish
Women and Change, 1900–1960* (Dublin: Woodfield Press, 2001), p. 152.
12   21–22 Nov. 1916; 24 Nov. 1916, RJD Ms (30).
13   10 Oct. 1919, RJD Ms (36).

Dublin during this period 1916–22. Like Frances Morrin in *Callaghan* she was 'a thoroughly dependable woman, who could be trusted always to fill a gap and never to make one'.[14] On 23 November 1916, for example, Jacob undertook errands for the NAVDF; it is likely that she was utilised more because she was on the spot rather than because of any qualities she was perceived to offer the organisation.[15] During the next three weeks she helped at the jumble sale at Liberty Hall, she did stocktaking work at the IWFL Library and took over in some capacity during Madeline's stay in hospital. This work involved setting up and working on the Liberty Hall stall at the Aonach held in the Mary Street Cinema. She also withdrew funds from the bank, paid wages on 9 December and interviewed the cutter involved in the making of 'the fancy shirts'.[16] Her own sense of unfamiliarity with the work came to the fore on 13 December when she was involved in the shipping of four dozen shirts to McDonagh's in Sligo that were barely ready for delivery at the requested time. McDonagh, she wrote, 'was not at all pleased with the shirts; I hope never to meet a harder person to please, than he is, but I suppose he found me a frightful fool'. However, once again she enjoyed the sense of community which she found in Liberty Hall; despite the debacle of the shipping incident she wrote how she 'stayed there till 6, & the girls sang Carrigdown & "I robbed no man I spilled no blood but they sent me to jail because I was O'Donovan Rossa and a son of Granuaile"'.[17]

Jacob was fully aware that her role was that of errand person. She noted on 9 December 1917 how she received a letter from Dr Lynn 'ordering me up to Áth Cliath to mind a stall for them at the Aonach, & saying the shirts could pay my railway fare'.[18] In Dublin for the 1918 Sinn Féin Convention she heard details from Madeline of the attempts of the women in the Rathmines Sinn Féin Club to ensure Hanna Sheehy Skeffington's nomination as a candidate for the Dublin Corporation election. Jacob very much followed Madeline around as she went to Liberty Hall and then up to Mary Street to meet a Mrs Power where Jacob 'was left in a parlour'.[19] When Jacob finally made the break from Waterford in late 1919 she was told by Hanna Sheehy Skeffington, with whom she was lodging, that if she wanted 'to be useful I might dust & sort out her books which are a bit untidy in reality if not in appearance'.[20] That Jacob

14 F. Winthrop, *Callaghan* (Dublin: Martin Lester, n.d. [1920]), pp. 119–20.

15 23 Nov. 1916, RJD Ms (30).

16 25 Nov.; 27 Nov.; 5–7 Dec.; 9 Dec.; 13 Dec. 1916, RJD Ms (30).

17 13 Dec. 1916, RJD Ms (30).

18 9 Dec. 1917, RJD Ms (32).

19 28 Oct. 1918, RJD Ms (35).

20 7 Oct. 1919, RJD Ms (36).

took this advice to heart and spent, for example, the afternoon of 21 October sorting Hanna's books in the drawing room, which she described as 'tough work', is evidence of her lack of purpose. On the morning of 20 October 1919 Dr Lynn called to ask her to go with her and the English pacifist, Edith Ellis, to the Mater Hospital to see the released hunger strikers: 'E. E. wanted to visit them, & the Dr was pressed for time & wanted me to stay with her & take charge of her'.[21] Jacob took a dislike to Ellis, particularly when Ellis later attempted to negotiate peace during the Civil War period. Much of this dislike appears to have been an instinctive recoil against her nationality:

> E. E. seems to be going around Dublin as a sort of secret diplomatic mission in her own person, being immensely important and having interviews with all sorts of people and talking guardedly of all sorts of secret peace moves that she knows of. The people she goes to or writes to wd not be half so accessible to an Irish pacifist who had some right to speak to them – will we ever learn not to bow down to the English? L. B. [Louie Bennett] and Miss Chenevix think the world of her, I believe. It puts me all on edge to be expected to discuss things with her.[22]

Again, like Frances Morrin in *Callaghan*, Jacob's sense of participating in a cause and the sense of personal independence she garnered from her life in Dublin was the reward for her helpmeet status:

> Frances had been timid at first, but she soon felt her feet firmly on the ground and began to enjoy her work. The independent life, full of incident and interest, the

---

21   20 Oct. 1919, RJD Ms (36). Edith Ellis came from a Quaker family in Leicester. She was imprisoned for three months in 1918 under the Defence of the Realm Act for publishing a pamphlet entitled *A Challenge to Militarism*. Malcolm Elliott, 'Opposition to the First World War: the fate of conscientious objectors in Leicester', *Transactions of the Leicestershire Archaeological and Historical Society* 77 (2003), p. 91. Eight hunger strikes began in 1919, including one involving 50 prisoners at Mountjoy. The strikers demanded prisoner of war treatment and when this was refused began a protest from their cells. The official response involving water hoses and manacles led to the strike. However, the prisoners were released as the government feared creating another martyr such as Thomas Ashe who died on hunger strike in 1917. George Sweeney, 'Irish hunger strikes and the cult of self-sacrifice', *Journal of Contemporary History* 28: 3 (July 1993), p. 427.

22   10 Feb. 1923, RJD Ms (43). Educated in Alexandra College, Helen Chenevix was one of the first female graduates from Trinity College Dublin. She was involved in the Irish Women's Suffrage Federation and with Louie Bennett organised the Irish Women's Reform League, which was established in 1911. In 1917 she was to the fore in reorganising the Irish Women Workers' Union with which she was to remain centrally involved. Angela Bourke et al. (eds), *The Field Day Anthology of Irish Writing*, vol. v (Cork: Cork University Press, 2002), p. 566.

gay comradeship, the sense of usefulness, the life of the Dublin streets, the society of her sister Beatrice, whose lodgings she shared, made up a pleasant whole, though some of the work might be such as nobody could hope to enjoy.[23]

FORGING RELATIONSHIPS: HANNA AND OWEN SHEEHY SKEFFINGTON

Jacob's time in Hanna Sheehy Skeffington's house does not appear to have been fraught with any tension, due possibly to the Hanna's absence on political work. Hanna, she wrote, 'was out except at meals'.[24] Indeed, summing up their living arrangement as Jacob proceeded to leave for Waterford again on 11 November 1919, Hanna created an analogy with her relationship to her husband: 'Hanna was remarking how little she had seen of me, & said it often happened the same with her & Skeffington if both were busy they would hardly see each other for weeks'.[25]

Jacob established one very meaningful relationship in this period, that with Hanna's son Owen Sheehy Skeffington. Jacob's diary offers evidence of a strong relationship between Hanna and her son. Despite this, it is clear from the diary that Hanna's political activism was not always conducive to being a dedicated parent and there were times, notably after Francis was killed, when she appeared to resent her parental role. On her first visit to Dublin after the rising Jacob noted how Hanna's father-in-law, Dr Joseph Skeffington, 'seems to be making himself very disagreeable to her & there may be danger of his trying to take Owen from her'.[26] Hanna and Owen's visit to Jacob in Waterford in June 1916 gave rise to the following diary entry: 'She seems to regard Owen somewhat as a burden – only for him she could easily have got herself killed at Easter, and she'd rather he was a girl anyway'.[27] Hanna returned to Dublin on 19 June while Owen remained with the Jacob family until 6 July. While certainly such references are the most extreme examples of Hanna's lack of maternal qualities, still it is clear that Owen spent much time by himself and was always waiting for his mother to arrive home from political meetings: 'We [with Owen] played cards till Hanna came in at 10 or so, & as usual when I wait to see her, I had to walk home'.[28] Andrée Sheehy Skeffington, although

23 Winthrop, *Callaghan*, p. 120.
24 7 Oct. 1919, RJD Ms (36).
25 10 Nov. 1919, RJD Ms (36).
26 15 May 1916, RJD Ms (29).
27 17 June 1916, RJD Ms (30).
28 13 Mar. 1922, RJD Ms (40).

in no way critical of Hanna's maternal skills, does testify in passing to Owen's disorientation following the death of his father and his loneliness when Hanna was engaged in pursuing justice from the British authorities. Andrée wrote of how when Owen came to visit her family during the summers, beginning in 1929, it was his first and only 'experience of normal family life'.[29] Hanna's sister, Mary Kettle, also seems to have had some misgivings as the following aside from Jacob's diary suggests: 'She disapproves of H's doings in the USA . . . fears her coming home because she'd get into jail & start hunger striking, & its no use talking or arguing with her, representing her duty as a mother.'[30]

Jacob, even after she moved into her own flat in September 1921, filled in for Hanna in many respects with Owen. On 17 March 1921 she recorded how she was invited to tea with Eva M'Curdy and had to bring Owen. Four days later she took Owen to the pictures with a number of his friends.[31] Returning to Dublin after spending Easter 1921 in Waterford she noted how no one, except the servant Bridget, was in when she arrived back to Hanna's house 'but Owen presently turned up from cricket or something & was glad to see me'. She noted how he was 'rather lonely' without his mother.[32] During this period Owen clearly relied on Jacob for company; she was always willing to partake in his games and activities and increasingly filled the role of a sub-stitute mother figure. This relationship gave her a feeling of value; it took on the form of an occupation:

> I called into the M'Curdys in the evening . . . Owen grudged my being away for that long from his confounded Banker [game]. It is very nice to have a kid that values your company so and leads you into romping.[33]

Hanna told her in 1923 that 'Owen is "gone" about me – and that's its [*sic*] seldom & slowly that he gets really fond of a person'.[34] In September 1922 Hanna visited Jacob in Waterford where she was spending some time after holidaying in Glenmalure, County Wicklow. Hanna was going to America, dispatched by de Valera as part of the women's mission to raise funds for

---

29   Andrée Sheehy Skeffington, *Skeff: A Life of Owen Sheehy Skeffington 1909–1970* (Dublin: Lilliput, 1991), p. 17, p. 19, p. 58.
30   26 Jan. 1923, RJD Ms (43). Mary Sheehy married Tom Kettle who was killed in the service of the British army during the First World War. She was active in many of the feminist campaigns of the early Free State.
31   17 Mar. 1921; 21 Mar. 1921, RJD Ms (39).
32   17 Apr. 1921, RJD Ms (39).
33   26 Apr. 1921, RJD Ms (39).
34   14 Sept. 1923, RJD Ms (44).

republican prisoners and their families. She was to travel with Kathleen Boland and Linda Kearns and needed Jacob to stay at Belgrave Road to look after Owen until she returned sometime in December. Jacob's response was to feel flattered.[35] Yet, despite her sense of gratitude at being chosen by Hanna to act in *loco parentis*, Jacob recorded the difficulties in looking after someone of Owen's age, noting how hard it was to make him do his homework 'in proper time without either sitting up late or needing to be called in the morning'.[36] She had to cope with all manner of child-related accidents, recording on 3 November that this 'was the night Owen put paraffin on his chilblains & used gloves to do it with, God knows why'.[37] The situation at Belgrave Road during this period of Hanna's absence was made more difficult for Jacob by the resignation of Bridget, after which she described herself working 'hard all these days, getting breakfast, setting the fire, marketing, cooking dinners. Owen much enjoyed the dinners I made him'.[38] Looking after Owen and feeling responsible for him continued for Jacob into the 1920s. In 1925, during the height of the local government elections Hanna was canvassing in Roscommon with de Valera as Jacob was designated to look after Owen who was ill with influenza. She recorded how she found Owen with a nosebleed which continued for some time. Although he was better the next day she was unwilling to turn up in Gardiner Street to fulfil her own commitments, afraid that Owen would be rendered unwell again.[39] It must be remembered that Jacob had no experience in running a house by herself, always being in a childlike role within her own family home. Despite such difficulties, however, Jacob appeared to thrive on the purposefulness of her role in looking after Owen.

During her period of residence with Hanna, Jacob worked on creating a finished typescript of *Callaghan* and did review work for her host, appraising amongst other works, Helena Concannon's *The Women of '98* and Katherine Tynan's autobiographical *The Years of the Shadow*.[40] On 21 January 1920, back in Waterford, *Callaghan* was ready to send out to publishers but it received no immediate success. By mid March she had received a negative response from Maunsel without any indication of the reasons for their disinterest. Advice led

35   24 Sept. 1922, RJD Ms (42). Linda Kearns had seen 1916 activity at the Hammam Hotel outpost. Kathleen Boland was the sister of Harry Boland, shot by the Free State in July 1922. Margaret Ward, *Hanna Sheehy Skeffington: A Life* (Cork: Attic Press, 1997), pp. 255–6.

36   11 Oct. 1922, RJD Ms (42). Owen was 13 in 1922.

37   3 Nov. 1922, RJD Ms (42).

38   12 Dec. 1922, RJD Ms (42).

39   5–7 Mar. 1925, RJD Ms (47).

40   Helena Concannon, *The Women of '98* (Dublin: M. H. Gill, 1919); Katharine Tynan, *The Years of the Shadow* (London: Constable, 1919); 31 Dec. 1919; 10 Oct. 1919, RJD Ms (36).

her to reject the Talbot Press as an alternative on the grounds of their cautious approach to finance and the fact that they utilised the same readers as Maunsel.[41] Jacob's contemplation of possible publishers was temporarily shelved by her visit to family friends in Chalfont outside Gerrard's Cross, Buckinghamshire in late May. During this holiday she visited London and in keeping with her wide approach to the politics of equality she attended the Fabian Summer School at Priorsfield, Surrey, for the fortnight commencing 31 July. These schools, begun in 1907, comprised a mixture of education and leisure activities.[42] During this period Jacob engaged in a medley of activities – lectures on how the Labour Party was going to transform England into a socialist state, on aesthetic fashions and a number of talks on Russia and Bolshevik government. A lecture on the 'Modern Novel' Jacob found '*awfully* interesting' and concurred with the contention relating to the 'inarticulate noises represented phonetically amidst the subject's thoughts' in Joyce's *Ulysses* that 'there was no need to be incomprehensible like that & it really served no good purpose'. English women radicals, Jacob noted, were no more self assertive than the Irish women she encountered in the Gaelic League and other mixed sex organisations. During the discussion after one lecture on the Labour Party several men, but hardly any women, spoke.[43] While in England Jacob made a number of attempts to get a passport, having earlier been refused one by Dublin Castle; she made enquiries at the White Star Office about travelling to Canada. Referring to Canadian emigration she was, she writes, suspected 'because I had an Irish accent & no ostensible business in Canada'. In a letter to Hanna she suggests that the earlier refusal to issue her a passport to visit relations in the United States 'may have something to do with my having sojourned in your house so lately'.[44]

Jacob returned to Ireland on 18 August 1920 without a passport, the London Passport Office having ascertained that Dublin Castle had not completed its inquiries about her.[45] By 20 September, having spent some time in Waterford, she was back in Dublin, staying once again in Belgrave Road with Hanna and Owen. Her first priority was to secure a publisher for *Callaghan* and she took the typescript to Bulmer Hobson in Harcourt Street; Hobson was one of the directors of Martin Lester Publishing. Although Hobson was more amiable than she had remembered him, she was miffed that 'in the course of our

41   21 Jan. 1920; 10 Mar. 1920; 22 Apr. 1920, RJD Ms (37).
42   See Patricia Pugh, *Educate, Agitate, Organize: 100 Years of Fabian Socialism* (London: Methuen, 1984), pp. 117–23.
43   1–6 Aug. 1920, RJD Ms (37).
44   Letter from Jacob to Hanna Sheehy Skeffington, 13 Dec. 1919, SSP Ms 33,608 (9).
45   28 June 1920; 30 June 1920; 9 July 1920; 14 July 1920; 22 July 1920, 17 Aug. 1920, RJD Ms (37).

conversation he didn't make one human remark about the book'. Similar to the Talbot Press, Hobson was concerned with the financial side of publishing, requiring her to shorten the book. He also remarked that he did not think the title was a good one.[46] The shortening process merely represented a half a day's work and amounted to the elision of 37 pages in total and by the 25 September the manuscript was again with Hobson.

Still settling in as a permanent resident in Dublin, Jacob next set about enrolling in the Dublin Metropolitan School of Art and began classes on 6 October 1920, recommencing the interest in jewellery making and metal work which had been the focus of her art classes in the Technical School in Waterford. Jacob also attended life drawing classes in the Art School and enrolled herself for private acting classes with Elizabeth Young. Young was an actress who was cast in a number of plays in the Abbey Theatre in the 1920s. She was a member of the amateur Dublin Drama League, formed in 1919 under the presidency of Yeats; she produced the League's presentation of H. Wiers Jennsen's play *The Witch* in February 1921. Jacob's diary indicates that she attended the rehearsals of this production.[47] In November she received proofs of *Callaghan* and noted how Elizabeth Young 'said I was improving'.[48] Within a matter of days Jacob had the proofs corrected and back with Hobson who published the book in December 1920, under the pseudonym Winthrop; Jacob offered no explanation for not using her own name.[49] This may have been down to a fear of failure; to hide behind a pseudonym can be seen as analogous to Jacob's unwillingness to foreground herself by assuming a leadership role in any of the campaigns in which she participated during this period.

Jacob craved the praise of her acquaintances and friends in Dublin's radical circles and certainly friends such as Hanna were aware of the novel. The *Independent* declared that the author failed to deliver on the book's potential: 'the whole story is but a sketch, a fragment, an episode, when enlarged to twice its length and thought out more carefully it could become a masterpiece.' The reviewer did concede that the style was 'very beautiful and the insight into character very wonderful' and he called on Winthrop to write a full-length modern Irish novel, taking a year if necessary to do it well: 'Then I shall be surprised if it is not really great'.[50] The anonymous reviewer in the *Irish Book Lover*, conceding that the book was 'pleasantly written', adopted a patriarchal

46 20 Sept. 1920, RJD Ms (37).

47 11–12 Aug. 1920, RJD Ms (37).

48 11 Nov. 1920, RJD Ms (38); 23 Feb. 1921, RJD Ms (39); Robert Hogan and Richard Burnham, *The Years of O'Casey, 1921–1926: A Documentary History* (Gerrards Cross: Colin Smythe, 1992), p. 48.

49 20 Nov. 1920; 18 Dec. 1920, RJD Ms (38).

50 *Irish Independent*, 24 Jan. 1921.

tone, subverting the text's claim to gender equality in the description of Frances as a 'charming little Suffragette'. The reviewer noted that the 'times and scenes depicted are too serious for humour to enter'.[51] Yet despite its topical appeal, the sales of *Callaghan* were slow and, ultimately, it was a commercial failure.[52] Jacob herself lost money on the book, having partly financed publication to the horror of certain family members, her cousin Lucy declaring: 'Oh *Rose*! you *must* have money to throw away!'[53] Jacob noted how the book received a 'glowing review' in the *Waterford Herald*.[54] Her immediate family in Waterford had no objections to the book, Tom and Dorothea both having read it as Jacob was writing it. However, the reaction of Jacob's acquaintances within the wider Waterford community was hostile, a hostility which arose from perceptions of anti-Catholicism in the novel. Visiting the Carstand Powers family over Easter she 'got gallons of abuse' and they considered that the novel would be 'the nightmare of my middle life & the regret of my old age':

> it's all an insult to Catholics, besides being bad grammar, C[allaghan] himself an evil minded ignorant disgusting cowardly ruffian, & everyone else ignorant & undesirable . . . I have no right to make Catholics use such horrible language because I've heard Protestants doing it.

The Carstand Powerses informed Jacob that the 'hotel Powers are raging about' the novel.[55] Offence could certainly have been taken to *Callaghan* from a Catholic perspective. Andy Callaghan, for example, declares that his idea of a non-sectarian Gaelic League 'is not to put two priests at the head of things just on account of their holy office'. However, the novel was more anti-English or even anti-Ulster Unionist than anti-Catholic. The opening scene of the novel sees Frances Morrin poke fun at a native of East Ulster with a 'craving for information relating to the condition of the southern provinces'.[56]

REPUBLICAN DUBLIN: 1919–21

The War of Independence broke out on 21 January 1919 with the ambush and shooting of two policemen at Soloheadbeg, County Tipperary, by six Volunteers; Jacob's new life in Dublin as an art student and novelist began in

---

51   *Irish Book Lover* XIII: 1/2 (1921), p. 21.
52   29 May 1922, RJD Ms (41).
53   12 Feb. 1922, RJD Ms (39).
54   9 Jan. 1921, RJD Ms (38).
55   9 Apr. 1921, RJD Ms (39).
56   Winthrop, *Callaghan*, p. 40, pp. 4–5.

the context of the escalating national struggle. The Waterford focus to her activism was sidelined from this point. When she returned to spend Christmas 1920 with her family she recorded the Black and Tan raid on the Sinn Féin premises in a very matter-of-fact manner which emphasised her distance; her focus was now squarely on the metropolis.[57] Hanna's house was raided at 1.15 a.m. on the morning of 5 October 1919, Jacob noting that the worst the soldiers found was discarded manuscript pages of *Callaghan*, notably Callaghan's anti-recruiting speech. That same morning Kathleen Lynn's house was also raided.[58] Jacob recorded Terence MacSwiney's death in her diary entry for 25 October 1920. MacSwiney had been arrested while Lord Mayor of Cork in March 1920. He began a hunger strike on 12 August, dying after 74 days without food.[59] She admired his bravery but was 'not sure about the rightness of hunger strikes always'.[60] When news of Kevin Barry's imminent execution emerged, Jacob was dispatched by Hanna to visit James Douglas,[61] head of the White Cross, to enquire if the Quakers could help. She also attended the Episcopal Gaelic Guild Committee in the company of Maighread Trench, and was informed that they should encourage the Protestant Archbishop to intervene. Although the Quakers sent a petition to the British Government asking for a stay of execution, this move was to no avail. Hearing that Lady Dockrell had influence with the authorities Jacob visited her but again to no advantage. Jacob was scathing of Lady Dockrell's submission to the will of her husband and her unwillingness to act on her own opinion: 'Objected to capital punishment on principle, but couldn't lift a finger without her husband's consent for fear of compromising him. She doesn't look at all that sort. She called Barry a coward too'.[62] This reference to Barry as a coward must have been a reference to the tactics of guerrilla warfare, Barry having killed three soldiers as part of an ambush at Monk's Bakery, Dublin. Jacob's outspoken support for Barry and MacSwiney and her association with those who were on the side of republican nationalism during this period even resulted in certain members of her family and friends distancing themselves from her:

> I got a letter from Helen in the evening, informing me that Mrs Fleming won't have me in her house any more, for fear detectives wd follow me & then she be suspected and raided. And Helen doesn't mean to come here any more either

57 8 Jan. 1921, RJD Ms (38).

58 4 Oct. 1920, RJD Ms (37).

59 Foster, *Modern Ireland*, p. 499.

60 25 Oct. 1920, RJD Ms (37).

61 James Douglas (1887–1954) headed the White Cross during the War of Independence and was a Senator during the periods 1922–36, 1938–43, and 1944–54.

62 29 Oct. 1920; 31 Oct. 1920, RJD Ms (38).

because Lin wd object – which seems to be going too far. I thought better of Lin
than to give way to such silly panic at other people's expense – I was very disgusted
about it altogether. It wdn't be half so annoying if it was on account of something
I had done myself.[63]

Jacob's diary recorded what would become the major republican touchstones
of the War of Independence – the events of Bloody Sunday, 1920: the murder
of 14 members of the British Army in their homes and places of rest on the
morning of 21 November 1920, and the Black and Tan reprisals as they shot
into the crowd during the match in Croke Park that same evening, killing 12
and injuring 60. These events Jacob later accorded central place in the plot
structuring of *The Troubled House*. What is interesting about Jacob's documen-
tation of these iconic events is the sense of excitement generated amongst so
many people, both those involved at various levels in the national campaign
and amongst onlookers. A Miss Little at the life class 'saw some of the shooting in Baggot St & seemed to enjoy it keenly, though not from any down on
the officers – simply as excitement'.[64] Jacob heard from Maighread Trench
how several Cumann na mBan women prayed outside Mountjoy on the
morning of Kevin Barry's execution on 1 November 1920:

> by her way of telling it & by her expression, it was clear to me that she at least had
> got some enjoyment out of it. Min Ryan came in & told all about MacSwiney's
> funeral in Corcaigh [Cork], & it was plainer still that she had enjoyed that. Hanna
> & I agreed that such things are a kind of emotional orgy. I know I am capable of
> such enjoyment myself, & it is revolting to think of.[65]

Such comments on how women in particular seemed to derive a sense of
excitement from the political atrocities of the national struggle would be once
more to the fore in Jacob's descriptions of the events surrounding the Treaty
split and the Civil War. During the attack on the Four Courts in June 1922
Dorothy Macardle directed Jacob, desirous of offering aid to the anti-Treaty
side, to the Red Cross premises in Gloucester Street. Jacob found her way to
Tara Hall, a Trade Union premises, full of girls making bandages and she

63   26 Oct. 1920, RJD Ms (37).
64   21–2 Nov. 1920, RJD Ms (38).
65   3 Nov. 1920, RJD Ms (38). Min Ryan (1884–1977) was one of four sisters active in the revolutionary
period. Min participated in the 1916 rising bringing food and messages to GPO. She married Treaty
supporter Richard Mulcahy in June 1919 and this in part may account for her decision to leave Cumann
na mBan and join Cumann na Soairse, the female organisation in support of the Treaty. Mc Coole, *No
Ordinary Women*, pp. 206–8.

joined in the work. During the morning wounded men were brought in while from out on the street firing was heard, and a large explosion broke one of the windows. Jacob noted how some 'of the girls were the C. na mb. type that love the whole thing in a horrible way'.[66] In Tara Hall again two days later Jacob noted how 'everyone seemed to be enjoying herself'.[67] Jacob did attempt to distance herself from any cathartic pleasure derived from the theatrical spectacle of republican mourning and, indeed, violence. However, at some level participation in the communal events of the Anglo-Irish and Civil War allowed her to feel the sense of involvement and emotional connection she did not have during 1916. During the burning of the Four Courts she described how she spent most of the afternoon of 29 June 'wandering round High St, Bridge St etc from a diseased spirit of curiosity'.[68]

Involvement in the street theatre of republicanism must be linked to Jacob's adoration of the heroes, dead and alive, of her republican canon. It is noteworthy that it was women in her account who predominantly 'enjoyed' the very public manifestations of the republican struggle – prayer vigils, funerals and demonstrations. Bearing witness to the struggle in this way women were allowed an outlet for pent up feelings that men more readily expressed in activism. Summing up the year 1921 Jacob wrote of this need to be part of a greater movement which underpinned her lack of core involvement and consequently clarifies her need to hero worship: 'I didn't mind hearing shots at night, even that time at Traigh Mhór [Tramore], & I was always wishing to be on the spot when things happened, as if I was the most callous person living'.[69] Hero worship became a form of activism by default as did recording the iconic events of the struggle. Jacob only testified to a sense of threat on one occasion; going home on 5 July 1922 at about 10 p.m. she encountered 'the most awful-sounding sniping progressing on all sides of me – a perfect orgy of it'. Encountering a man coming up Camden Street she enquired if there was much shooting in that area:

> & was told with a cheerful smile, 'Oh any amount' – just as if I wanted it. I went on, and shots kept crashing all round as it seemed, though I saw nothing. I tried to get across in to H. [Harcourt] St, but a woman in a lane warned me not to, saying it was worse there. I got home by Cuffe St at last, all safe, but it was the terrifyingest ten minutes I spent during the war.[70]

66   30 June 1922, RJD Ms (41).
67   2 July 1922, RJD Ms (41).
68   29 June 1922, RJD Ms (41).
69   Summation 1921, RJD Ms (40).
70   5 July 1922, RJD Ms (41).

Fully resident in Dublin Jacob involved herself at committee level in many of the multifaceted organisations working for Irish cultural and political independence and for women's rights. Her diary confirms the close connections between the personnel of such organisations that often transcended ideological tensions. For the most part, Jacob's political activism prior to the outbreak of the Civil War was confined to attending committee meetings in between attendance at art school and her writing activities. She helped Kathleen Lynn by visiting infants around Dublin, a form of work she despised: 'I went visiting some of Dr Lynn's babies – beastly back-woods places they do live in but they seem thriving'.[71] In January 1921, she committed herself to monthly visits but refused to take on more than ten cases.[72] She sought White Cross work from James Douglas but it was Maud Gonne who introduced her to James MacNeill,[73] the honorary Secretary, who sent her to the Mansion House to address envelopes with the other voluntary workers. The White Cross was established in 1920 to aid the victims of the Anglo-Irish War. Kathleen Lynn, who wrote to Griffith following her release from prison about setting up such a society, envisaged it as an organisation 'such as there had been during the time of the Land League', probably a reference to the role of the Ladies' Land League. Lynn wrote how the White Cross had no connection to any of the component organisations that ultimately merged in the NAVDF, although there were cases of joint membership. Although the fund was designed to aid cases of distress on both sides of the political divide, Lynn noted how it tended to be those on the republican side who were relieved.[74] Jacob soon was entrusted by Gonne with investigating relief cases for the White Cross, conducting such work throughout 1921 and into the next year, visiting the Trades Hall in Capel Street, for example, on 4 February 1922 'to see a boy, to make out was he a case of permanent disablement, which he wasn't'.[75]

INTERNATIONALISM AND NATIONALISM

On 1 December 1920 Jacob joined the Irish Women's International League for Peace and Freedom (WILPF) established in 1915. The Irish branch (IIL), meeting at 39 Harcourt Street, produced its own synthesis of the key

---

71   18 Nov. 1920, RJD Ms (38). With ffrench Mullen, Lynn established St Ultan's Infants' Hospital in 1919. For Lynn's account of the need for such a hospital see Dr Kathleen Lynn, BMH WS 357, p. 10.

72   20 Jan. 1921, RJD Ms (39).

73   Brother of Eoin MacNeill, co-founder of the Gaelic League, James MacNeill was the first Governor General of the Irish Free State.

74   Dr Kathleen Lynn, BMH WS 357, pp. 10–11.

75   24 Jan. 1921; 14 Feb. 1921; 15 Apr. 1921, RJD Ms (39); 4 Feb. 1922, RJD Ms (40).

discourses of the period. Demands for female equality blended with the pacifist ideals of the organisation and the nationalist discourse of the period. After the Rising the IIL worked to have Ireland recognised as a separate nation by the International Committee of Women for Permanent Peace with which it was affiliated. An editorial in the *Irish Citizen* summed up the manner in which the discourse of nationality blended into internationalism and pacifism.

> For we are helping to give Ireland international importance and responsibility by basing her claim of independence on a moral principle essential to the progress of a constructive civilisation throughout the world: we are helping to educate the public opinion of the world in favour of the practical application of the principle of nationality as a means of avoiding much crime, much bloodshed, much suffering: and we are thereby helping to promote the twin causes of internationalism and humanitarianism.[76]

The multi-layered concerns of the IIL clearly appealed to Jacob. In 1917 the body drafted a petition to the Board of Education calling for Irish history to remain on the programme for the King's Scholars.[77] When the IWFL was described to Jacob as 'one of the most truly national organisations in Ireland' she vehemently denied the plaudit 'on the ground of their neglecting the language'.[78] The IIL, by contrast, was more suitable to Jacob's desire for a holistic approach to the nationalist and feminist struggles of the period. That being said, Jacob would never satisfactorily reconcile her commitment to pacifism with her support for the politics of republican violence. In January 1922 the IIL joined other feminist societies in pushing for an extension of the franchise to women over the age of 21 before the vote on the Treaty took place. Representatives of the various women's organisations met on 27 January to demand interviews with both Griffith and de Valera.[79] The coming together of the various feminist organisations at this time proved fraught with tensions as the following extract from Jacob's diary highlights. The IWFL, on the basis of its perceived truckling to an alien parliament in the past, was placed in a defensive position:

> found Mme M[arckievicz] telling Mrs C. [Connery] that C. na mb. wanted to have their deputation all alone. Mme M. & Mrs C. are not intended to talk together on politics, they are sure to get into a row. C. na mb. feels that the IWFL

76   *Irish Citizen* 4: 14 (Oct. 1916).
77   *Irish Citizen* 4: 45 (Mar. 1917).
78   30 Sept. 1917, RJD Ms (31).
79   25 Jan. 1922; 27 Jan. 1922, RJD Ms (40).

disgraced itself in the past by asking votes from England – that made good ground-work for getting annoyed, as Mrs C. distinctly did.[80]

De Valera received the deputation on 17 February with Jacob as the only representative of the IIL. Although civil, de Valera was not helpful, 'said we shd do best to get one of the majority to introduce the bill – true but impossible. We were rather disappointed with him'. Griffith proved to be no more satisfactory when the deputation met him on the afternoon of 24 February. Indeed, Griffith did not project the same air of civility that was a feature of the de Valera interview. Jacob had early testified to the fact that all the women in the Dáil were anti-Treaty, 'except Mrs Pearse, who wobbles according to what people tell her'.[81] Griffith's obvious knowledge of this united anti-Treaty front amongst the six female Dáil deputies clearly influenced his belief that to grant a franchise extension was to endanger the Treaty and the result was a fractious atmosphere:

> G. started by saying the Dáil had no power to alter the franchise, & it wd take 8 months to make a new register, and after a good deal of discussion (the C na mb people & he getting cross & Hanna always amiable) ended by defying us to do our worst, & saying we, or nearly all of us, were really out not for votes but to wreck the Treaty . . . He looked worried & was quite cross. He started every sentence with To be perfectly frank – which always heralds something nasty.[82]

Despite the unsatisfactory interviews the women of the joint societies continued to campaign and Jacob spent most of the morning of the 28 February with Meg Connery and Mrs Johnson handing out leaflets about the franchise extension to people going into the Dáil.

On the international front, in May 1921, Jacob was elected with Lucy Kingston as a delegate to the International Congress of the WILPF in Vienna. Kingston, also a Quaker, was heavily involved in the WILPF and would participate actively in many of the feminist organisations in the early Free State, notably the Irish Women's Citizens and Local Government Association. This trip to Vienna with Kingston began one of Jacob's closest friendships, ultimately resulting in the two sharing living space in the 1950s.[83] Jacob was to

---

80   6 Feb. 1922, RJD Ms (40).

81   11 Jan. 1922, RJD Ms (40).

82   17 Feb. 1922; 24 Feb. 1922, RJD Ms (40).

83   For details of Lucy Kingston's life and politics see Daisy Lawrenson Swanton, *Emerging from the Shadow: The Lives of Sarah Anne Lawrenson and Lucy Olive Kingston Based on Personal Diaries, 1883–1969* (Dublin: Attic, 1994).

pay the majority of her own expenses, [84] leaving Dublin to travel via London on 5 July. En route back to Ireland she spent a few days at the Fabian Summer School. Back in Dublin on 6 August Jacob's work for the IIL during the early autumn of 1921 comprised arranging discussions on the League of Nations and handing out leaflets about the Russian famine with Louie Bennett. The retort of many to their appeal for aid for Russian victims was 'what about trouble & poverty here'. The IIL response was that all money was spent on Irish produced foodstuffs. [85]

Jacob, however, was not immune to the poverty and suffering of those around her in Dublin and, indeed, had not been during her earlier life in Waterford. On 4 March 1918 she attended a nascent women's trade union meeting in Waterford that her sister-in-law, Dorothea, had encouraged the Trades Council men to 'get up'. Jacob herself tried to get trade union activist, Helen Chenevix, to speak at it but she was unable to come until the following Thursday. Jacob met Chenevix first in her capacity as union activist, but the two would be fellow members of the IIL in the 1920s. The next morning Jacob went, also with Dorothea, to the food depot in Barrack Street, Waterford, to learn to make meat pies. [86] Later that year, in May, she acted as guide and companion to a Mrs Callender who, staying with Tom and Dorothea, was in Waterford to organise the Irish Women's Workers' Union. [87] Through these experiences, Jacob began to gradually form an understanding of the economic plight of lower-class women, initially in Waterford. A fellow nationalist activist, Miss Hoyne, 'told me frightful things about Robertson Bros: – girls making only 5/- a week, & being paid only 1/5 for making children's frocks. And she can't get it published anywhere'. [88] Her attendance as a non-member at many of the meetings of the Waterford branch of the MWFL had also provided Jacob with a knowledge of the prevalence of poverty, particularly as it related to women and children. On 16 April 1917 Chenevix lectured on child welfare, discussing baby

---

84   18 May 1921, RJD Ms (39).

85   24 Oct. 1921; 18 Oct. 1921, RJD Ms (40).

86   4–5 Mar. 1918, RJD Ms (33).

87   17–18 May 1918, RJD Ms (33).

88   29 Nov. 1918, RJD Ms (33). The poor wages paid to women were also occasionally a subject at suffrage meetings in Waterford. In January 1912 Miss Helga Gill spoke on women and the vote in Norway and contrasted the situation to Ireland. In Ireland, without a vote, women were powerless to influence their economic well being resulting in lack of equal pay for equal work. The speaker cited the example of women post office workers. She noted that the 'latest move on the part of the Government was to economise in the Post Office department at the expense of women. They were going to introduce a new class of women clerks into position and reduce the wage bill below anything they had given yet to women'. *Waterford Standard*, 31 Jan. 1912.

clubs, milk depots and issues around education; Jacob was 'surprised at how interesting it was'. In particular, she was horrified at the facts Chenevix presented as to the relative number of male and female school inspectors.[89]

Of course, Jacob's knowledge of and involvement in movements to alleviate poverty had, as noted, its genesis in her Quaker heritage. She regularly attended poor relief committees in Waterford throughout her 20s and early 30s.[90] She thus brought aspects of her Quaker background to bear on her growing feminist and nationalist activism in this period. On 12 December 1916 she gave a lecture on individual rights to the IWFL and included animals in her delineation of the rights of all sentient beings: 'common men – women – animals'. She was appalled that the only man at the lecture, Conrad Peterson

> talked helpless rot about the callousness of humanitarians to human suffering, & various animals being more regarded than men, & nobody quite grasped the base idea of it all, that animals are citizens of the world with rights not connected with our convenience.[91]

Despite her cultural connections to the values of the Society of Friends Jacob resigned as a member in February 1917.[92] This resignation was due to a lack of personal faith. This was not a sudden crisis of faith. A number of Friends tried to persuade her to rescind her resignation. Unlike them, however, she did not perceive the world as 'empty and wretched . . . without Christ' and she had never 'heard him talking . . . and felt his presence'.[93] Despite such a frank avowal of her lack of faith and her resignation from the Society of Friends she continued to attend many of the social and intellectual functions, such as essay meetings and debates, going with her mother to the 'Six books' evening at the Meeting House in November of that year.[94] However, as she fully immersed herself in Dublin life and turned towards life in a Free State, Jacob's links with the Waterford Friends became increasingly limited to her immediate family.

89   16 Apr. 1917, RJD Ms (31).
90   See, for example, 2 Nov. 1916, RJD Ms (30).
91   12 Dec. 1916, RJD Ms (30).
92   24 Feb. 1917, RJD Ms (31).
93   26 Feb. 1917, RJD Ms (31).
94   13 Nov. 1917, RJD Ms (31).

'THE TROUBLED HOUSE'

Jacob's holistic sense of revival facilitating and fuelling political and feminist advancement in Irish society is evident in her novel, *The Troubled House*, written in the early years of the Free State, although not published until 1938.[95] Jacob's first title for this novel of Dublin set in the period 1916–21 was *A House Divided*. The change in title better reflects her authorial purpose; a troubled house has greater potential for the resolution of tensions than a divided house. Although the divisions existing within the Cullen household act as a micro-cosm of the political and cultural schisms permeating the wider Irish society, the novel's ultimate resolution of divisiveness suggests that, in Jacob's view, intersecting ideals premised on Irish cultural, political and feminist rejuve-nation had in this period the potential ultimately to transcend splintering opinions. As in *Callaghan*, Jacob used the diary as a form of 'sketchbook' which she worked from in creating the fictional canvas of *The Troubled House*; her own centrality in the diary is then embedded in the fictional text. The fictional text allowed her, a fringe activist, to fully articulate her views on republicanism and the position of women in an independent polity. The following extracts from the diary and the novel offer an example of how her lived experience during the revolutionary period acted as the basis of her fictional work of that time. On 25 November 1920 Jacob went down to the quays to look at the funerals of the British Army men killed on Bloody Sunday recording the following account:

> I must say what came into my mind on seeing the 9 – or more – coffins was 'are there any more of your English dogs that you want to be slain?'
> There were lorries of soldiers & b. & ts going round, who noticed after a bit that hardly any men took their hats off to the funeral, & then they took to bullying, shouting out in the most truculent style 'Off with those hats!' & as I afterwards learned, throwing hats into the river if they were not taken off, but I saw none of that; the meek men being in the majority where I was.[96]

Maggie Cullen witnesses the same scene in the novel although from a more central position to that of Jacob's:

95 On 1 July 1924 Jacob recorded that she had finished the novel a few weeks previously and was engaged in a rewrite. RJD Ms (46).
96 25 Nov. 1920, RJD Ms (38).

The British soldiers roar at the crowd to remove their hats.

The words can be set down, but the fierce bullying tone of them is indescribable. It brought home to me, almost for the first time in my life, what insult is. The officers moved around the outskirts of the crowd, brandishing revolvers, shouting and threatening men with their canes. Their truculent faces were close to us and the men near us were raising their caps a quarter of an inch from their heads. I was trembling all over with the craving to strike one of those red arrogant faces.[97]

Within the Cullen household divisive political views initially work to tear the family apart. Maggie Cullen's sons, Liam and Roddy, are activists in the Anglo-Irish War; Roddy, as a young boy, fills the function of messenger. Their brother, Theo, although he hates England, is a confirmed pacifist, while Maggie's husband is a supporter of the Irish Parliamentary Party and completely opposed to the supremacy of the physical force ethos in contemporary Irish politics. The novel reverberates with a sense of the influence of the cultural revival or the manner in which revivalist attitudes became lived experiences or an integral strand in the evolution towards national and individual advancement. Maggie talks of the interests of her husband's nephew, reared in a Southern Unionist family:

> horse-racing and Rugby football; who seemed to judge everything in terms of money; who would not know the difference between Dáil Éireann and the Oireachtas of the Gaelic League. I had no tolerance for these young people; I felt that they were missing all the opportunities of their youth for want of soul and spirit.

The idealism of the revival in its cultural and political manifestations exists in the novel as a counter to the jaded politics of the Irish Parliamentary Party and the materialism and bourgeois nature of non-nationalist Ireland. By contrast with their cousins, Maggie's sons are GAA followers and, indeed, Roddy witnesses the shooting in Croke Park on 20 November 1920. Theo has been named after Wolfe Tone. Even the domestic animals who make appearances in the novel exist within a context where Ireland's past is revered and used as the vehicle to shape the present and direct the future configurations of an independent Irish society. The cat belonging to the artist, Nix, for example, is named Silken Thomas, while the cat in Liam's lodgings is called Mick for Michael Collins. The idea of the Irish national struggle as an unbroken tradition, linking dead generations with those of the present, is offered in such domestic details.

97 Rosamond Jacob, *The Troubled House: A Novel of Dublin in the 'Twenties* (Dublin: Browne & Nolan, 1938), pp. 95–6.

Maggie, as a woman in a male-dominated family comprising different nationalist opinions, struggles to find an existence of her own. Maggie's apparent lack of autonomy as the novel opens acts as a symbol of how the feminist programme was relegated a fringe position in the nationalist and cultural discourse of the period. Maggie recognises that she is defined as wife and mother:

> It came to my mind . . . what a queer thing it was that my life should spend itself thus, almost entirely in love and care and fear and thought and anxiety over three men and a boy. Was I nothing but a being relative to them, without real existence of my own? Each one of them led his own life, had his centre in his own soul, as a human creature should, but I had no purpose or driving force in myself; nothing that was independent of them. It seemed absurd, futile, unworthy.[98]

Yet Maggie's absence from her family in the care of her ill sister in Australia facilitates her trajectory towards self realisation; absence distances her from her primary role as mother. She leaves Ireland for two years returning shortly after the death of Terence MacSwiney in October 1920. By this time, Jim Cullen has evicted his son, Liam, from the family home because of his activism in the service of the IRA. Jacob's discussion of Liam's politics shows her increasing willingness to subject her beliefs to scrutiny and critique; this is even more the case than in her earlier novel. In such an analysis she elaborates on issues touched upon in her diary, particularly the question of the exposure of the young to violence; this is discussed in her portrayal of the activism of Roddy and through Maggie's reminiscences on the youthful Liam who lived 'for excitement'. When the Rising broke out Liam 'ran off and spent five days spying and carrying messages for the Volunteers. He wasn't 16 then and looked less, so he was able to slip off and get home after the surrender. I don't think he ever enjoyed anything so much in his life'.[99] Jacob suggests that many of those who joined the Volunteers and later the IRA were caught up in a communal excitement that acted almost as a drug on susceptible personalities. Through her characterisation of Liam she suggests the toll of violent activism on the individual rather than its benefit to the national cause, the latter so much a part of the rhetoric of Volunteer recruitment. Maggie's description of her first meeting with Liam on her return emphasises how his involvement in the Anglo-Irish War has damaged him as an individual by truncating personality development in certain areas. Jacob, in this way, removes the focus from national collectivity:

98　Ibid., p. 91.
99　Ibid., pp. 13–14.

His grey-green eyes were – or looked – deeper set than I remembered them; his mouth looked years too old; every feature showed some subtle evidence of conflict and experience. But it was a partial, uneven development of mind and character that I saw. Liam had grown up like an untrimmed hedge; some branches shooting up strong and vigorous, others growing crooked, some scarcely growing at all.[100]

The Troubled House is then an exercise in exposure; Jacob is concerned to lay bare the pathology of republican violence and the problematic consequences of the impetus to collectivity embedded in the republican discourse and actions of the revolutionary period. Fitzpatrick's statement on nationalism in the period 1916–18 can equally be applied to the period of the Anglo-Irish War: 'A nationalist might express his allegiance by dying for Ireland, killing for her, subscribing money or services for her upkeep, voting for her or talking about her. Each mode of expression involved collective rather than individual actions'. He continues: 'Idiosyncrasy and individuality were almost unknown among Irish nationalists; submission to collective discipline, was commonplace'.[101] During the revolutionary period the image of the self-sacrificing hero was one of the dominant nationalist tropes. Contemporary accounts of the public displays of nationalist support, as for example, during the funeral events around the death of Terence MacSwiney stressed the homogeneity of the Irish public;[102] the individual was subordinated to the communal. Jacob's text at one level suggests that this has negative and destructive ramifications, a fact that emerges in Dolan's analysis of the events of the morning of Bloody Sunday, 1920. Dolan states that amongst historians there has been 'no real consideration of killing and its effects on a band of largely untrained young men in a guerrilla war'.[103] Jacob's novel is an interesting near contemporary fictional attempt at such consideration. It is clear from certain asides in Jacob's diary that the issue of the effects of war on the individual rather than the collectivity was not altogether ignored amongst contemporaries. Jacob noted the discussion between George Russell and Markievicz on the 1921 Treaty. Russell, she wrote, 'spoke well of the demoralising & brutalising effect of being at war' although she did reductively add 'but you can't take a man very seriously on politics who says he doesn't care where he is governed from as long as the people are happy'.[104] Attending the

100 Ibid., p. 17.

101 David Fitzpatrick, 'The geography of Irish nationalism, 1910–1921' in C. H. E. Philpin (ed.), *Nationalism and Popular Protest in Ireland* (Cambridge: Cambridge University Press, 1987), p. 404.

102 Paige Reynolds, 'Modernist martydom: the funerals of Terence MacSwiney', *Modernism/Modernity* 9: 4 (2002), p. 542.

103 Anne Dolan, 'Killing and Bloody Sunday, November 1920', *Historical Journal* 49: 3 (2006), p. 791.

104 18 Dec. 1921, RJD Ms (40).

court-martial of Markievicz at the Royal Barracks in December 1920 Jacob commented that one witness: 'was a young officer who had been in the raid when the box was found, & he gave the impression of being almost half witted with nervousness & stiffness'.[105]

Liam Cullen in *The Troubled House* is no Frank Teeling, a man whose service to the State had been to learn 'to kill without question'.[106] However, Theo's conversation with Maggie highlights the manner in which Liam's activism has impacted on him as an individual. The suggestion is that his personality made him particularly vulnerable to the discourse of communal service and martyrdom that was a feature of the IRA in the Anglo-Irish War. Markievicz's introduction to the Fianna Handbook, for example, called on the young to remember those across the world who died for freedom, continuing:

> The spirit of Ireland is free because Ireland's children have never shirked to pay the price. The path of freedom may lead us the same road that Robert Emmet and Wolfe Tone trod. Treading in their footsteps, we will not fear, working as they worked we will not tire, and if we must die as they died we will not flinch.[107]

In *The Troubled House* Theo indicates how this discourse of martyrdom and personal sacrifice have been absorbed within the psyche of a generation of nationalists:

> Mother, these people have an extraordinary power of dealing with that sort of thing. It's not that they don't feel they'll do anything for each other. It's as if they had a vision or something, that gives them security or as if they were under the power of a drug. I don't know which it's most like. Lots of them, of course, depend on religion, but it's not like that with Liam, nor with a good many of his friends.[108]

The reference to the manner in which collective action acted as drug is underscored later in the novel when Theo is to be hanged by the British authorities, unless Liam turns himself in. Maggie notes when Liam determines on a plan to rescue Theo from prison:

---

105 2 Dec. 1920, RJD Ms (38).
106 Dolan, 'Killing and Bloody Sunday', pp. 789–90. Teeling, who was involved in the IRA attack on British soldiers on 20 November, shot William Johnson on 27 March 1923 for bringing a bag of tomatoes into the bar at the Theatre Royal.
107 *Fianna Handbook* (Dublin: Patrick Mahon, 1914), p. 8.
108 Jacob, *The Troubled House*, p. 21.

On the heels of this hope, I realised how little, even in his most dangerous doings, Liam had ever really considered the possibility of getting hanged. He would risk anything, but seldom or never would his mind occupy itself with probable consequences he was nothing but a child.[109]

Liam was part of the IRA responsible for the murder of the British Army personnel on the morning of Bloody Sunday, 1920. Foregrounding her theme of the impact of republican violence on the individual, Jacob represents Liam as traumatised. Andy Callaghan and his wife help the troubled young man. In this way *Callaghan* and *The Troubled House* are linked and mirror the trajectory of the republican struggle, focusing on 1916 and the Anglo-Irish War respectively. Liam's childlike attitude to violence comes to the fore during this period of the novel in a scene reminiscent of the portrayal of Johnny Boyle who has killed Robbie Tankcred in Seán O'Casey's *Juno and the Paycock*, set during the later conflagration of civil war. Jacob saw this play at the Abbey in March 1924 when she was engaged with the first draft of the novel and made reference to just that scene in a play she otherwise decried as 'beastly . . . nearly all snarling and wrangling of horrid worthless people . . . The happiest moment in it, to my mind, was when the 2 IRA men with revolvers came in and dragged out that *intolerable* Johnny to be shot, just after he had surpassed himself in beastliness to his mother & sister'. [110] Following his participation in the events of the morning of Bloody Sunday Liam, like Robbie, cowers in his room in Nix's apartment, beset by demons unleashed by his participation in violent activity. As Nix opens the door to bring him food he cringes: 'Stop! Stop don't let her open the door!' he cried. 'He's in there if it's opened I'll have to kill him again. Stop her! Don't you hear him? Screaming?' As Juno must take responsibility for Johnny so the women who shelter Liam must have strength and presence of mind when he has none.[111]

When the Cullen family discover that Roddy has not only carried ammunition and messages regularly for Liam's company but had once taken part in an armed military operation, Maggie's concern for his development as a person echoes Jacob's reservations on exposure of the boys of the Fianna to violence at a young age:

> it trains you to be clever at deception and to look on killing as a matter of course, or a game. It accustoms you to the facts of war while you're too young to realise what war is. I don't want you to grow up just a good soldier; I want you to grow up with

109 Ibid., p. 195.
110 7 Mar. 1924, RJD Ms (45).
111 Jacob, *The Troubled House*, p. 102.

a free mind, not one that's been hardened and bent in a certain direction by doing work that is only questionably right for anyone, while you're still almost a child.[112]

Jacob initially then problematises the notion of homogeneity created by the iconography and through the theatre of the revolutionary struggle, epitomised in such public displays of collective mourning following the death of MacSwiney. In fact, the novel opens to the backdrop of that death. In America at the time de Valera declared that MacSwiney's 'people . . . were waiting to make sacrifices as he did'.[113] Jacob suggests that this notion of martyrdom, absorbed into the consciousness of the nation, became unhealthy at the microcosmic level of the individual. Dolan, indeed, gives graphic details of the impact of the killings on the morning of Bloody Sunday on those who participated, giving evidence of nervous breakdown, alcoholism and even men who, in the words of one member of the Free State army personnel, became 'stark mad', drink unleashing the latent effects of atrocity on the individual.[114]

Jacob's critique of republican violence in the novel is, however, undercut in a number of ways. Firstly, *The Troubled House* is replete with descriptions of sacrifice in the service of the cause, the overarching tone being one of admiration. Theo is involved in a raid on a British Army barracks, having gone to fulfil the injured Liam's obligations to the IRA. Subsequently captured, he is imprisoned in Kilmainham Jail and describes his fellow prisoners with affection; he is imbued with admiration for the manner in which the personal is subordinated to the political:

> A lot of them have made complete sacrifice of their worldly prospects, broken off University courses, lost their jobs with their eyes open, etc., and some of them are married, with children to support it makes me think of that bit in Wolfe Tone's speech at his trial: 'I have sacrificed all my views in life; I have courted poverty; I have left a beloved wife unprotected and children whom I adore fatherless.'[115]

The analysis of the impact of violence on the killer or activist is also subverted by Maggie's recognition of the need for individual sacrifice and personal subjection to the pathology of violence if Ireland is to gain full independence. When her husband dismisses IRA guerrilla violence as a 'peculiarly cruel and dastardly form' of warfare, Maggie responds by subordinating her son's psychic health to the greater good of the nation-in-waiting.

112 Ibid., p. 68.
113 Quoted in Reynolds, 'Modernist martyrdom', p. 548.
114 Dolan, 'Killing and Bloody Sunday', pp. 807–8.
115 Jacob, *The Troubled House*, p. 180.

We've never had a chance to form an army that the British would recognize. If our men wore uniforms, they wouldn't be treated as belligerents; in fact, wearing their uniform is a capital offence by British law, and you know it. It's absurd to blame them for fighting in the only way that gives them a ghost of a chance.[116]

Maggie thus evokes and validates the dominant communal discourse of the revolutionary period. By doing this she is at once the good Irish nationalist mother sending her sons out to fight for Ireland, but in doing so, she also eschews the supposedly 'authentic' maternal instincts of protection, opting instead for the safety of the political entity in gestation. Her domestic role as mother has been rendered secondary: her political opinions take precedence as she ignores the toll of violent activism on Liam. She is not then symbolic of the traditionally passive nationalist mother and, in this way, she could be seen to be moving towards self actualisation. Maggie squarely faces the toll of violence on the individual psyche at no stage seeking to minimise or ignore this reality but, as the following passage indicates, her sense of nation takes precedence over her sense of family.

I began to wonder whether his and Theo's real interests were suffering any injury from the war. Suppose them both to die before it was over would not that be preferable to the life of many men? It would be a better death than most people can expect. Suppose them to survive it, Theo at least would be unharmed, and would not anyone value retrospectively such years as Liam was passing through as among the best worth having of his life? . . . Could war improve a human being so? If certain good qualities were developed by it, must not bad qualities be developed also? Liam's face looked very pure, refined and steadfast now, but I had lately seen it distorted with passion. I knew there were capabilities for evil in him which his present life must foster and which showed no mark upon his sleeping face. Yet I did not wish him out of the IRA. Above all, I could not wish him like some other young men I knew, who 'kept out of politics,' and lived exclusively in their own little spheres of work and amusement, indifferent to the crisis that was convulsing their nation under their eyes.[117]

Maggie describes her 'sympathy with the boys' interests'.[118] This sympathy is not as a mother but as a fellow citizen in the imagined community. Her

116 Ibid., p. 39, p. 40.
117 Ibid., pp. 117–18.
118 Ibid., p. 173.

politics have led to her estrangement from her husband; again her beliefs and her willingness to overtly state them have undermined her role as wife and mother. The distorting effects of politics and violence on the family and her own role as mother is something she recognises and struggles with when she considers Theo's impending execution:

> It seemed to me absurd almost to the point of impossibility that I should be unable to protect my own child from danger. Was he not mine? Had I not the right to bring him safe through the world in the face of every enemy? If I had not, it seemed a mockery to call me his mother. I could not acknowledge that he was an entity as independent of me as if I had never borne him.[119]

In this passage Maggie goes straight to the heart of the dilemma of the ideology of domesticity premised on the concept of the moral mother. Maggie, as moral mother, is supposed to hold herself responsible for actions over which she has no power.[120] However, by acknowledging her children as independent entities, Maggie frees herself from the constricting potential in maternal responsibilities and takes ownership of herself as an individual. Her response to Liam's tales of danger while on the run indicates her participatory role as a citizen of the nation to be born from such violence rather than a submissive maternal role of worry and impotence. She, like Liam, is an entity in the imagined nationalist community of the period; she is brought into the action and is 'enchanted' too:

> He had been out of Dublin for nearly two months . . . and he had to relate tales of adventure and hairbreadth escapes, down in the country, which would have chilled my blood if his enjoyment of the experiences had been less exuberantly plain . . . I sat listening in a sort of enchantment as he talked, feeling as if ninety-eight had come again and Miles Byrne was telling me his adventures.[121]

The emphasis on Maggie's role in the public sphere of politics rather than in the private sphere of maternity is highlighted again towards the close of the

---

119 Ibid., p. 195.

120 For this concept of the powerlessness of the mother who is held to high ethical standards under the ideology of separate spheres see, for example, Helen M. Buss, 'A feminist revision of new historicism to give fuller readings of women's private writings' in Suzanne L. Bunkers and Cynthia A. Huff (eds), *Inscribing the Daily: Critical Essays on Women's Diaries* (Amherst: University of Massachusetts Press, 1996), pp. 86–103.

121 Jacob, *The Troubled House*, pp. 234–5.

novel. Walking towards Grafton Street she describes the psychological effect of the Truce on the imagined community. That she is part of that community, that she has an existence in the public sphere, is emphasised by the use of the possessive 'our streets' and in the manner in which her response to the soldiers they pass mirrors that of her sons:

> We passed British soldiers in couples and groups . . . soon I began to notice how Liam and Roddy looked at their approach, how they never would move aside an inch to make room for a soldier, whether he came from left or right, and I woke up. Of course, they had no right in our streets, they were an army of occupation; their presence there was aggression and insult. Before we came near Grafton Street I was longing to shoulder every one of them off the pavement.[122]

That the novel ultimately aligns itself on the side of republican violence is also clear from the portrayal of the pacifist position through the character of Theo. Theo's description of how the British Government could be forced to concede independence through nationwide passive resistance reads as idealistic and, crucially, is dismissed as such by Maggie who, while she admires him taking a principled stance, questions the use of the tactic against 'an army of occupation':

> It could absolutely paralyse them if it was worked right. There should be a complete boycott of them, so that they'd have to take all their supplies, and their accommodation and transport, by force, and if the people were willing to be killed rather than give in, and to be entirely loyal to Irish law and ignore British, whatever it cost them, and carried on their own institutions unitedly in defiance of what the British might do, you'd very soon find the British asking for a parley, partly because a large section of decent opinion in England would demand it.[123]

Furthermore, Theo is increasingly unable to maintain his commitment to both pacifism and republicanism, reflecting the tensions within Jacob's personal commitment to both ideologies. When Theo's father suggested that the officers who fired into the crowd in Croke Park on 20 November may have gone to the venue to find information about the morning killings of British soldiers and may have been shot upon and fired back creating panic, Theo is indignant, leading to the following exchange:

122 The truce came into effect on 9 July 1921. Jacob, *The Troubled House*, pp. 260–1.
123 Jacob, *The Troubled House*, p. 35.

Who said they were fired at?

It's the natural supposition.

Yes, for those who start with the assumption that the British authorities can't commit a crime. You're assuming an excuse for them that you'd never assume for the IRA in fact, you wouldn't even admit that the IRA had a right to fire back if they were fired on. Also, you're ignoring what Jack said about the machine guns at the gates. Supposing a few revolvers were fired at them, did that give them the right to turn machine guns on a crowd of men, women and children?[124]

In this exchange Jacob recorded the confusion around the events in Croke Park as the British Army argued at the time as to who fired first.[125] The manner in which Maggie resolves Theo's move towards violence as he involves himself in an IRA raid on an army barracks sums up Jacob's own position.

But the more I considered his behaviour of to-night, the more excusable and inevitable it appeared. As long as the whole energy of the Republican movement was thrown into the military campaign, such things must happen. Theo with his Republican sympathies and without the power to create a passive resistance in the midst of war, could not always stand aloof while others were risking life and limb and livelihood; he must break out occasionally, even at the cost of being inconsistent; even if his principles did suffer a temporary eclipse.[126]

Theo escapes Kilmainham dressed as a Black and Tan; from a safe house he engages in White Cross work. His demeanour on escape allows Maggie to reconcile any doubts she may have had on his abandonment of his pacifist beliefs:

noting how much happier, more confident and at ease he looked than in the weeks before the raid. There was no sign about him of strained nerves or mental illness of any kind; his face was thinner than it used to be, but it has a new look of poise and inner harmony, and joyful subdued excitement gave a warmth of colour to his cheeks and a dancing gleam to the clear darkness of his eyes.

. . .

Mother, I want to tell you, now that it's all over – I wouldn't have missed it for anything.[127]

---

124 Ibid., p. 83.
125 Dolan, 'Killing and Bloody Sunday', p. 791.
126 Jacob, *The Troubled House*, pp. 116–17.
127 Ibid., p. 222.

By the end of the novel, Jim, the supporter of the old Home Rule ideal, is dead, having been killed in an ambush spearheaded by his son Liam. Although, as Doyle states, 'Liam's act of patricide suggests the need to remove the old establishment in order to make way for the emergence of a new nation',[128] it is noteworthy that Jim makes terms or peace with his more radical wife. In some ways he has been won over to the righteousness of the republican cause by the brutal treatment meted out to Theo when in Portobello Barracks. Maggie feels no animosity towards Liam for his act of patricide. Instead, she shares with him and her younger son, Roddy, a sense of national ownership following the Truce in the Anglo-Irish War. Her response to her husband's death is cold: 'I did not mourn Jim as I would have if our marriage had been perfect, but he was my dearest, closest, equal friend, who had shared my life for a quarter of a century, and losing him I felt only half myself'.[129] No evidence serves to buttress this latter statement; on the contrary by the end of the novel Maggie has gained a sense of personal independence as a woman and as a mother that mirrors the expectation of political independence. Jim's death is also then symbolic of Jacob's belief in the need for a reorganisation of society on gender lines. By the end of the novel Maggie has resumed life within her family surrounded by her sons but without her husband. She has not rejected her family but has realigned her own role as an individual within it. The novel does not then denounce marriage as an institution but argues for equality between partners and the right of women to be both mothers and independent beings.

The novel closes with a focus on the artist Nix and the few literary critics who have examined the novel place emphasis on this character.[130] Nix lives a bohemian life by the standards of the time, conducting casual affairs with a frank directness. A woman who would kiss a man 'for fun, while he was trying to make up his mind whether to kiss her for fun or not'. She's a new woman, that's all, Maggie concludes. There will probably be more like her, as time goes on. The prospect of increasingly alternative lifestyles for women in an independent Ireland premised on revivalist ideals around language, art and personal freedom held out by Jacob's novel seems most obviously encoded in the character of Nix. Certainly in the character of Nix Jacob recorded her experience of the exotic and the bohemian in revivalist and revolutionary Dublin when measured against her experiences in Waterford. That Nix is an

128 Damian Doyle, 'A bio-critical study of Rosamond Jacob and her contemporaries', unpublished PhD thesis, University of Colorado, 2000, p. 44.

129 Jacob, *The Troubled House*, p. 258.

130 Meaney 'Women and writing, 1700–1960'; Meaney, 'Regendering modernism: the woman artist in Irish women's fiction'; Doyle, A bio-critical study of Rosamond Jacob'.

artist, of course, is important because this was the role around which Jacob sought to construct her own sense of purpose. Such prospects testify to Jacob's sense of struggle and, ultimately, hope of finding an existence for herself at a period of transition in Irish society, as the occupied nation became the post-colonial society of the Free State. As if needing to symbolically embrace this struggle Jacob made a decision to wear 'breeches' and get her hair bobbed as she sought to forge a role in the new State as a writer and feminist republican activist.[131] However, to focus on Nix as the key figure in the novel is to misunderstand Jacob's aspirations in the new State. One line in particular offers the key to emphasis of the novel. Maggie Cullen reflects on her own role as mother, using Nix's life as a counter:

> My energy had all gone into one channel; I could not liberate enough of it to concentrate on any life of my own. But was it necessary for wives and mothers to be like that? I could not believe it. I thought with envious admiration of Miss Carroll and Nix Ogilvie, with their souls in their own work; *I would have felt a deeper admiration still had I seen them steering the same course though possessed of husbands and children.*[132]

Importantly, Jacob aspired to neither of the extremes of female existence she presented in her novel – selfless domesticity and self-absorbed individuality.[133] Instead, passages like the one above might suggest she believed it was possible to be a woman, a mother and an individual. In this way, by the close of the novel, Maggie who has come some way to this existence could be closer to Jacob than Nix, and better reflect Jacob's own hopes in the new nation.

131 19 May 1923, RJD Ms (44); 26 Nov. 1924, RJD Ms (46).

132 Jacob, *The Troubled House*, p. 91. My italics.

133 Nix's self-absorbed nature, it should be noted, is portrayed through the eyes of Maggie Cullen who fears her influence over her son, Theo. Yet Nix's outspoken manner and her willingness to enunciate opinions were traits Jacob admired. The following comment on Nix by Theo sums up these qualities: 'It's her mind, really that fascinates me . . . Other girls seem to be all cut in a pattern – too lazy to think, afraid to say anything they think men won't like, or that's different from what other people are saying. . . . Her mind goes through things like a spear, she doesn't know how to be false, and she doesn't give a damn for what anyone thinks.' Jacob, *The Troubled House*, p.270.

FIVE

SINGLE WOMEN, SEX AND
THE NEW STATE

—

Despite her initial optimism, Jacob, like Constance Moore, in her autobiographical unpublished novel, 'Third person singular', written in the 1930s, found
it difficult to establish a meaningful role for herself in the new state. Jacob wrote
her own fears into the character of Constance, including the manner in which
she believed others perceived her. The character, Hugh MacNevin, is aware that
people in the village do not 'as a rule' like Constance as much as his sister Emily:
'She's rather queer, but she's a good sort really'. Douglas McGinley, whom Jacob
met at Gaelic League meetings in the 1920s, commented on the difference
between her friend, Helen, and herself: 'You [Helen] don't look as if you cd ever
be a decent pal to a fellow, & Rose looks as if no fellow wd ever have the courage
to try to be a pal to her'.[1] Peadar O'Donnell[2] remarked similarly on the manner
in which Jacob's demeanour was initially off putting: 'he said he felt a cold
draught all round me that made him feel it necessary to investigate a bit before he
cd be comfortable with me. I suppose that's what George [Gilmore][3] feels, and
all other men'. O'Donnell further referred to how he 'used always to feel a sort of
"subdued hostility" about me'.[4] Jacob herself put her off-putting manner down to
her fear of men but did not elaborate.[5]

Untrained for any profession, as so many of her female contemporaries,
Jacob supplemented the allowance she received from her family with her
meagre earnings from journalism and literature. The earnings Jacob received

---

1   30 Jan. 1927, RJD Ms (55).

2   The writer Peadar O'Donnell was a prominent IRA leader in the 1920s and 1930s. O'Donnell was
also prominent in Saor Éire and the Republican Congress. Among his most notable editorial positions
was with *An Phoblacht*, 1926–9 and *The Bell*, 1940–54.

3   George Gilmore was one of the notable Protestant leaders in the IRA in the early decades of the
Free State having had a minor role in 1916; at the 1933 IRA Convention he was listed as Staff
Commandant with a full-time position in the IRA. Gilmore was a supporter of the 1934 Republican
Congress. Brian Hanley, *The IRA, 1926–1936* (Dublin: Four Courts, 2002), p. 20, pp. 192–3.

4   9 Nov. 1934; 1 Dec. 1934, RJD Ms (76).

5   Summation of 1934, RJD Ms (76).

from her literary endeavours were especially scant during the 1920s and 1930s as her novels failed to sell or remained unpublished. As late as 1947, £68 interest on a legacy of £300 towards publishing expenses in her Aunt Hannah's will was a welcome addition.[6] As a single woman with no qualifications and a very limited income, Jacob lived a relatively frugal life and her concern with money and resources is arguably reflected in the huge amount of detail given to food in her diary. She regularly listed what she served visitors when they came for tea and noted what she herself was offered in turn. Frank Ryan wouldn't eat sardines or cheese but did eat cake![7] Of course, this attention to the details of food and hospitality also reflected the economic state of Ireland during her adult lifetime, particularly during and immediately after the Emergency.[8]

In 'Third person singular' Constance, ageing and having failed to find a 'happy love affair', by night found herself 'questioning the value of life'.[9] In December 1928 Jacob's housemate, Florence, told her that she 'ought to have gone out and trained for something 20 years ago'. Florence suggested that she begin work on a history of the United Irishman. Jacob had begun this history already, noting in January 1927 how she went to the National Library to read Jackson's trial to begin preparation for such a work.[10] By September she had enough material to begin writing but was unable to progress as she was still at work on *The Troubled House*.[11] Florence's suggestion was the basis for the discussion between housemates Constance Moore and Emily MacNevin in 'Third person singular'. Emily tells Constance, brooding on her unrequited love for Hugh MacNevin, that she needs a profession. When Constance responds that she 'doesn't care about anything . . . yet I hate feeling inferior to all people who work', Emily suggests she write a historical treatise. Constance decides on a history of Aodh Ruadh O'Domhnaill.[12]

Jacob's position as a single woman was not a life choice. She was by no means opposed to marriage and appeared to view it as a natural stage in the life cycle, although, as noted, she believed that her radical views on women's rights led to a perception of her as anti-marriage. This comes strongly through

6   13 Dec. 1947, RJD Ms (126).
7   18 Nov. 1926, RJD Ms (54).
8   Clair Wills discusses the role of Maura Laverty both on the radio and in writing in educating homemakers in the use of alternative foodstuffs during the Emergency. Her popular novel, *Never No More* (1942) contained recipes using innovative foodstuffs available locally. Clair Wills, 'Women writers and the death of rural Ireland: realism and nostalgia in the 1940s', *Éire-Ireland* 41:1 (2006), pp. 201–3.
9   Rosamond Jacob, 'Third person singular', RJP, p. 11, p. 85, p. 2.
10   12 Jan. 1927, RJD Ms (55).
11   1 Sept. 1927, RJD Ms (58).
12   Jacob, 'Third person singular', pp. 97–9; 26 Dec. 1928, RJD Ms (61).

in the manner in which she depicts perceptions of Constance and Emily as two women sharing living space in 'Third person singular'.

> When I meet women like Miss Moore and the doctor, said Mrs Ambrose thoughtfully, women living alone together, I often wonder if they like it, if they're glad or sorry not to be married . . . Connie rather needs some sort of object, but she wouldn't have any use for a husband. She despises men.

This testifies to a very stratified thinking in society, the notion that women who demanded equality of rights were by definition anti-men. Yet Constance declares that 'nothing interests as much as men'.[13] Jacob was by her own admission jealous when her close friend Helen got engaged to Douglas McGinley. 'I hate and loathe engaged couples', she wrote, '& it's rather the limit to have to put one's only sitting room at the disposal of one, when one used to be one of the party'. Jacob's sense of isolation was manifest in her plea to Helen 'not to put D. before me'.[14] She desired to 'have a man to go to things with'. Although Helen would, she believed, be scornful of any man who would choose to spend time with her, 'it wd be like heaven to have a nice man obviously liking to be with me'.[15]

Jacob's case was a twentieth-century version of the problems of single women highlighted by Isabella Tod in 1874. Tod argued for an improvement in the education of middle-class girls to allow them provide for themselves, highlighting the false assumption that all women were and could be provided for in marriage.[16] Indeed, Helen's engagement to Douglas by the late 1920s had practical ramifications for Jacob as the two lived together up to this point. In September 1929 Helen informed her that she would rather pay the entire rent on the flat as she wanted to be free to have Douglas visit without worrying about Jacob's sense of exclusion. Hanna came to the rescue and suggested that she stay with her until Florence, Helen's replacement as a housemate, was able to share a flat. This Jacob described as 'a great relief'; she did not have to continue to look for furnished rooms.[17]

When Jacob moved in with Florence in November 1929 she was dismayed that she was to be four days alone in the flat and equally dismayed at Helen's lack of sympathy for her loneliness. Helen felt that Jacob should not expect

13   Jacob, 'Third person singular', p. 86, p. 99.
14   4 Feb. 1928; 8 Feb. 1928, RJD Ms (59).
15   10 Dec. 1934, RJD Ms (76).
16   Isabella M. S. Tod, *On the Education of Girls of the Middle Classes* in Maria Luddy (ed.), *Women in Ireland 1800–1918: A Documentary History* (Cork: Cork University Press, 1995), p. 109.
17   16 Sept. 1929; 23 Sept. 1929, RJD Ms (62).

Florence to be a companion.[18] Jacob's failure to marry put full pressure on her own resources which were limited given her lack of sustained formal education and the lack of a space in Irish society where single women could access fulfiling forms of social engagement and create a meaningful existence without a spouse. Indeed, one of the problems at many of the social gatherings Jacob attended was an excess of females over males. While not quite as dramatically described, her account of the issue was akin to George Moore's 1886 fictional account of the problems of the Anglo-Irish marriage market in *A Drama in Muslin*. In the Shelbourne Hotel drawing room the situation is crudely summed up by an unnamed hopeful on the marriage market: 'the worst of it is that the stock is for iver [*sic*] increasing, every year we are growing more and more numerous, an th' men, oh! th' men seem to be getting fewer'.[19] The overt concern of Moore's novel is an analysis of what Oliver MacDonagh has described in the context of Jane Austen as the 'career marriage': the desperate, soul-destroying female attempt to find security in marriage or wither into the meaningless obscurity of spinsterhood.[20] In many respects Jacob's position as a single woman in the first half of the twentieth century did not differ greatly from the nineteenth-century context. Peadar O'Donnell diagnosed her problems in the course of a casual discussion in November 1934 as ones stemming from living 'too much without vital things to do'. Hanna, by contrast, was amazed to learn of Jacob's growing loneliness believing that she had too many internal resources to be a candidate for depression. Yet on 13 October 1936, the day of her 48th birthday, Jacob described herself as 'miserably lonely'.[21] Constance in 'Third person singular' hated birthdays and described them as crowding in on her, 'heralding middle age, when a happy love affair for her would be impossible'. This was the thing Constance 'always longed and hoped for' and 'the gradual blotting out of this hope was the thing she dreaded most of all in the dreary prospect'.[22]

O'Donnell encouraged Jacob to take her writing seriously and agreed to read her work. He disparaged 'Third person singular' as too full of self-pity. Fulsome in his praise of *The Troubled House*, he still believed that it was not the type of material his English publishers would take and advised her to try to have it serialised in some paper.[23] Jacob took his advice and on 26 May 1936 she received

18   13 Nov. 1929, RJD Ms (63).

19   George Moore, *A Drama in Muslin* (Gerrards Cross: Colin Smythe, 1981), p. 153.

20   Oliver MacDonagh, *Jane Austen: Real and Imagined Worlds* (New Haven: Yale University Press, 1991), p. 33.

21   9 Oct. 1936; 13 Oct. 1936, RJD Ms (80).

22   Jacob, 'Third person singular', p. 1.

23   7 Nov. 1934, RJD Ms (76); 27 May 1935; 29 May 1935, RJD Ms (77); 10 Feb. 1936, RJD Ms (78).

a letter from the *Irish Press* agreeing to serialise the book. The first instalment was published on 18 June 1936. This, together with the news that Harrap would publish *The Rise of the United Irishmen*, were the great personal events of 1936, giving her 'a grand sense of justifying myself & being good for something, a relief from the confused sense of failure I have most of the time'. Indeed, when she informed her Aunt Mary of the news of the impending publication of *The Rise of the United Irishmen* 'she said kindly that it wd be an occupation'.[24]

Much of Jacob's life in the 1920s and 1930s then revolved around an attempt to live a meaningful existence in a society in which she was increasingly invisible as a single woman. She described a Gaelic League céilidhe of 5 April 1925 as 'the best ever' because unlike the usual situation where women outnumbered men, there were only four women at the event and a 'rising number of men . . . I had to dance *everything*'.[25] Women's powerlessness at social events, their dependence on male invitation before they could participate in dances might seem trivial but should not be underestimated as a source of irritation to intelligent women. Jacob had earlier fictionalised the situation in the dance scene in *Callaghan*. Frances is reduced to admiring Callaghan from the periphery of events, wishing that he would ask her to dance. Instead of the desired scenario she is introduced to a young man named Murray and 'had to waltz with him'. Frances is sufficiently perceptive to note that girls were forced to pretend to enjoy dances even if they did not receive any invitations to participate. Later in the novel, as Frances and Callaghan work through the various misunderstandings that have kept them apart, she entreats him to understand the powerlessness of women: 'If men would only keep it always in mind that a woman can't take the initiative'.[26] Jacob did attempt to provoke a more proactive response from the women who attended social events at the Gaelic League but was frustrated by entrenched passivity as the following account indicates:

> I suggested the women choosing partners to Gearoid & he was quite agreeable but F. Ryan, who was M. C., only proclaimed it for one dance, & then I had to practically *force* even Helen & a couple of others who supported the idea onto their feet – having chosen my own partner. It was a 16 hand reel, & it was with difficulty it was collected – the girls there are a miserable lot.[27]

---

24 Summation of 1936; 19 Jan. 1937, RJD Ms (80).

25 5 Apr. 1925, RJD Ms (48).

26 F. Winthrop, *Callaghan* (Dublin: Martin Lester, n.d. [1920]), pp. 104–5, p. 153.

27 25 Oct. 1925, RJD Ms (49).

THE 'AFFAIR'

Jacob's affair with Frank Ryan may be considered to add a further layer of meaning to her life and politics from the mid 1920s. This affair began in 1928 when Jacob was 40 and Ryan 26, continuing with varying degrees of intensity and disengagement until the mid 1930s. The affair offers an insight into the position and perception of single women in Irish society and into contemporary Catholic sexual morality, one of the cornerstones of the new state's identity in the 1920s and 1930s. In the context of the dominant Catholicity of the new state Jacob and Ryan's relationship was scandalous. The affair needs to be examined initially at the level of contemporary perceptions, with a consideration of how the participants viewed their actions and the mechanisms and subterfuges they engaged in to keep the scandal from breaking. The wider perceptions and ramifications of the affair are interesting for what they say about women who did not fit neatly into the dominant domestic paradigm of wife and mother. In January 1918 Jacob lamented the absence of a male relationship and lack of a baby to her secret diary.[28] Jacob did briefly mention the idea of adopting a baby in November 1924, but this was something she never again referred to.[29] More usually Jacob was conscious of herself as unusual in her ambivalent attitudes to the desirability of motherhood and mindful of how she was perceived by other women as 'unnatural'.

> Somehow we go onto babies, & I horrified Dr M'C [M'Cormack] with making out that they gave lots of trouble & hard work – in short that they had a very pronounced seamy side. She got quite annoyed with me. She knows perfectly that if you train them right they are very little trouble, & that no natural woman minds the trouble or has any difficulty in looking after crowds of them.[30]

It was, of course, not just other women who would have considered Jacob's ideas on children and childcare unnatural; in 1927 Kevin O'Higgins depicted

28 Jan. 1918, RJD Ms (171).

29 3 Nov. 1924, RJD Ms (46). Of course, Jacob made this comment in the context of the lack of legal adoption in the south of Ireland until the 1950s. When legal adoption was introduced in that decade single women were not permitted to adopt. Diarmaid Ferriter, *The Transformation of Ireland 1900–2000* (London: Profile Books, 2004), p. 324. The 1926 Adoption Act in England did permit single women to adopt although doubts as to the suitability of single-parent adoptions were raised increasingly by the 1950s. Katherine Holden, *The Shadow of Marriage: Singleness in England 1914–60* (Manchester: Manchester University Press, 2007), pp. 142–4.

30 20 Jan. 1925, RJD Ms (47).

as abnormal any woman who did not adhere to the domestic image of women.[31] In March 1931, at a People's Rights Association committee[32] Jacob recorded how 'John B. [Brennan] of course had that damned child with her, it's a sort of madness'.[33] Jacob, although she loved her niece and nephews and their offspring, had no real affinity with children. She taught Irish dancing and Irish language to children under the auspices of the Gaelic League in the mid 1920s but she described the group on one occasion as a class of 'ignorant kids' and the work as 'tiresome'.[34]

McGarry states that Jacob was a believer in free love but Ryan's Catholic sense of morality inhibited him.[35] Ryan's inherent belief that he was committing a sin in having a sexual relationship with Jacob and was therefore a source of scandal caused him to insist on absolute secrecy even to the point of ignoring Jacob at social gatherings. Ryan's sexual inhibitions are noteworthy when placed against his absolute willingness to stand against the Catholic Church in the area of politics; a republican enthusiastically committed to the use and necessity of physical force, he was opposed to the influence of the Catholic Church on politics.[36] Jacob herself did not manifest even the slightest sense of wrong doing in connection with the affair. However, the attitudes of friends and family beyond the parameters of her activism highlights the problems women of the period faced in living any type of life which deviated from the dominant beliefs on the position of women in Irish society. Even aside from her affair with Ryan, of which it is not clear if they were fully aware, members of Jacob's family and wider social circle viewed her intellectual and activist life in Dublin with suspicion. This was compounded when she was arrested and incarcerated in Mountjoy in early 1923 during a raid on Hanna's house, an experience discussed more fully in the next chapter. Even Sheehy Skeffington, a close friend, viewed her as slightly skittish, warning her during the War of Independence against signing any document at the command of soldiers: 'She seemed to think I might be induced to do it if the demander

31   Maryann Valiulis, 'Neither feminist nor flapper: the ecclesiastical construction of the ideal Irish woman' in Mary O'Dowd and Sabine Wichert (eds), *Chattel, Servant or Citizen: Women's Status in Church State and Society* (Belfast: Institute of Irish Studies, 1995), p. 169.

32   This was the new name for the Women's Prisoners' Defence League which had been banned earlier that year.

33   8 Mar. 1932, RJD Ms (69). The child Jacob refers to is Finian, born in 1917, during Sidney Gifford's [John Brennan] brief marriage to the Hungarian, Arpad Czira. Sinead McCoole, *No Ordinary Women: Irish Female Activists in the Revolutionary Years* (Dublin: O'Brien, 2004), pp. 166–7.

34   5 Feb. 1926; 11 Feb. 1926, RJD Ms (51).

35   Fearghal McGarry, *Frank Ryan*, 2nd edn (Dublin: UCD Press, 2010), p. 5.

36   Ibid., p. 9, p. 14.

were handsome'.[37] Allied to the perception of Jacob as politically non-con-
formist and even irresponsible, her single status caused her to stand apart in
an Ireland where the ideology of domesticity was promulgated by Church
and State alike. Historians have absorbed the notion of the relationship as
scandalous; the secrecy with which the two conducted their liaison has led to
its description as an affair despite the fact that the word was used by neither
party, and neither Ryan nor Jacob were committed to any third person. Thus
the relationship is encoded in the dominant morality of the Free State and has
been so transmitted into the historical record.

For Jacob, a single woman involved at the fringes of illegal republican
activities, to have an affair with the charismatic and elusive Ryan was to court
scandal and to situate herself even further outside the pale of respectable Irish
society. Although she does not discuss details such as whether they used
contraception or not, Jacob would have had relevant knowledge, in the abstract
at least. Up to the time of the 1929 Censorship Act newspapers in Ireland
carried advertisements for mail-order contraceptive devices with full details
on their use, aimed in particular at women, promising sexual pleasure without
the anxiety of an unwanted pregnancy.[38] However, Jacob in many respects was
naïve even in her late 30s; she conducted the affair with Ryan in a manner that
emphasised the romance and adventure she associated with the covert and the
clandestine. Her upbringing in Waterford was cosseted and despite her
activism in Dublin she still moved as a single woman sheltered by a network of
family and friends.

An examination of this affair, however, offers much more than a
voyeuristic glance at illicit sexual activity; the affair can be viewed as a vehicle
to examine the position of single women in Irish society in the 1920s and
1930s. An examination of the fear and dread of scandal can act as a means of
examining alternative lives in contemporary Irish society, lives which did not
conform to the prevailing ethos of Catholic morality and the domestic image
of women. The manner in which Jacob and Ryan's relationship was elided
from, or 'othered' by, the historical record and from family history must be
considered. Scandal was translated into silence and denial and this mutation
has affected the manner in which Jacob, particularly, has been treated in Irish
historiography. Damian Doyle's work on Jacob does not mention the relationship, despite, or perhaps because of, his access to Jacob's autobiography held

---

37 20 Dec. 1920, RJD Ms (38).

38 Sandra McAvoy, 'The regulation of sexuality in the Irish Free State, 1929–1935' in Greta Jones and
Elizabeth Malcolm (eds), *Medicine, Disease and the State in Ireland, 1650–1940* (Cork: Cork University
Press, 1999), p. 255.

in private family hands.[39] Political biographies of Ryan have mentioned the 'affair' in passing, but there has been no sustained analysis of how the relationship acts as a symbol of the problems attached to any attempt to seek alternative lifestyles beyond the dominant and patriarchal discourses of Church and State.

Jacob met Ryan in October 1925 when he began teaching advanced night classes in the Gaelic League. Her immediate reaction to meeting him was on a physical level: 'F. Ryan teaching at the class – charming to look at, & quite possible to understand but no conversation'.[40] This description sums up what was to be Jacob and Ryan's relationship. McGarry writes that 'part of the attraction for Ryan may have been for a physical relationship without emotional ties'.[41] In January 1926 Jacob wrote: 'Proinnsias [Frank] is delightful to look at – and to listen to – I fear he will spoil me for all other teachers'.[42] Rather than spoiling her for other teachers, more correctly, Jacob's growing attraction to Ryan ensured that she forged no other meaningful sexual relationships. For a time in 1929 she attempted to develop a relationship with Séamus, a fellow Gaelic League member, but this was arguably less an attempt based on attraction than a realisation that the relationship with Ryan was not going to develop: 'I have rather failed with Séamus as far as satisfying myself is concerned (when he was ill that time it grew very clear to me that I didn't want him) and must confine myself to trying to be a friend to *him*'.[43] Similarly she conducted what she described as a 'cold-blooded experiment' with Robert Brennan in late 1930: 'About 9 Bob B. turned up and was not good, & I was a bit easy going, but frightened him with threats of impending people'. Again, Jacob had no real attraction to Brennan and could not help comparing him to Ryan: 'oh the difference between the touch of him & B – the intoxication of him in comparison'.[44] Yet it is possible that Jacob continued her 'experiment' with Brennan over a number of years. In June 1932 she recorded the following: 'About 10.15 Bob B. turned up ... He says he doesn't want a woman physically unless he likes her mentally – glad to hear it'.[45]

39   Damian Doyle, 'A bio-critical study of Rosamond Jacob and her contemporaries', unpublished PhD thesis, University of Colorado, 2000; D. Doyle, 'Rosamond Jacob' in Mary Cullen and Maria Luddy (eds), *Female Activists: Irish Women and Change 1900–1960* (Dublin: Woodfield Press, 2001), pp. 169–92.

40   26 Oct. 1925, RJD Ms (49).

41   McGarry, *Frank Ryan*, p. 5.

42   25 Jan. 1926, RJD Ms (51).

43   Summation of 1929, RJD Ms (63).

44   7 Nov. 1930; summation of 1930, RJD Ms (65).

45   9 June 1932, RJD Ms (68). Angela Bourke discusses Maeve Brennan's fictional portrayal of the 'emotional climate in her childhood home'. The Derdons and the Bagots are, in the words of Bourke, 'frozen in their twisted postures of mutual incomprehension'. However, Bourke cautions the reader

Ryan was Jacob's first real relationship. Prior to this she had developed crushes on various men – Geoffrey Coulter, the Gaelic Leaguer, Brian McGinley and both Farrington brothers, Tony and Ben. For a brief period in 1924 it appeared as if the relationship with Coulter might develop, certainly she was interested in him on a physical level and enjoyed the sense of intrigue his presence in an all female flat lent her:

A WIL [IIL] committee after tea, and I had asked Geoffrey in at 9.45, & when he came at 9.55 the blighters hadn't gone yet & I had to put him in my bedroom for a few minutes. He was as quiet as a mouse, but left a reek of tobacco in the passage that they couldn't but notice as they were going out. Then I brought him in and he stayed talking & eating biscuits till 12.30, when I put him out – wd have been tempted to ask him to stay the night only Lydia knew he was here.[46]

She interacted with McGinley at Gaelic League activities and talked about attending some of these social functions 'actuated by a craving to see Brian M'Ginley again'; but this was before the relationship with Ryan became physical.[47] Brian was 'the only decent looking' man in the Gaelic League branch until she began to take more notice of Ryan.[48] Jacob did admit that teachers who filled in during Ryan's absence on political matters were better; Séamus Ó Clérigh who took the class on 8 February was, she wrote, 'really a better teacher, being more searching, & not being deaf'.[49] Still she craved praise from Ryan, commenting in her diary when he commended her essays. Even before the 'affair' started, the power balance in the relationship was in inverse relationship to the difference in age between the two. It was he who had the power to pay her attention or not at social gatherings. This, of course, was partly a reflection of expectations as to the contemporary social role of men and women. Going to a UCD republican club céilidhe organised by Ryan on 12 May 1926 she noted how 'P. never came near me, of course'.[50] However,

against assuming a true account; rather Brennan's stories were, she argues, born out of her need to express certain feelings 'at the time she wrote'. Nevertheless, it is clear from Bourke's biography that Robert Brennan, anti-Treaty in politics, was absent on political business for much of the period after 1922. Jacob's assertion of some form of a sexual relationship with Brennan may add a further layer to the discussion of Maeve Brennan's parents' relationship so interestingly portrayed by Bourke. Angela Bourke, *Maeve Brennan: Homesick at the New Yorker* (London: Jonathan Cape, 2004), pp. 92–3.

46 30 Oct. 1924, RJD Ms (46).
47 19 Jan. 1926, RJD Ms (51). See also 30 Jan. 1926.
48 10 Feb. 1926, RJD Ms (51).
49 8 Feb. 1926, RJD Ms (51).
50 12 May 1926, RJD Ms (52).

Jacob's social ineptness and the likelihood that the relationship between the two meant more to her than him also explained the power differential that would, indeed, widen over the years.

The Gaelic League céilidhe became increasingly a source of both pleasure and pain to Jacob as she craved recognition from Ryan. Discussions and dances with him at such events were meticulously recorded or the lack of them noted in her diary; 'Proinnsias is lovely to dance with' she observed in the entry for 7 February 1926. 'It annoys me,' she wrote, on 14 February 1926, 'not to dance with Proinnsias, whether he's drunk or sober'.[51] A strict teetotaller, Jacob's opposition to drink did not militate against her growing attraction to Ryan. She enjoyed and revelled in his consciously wild boy image:

> Proinnsias came with Helen & me to Stephen's Green, telling us how he first got drunk, . . . wild incidents of the wars . . . Deliciously told – the thought of P. as an armed desperado is very intriguing.[52]

Ryan's ability to impart a sense of adventure was heightened for Jacob when he secretly passed her 'a flat leather case with something hard in it' to keep for him for the duration of the language class on 22 March 1926. Taking it and putting it between her books she enjoyed the sense of mystery he imparted and the implicit bond it created between them. He had, she recorded, 'all the air of a man offering you a parcel before the Black and Tans arrive'. 'I love the way he turns to me', she wrote over a year later, 'beginning with the leather case incident last spring. He certainly must know I'm fond of him'.[53] Three nights later as the two sat together correcting her essay she revelled in the idea that the rest of the class 'appeared to find us a very compromising & amusing spectacle'.[54] The two increasingly flirted with each other, Ryan teasing Jacob about possible indiscretions: 'I had a nice swing with P.; he said "Did Dubhglas go home last night?" I said "He came home with me" & P. put his hand to his forehead and passed away with shock, into the arms of those behind him'.[55] Jacob experienced that sense of early infatuation when all aspects of the other person intrigued and gave pleasure. When there was some banter at a Gaelic League event that Ryan would 'look well stripped', Jacob responded internally: 'God knows he would'. On trial for IRA activities in October 1928 Jacob described how he 'certainly did "adorn the dock" – I never saw him look

51   7 Feb. 1926; 14 Feb. 1926; 15 Feb. 1926, RJD Ms (51).
52   5 Mar. 1926, RJD Ms (51).
53   1 May 1927, RJD Ms (56).
54   22 Mar. 1926; 25 Mar. 1926, RJD Ms (51).
55   19 Dec. 1926, RJD Ms (55).

handsomer . . . he made everyone else look insignificant'.[56] Even his accent drew admiration from her: 'A Limerick accent', she wrote, 'beats all, especially when he can't say th'. His letters 'are exactly like himself, you can nearly see them sparkle'. [57]

Jacob and Ryan's relationship proceeded slowly. He read and commented on *Callaghan*, liking the protagonist but feeling that she had included 'some nasty things about religion', continuing that he himself 'wd like to disbelieve in God but couldn't'.[58] By November 1926 he was turning up at her doorstep in the middle of the night although at this point he slept on a mattress. Despite Jacob's love of the adventure of Ryan she worried when he was on the run from the Free State authorities after the 1926 Poppy Day riots that her flat would be raided.[59] By early January 1927 Ryan's activities meant that he had lost his job in Mountjoy School. He was unable to pay his rent and was 'afraid of his landlady'. Jacob described how she 'lay in ambush for P. in the [Gaelic League] office and tried to lend him cash but he wdn't have it while he has no prospect of work'.[60]

'A ROOM OF ONE'S OWN'

Ryan increasingly visited in the middle of the night which brought Jacob into conflict with Dorothy Macardle with whom she shared a flat in Herbert Place, in the second half of the 1920s. Macardle perceived Jacob to be unaware of appropriate behaviour in this regard. Jacob records how she 'raged to me' and

> called me into her room to blast me – she was in a wild temper – I was to tell 'that young man' that he was never to do it again – it was indecent – no flat for a man to be in – we agreed not to have visitors without asking each other's leave – Mrs O. F. wd have a right to complain . . . I never thought she was such a prude, or so unbearingly selfish.

This conflict between Macardle and Jacob over visitors, in this context, the suitability of single women entertaining men, highlights the almost childlike status forced on unmarried women. The protagonist in Mary Lavin's 1951 short story 'A single lady' vehemently resented 'the suggestion that a woman

56 26 Oct. 1928, RJD Ms (60).
57 7 July 1926, RJD Ms (53).
58 17 Oct. 1926, RJD Ms (54).
59 Poppy day riots were directed against the perceived Imperialist ceremonies of Armistice Day.
60 9 Jan. 1927; 14 Jan. 1927, RJD Ms (55).

should be regarded as in any way ignorant of certain matters just because she was single'. Despite her university education and her middle age, 'it seemed as if people supposed she knew nothing when it came to talking about certain things'.[61] Even very young married women were accorded respect and rights denied to older single women in Irish society.[62] As Ferriter points out, in William Trevor's short story 'The ballroom of romance', Bridie's father still referred to her as a girl despite the fact that she was 36.[63] Although her Protestant neighbours disapprove of Frances's marriage to Andy Callaghan they no longer consider her a 'foolish girl' as they had with regard to her activism in the suffrage cause.

> Now their manner to her . . . had become perceptively colder, and somehow, at the
> same time, more respectful. She was no longer a foolish girl, but a woman . . .
> Think what they will of the match, there are few people whose respect for a
> woman is not increased by the news of her engagement.[64]

The inability of single women to draw down mortgages, coupled with the lack of training to equip them to earn sufficient income, forced many such as Jacob to share their living space. Throughout her life Jacob was vulnerable to impermanent and inadequate living conditions. In November 1924 she had been, for example, forced 'clear out' of the flat she shared with Josephine Webb. Family members who inherited the property on the latter's death quickly sold it, forcing Jacob to make alternative arrangements. Early in 1925 she moved to Osborne Villas. When this did not work out she stayed for a time with Hanna Sheehy Skeffington while hoping 'to hear of some accommodation', moving to 24 Leinster Square at the end of March 1925. Later that year she moved into the flat in Herbert Place with Macardle.[65] Lacking 'a room of one's own', Jacob's uneasy position in a society that venerated home and family was even more pronounced. At the end of 1926 she commented with relief 'No house moving, thank God'.[66] Jacob's need for a room of her own was much more mundane than the need articulated by Virginia Woolf in 1929. Woolf argued the need if women were to be able to write; Jacob's lack of personal space and

---

61   Mary Lavin, 'A single lady' in Angela Bourke et al. (eds), *The Field Day Anthology of Irish Writing*, vol. iv (Cork: Cork University Press, 2002), p. 993.

62   Marjorie Howes, 'Public discourse, private reflection, 1916–70' in Bourke et al. (eds), *Field Day Anthology*, vol. iv, p. 929.

63   Ferriter, *The Transformation of Ireland*, pp. 494–5.

64   Winthrop, *Callaghan*, p. 169.

65   9 Nov. 1924, RJD Ms (46); 13 Mar.; 30 Mar. 1925, RJD Ms (48).

66   Summation of 1926, RJD Ms (55).

a home of her own as a single woman condemned her to uncertainty and transience – to living in a space that was not a home by the standards of the discourse of the period. By the terms of that discourse the spaces Jacob lived in throughout her life were waiting rooms; the single woman, who had left the parental home, waited in an ante-room or enclave to step into her own home as a married woman.[67]

Full autonomy was not allowed women such as Jacob by a society that refused to recognise the needs of single women, viewing them instead, in instances, as childlike, superfluous and unproductive. In 1918 Jacob wrote how her friend Charlotte 'strongly advised me to go away from home somewhere & get work, & said that it is the only way to find people that really want to be friends with you & to feel natural instead of superfluous'.[68] Jacob's enjoyment of the company and environment of Hanna and Owen Sheehy Skeffington reflects her own lack of a home, a situation typical of other women in the period. As late as 1948 she described visiting an R. Mills at 28 Herbert St 'where she has a small room & a dark kitchenette, high up'.[69] Minding Owen in 1924 she described how 'delightful it was to be in that milieu again'. She notes that it was 'strange how ready I am to do housework there'.[70] Indeed, Jacob achieved none of the ideals associated with domesticated women. She was not tidy by nature and one of the causes of her quarrels in sharing a flat with Helen was what the latter depicted as her lack of household order and even cleanliness. Helen, even after she no longer shared with Jacob, criticised her for not washing her dishcloths enough, something Jacob saw as 'damned impertinence'.[71]

The day following the encounter with Macardle, Jacob was forced to tell Ryan 'not to come again for the present because of Dorothy's behaviour '.[72] She had to 'fight to make Macardle consent' to her brother Tom staying in the flat in April 1927: 'Men are so noisy – she knew she wd lose her sleep with him'.[73] Indeed, the problem was not just male visitors. She noted on 19 February 1927 how Helen and herself 'actually dared to talk at supper, under Dorothy's room, & she came down & scolded us'. Earlier that month, Macardle's absence allowed the two women to 'have the privilege of speaking above our breath'.[74] Macardle's intolerance notwithstanding, Jacob's spiky personality,

67 Virginia Woolf, *A Room of One's Own* (New York: Harcourt Brace Jovanovich, 1991).

68 19 July 1918, RJD Ms (171).

69 12 Apr. 1948, RJD Ms (128).

70 2 Aug. 1924; 4 Aug. 1924, RJD Ms (46).

71 15 Feb. 1939, RJD Ms (86).

72 17 Oct.; 10–14 Nov. 1926, RJD Ms (54).

73 14 Apr. 1927, RJD Ms (56).

74 19 Feb.; 4 Feb. 1927, RJD Ms (55).

in particular her candid willingness to state her opinions with no sense of nuance or recognition of context, would account for many of the problems she encountered in sharing living space. The following contretemps with Helen offers an insight into how others perceived her:

> Helen in the course of telling me about the girl that was so scandalously late for the bus at Belfast . . . mentioned the man in charge of her saying 'I'm thro with women', & when I foolishly said that was a silly remark, she fell on me for my objectionableness in taking men's anti-women remarks seriously . . . taunted me with . . . not being the sort of person to get invitations for such sprees.[75]

Again, Jacob was aware of her shortcomings and the manner in which they influenced people's perceptions of her. All this she wrote into the character of Constance seen through the eyes of Hugh MacNevin:

> Connie is queer, he repeated. She's shy and it's a funny thing, but she never seems to have learnt just how to behave. She'll say the most hopeless things without dreaming of harm . . . and then wonders why people are so easily offended. She has extraordinary ideas too. She's as prickly as a furzebush, and there's not a custom or an institution in the world she hasn't something against. But she's alright when you get to know her.[76]

Jacob did not have an ability to transcend the serious and was highly critical of flippant behaviour, particularly from women. Her attitude to the women who attended the south Dublin election meeting in December 1924 offers an example of this in context: 'Those girls there behave disgustingly, shouting nicknames at the men coming in, & no one checking them'.[77] This example indicates an inability to view the world through anything other than a self-lens.

Yet the rows documented by Jacob indicate the manner in which these women were in certain ways developmentally frustrated by virtue of the way in which society was organised. The rows evidence how adolescent jealousies persisted in grown women. As late as 1934 Jacob expressed a juvenile jealousy of the manner in which Helen monopolised George Gilmore, 'she knowing how I liked him, & having plenty of men of her own'. Jacob, having little self-esteem, believed that Helen had 'superior attractions' to her – 'liveliness and

75   9 Aug. 1935, RJD Ms (77).
76   Jacob, 'Third person singular', pp. 85–6.
77   15 Dec. 1924, RJD Ms (47).

self-confidence and quickness'.[78] Jacob considered, like Constance Moore, that she had 'no natural feminine instinct for dealing with men'.[79] By 1928 Jacob was sharing a flat with Helen, engaged by this date to Douglas McGinley. Jacob found the situation of Helen's engagement difficult and indeed behaved as Macardle had to her over Ryan: 'Had it out with Helen re D & his behaviour & his staying till 12'.[80] Douglas McGinley's dislike of Jacob apparently sprang from his belief that she was in love with him.[81] However, the real issue at stake was the lack of personal space and self-autonomy. McGinley's problems with Jacob and *vice versa* would have been less contentious had Jacob, as a woman in her 40s, not been forced to share a living space with his fiancée. Yet the issue is even more complex. While sharing living space was a financial necessity it was also a psychological necessity for single women, an emotional bulwark against the encroaching loneliness of middle and old age. Despite all her rows with Macardle over visitors Jacob noted the absence of Dorothy and Florence from the flat on the night of 1 March 1927, writing, 'I was alone for most of the evening and horribly lonely'. The following evening brought more of the same: 'Lucy called in the afternoon & sat talking a while. After that another beastly lonely evening – both D. and F. out'.[82]

Jacob had to sneak Ryan into the flat due to Macardle's hostility. The latter's absence on a rest cure on 18 November 1926 allowed the two to share a cosy meal by the fire and it is clear that an intimacy was developing. 'He had a delicious comfortable friendliness about him that evening, and was of course a continual pleasure to the eye & ear.' Ryan, on the run in late November ignored the potential conflict he would create between Macardle and Jacob and continued to turn up looking for shelter.[83] Indeed, the sense of shared hostility to, and even getting one over on, Macardle enhanced the bond. Ryan and Jacob did not begin a physical affair until 1928 and uncharacteristically it was she who made the first move. This move was born out of growing frustration and a sense of exclusion consequent on Helen's engagement to Douglas McGinley.

P. sat talking of Tourist work – printing, etc, till 11.35, then when he started to go I asked him to stay the night with me. He was perfect – didn't shirk it – shut the door refused with obvious reasons, looking painfully miserable – admitted he'd

78 16 Feb. 1934, RJD Ms (74); Summation of 1934, RJD Ms (76).
79 Jacob, 'Third person singular', p. 101.
80 22 Nov. 1928, RJD Ms (61).
81 11 Dec. 1928; 8 Feb. 1929, RJD Ms (61).
82 1–2 Mar. 1927, RJD Ms (56).
83 18 Nov.; 26 Nov. 1926, RJD Ms (54).

like to – any man would like to accept such an invitation – I cdn't argue it, he was so unhappy over it – then he did take me and kiss me, and when I made to stop, he pulled me down on the sofa and lay there, holding me tight, partly on top of me, his face against mine, all hot and panting and deliciously excited, showing most plainly *how* tempted he was, for more than half an hour.[84]

It is clear from Jacob's account in the 'secret' diary that both she and Ryan were very inexperienced sexually.

I got him into the other room & into bed – kept his shirt on, but when I was naked he took me in his arms, standing & then got into bed & I cd feel his lovely skin all over – but he's still inexperienced & I couldn't get right, except once when he hurt like hell.[85]

A feature of Jacob's diaries in these years is a précis of the year past. For 1928 she makes reference to the events of the 18 July writing how she 'had ¾ of an hour in heaven'. By October Ryan was committed to Mountjoy for trial on the charge of being a member of the IRA, supporting documents having been found in his desk at the Tourist Association,[86] and Jacob plainly felt his absence. A céilidhe on 14 October was described as 'horrible without P.'. The next day she went to Mountjoy but found he had a visitor already. The result was that she spent 'the afternoon missing appointments & making mistakes . . . Strange what a fearful effort of moral courage it is to me to go up to Mtjoy & ask for Proinnsias – just because I care so much for him'.[87] At some level her sense of affection was reciprocated. Ryan wrote to her from Mountjoy informing her in a letter of 10 September 1928 that he would appear before the dock in Green Street some time in the next week and hoped to 'get a "gawk", at all my pals'. 'When I get out,' he continued, 'I'll give you all the news of this place. There have been *some* changes in five years . . . Keep the Branch alive for the winter; I'll be there in the spring'.[88] In many respects this is the letter of a friend rather than a lover but a letter the following year, headed, 'the night before the morning after', suggests a greater intimacy:

84   18 July 1928, RJD Ms (60).

85   RJD MS (171).

86   Adrian Hoar, *In Green and Red: The Lives of Frank Ryan* (Dingle: Brandon, 2004), pp. 46–7.

87   14–15 Oct. 1928, RJD Ms (60).

88   Ryan to Jacob, 10 Sept. 1928, RJP Ms 33,130.

Demolished:

Reams and reams of paper,

Six eggs,

Two loaves,

One cake,

Some butter

One bowl sugar,

A few pinches of tea,

A grain of salt, and

One plate.

All but the last item are irrecoverable. The last will be found in the dust-bin. It clung to the Tea-pot at washing-time. As I didn't observe its ivy-like affection, and as the tea-pot didn't reciprocate it, it committed suicide on the gas-range. This tragedy having happened after my last meal, I did not consider it necessary to appoint a successor or substitute to it.

I was quiet as a mouse and I hope not as destructive as one. If any other plate (except the china one) is missing, try the pawnbrokers.[89]

'THE END OF THE AFFAIR'

Released in February 1929 Ryan began to disengage from Jacob. Despite the affectionate tone of the above letter, he wanted the relationship to remain secret and the clandestine nature of the affair began to take its toll on Jacob. Increasingly she recorded nights and times spent waiting for him to visit to no avail. On 2 March 1929 he arrived around 8 p.m.:

took me out to the garage as the only quiet place, & made love eagerly for nearly an hour there. Just he was in the mood for it – wanted it – but it was a horrid uncomfortable place. I got a bit further anyway – could hardly believe my senses at first it was such a surprise.

The next night at the Gaelic League céilidhe he 'had a shy fit & wdn't speak to me'.[90] Jacob progressively fell into a semi-domestic role vis-à-vis Ryan, offering him shelter, food, even doing his mending for him. At an early stage

---

89 Ryan to Jacob, 30 Mar. 1929, RJP Ms 33,130.
90 14 Feb. 1929; 2–3 Mar. 1929, RJD Ms (61).

in their acquaintance she wrote that he was 'the kind of man you would love to be taking care of and petting'.[91] She herself became increasingly frustrated by the constricted nature of the relationship. 'Gave him dinner – he was absorbed in articles for Bulletin . . . but that T. girl & others – Hanna Ethne, T. girl again – seemed to be around *all* the time . . . No comfort in him in all.' Four days later 'he turned up at 3, to spend a couple of nights here. But hellishly busy, of course . . . got no good of him at all . . . lovely night, but I was thoroughly wretched'.[92] On 12 April 1929 she arrived home at 11.30 p.m. to find Ryan waiting for her.

> He stayed till 12 or so talking almost all business . . . then got affectionate again, but *would* return to the garage – confound him – a little while there, couldn't get him back to a comfortable room – wouldn't be fair – I think he's mad.[93]

Jacob's life increasingly revolved around the chance of contact with Ryan, physical or otherwise. A visit to Macardle in June 1929 was cut short because she was 'afraid to stay late for fear P. wd come – of course he didn't *because* I came home'. Her lack of power in the relationship was beginning to impact on her quality of life. Repeatedly he placated her with promises to come 'some evening next week'. Gaelic League meetings were recorded as 'dreary' without his presence. His silence on occasions when he did visit made her 'uneasy & miserable'.[94] She lived for the increasingly rare occasions as that of 24 November 1929 when she met the 'black panther' in one of his affectionate moods at a céilidhe in Ely Place.

> had the very rare pleasure of dancing with him – wanted to speak to me. Did so after on the stairs – could I go home? I did, in the pouring rain, & he met me on the corner. As soon as we were in, & he was assured there was no danger of F. coming in – out with the light, and oh he was lovely – but how insanely ambivalent he is – This must stop! – Do you think I'd come here if I didn't like it? If only he hadn't always to be somewhere else so soon. He was so miserable, so sick with himself, so ashamed & downhearted, over things in general, he never was so

91   23 Mar. 1926, RJD Ms (171). In her earlier relationship with Tony Farrington Jacob similarly took pleasure in providing him with sustenance and nourishment in a fashion that underscored the ideology of separate spheres. In October 1915 she wrote: 'I had the pleasure of heating milk for him, & of seeing him eat about 4 pieces of gingerbread one after the other'. RJD Ms (171).

92   15 Mar. 1929; 24 Mar. 1929; 28 Mar. 1929, RJD Ms (61).

93   12 Apr. 1929, RJD Ms (61).

94   11 June 1929; 25 Sept. 1929; 27 Sept. 1929, RJD Ms (62); 29 Oct. 1929, RJD Ms (63).

heartbreaking before, but he let me pet him and say anything I liked – he was delicious beyond words, if only he'd be reasonable & articulate – but its so cruel not to be able to give him any comfort beyond the moment, to have him blame himself for giving way to his desires instead of letting me be permanent friends.[95]

Yet despite such guilt, or maybe because of it, Jacob did not see him for over a month after the night of the 24 November and her frustration with the situation was palpable. 'No sign of the panther & not a word – I'd give a lot to know why he can't write, & how he can't see the horridness of such behaviour'.[96] In summing up her relationship with Ryan during 1929 Jacob wrote how she

had hell from him, in suspense, disappointment and starvation, but I had a few heavenly hours to make up – but if only his soul was more friendly – I sometimes feel that as he wants me physically he doesn't want me to talk to – the shyness & the sense of sin he seems to get, & I helpless to prevent it.[97]

This situation continued throughout 1930. On 18 February she wrote:

Went home & waited for P. He didn't turn up until nearly 11. Talked a while about the paper . . . then I supposed I knew why he'd come – I sure will guess in future, but I think its too bad never to come *except* for that. It's not fair.[98]

Willing to have sex with her in private, Ryan began increasingly to ignore her at public occasions, a fact she was unable to come to terms with: 'I hate the way he'll never come and talk to me at a céilidhe, but treats me like the most casual acquaintance.[99] The ironic thing was that Ryan himself had in the words of Hoar 'endured the torment of an unrequited love' for Elgin, the sister of Tom Barry.[100] Possibly Ryan's attachment to Barry had not dissipated and this may explain his treatment of Jacob who recorded on 8 March 1930 that she did not go to the Cumann na mBan céilidhe 'because I felt sure P wd be there, probably with E. B., and I couldn't stand the way he treats me at a céilidhe'. It is quite likely that E. B., whom Jacob does not identify further,

95 24 Nov. 1929, RJD Ms (63).
96 23 Dec. 1929, RJD Ms (63).
97 Summation of 1929, RJD Ms (63).
98 18 Feb. 1930, RJD Ms (63).
99 2 Mar. 1930, RJD Ms (64).
100 Hoar, *In Green and Red*, pp. 31–2.

was Elgin Barry.[101] Although Jacob does not mention any problem with the age difference between the two, possibly this may have been something Ryan was uncomfortable about. Jacob did note how Douglas McGinley teased her on one occasion at a Gaelic League céilidhe with the words 'Ah he's only a child'.[102] Ryan himself wrote to her in September 1927: 'I'm twenty-five years today. Before I'm twenty-six I hope to have straightened out much of this crooked life of mine, and to have got beyond the talking stage in many things.'[103] While this was not a reference to their relationship, it does suggest that he was aware of how his life in certain respects did not conform to expectations, whether his own or others is not clear.

Yet Ryan clearly had some level of attraction to Jacob that he found difficult to shake. Of course, a more cynical reading might be that she was willing to be physically intimate with him on his terms. She never pressed him to make the relationship public; there was never any talk of it as a permanent arrangement leading to marriage. In August 1930 she recorded an increasingly rare night of happiness:

> He began to leave at 11, & then changed his mind and spent another half hour, quite differently . . . He was as inaccessible as usual, appeared to acquiesce but finally asked me not to talk, & had the air at one time of depression but when we parted I never saw him smile so happily at such a time – a smile that didn't look a bit as if his conscience was troubled.[104]

In the secret diary she was even more explicit:

> At last, and all of his own doing, to be in his arms again, to feel his satin skin and stroke his hair and feel him pant, and hold him – and I never got such a sweet, straightforward kiss as when he went in the light . . . without that unhappy guilty air he had before.[105]

A few months later, in October, Jacob tried to initiate a conversation 'about ourselves' but it appears as if Ryan took refuge in his deafness to frustrate her attempts.[106] Jacob did discuss her relationship with Ryan with family friend, Ned Stephens. The conversation revolved around Ryan's 'inhibitions' and

101 8 Mar. 1930, RJD Ms (64).
102 16 May 1926, RJD Ms (52).
103 Ryan to Jacob, 1 Sept. 1927, RJP Ms 33,130.
104 2 Aug. 1930, RJD Ms (65).
105 30 Aug. [1930] RJD Ms (171).
106 7 Oct. 1930, RJD Ms (65).

Ned represented his sense of post-coital guilt as 'the regular thing after doing that if yr conscience is against it. And the other person becomes a symbol of yr sin. He understood the difficulty of talking to him too'.[107]

Ryan disengaged even more in 1931 and Jacob went through nights of torment as she watched him ignore her or flirt with other women. She stated how there was one advantage in dancing the Walls of Limerick with him – a dance that involved changing partners: 'He *could* flirt with other women in it, but at least he couldn't *keep* flirting with one'.[108] Even earlier in the relationship she noted how he engaged with other women, on one occasion describing how women 'stuck to him like burrs'.[109] Happy to see him in April 1927 she was yet irritated that 'he gassed to Helen in that way that seems a necessity with him if there's a girl present though sometimes there's a kind of mechanical air about it'.[110] Summing up 1932 she wrote:

> As for P. he is in some ways dearer than ever, but I've seen very little of him . . . I had only three spots of love, the last one the best; – I seldom had a lovelier evening than that, – but there was an awful time when I had given him the letter & thought he was never going to answer. He is *friendly*, tho, I don't feel so much fear that I'm just a nuisance to him.[111]

Ryan continued to call late in the night in early 1933, clearly spur of the moment, more than likely these were drink induced visits. He appeared according to Jacob on one such occasion, 'very reckless and hard to deal with'. However difficult he was to deal with, her feeling on seeing him was one of pleasure: 'The peace and comfort of having him without fear of his getting up and going off was heavenly. I don't think I slept at all any more, but he did, and was lovely to feel . . .'. Six days later, however, she resolved never to stay at home again for him when he did not arrive as promised to tea.[112] In late March she was roused at 1.15 a.m. and opening the door, Ryan fell in drunk, not knowing where he had been from 11.30 a.m. when he had left a Sweepstakes dinner.[113] 'He was pretty quiet for a good while, and then woke up & got wild – also for a long time'. She wished that he could have arrived some time when

107 18 Dec. 1930, RJD Ms (65).
108 28 Feb. 1931; 13 Mar. 1931; 27 Mar. 1931, RJD Ms (66).
109 27 Oct. 1929, RJD Ms (63).
110 5 Apr. 1927, RJD Ms (56).
111 Summation of 1932, RJD Ms (71).
112 20 Jan. 1933; 26 Jan. 1933, RJD Ms (72).
113 The Irish Sweepstakes were established under Free State legislation in 1930 to raise funds for voluntary hospitals in crisis since the 1910s. See Marie Coleman, *The Irish Sweep: A History of the Irish Hospitals Sweepstake, 1930–87* (Dublin: UCD Press, 2009).

she did not have a cold and also wished she had the strength of mind to refuse him entry when he arrived drunk.[114] While he arrived sober at 1.15 a.m. on 23 November and was 'lovely in ways', Jacob hated his morning silence.[115] However, the relationship preyed less on her mind by the end of 1933:

> As to P. I had the thing I wanted 3 times, and will be the better for it for ever. I had good talks but very few, and much less of him . . . but I am getting to mind that a little less, I think, except sometimes when it is awful.[116]

Jacob was slightly more critical of Ryan by this date, noting how he complained when other people let him down but failed to keep his own appointments; when challenged he indignantly claimed 'he cdn't be in 10 places at once'. His request, via his sister Eilís, that Jacob provide a Manchester Martyrs cutting for him at a night's notice for a lecture he was giving provoked a desire that 'something wd show him how exigent & inconsiderate he is'.[117] Silence was also a feature of Ryan's visit in March 1934. Despite the silence Jacob experienced 'the usual breathless electric feel for a long time' when he 'began to love me'.[118] By December 1934 Ryan was not only silent when he arrived 'in the small hours' but 'chilly'.[119] At the end of that year she asked herself if she would 'ever know a little more about him in his own soul'. In early February 1935 Ryan arrived, again in the small hours of the morning, stayed for about an hour and 'chased the loneliness'.[120] In July, arriving sometime between two and three for sex, he refused to stay for breakfast, afraid to make a sound.[121]

By the end of 1935 the affair was effectively over. Since October Ryan had not visited except on business. She concluded by saying how he 'carries on the good work and I admire him publicly more than ever', adding 'I'm very lonely for a man with time to be a real friend to me'.[122] She recorded at the end of 1936 how he arrived, sat reading and talking for an hour or more, but had 'no ulterior motive'. Ryan did not even inform Jacob when he left to fight in the Spanish Civil War in December 1936. She notes that she met him in Peadar O'Donnell's

114 25 Mar. 1933, RJD Ms (72).
115 23 Nov. 1933, RJD Ms (73).
116 Summation of 1933, RJD Ms (74).
117 19 Nov. 1934; 22 Nov. 1934, RJD Ms (76).
118 23 Mar. 1934, RJD Ms (74).
119 7 Dec. 1934, RJD Ms (76).
120 Summation of 1934; 14 Feb. 1935, RJD Ms (76)
121 21 July 1935, RJD Ms (77).
122 Summation of 1935, RJD Ms (78).

house on the 7 December and 'had no notion that that was the last I'd see of him before he went to fight in Spain, damn him'.[123] Jacob listened attentively to Ryan's broadcasts from Spain, noting his 'lovely voice' – old habits died hard![124]

A NON-BELIEVER IN A CATHOLIC STATE

Jacob's position as non-Catholic in 1920s and 1930s Ireland certainly contributed to her sense of exclusion. The homogeneous nature of the Free State, the sense of shared culture based on a patriarchal-style Catholicism, forced her as a woman and a non-believer from a non-Catholic background to adopt a tone of ironic detachment, which bordered at times on a sense of superiority. The newspapers, she claimed, recorded the centenary Catholic Emancipation celebrations in 1929 'in pious hysterics'. She noted also that there were '5 columns about the men in the procession, 6 lines about the women'.[125] The official Mass at the Eucharistic Congress three years later similarly drew attention to the patriarchal tone of Irish Catholicism so hated by Jacob. Mrs Kettle was a subject for admiring conversation between Sheehy Skeffington and Jacob when she defied the Town Clerk's claim that no women could go to the official Mass at Marlborough Street.[126] A casual conversation with friends in Delgany in October 1925 revolved around the idea of setting up 'a liberty league to unite progressive people against Church tyranny'.[127] At a Radical Club committee meeting six months later she succeeded in her proposal to have a ten minute talk on the effect of religion on Irish culture, determined to 'vindicate our right to discuss religious topics freely', some members 'having spoken as if religion should be barred'.[128] To Jacob's chagrin, issues of contraception and divorce debated at the IIL provoked controversy. Mrs Dix[129] refused to allow discussion 'of anything the Catholic Church (or any church) has pronounced against'. That was 'her idea of how to be non-sectarian'.[130] A typical conversation at tea in Jacob's flat revolved around 'making the country safe for irreligion'.[131]

---

123 11 Nov. 1936; 7 Dec. 1936, RJD Ms (80).
124 10 Jan. 1937, RJD Ms (80).
125 24 June 1929, RJD Ms (62).
126 27 June 1932, RJD Ms (69).
127 5 Oct. 1925, RJD Ms (49).
128 17 Apr. 1926, RJD Ms (52).
129 Una M'Clintock Dix.
130 29 May 1925, RJD Ms (48).
131 16 July 1927, RJD Ms (57).

Although Jacob was a non-believer she manifested a cultural sense of Protestantism. Jacob had a tendency to think in syllogisms; as she equated republicanism with a commitment to progressive legislation in the 1920s, a concern of the following chapter, so she considered non-Catholics as more liberal minded, indeed berating those who did not follow such a hypothesis. During a conversation in 1925 on divorce in the home of anti-Treaty activist and propagandist, Frank Gallagher,[132] she noted how it was 'disgraceful that only one Protestant – Thrift – wd defend the right to divorce . . . Johnson & Blythe[133] both against it, as if they had no more sense than Catholics.'[134] She herself regularly decried the divorce ban as anti-liberal, declaring with self-admiration that herself and Hanna discussing the topic was 'rather too much' for Aodh de Blácam.[135] Jacob's opposition to organised religion but in particular her anti-Catholicism, in part explains her alignment with forces perceived to be anti-Church. For Jacob people were, reductively, either secular minded or in thrall to religion, Louie Bennett, for example, having 'a natural secular mind' and accordingly 'expressed much of my own feelings'.[136] A visit to Macardle who was in bed with a chill in 1930 led to one of their favourite conversations – de Valera – this time a discussion on the 'Catholic church & its effect on people'.

> She said a terrible thing – that he had the finest character she knew, but she always felt half its capabilities were smothered & kept from functioning by being a Catholic. I was much impressed. She thinks its much worse for leaders than for ordinary people – cripples their special qualities.[137]

---

132 Frank Gallagher (1893–1962). For details of Gallagher's propaganda see Graham Walker, '"The Irish Dr Goebbels": Frank Gallagher and Irish republican propaganda', *Journal of Contemporary History* 27: 1 (Jan. 1992), pp.149–65.

133 William Edward Thrift, a future provost of Trinity College, was one of only two dissidents who voted in the Dáil against the proposal by Cosgrave on 11 February 1925 to revise standing orders to disallow the introduction of divorce bills. A Protestant, Ernest Blythe was Minister for Local Government in the first Free State government. Thomas Johnson was the leader of the Labour Party. For details on this vote see David Fitzpatrick, 'Divorce and separation in modern Irish history', *Past and Present* 114 (Feb. 1987), pp. 172–96.

134 31 Jan. 1925, RJD Ms (47).

135 3 Apr. 1924, RJD Ms (45). Aodh de Blácam (1890–1951) was a convert to Catholicism and a writer in support of the language movement. In later years he was a member of the Fianna Fáil executive. Seamus Deane (ed.), *The Field Day Anthology of Irish Writing*, vol. ii (Derry: Field Day, 1991), p. 955.

136 21 Jan. 1934, RJD Ms (74).

137 23 Mar. 1930, RJD Ms (64). Macardle ceased to identify herself as a Catholic from the 1920s, angered by the Church's excommunication of civil war republicans. Nadia Clare Smith, *Dorothy Macardle: A Life* (Dublin: Woodfield Press, 2007), p. 42.

Throughout the period Jacob lost no opportunity to highlight her antagonism
to the religious homogeneity of the Free State. She described the first number
of the Fianna Fáil paper, the *Irish Press*, of 5 September 1931 as 'not bad, but
very holy of course with a perfectly extraneous priest stuck into the middle of
the starting the machinery photo'.[138] Jacob and Macardle both objected to the
denunciation in the paper on 7 December of an article on the need for birth
control published in the *Sunday Times*. Macardle interpreted the condemnation as indicative of

> the arrogant narrow rudeness to all non-Caths. . . . She was very downhearted over
> the paper altogether, with the sectarian blight over it, and F. F. and the country.
> Never heard anyone speak better. Like me, she had got the *Sunday Times* &
> thought the article excellent.[139]

CONSTRUCTIONS OF SEXUALITY IN THE FREE STATE

Irish historians have failed to focus on sexually active women in the early Free
State, focusing instead on Church and State attempts to deny expressions of
sexuality although, in contrast, Diarmaid Ferriter's *Occasions of Sin* is concerned
with the 'complexity of Irish sexual history'.[140] While this remark on lacunae
within the historiography has been made in the context of the failure to examine
fully the sexual activity of prostitutes, it should also be extended to women like
Jacob who failed for whatever reason to marry but were not content to live a
life of celibacy.[141] This was problematic in the early decades of the Irish Free
State. The standard cultural fears of post-colonial states were heightened in
the Irish context by the partitioned nature of the new political entity that was
the Free State. Furthermore, a fear permeated the ranks of Irish-Ireland that
although political independence had been achieved Ireland was increasingly
enslaved to English cultural values and norms. The impulses behind the
Censorship of Publications Act, 1929, were twin: moral and cultural.[142] In
'Suggested tariff on imported newspapers and magazines' published in *Studies*

138 5 Sept. 1931, RJD Ms (67).

139 7 Dec. 1931, RJD Ms (68).

140 Ferriter, *The Transformation of Ireland*, p. 322; Diarmaid Ferriter, *Occasions of Sin: Sex and Society in Modern Ireland* (London: Profile Books, 2009), p. 1.

141 This failure has been recently rectified with the publication of Maria Luddy, *Prostitution and Irish Society 1800–1940* (Cambridge: Cambridge University Press, 2007).

142 Terence Brown, *Ireland: A Social and Cultural History 1922–79* (Glasgow: Fontana, 1981), pp. 69–70.

in 1927 Fr R. S. Devane called for legislation to stem the tide of immoral
literature flowing into Ireland. This article posited a polarised view of
England and Ireland common to nationalist discourse.[143] To create and sustain
a healthy, pure-minded and sexually conservative Irish population it was necessary to preserve Irish society from contaminating English cultural mediums
preoccupied with sex and immorality. The first draft of the Censorship of
Publications Act has been described as equating sexual passion with sexual
immorality.[144] The fact that almost a quarter of the *Report of the Committee on
Evil Literature*, published in December 1926, was concerned with issues
around contraception and fertility control indicates the fear of uncontrol-
led sexuality; knowledge of birth control was considered to promote sexual
promiscuity.[145] The authentic Ireland was a 'realm of purity' and had to be
maintained as such. A 'new romance of the nation' would place new demands
on constructions of Irish sexuality.[146]

Jacob was fully immersed in the debate on censorship and conscious of the
primary impetus to control and regulate sexuality. She offered details, for
example, of a lecture on 'The cult of the abnormal in literature with special
reference to *Ulysses*' at a Radical Club meeting where the speaker, MacManus,
talked 'awful tosh, everything abnormal was vile, morbid, filthy . . . At times
you'd think it was the Catholic Bulletin talking'.[147] It should, of course, be
noted that when Jacob herself read Joyce's text, which Hanna brought back
from a visit to Paris, she questioned why he was 'so fond of pure ugliness'.[148]
Jacob recorded details of censored books successfully brought into Ireland
from abroad; in August 1930 she received Bertrand Russell's *Marriage &
Morals* from a friend returned from England.[149] She was horrified when the
Irish Press omitted sections from *The House Divided* when they serialised it in
1936. The phrase 'Lying on the floor in her petticoat' was removed and the
word 'sexless' changed to senseless.[150] Ward writes how the ban on the sale of

143 'Suggested tariff on imported newspapers and magazines', *Studies* XVI (Dec. 1927), pp. 545–63.

144 Howes, 'Public discourse, private reflection, 1916–70', p. 929.

145 Michael Adams, *Censorship: The Irish Experience* (Alabama: University of Alabama Press, 1968),
p. 35; Sandra McAvoy, 'Sex and the single girl: Ireland 1922–1949' in Chichi Aniagolu (ed.), *In From
the Shadows: The UL Women's Studies Collection*, vol iii (Limerick: Women's Studies and Department
of Government and Society, University of Limerick, 1997), p. 57.

146 Siobhán Kilfeather (ed.), 'Sexual expression and genre, 1801–1917' in Bourke et al. (eds), *The Field
Day Anthology of Irish Writing*, vol. iv, p. 826, p. 827.

147 16 Jan. 1926, RJD Ms (51).

148 15 June 1926, RJD Ms (51).

149 4 Aug. 1930, RJD Ms (65). Bertrand Russell, *Marriage and Morals* (New York: Horace Liveright,
1929).

150 15 July 1936, RJD Ms (79).

contraceptives under the Criminal Law (Amendment) Act 1936 did not provoke a response from the various female activist organisations. Although this may have been the case in public, Jacob's diary testifies to how the topic was one for debate throughout the 1920s in many of the feminist committees and organisations she attended, she herself hosting such a debate over tea on 22 May 1925: 'Fierce discussion, all for divorce except Mrs S. [Stephens] who was mildly against it. Stories of un controlled-birth horrors & clerical influences (Mrs Le B [Brocquy]) to curdle your blood'.[151] On 23 January 1929 Jacob spoke for the availability of birth control information at a Censorship debate attended by, she claimed, about 200. Those like her were condemned by one speaker for 'loose talk about limitation of families' and they were referred 'for guidance on the matter' to *The Republic & the Church*.[152] A 'waste of woman doctor' was for Jacob the case of a Dr M'Cormack who refused to acknowledge the need for contraceptive advice to mitigate the demands of large families on the health of women and the lack of individual attention to children.

> She talked about large families, re maternity patients of hers with 4 babies in 3 years sort of thing, and defended that – saying how much worse contraceptives were on the nerves & mind than a child every year for the body & mind – body & mind of the mother; she didn't seem to think it could do any harm to children at all. She is curious when she talks like that.[153]

The regulation of female sexuality in particular was crucial to the emerging self-image of the Irish nation; the burden of virtue was placed on Irish women; sexual propriety and chasteness were primarily the responsibility of women.[154] One of the chief concerns of the new government was to establish stability and order after the turbulent years of the independence struggle. In this context unregulated sexuality symbolised chaos.[155] Consequently the expression of sexuality had political connotations. State and church attempts to confine expressions of sexuality within marriage were linked strongly to the cultural and political insecurities of the new post-colonial Irish Free State. The stability of the Catholic state was predicated on women within the home

151 22 May 1925, RJD Ms (48). Sybil Le Brocquy (1892–1973) was a playwright with a particular focus on the life of Jonathan Swift and Vanessa.

152 23 Jan. 1929, RJD Ms (61). Jacob attributes this publication to Father M'Glade but it is probably John McClory, *The Republic and the Church: A Series of Lenten Lectures mainly on Divorce and Birth Control* (London: B. Herder, 1927).

153 31 July 1924, RJD Ms (46).

154 Valiulis, 'Neither feminist nor flapper', p. 172.

155 Howes, 'Public discourse, private reflection, 1916–70', p. 923.

and sexuality confined within the bounds of marriage. The definition of Irishness was heavily premised on strict adherence to Catholic social teaching.[156] Concern was expressed about the rising number of unmarried mothers, the relaxation of sexual morals and the sexual abuse of young children. There was also a fear of increased sexual activity among single women who were not prostitutes. Both the Committee on Evil Literature and the Carrigan Committee of 1930–1, which was to 'Enquire into the Criminal Law Amendment Acts (1880–5) and Juvenile Prostitution', expressed a belief that the purveyors of contraception targeted the unmarried in the Free State.[157] By these standards women such as Jacob had no legitimate right to develop any sense of sexual autonomy beyond the limits of a dominant conservative definition of sexuality that insisted on the normative version within marriage. A perception among historians underlies the literature on marriage patterns and the history of sexuality that those who found the sexual conservatism of the post famine period and the early decades of the Free State restricting were those who tended to emigrate. Furthermore, the treatment of issues around marriage, illegitimacy rates and emigration is premised on a heavy focus on women in rural Ireland.[158] Alternatively, information on women and sexuality comes via state files at the Central and Circuit Criminal Courts where women gave testimony on abortions and sexual assault.[159] In other words, information only entered the public domain when sexual activity was non consensual or resulted in problematic pregnancies. There is little information available or discussed about sexually active women such as Jacob who did not sustain unwanted pregnancies but whose sexual activity did not fall within the norms dictated by Church and State. Indeed there is a fuller recognition of lesbian relationships than heterosexual relationships outside the bonds of marriage. When single women are considered in historiography it tends to be in the context of emigration with less discussion of women like Jacob who wanted to remain in Ireland but who were fringed by their non-marital status. In *Erin's Daughters in America*, for example, Hasia Diner discusses the late marital age of Irish female emigrants relative to women in other immigrant groups, and concludes that this reflects a reluctance to marry to preserve living standards or personal autonomy.[160]

156 Ibid., p. 924.

157 McAvoy, 'Sex and the single girl', pp. 55–7; McAvoy, 'The regulation of sexuality', p. 256.

158 See Howes, 'Public discourse, private reflection, 1916–70', p. 924.

159 See McAvoy, 'Sex and the single girl', pp. 62–4.

160 Hasia Diner, *Erin's Daughters in America: Irish Immigrant Women in the Nineteenth Century* (Baltimore: Johns Hopkins University Press, 1983).

THERAPY

But what then of women such as Jacob, living in an urban context, that remained in the State, who arguably wanted to marry but did not have the opportunity. The State and Church directed insistence on a 'normative' and constricting version of sexuality created a tension for Jacob between her public and private status as sexual being. This tension may explain her attempt to seek out therapy around the time period in which the relationship with Ryan became physical, although she had shown evidence of knowledge of Freudian ideas from much earlier. By the end of September 1927, a few weeks before her 39th birthday, Jacob had entered into a correspondence with a Mrs Hartley, an analyst in London. During the period of her infatuation with Tony Farrington in 1915 she recorded a very notable comment in the alternative diary. This offers a key to understanding the manner in which she absorbed the conflict created between her private sexual needs and public discourse. Jacob believed that her sexual feelings were not consistent with the essentialist attributes accorded to women in society. In this she then seems to have assimilated, at a latent level, key concepts of the ideology of separate spheres, despite all her pronouncements on gender equality. Under the ideology of separate spheres women were not expected to have sexual feelings; they were passive, meek and chaste. Jacob clearly experienced physical attraction for Tony Farrington and she problematised this in the following way:

> I certainly am in some ways a man in disguise – a man turned inside out. My love for Tony is more masculine than feminine; I love him, not spiritually & patiently & unselfishly as a woman is supposed to love a man, but physically and impatiently & selfishly, as a man loves a woman. The idea of his being happy apart from me has no charms for me at all. I'd rather have him unhappy near me than happy far away. It's more a craving & a passion for him than proper love. And the very fact of picking someone younger than myself to love is like a man.[161]

The feelings of being at odds with what was expected of women would later manifest itself in her relationship with Ryan who was also much younger than her. The tension between private feelings and expected behaviour is reflected in the character of Constance in 'Third person singular'. Constance is viewed by her friend Emily as abnormal because of her interest in men and her desire for a relationship. The abnormality in this context is the fact that Constance, despite her single status, is a sexual being.

161 RJD Ms (171).

Now see here, Emmy, I won't be looked at in that shocked way. I've said nothing to shock anyone. I know I take too much interest in Masculinity, because I'm starved of it, but I'm nearer the right and normal than you are, with your vacant cavity where sex ought to be. You're a kind of monstrosity.

But lots of women live without men and are perfectly happy, Emily replied, and I never in my life heard any woman talk like you.

Because they've been taught to be ashamed to. And the happy women you talk of either were unnatural, like you, or else they'd had as much as they wanted.[162]

Even aside from the issue of sex, Jacob noted how the organisation of Irish society along rigid gender lines militated against single women's interaction with men on an intellectual level. On 20 October 1939 she gave a talk on C. P. Gilman's *The Man-Made World*. This work by Charlotte Perkins Gilman, published in 1911, distinguished male and female traits and ascribed the ills of the world to patriarchy. At the talk the chairperson, Jacob noted, very sensibly 'talked of the hardship of the lack of men's society to celibate women . . . Mrs Nichols thought that meant their need of sex, very stupidly, & [the chair] agreed with me that women want men's companionship more than men want women's'.[163]

What also compounded Jacob's growing isolation and sense of being at odds with her environment in the decades after independence was a growing tension with her sister-in-law, Dorothea. At the core of this acrimony were Jacob's views on gender and her belief that men and women could and should engage in intellectual discourse. Very close to her brother Tom, who took over the family Real Estate business in Waterford, Jacob's visits to his home were increasingly difficult and fraught with strain as a result of the deteriorating relationship between herself and Dorothea. Dorothea took to writing letters highlighting the problems she perceived in Jacob. On 12 March 1925 Jacob noted: 'Powerful letter from D. about my not facing facts, etc – all her conceptions of Mamma & me & what we said to each other, which she treats as accepted facts'.[164] Dorothea viewed Jacob as too uncompromising in regard to her ideas on equality and was suspicious of her political activism.

> D. had a lot of chat (unprovoked) to the effect that I should be content to be intellectual and not want people to dance with me as well. She has that notion about women that it is unreasonable of them to wish both mind & body to be used & pleased – of course a man may always cultivate both.[165]

162 Jacob, 'Third person singular', p. 99.
163 20 Oct. 1939, RJD Ms (90).
164 12 Mar. 1925, RJD Ms (48).
165 12 Sept. 1926, RJD Ms (54).

The situation came to a head in early 1927 and Jacob was very hurt when Tom appeared to take Dorothea's view, questioning her life choices and suggesting therapy. What sparked the confrontation was a talk by the playwright T. C. Murray, on modern Irish drama at the Waterford Literary Society. Coming home Dorothea noted that the girls in Synge's *The Playboy of the Western World* made a hero out of Christy Mahon to which Jacob retorted 'And not the girls only by any means'. Jacob later discovered that Dorothea saw this as 'an instance of the obsession which makes it nearly impossible to talk to me'. The next day the situation reached crisis.

> Went back to the Limes & began talking of Maya – Tom started on how men can't stand her & when I said it was partly their own fault, he rounded on me and told me I was like her & it was getting impossible to talk to me because of my anti-men obsession and they (he & D.) were very worried about me, fearing I wd get like Aunt Is; I was so full of grudges against life.

This entry is an interesting example of the binary thinking which feminist thought gave rise to in the period. The manner in which Jacob rigorously watched for, and refused to ignore, incidents and utterances of gender inequality led to a perception that she was anti-men; even her brother – probably the individual she was closest to – articulating such a viewpoint. Yet what Jacob wanted was a re-organisation of society on gender lines. Instead of the artificiality of gender relations under the ideology of separate spheres she desired natural interaction between men and women on the basis of a common humanity. When Jacob noted that people in Dublin could get on well with her, Tom agreed but asked what sort of people they were.

> It turned psychological then – they think I am wasting and frittering my life among these intolerable Dublin people . . . I shall presently come to associate that house with beastly talk and an atmosphere of constant disapproval, and it is pretty tough to have Tom in it as well as D. They said it was impossible to be interested in the sort of life I lived in Dublin; evidently as long as I am myself I shall be wrong. They talked fairly intelligently, psychologically, about sex, and were very anxious I should get analysed.[166]

By the end of the second decade of the twentieth century there was a large amount of material about psychoanalysis available to the educated public in

166 4–5 Jan. 1927, RJD Ms (55).

Britain in general interest periodicals.[167] And Jacob took the suggestion to see an analyst seriously, discussing the matter with Lucy Kingston on her return to Dublin. Lucy advised her to go to London rather than Germany, the latter being too long a journey without knowing anything of the analyst in advance.[168] Jacob began therapy through correspondence with Mrs Hartley who appeared to diagnose on the basis of Freud's theory of the unconscious and how it influenced everyday thinking and actions.[169] On 5 October 1927 she received a further letter from Mrs Hartley admitting that it would help to meet her in person.[170] Jacob travelled to London on 17 October for a ten-day stay. She left little detailed account of the sessions. What she has noted in her diary suggests that a traumatic episode might have occurred in childhood.

> Talked about my notes to her, childhood sexuality – what's wrong with me is having no latent period of sex wh kids ought to have between 2 and 10. She thinks seeing nakedness might be bad for kids, inflaming their sex feelings – this apparently happened with me, then prohibitions or rebukes wh gave me the permanent sense of repressed guilt about male genitals.[171]

Jacob disliked Mrs Harley's notions around the different roles of men and women, believing her to be akin to Dorothea in that regard. In particular, she disapproved of her perception of women as superior to men 'which result in their practical subordination' and the 'idea that all except personal relationships shd be left to men. It was woeful to hear her'. Yet she approved of the fact that 'she has no orthodox sex morals which is a blessing – doesn't disapprove of masturbation even'.[172] During this analysis both Jacob's father and Ryan were mentioned. We have no independent details of Hartley's view of Jacob. What we can say is that the manner in which Jacob summed up Hartley's comments is akin to her earlier comments in the context of her discomfort with the feeling engendered by her attraction to Tony Farrington. Jacob at this point still believed that her sexual desires were not consistent with society's view of women.

---

167 Dean Rapp, 'The early discovery of Freud by the British General educated public, 1912–1919', *Social History of Medicine* 3: 2 (Aug. 1990), pp. 220–1.

168 13 Jan. 1927, RJD Ms (55).

169 28 Sept. 1927, RJD Ms (58).

170 5 Oct. 1927, RJD Ms (58).

171 18 Oct. 1927, RJD Ms (58).

172 19 Oct. 1927; 21 Oct. 1927, RJD Ms (58).

Feeling myself failing as a girl – woman, I unconsciously tried to be a boy instead – this turning to the male strengthened by sympathy with Papa & admiration of him. So hindered by this in my development that puberty, (period of greatest emotional adjustment) the conflict got too hard for solution and an arrest took place, so that emotionally I am still an adolescent.

Jacob appeared to take comfort in the concept of arrested development that resulted in 'an ego still uncertain, over-occupied with itself, too assertive & too unsure'. Jacob noted Hartley's analysis in this context:

she said that this turning away from normal development to try to be a boy is one manifestation of a very deep trouble, like boils showing trouble inside . . . Failure to accept self means revolt, divided action & arrest of growth.[173]

Hartley used the language of penis envy and castration complex in her analysis of Jacob. She responded to Jacob's sense of exclusion when Helen became engaged in February 1928, objecting to her 'desire to get whatever I cd, and I did see that it was harmful but its very hard to give up wanting *anything*'.[174] Jacob's analysis came to an abrupt end when Mrs Hartley died in June 1928. That same month her Aunt Hannah also died, and after the funeral she perused letters she had sent to her in the light of Mrs Hartley's reading. Reading the letters:

puts me back utterly in the past & made me decide I must stop trying to keep, hoard, remember things – let them come & go, not try to hold them so, & I might lessen that grabbing, hoarding habit which I think keeps things away from me. To begin with, I stopped keeping this diary at the length I used.[175]

Her sister Betty, who died in infancy, was mentioned during analysis as 'the most important thing yet, accounting for my jealousy & lack of self-confidence', while Tom's status as the older child strengthened these feelings and lacunae. Jacob noted how Mrs Hartley 'is greatly impressed at the general circumstances of my childhood – the handicap they gave me'.[176]

Jacob's short-lived attempt at therapy is evidence of her desire to forge meaningful emotional and sexual relationships; her fear that not to do so

173 Notes at end of diary, RJD Ms (59).
174 8 Feb. 1928, RJD Ms (59).
175 19 June 1928, RJD Ms (60).
176 18–22 Oct. 1927; Notes at end of diary, RJD Ms (58).

would render her existence less than whole was one she increasingly believed realised in later life. The stratagems she employed in an attempt to mitigate feelings of inadequacy need to be interrogated to allow focus on the individual perspective in Irish society as opposed to a focus on purely political trajectories and discourses in the period. The role of cultural and social events in contributing to politicisation has been under examined in the historical record.[177] The social and cultural events attended by Jacob offered a sense of community and an outlet for a single woman increasingly struggling with the feelings of uselessness and loneliness described in this chapter. Jacob's adherence to the broad range of republican and left-wing political ideas of the left in the 1920s and 1930s cannot be divorced from her need to socialise and feel a part of something on a human and personal level. Jacob had travelled to feminist and nationalist activism via involvement in the cultural organisations of the revival period. The paradigm of Jacob's early twentieth-century activism was replicated in the early Free State period. Cronin notes the manner in which the Blueshirts 'acted as a family' in the period. Members joined with people of similar age and political affiliation.[178] A similar point can be made about the broad republican and feminist left in the 1920s and 1930s. Jacob's diary evidences how the issues of everyday life – invitations to tea, dining out in Dublin, dances, and literary evenings – merged with the political affiliations and principles discussed in the next chapter.

177 Mike Cronin, *The Blueshirts and Irish Politics* (Dublin: Four Courts Press, 1997), p. 15. Cronin discusses how the Blueshirts, in the tradition of the Fenians, offered an inclusive social programme comprising marches and sports days to inculcate a sense of identity and to provide a social outlet.
178 Ibid., p. 134.

SIX

POLITICS

1922-36

—

The frustration of the aspiration to gender equality ensured that the 1920s and 1930s was an era of disillusionment for radical Irish women. This was mirrored by the sense of betrayal felt by a number who refused to accept the Treaty. Those women who refused to join Fianna Fáil in 1926 and those who briefly joined further experienced the prevailing sense of perfidy. The latter quickly exited the newly formed party once de Valera's true parliamentarian and patriarchal proclivities emerged redolent with tactics of democratic compromise and a perceived refusal to bring the 1916 ideal to completion. For a number in the Free State, feminist and republican causes became linked as those individuals mourned what Lee describes as the failure of 'historical expectations'.[1] It has been noted that the failure of women to advance to levels of political and economic equality in Ireland in the 1920s and 1930s should not be viewed as an example of Irish exceptionalism. Women elsewhere in Europe and in America similarly experienced a frustration of expectations following the granting of the franchise.[2] However, it is necessary still to consider how people like Jacob interpreted perceptions of gender and political oppression. As Leerssen writes, history 'is not just an accumulation of events, but crucially also the human experience of those events'.[3]

Jacob's perception of repression in Ireland in the 1920 and 1930s was holistic and her response was equally multilayered and, at times, contradictory. Her affair with Ryan and her own political beliefs saw her move in political and

1   J. J. Lee, *Ireland 1912–1985* (Cambridge: Cambridge University Press, 1989), p. 173.

2   Mary Daly, '"Oh, Kathleen Ni Houlihan, your way's a thorny way!" The condition of women in twentieth-century Ireland' in Anthony Bradley and Maryann Valiulis (eds), *Gender and Sexuality in Modern Ireland* (Amherst: University of Massachusetts Press, 1997), p. 108.

3   Joep Leerssen, *Mere Irish and Fíor-ghael: Studies in the Idea of Irish Nationality, its Development, and Literary Expression Prior to the Nineteenth Century*, 2nd edn (Cork: Cork University Press in association with Field Day, 1996), p. 4. MacDonagh similarly writes 'every concept of reality is unique, and may be burning glass upon the past if angled correctly'. Oliver MacDonagh, *The Nineteenth Century Novel and Irish Social History: Some Aspects* (Dublin: National University of Ireland, 1970), p. 20.

social circles in which a commitment in varying degrees to violent politics
clashed with her own belief in the efficacy of achieving political change
through pacifist means. One of the chief results of civil war defeat, reinforced
by Cumann na nGaedheal's coercive policies, was to establish the active
republicans who remained into 'a close-knit community'. Work, activism and
social life for many took place with few divisions within republican circles.[4]
Conflicting politics and ideals, however, were still prevalent within republicanism. The IRA during this period manifested support for opposing ideas;
the commitment to militarism acted as a glue holding supporters of disparate
beliefs and aspirations together.[5] Of course, the most blatant contradiction
must be seen in an organisation dedicated to securing full political freedom for
Ireland but opposed to majoritarian democracy.[6] Ryan and Peadar O'Donnell
initiated the 'no free speech for traitors' campaign in November 1932 and
people like Jacob signalled their tacit support for such a campaign by their
attendance at meetings that led to clashes between the IRA and members of
Cumann na nGaedheal and the Army Council Association. Neither Jacob
nor Ryan appeared to notice the irony in this campaign when measured
against their own fervent cries of oppression under legislation such as the 1927
Public Safety Act and following the sustained government move against the
IRA in 1931. Yet earlier Jacob had been quick to denounce as hypocrisy the
public condemnation of the shooting of British soldiers in Cobh by men in
Free State Army uniforms in March 1924. 'Strange & cruel, but people in
public positions did go into mad hysterics over it, murdering Republican
prisoners was no harm beside it apparently.' Three days later she attended the
Dáil and was vehemently critical of Cosgrave who 'rake[d] the dictionary for
all the most violent words to denounce murder'.[7]

4   Fearghal McGarry, *Frank Ryan*, 2nd edn (Dublin: UCD Press, 2010), p. 4.

5   Four separate tendencies have been isolated within the IRA in the 1920s and 1930s: 'apolitical
militarists, conservative supporters of Sinn Féin, socialists and a broad layer committed to armed force
but receptive to radical policies', the reality being even more complex. Ryan and Michael Price, for
example, who had no affinity with socialism in the early 1930s, were instrumental in the founding of
the Republican Congress in 1934. Brian Hanley, *The IRA, 1926–1936* (Dublin: Four Courts Press,
2002), pp. 175–6.

6   Ibid., p. 179.

7   22 Mar. 1924; 25 Mar. 1924, RJD Ms (45). During the incident one man was killed and another 23
persons injured, including five civilians, two of whom were women. On 25 March Cosgrave declared
in the Dáil: 'It is almost inconceivable that any civilised country could produce even four men who
could plot and carry out a deed so foul and so callous. The annals of savagery may be searched, but I
doubt if any worse instance of murderous cowardice can be found.' *Dáil Éireann Debates*, vol. 6,
25 Mar. 1924.

For Jacob the causes of feminism and republicanism had a symbiotic relationship and thus her sense of repression in the Free State was multi-focused. The Cumann na nGaedheal governments of the 1920s and the Fianna Fáil governments of the 1930s both withdrew rights from women and incarcerated the republican activists with whom she interacted. A solution to these issues lay for Jacob in an increasing move towards the left-wing politics of the period. With this answer she followed the political trajectory of members of various disillusioned or marginalised groups in the late 1920s and early 1930s. This move towards the subterranean counter culture of the left undercuts the generalisations sometimes made about the feminist movement in the Free State, as focused on mainstream political parties.[8]

Jacob's increasing republican and feminist marginalisation was underscored by her developing personal isolation as friends and family members married and established new lives. On the basis of her portrayal of the female artist Nix, in *The Troubled House*, Jacob has been described as having 'inherited the exhilarating sense of possibility which characterised the New Woman writers'. The novel has been described as 'optimistic': 'there will be more like Nix, and its approbation of alienation (Nix's as an artist, Theo's as a pacifist) contrasts bracingly with the despair this condition induces in so many of her contemporaries'.[9] However, the novel was written in the early years of the Free State's existence when the anti-climatic nature of life in an independent Ireland had not fully manifested itself. The novel's sense of potential must be contrasted with the very real feelings of personal alienation Jacob experienced as a single woman and a marginal female activist in the years that followed. Moreover, Jacob's Nix is atypical in her writings and Jacob herself occupied a curious space, mediating between the female activist and the New Woman of modernism. Despite her flirtation with the figure of the female artist, Jacob never transcended the national or the political. She never managed to situate herself at the level of 'universal truths or artistic individualism . . . the important enabling strategies for women artists throughout the period', remaining tied to the 'national and communal levels'.[10] She can be categorised in the period by political, national and family links and not, therefore, by ideas of self-definition. Jacob does not then fit Meaney's conceptualisation of the New Woman writer.[11] The optimism critics have seen mirrored in her characterisation of Nix was not borne out by Jacob's actions. Individual need and

8   Daly, 'Oh, Kathleen Ni Houlihan', p. 108.

9   Gerardine Meaney, 'Identity and opposition: women's writing, 1890–1960', in Angela Bourke et al. (eds), *The Field Day Anthology of Irish Writing*, vol. v (Cork: Cork University Press, 2002), p. 979.

10   Ibid., p. 1,071.

11   Ibid.

aspiration of the type preached early in the century by Dora Marsden in *The Freewoman, The New Freewoman* and *The Egoist* were sacrificed in Jacob's case to the 'Cause', indeed, various causes: feminist, republican and the various left-wing offshoots of the 1920s and 1930s.[12]

The Juries Acts of 1924 and 1927 established the government as the arbiter of citizenship. Kevin O'Higgins explained that women could be exempted from jury service because the government was not obliged to impose the duties of citizenship equally.[13] Sheehy Skeffington repeatedly drew attention to the fact that republicans were sent to jail in Ireland during the 1920s by juries comprising only men. Ward points out how for Sheehy Skeffington anti-feminism and anti-republicanism were synonymous.[14] Jacob perceived the situation similarly. In her history of the rise of the United Irishmen[15] she discussed the trial of Hamilton Rowan in January 1794 for distributing copies of the United Irish address to the Dublin Volunteers of 1792. Jacob notes that John Giffard, sheriff of Dublin, packed the jury against Rowan. She remarks on the manner in which the United Irishmen adverted to Giffard's actions when they presented Rowan with an address in February 1794. They commented, she declared, on 'the jury scandal in terms which show that they regarded trial by jury as the very foundation of civil liberty'.[16] The attempt by O'Higgins to remove women from juries in early twentieth-century Ireland was then an attempt, according to Jacob, to place women at a remove from matters relating to life and civil liberty – fundamental issues of citizenship.

Jacob's perception of the repressive attitude towards women's rights in the early years of the Free State was bound up with her overall sense of an atmosphere of censorship and a political discourse of control and coercion emanating from the Cosgrave government. Although historians have placed the 1923 Censorship of Film and the 1929 Censorship of Publications Acts in the wider context of a wave of censorship which prevailed across Europe, for people like Jacob living the specific Irish experience it was impossible to

---

12   For Dora Marsden see Angela K. Smith, *Suffrage Discourse in Britain During the First World War* (Aldershot: Ashgate, 2005).

13   Maryann Valiulis, 'Engendering citizenship: women's relationship to the state in Ireland and the United States in the post-suffrage period' in Maryann Valiulis and Mary O'Dowd (eds), *Women and Irish History* (Dublin: Wolfhound, 1997), p. 167.

14   Margaret Ward, *Unmanageable Revolutionaries: Women and Irish Nationalism* (London: Pluto Press, 1995), p. 165.

15   This was initially serialised in 1928 in *An Phoblacht*.

16   Rosamond Jacob, *The Rise of the United Irishmen 1791–94* (London: George G. Harrap, 1937), pp. 221–2.

perceive the wider historical trends so evident in retrospective.[17] The following diary entry conflates her horror at censorship, at the ban on the divorce
from 1925 and at the attempt by Kevin O'Higgins to remove citizenship rights
from women.

> Whole jury panel for Dublin called – not one woman on it . . . talked with
> Mortished . . . & he told me of . . . their deputation yesterday. They came away
> boiling. Told that Wells, Shaw, Russell, etc wd be banned . . . State is to be
> mentally governed by authority; any attack, for instance, on institution of
> marriage, will be banned, things are worse even than he feared.[18]

To this list of oppressive measures can be added Jacob's objection to the ban
on contraceptives discussed in the previous chapter.

Such lack of respect, as Jacob saw it, for individual freedoms and the failure
of the government to recognise women as full citizens was bound up with her
belief in the lack of political freedom in the Free State. Jacob conflated discriminatory legislation against women with repressive measures against republicans,
notably the oath of allegiance incumbent on all public employees, which she
described as discriminating against 'honest republicans'.[19] Such repressive
measures were, she believed, escalated following the assassination of Kevin
O'Higgins in July 1927, with the introduction of a Public Safety Bill and an
Electoral Amendment Bill under which Dáil candidates would surrender their
seats if they did not take the Oath of Allegiance within a specified time:

> This day's paper had the first account of the government's proposed legislation for
> preventing nomination of candidates unless they take the oath of allegiance, for
> destroying the people's power of initiating legislation, & for dealing in a more
> martial law & irresponsible way with 'treason'. Thus Republicans are encouraged
> to pursue peaceful methods.[20]

17 See, for example, Michael Adams, *Censorship: The Irish Experience* (Alabama: University of
Alabama Press, 1968); Senia Pašeta, 'Censorship and its critics in the Irish Free State, 1922–1932', *Past
and Present* (2003), pp. 193–218; Peter Martin, *Censorship in the Two Irelands 1922–1939* (Dublin: Irish
Academic Press, 2006).
18 Probably Ronald James Patrick Mortished, author of amongst other similar works, 'Ireland, the
League and the Empire', *Foreign Affairs* 8 (1926), pp. 364–6.
19 30–31 July 1925, RJD Ms (48).
20 21 July 1927, RJD Ms (57). Jacob's reference to the people's power of initiating legislation refers to
the attempt by de Valera in 1927 to raise a petition to have the oath abolished. Under the 1922
Constitution the people had the right to initiate legislation or make constitutional amendments. The
first stage was a proposal signed by 50,000 registered voters.

Such measures all emanated, she believed, from a government directed by Catholic morals and committed to censorship and repression. Jacob in the 1920s equated progressive social and political ideals, within which she included a commitment to female equality, with republicanism. In 1926 the annual Congress of the WILPF was held in Dublin. Jacob, one of the chief organisers, noted how it was only republican members of the IIL who voted for any advanced measures, notably a resolution against special protection for women in industries.[21]

For a time Jacob deferred the realisation of her expectations in the area of full female participation in the State, believing that a republican government under de Valera would usher in the type of society she envisaged.[22] *The Rise of the United Irishmen* describes Tone as the first to conceive 'the idea of a democratic state . . . which should be, not a new British colony developing into independence, but the historic Irish nation'. Although Jacob criticised on more than one occasion the assumption of the United Irishmen that 'there is but one sex in history and that male', implicit in her flawed analysis was a belief that present-day republicans had transcended such an assumption.[23] On 1 August 1926 she noted how de Valera had 'learned to say men and women without prompting'.[24] Earlier in July 1924, present at the Sinn Féin offices at 23 Suffolk Street the day following de Valera's release from prison, Jacob noted the huge welcome he received, the shouts of 'Up de Valera! Up the Republic!' She commented: 'It was glorious. I hope he won't ever go & do something that will spoil the recollection of that five minutes'.[25] Such was, however, to be the case; for women such as Jacob a de Valera-led government was to solidify their alienation from the Irish State. When Fianna Fáil proved to be just as, if not more, discriminatory to women in Irish society and equally

21   13 July 1926, RJD Ms (53).

22   For the women of Cumann na mBan, recognition of the Republic was linked to acknowledgment of equality for women – to the full implementation of the ideals enshrined in the Republican proclamation. They were conscious, Ward argues, that members of the pro-Treaty side would not alleviate their political and social oppression as women. On the other hand, they had no clear idea of the different social and economic structures that would distinguish a republican government from the Free State government. Yet, Ward argues, in this 'limited sense Cumann na mBan's rejection of the Treaty was at least partly based upon some feminist understanding of its implications'. Ward, *Unmanageable Revolutionaries*, p. 178.

23   Jacob, *The Rise of the United Irishmen*, pp. 58–9, p. 67. The review of the book in the *Waterford News* in September 1937 criticised Jacob for mentioning the subjection of women during the period. 8 Sept. 1937, RJD Ms (82).

24   1 Aug. 1926, RJD Ms (53).

25   17 July 1924, RJD Ms (46).

as authoritarian as the Cosgrave-led governments, Jacob turned towards left-wing republicanism while maintaining her internationalist outlook. The left had much to attract Jacob. There was a shared commitment to many of the ideals that galvanised Jacob, in particular a commitment to social and gender equality. Peadar O'Donnell, for example, had in 1918 agitated for equal pay increases for women workers in the Monaghan Asylum and criticised the Derry trade union movement for failing to support women workers in the 1920 shirt cutters' strike.[26]

THE STREET THEATRE
OF REPUBLICANISM

When the terms of the Anglo-Irish Treaty were published in December 1921, Jacob wrote: 'Terms of the peace Treaty in the papers – seemed to me very poor. I was surprised at Griffith & Collins'. Two days later she was more optimistic on the basis of de Valera's position: 'De Valera's statement that he couldn't recommend the Treaty illuminated the atmosphere & made me feel able to hold up my head again. I never thought he had it in him . . . I didn't think he would ever trust his judgement against Griffith & Collins.'[27] Very quickly and enthusiastically Jacob became involved in anti-Treaty politics and organisations. Earlier, as hostilities escalated before the outbreak of the Civil War, she had been part of the women's delegation comprising the various feminist societies who attempted to broker peace, meeting both Cosgrave and the Republicans. Once again, Jacob participated in the role of onlooker: 'I went for the interest of the thing & had nothing to say of my own'.[28] As the conflict emerged into the open she attended meetings to discuss the treatment of republican prisoners in Mountjoy, listening to such speakers as Bridie O'Mullane who had been arrested and sentenced in October 1919 for inciting the murder of policemen.[29] The refusal to grant prison access to family members of the incarcerated led to the establishment in August 1922 of the Women Prisoners' Defence League (WPDL): Charlotte Despard was President with

26 Donal Ó Drisceoil, *Peadar O'Donnell* (Cork: Cork University Press, 2001), p. 13, p. 16.

27 7 Dec. 1921; 9 Dec. 1921, RJD Ms (40).

28 1 July 1922, RJD Ms (41).

29 Following her release O'Mullane acted as a full-time organiser for Cumann na mBan and was active on the anti-Treaty side during the civil war. In November 1922 O'Mullane was arrested and incarcerated in Mountjoy, Kilmainham and the North Dublin Union. Sinead McCoole, *No Ordinary Women: Irish Female Activists in the Revolutionary Years* (Dublin: O'Brien, 2004), pp. 194–6.

Maud Gonne as Secretary. To become a member you had to have a family
relationship to a prisoner and pay a halfpence weekly. The organisation publicised details of the treatment of prisoners.[30]

In publicly marking the execution of republican prisoners and by holding
vigils outside Irish prisons the WPDL were to the fore in promoting the
concept of republican politics as spectacle or street theatre.[31] Protest at the
incarceration of the individual served as a vehicle for the demonstration of a
public republican culture that laid claim to geographical space within the city.
By rendering itself publicly visible the republican community in this way manifested its strength and resilience. The harsh treatment of women in Free State
jails which led to hunger striking was denounced on the streets of Dublin. The
women who orchestrated the vigils outside Mountjoy, who maintained safe
houses and who sheltered men on the run during the Civil War, underscored
the fact that the republican opposition to the Free State Government was not
safely contained as a parliamentary opposition. Republican opposition had
invaded the domestic sphere or, alternatively, the domestic sphere was increasingly, in this context, indistinguishable from the public sphere. The republican
opposition was porous, diffused throughout the population. Public spectacle –
violence or vigil – was used to demonstrate the republican presence at certain
flashpoints and at key geographical spaces.

The significance of the role of women in the WPDL, who were to the fore
in this public demonstration of republicanism, has possibly been underrated
or elided. The fact that members needed a familial connection to one of those
incarcerated in the jails of the Free State meant that these women have not
been viewed as active participants in the republicanism of the 1920s, but,
instead, in terms of their family or domestic role. The manner in which those
within the wider republican community without such a familial connection to
the prison site, such as Jacob, could still participate in the vigils and public
events hosted under the auspices of the League needs to be considered.
Although women's political roles expanded in Ireland during the revolutionary
and Civil War periods, there was nothing amounting to full equality. Women's
entry into the public sphere of revolutionary politics was often roundabout,
couched in the language and constructions of domesticity and often its full

---

30   Ward, *Unmanageable Revolutionaries*, p. 190. Charlotte Despard (1844–1939) was a philanthropist
and a suffrage and labour activist in England. She moved to Ireland in 1921 and was involved in the
politics of the republican opposition to the Free State. See Margaret Mulvihill, *Charlotte Despard*
(London: Pandora Press, 1989).

31   Nicolas Allen's recent work considers aspects of the 'culture of staged protest' in the 1920s. Allen
discusses the manner in which 'civic space was shaped by public rallies, theatre riots and ceilidhs'. Nicolas
Allen, *Modernism, Ireland and Civil War* (Cambridge: Cambridge University Press, 2009), p. 42.

significance in the wider canvas of revolutionary activism in Ireland ignored or fringed. Public vigil in honour of family members brought women of the WPDL and other female activists subversively into the visible public domain. Their discernible presence, acting as the fulcrum of republican street theatre, served to underwrite the uncontained nature of the threat to the authority of the Free State.

As in the period before 1922, the cathartic nature of republican demonstration emerged strongly as a feature of Jacob's political activities. As in earlier years, she enjoyed the sense of belonging and solidarity, although not without her usual critical edge. She attended a procession on the afternoon of 12 November 1922 from Mountjoy in support of the incarcerated Mary MacSwiney, commenting superciliously: 'Some girls couldn't be torn away from their occupation of [jeering?] the soldier at the gate even to walk in the procession'.[32] This sense of condescension was reflected in her account of an earlier visit to Mountjoy with Meg Connery:

> We found a very bullish crowd of relatives outside the prison gates, lots of noisy kids about & some standing inside the grounds, having climbed the wall, shouting up to the prisoners in D wing, who had taken the iron bars out of their windows & were leaning out or sitting on the sills. It was a rather absurd scene, & I never saw anything more raffish and unimpressive.[33]

Mary MacSwiney was arrested on 4 November 1922 under the Emergency Powers Act, accused of delivering seditious anti-Treaty speeches. Imprisoned without trial she immediately began her hunger strike as a protest against British hegemony in Ireland.[34] Just a week after Jacob's participation in the MacSwiney procession she again travelled to Mountjoy, this time to see Annie MacSwiney who was now also on hunger strike outside the gates of the prison, having been refused permission to see her sister. The next day Jacob went to see, amongst others, James Douglas to enquire if he could wield any influence on the Government to procure the release of Mary MacSwiney.[35] In the event MacSwiney was released without explanation on 28 November.[36]

32 12 Nov. 1922, RJD Ms (42).

33 4 July 1922, RJD Ms (41).

34 George Sweeney, 'Irish hunger strikes and the cult of self-sacrifice', *Journal of Contemporary History* 28: 3 (July 1993), pp. 428–9.

35 20–21 Nov. 1922, RJD Ms (42).

36 It has been suggested that Richard Mulcahy, Minister for Defence, argued that leniency would reflect best on the Free State Government, particularly following the executions of 17 November. Charlotte Fallon, *Soul of Fire: A Biography of Mary MacSwiney* (Cork: Mercier Press, 1986), pp. 92–3.

Jacob found herself within the walls of Mountjoy in January 1923. Minding Hanna's house she had agreed that the republicans could set up a typing station on the premises. In doing this she believed she was following Hanna's wishes, the latter having told her to give shelter to any republicans on the run.[37] Whatever her intentions at the time, retrospectively Hanna was annoyed. On 8 February 1923, shortly after Jacob's release, Owen visited her for tea bearing a letter from his mother 'which made me feel awful, she was in such a panic about him & disapproved so of the office'.[38]

Jacob's diary account of her incarceration betrays no sense of distress. Indeed, the gossipy tone of the entries suggests that she enjoyed the sense of community the prison experience engendered similar to the manner in which she enjoyed the communal nature of political activism.[39] When she was released at the end of January her diary sounded a note of regret: 'M Skinnider's drill class started on Monday . . . I wished they had started the class sooner; I only got 4 days of it'.[40] When fellow inmate, Mrs Cogley, was released she wrote how it 'was nice to see a Mountjoy face again and hear of things since I left'; the two gossiped about the strong dislike taken by many prisoners to Macardle.[41] Despite the dislike of Macardle among those within Mountjoy, Jacob's friendship with her began from this point. She met Macardle's father to give him news of how she was coping with imprisonment. Jacob did not blink when Sir Thomas Callan Macardle declared that jail 'will be good for her in some ways, that she has led too purely academic a life always among the same sort of people'.[42]

Jacob's 'jail journal' is filled with petty details of cliques, rows and the banalities of day-to-day prison life; at a concert there 'were sweets in a bucket passed round by M. Deegan,[43] but of course they were frightfully robbed the first time they came within reach of M. Skinnider, and that corner of the room had to be passed very carefully afterwards'.[44] Classes were held in Irish language, French, drama and home nursing, Jacob being delegated to organise

37   Damian Doyle, 'A bio-critical study of Rosamond Jacob and her contemporaries', unpublished PhD thesis, University of Colorado, 2000, p. 39.

38   8 Feb. 1923, RJD Ms (43).

39   This was a common experience of both male and female prisoners in the civil war period, although more has been written of the former. English describes O'Malley's experience as akin to 'university life' and discusses the sense of intimacy and shared purpose. Richard English, *Ernie O'Malley: IRA Intellectual* (Oxford: Oxford University Press, 1998), p. 25.

40   25 Jan. 1923, RJD Ms (43).

41   12 Feb. 1923, RJD Ms (43).

42   4 Feb. 1923, RJD Ms (43).

43   Maura Deegan was later involved in the riots in April 1923 as prisoners from Mountjoy were removed to the North Dublin Union. McCoole, *No Ordinary Women*, p. 123.

44   14 Jan. 1923, RJD Ms (43).

talks and debates on Saturdays and to organise a beginner's class in Irish.[45] The debate on 21 January was that 'in all matters relating to the community, without exception, the will of the majority shd prevail'. Because there were no sweets there was 'no brawling'.[46]

Republican society on the outside was reproduced at a micro level within the walls of the prison. Jacob's diary offers the reader no preamble to her imprisonment; the raid on Hanna's house is not mentioned although there is a break in the entries. When the diary resumes the reader is not immediately aware that Jacob is recording events in prison and the first prison entry reads as so many of her earlier accounts of republican life in Dublin, complete with tea and gossip.

> There was a dance this night in the hall ... The band sat on the spiral stairs and did splendidly with combs and a tin box & 2 knives ... I had tea with Dorothy & Madame this evening; Mrs Cogley was there too. We were talking about Cosgrave's egregious answer to the last local body's pleas for peace, taking it for granted, among other things that everyone who wants peace is a republican.[47]

As within the wider republican society, Jacob was a fringe figure during her time in prison, although it should be noted that this was brief as she was released on 25 January.[48] Again the tone of the diary is very much one of reportage. Key figures emerged within the prison hierarchy.[49] One such clique developed around the 'Humphrey's[50] crowd [who] were locked in their cell all day, because they turned out the extra bed & broke it yesterday, & barricaded their door last night so that it couldn't be put in again'.[51] This group favoured constant conflict with prison authorities and in an objection to overcrowding barricaded themselves in their cell, refusing to admit new prisoners.[52] These women clearly had

45   19 Jan. 1923; 25 Jan. 1923, RJD Ms (43).

46   21 Jan. 1923, RJD Ms (43).

47   6 Jan. 1923, RJD Ms (43).

48   Family members had Jacob sign a release document undertaking not to work against the Free State Government. For details of this document see McCoole, *No Ordinary Women*, p. 102.

49   Oonagh Walsh notes how the hierarchy of Cumann na mBan outside the prison was replicated within. Oonagh Walsh, 'Testimony from imprisoned women' in David Fitzpatrick (ed.), *Revolution? Ireland 1917–1923* (Dublin: Trinity History Workshop, 1990), pp. 76–7.

50   Both Nell Humphries and her daughter Sighle were in jail during this period following a raid on 4 November 1922 on their family home in which the anti-treatite Ernie O'Malley was hiding. McCoole, *No Ordinary Women*, p. 95.

51   9 Jan. 1923, RJD Ms (43).

52   McCoole, *No Ordinary Women*, pp. 100–1.

power within the prison: 'Tonight 5 women from Dundalk were brought in. P's[53] orders were that the small cells were to be asked if they wd receive them, & if they refused, they could go on the landings. The council met today & decided that for the present anyway there is to be no fight'.[54] The incarcerated were able and willing to assert themselves and from Jacob's account were able to maintain their power and dignity through solidarity and communality:

> Strange noises went on upstairs last night, & 7 soldiers were here besides P. this morning we heard that he had attacked the Kerry cell on the top landing – M Comerford was in bed on the landing, & he told her to get up & dress, and when she had done so, he got the door opened. The inmates came out, (of themselves or by force, I don't know which) P. & the soldiers put in the extra bed and threw the 7 inmates & M. Comerford after it. Miss Higgins[55] broke a basin by accident; & this morning we hear that Esther Davis[56] threw the bits out of the gashole at Miss Phillips[57], & abused her. They cheered & sang songs up there when the soldiers were leaving. Today the whole top landing is locked up.[58]

Three days after her release Jacob attended a meeting in O'Connell Street to recount her prison experience but was castigated by Gonne and Despard because she failed to 'pitch it half strong enough'.[59]

Jacob continued to record the religiosity associated with the republican theatre of defiance. In October 1922 the Catholic church issued a joint pastoral excommunicating those who persisted in anti-State activities. This made it all the more important for Republicans to convince onlookers of their essential Catholicism.[60] Those who participated in the procession to Arbor Hill and Mountjoy on 16 December 1923 sang hymns as they passed along the quays,

---

53   This probably refers the Deputy Governor, Paudeen O'Keefe, who looked after female prisoners. Ibid., p. 100.

54   9 Jan. 1923, RJD Ms (43).

55   Wardress in Mountjoy. McCoole, *No Ordinary Women*, p. 113.

56   In Mountjoy for hitting a policeman. Ibid., p. 111.

57   Probably another wardress.

58   10 Jan. 1923, RJD Ms (43).

59   28 Jan. 1923, RJD Ms (43).

60   Charlotte Fallon, *Soul of Fire: A Biography of Mary MacSwiney* (Cork: Mercier Press, 1986), p. 90. In October 1923 it was mooted at the Sinn Féin Árd Fheis that in support of the republican hunger strikers the rosary should be publicly said across the villages and towns of Ireland for a period of seven days. English, *Ernie O'Malley*, p. 90.

stopping to pray at the Royal Barracks for de Valera's release.[61]Although Jacob, as noted, enjoyed the sense of shared participation, her anti-religious outlook meant that at best she viewed such outpourings of religiosity with some scepticism. Indeed, a year later, in 1924, she described as 'awful' the scenes in O'Casey's *Juno and the Paycock* 'when the women got eloquent in prayer'.[62] When she followed the bodies, returned to their families in 1924, of executed republicans, Liam Mellows, Joe McKelvey, Rory O'Connor and Dick Barrett,[63] from Mountjoy to the hall in Hardwicke Street, Jacob was irritated by the lack of names on the coffins but was relieved that 'they were not in a church'. When Childers, as a Protestant, was left alone in the Hall, the other bodies being buried from White Friars Church, Jacob noted wryly: 'Pity they weren't all left there'.[64] At the time of the executions she described Childers's fate as the 'worst public thing done by Irishmen for a century I think'. However, it was the execution of Mellows whom she had known in Waterford in the pre-revolutionary period that really impacted on her: 'All this time I'd been congratulating myself that Mellows was safe anyway, whoever they might catch. It was awful. I can't see that there is any further height of atrocity left for the FS government to reach'.[65]

On 27 April 1923 de Valera issued the order to ceasefire. Jacob supported the declaration believing that it 'put all the onus of continuing the war on the government'.[66] And in fact, the ceasefire initially led to the internment of further prisoners.[67] However, by November 1923 the Cosgrave government began to release republicans after the death of two men on a hunger strike that began on 13 October.[68] As prisoners were released Jacob met trains and participated in providing halfway houses for men en route from Dublin prisons to

61   16 Sept. 1923; 17 Oct. 1923, RJD Ms (44). Smith discusses the manner in which the commemoration of the seventh anniversary of the execution of the leaders of 1916 by the women in Kilmainham Jail was similarly imbued with religiosity. Nadia Clare Smith, *Dorothy Macardle: A Life* (Dublin: Woodfield Press, 2007), p. 42.

62   7 Mar. 1924, RJD Ms (45). In Act Two Mrs Tancred mourns her son, an anti-Treaty casualty of the civil war invoking the support of the 'Mother o'God' the 'Blessed virgin' and the 'Sacred Heart of the Crucified Jesus'. Sean O'Casey, *Juno and the Paycock* in John P. Harrington (ed.), *Modern Irish Drama* (New York: W. W. Norton, 1991), p. 235.

63   These men were executed in 1922 by the Free State government, in retaliation for the murder of Seán Hales, TD, and the wounding of Pádraic Ó Maille, TD.

64   28–29 Oct. 1924, RJD Ms (46).

65   24 Nov. 1922; 7 Dec. 1922, RJD Ms (42).

66   29 Apr. 1923, RJD Ms (44).

67   Ward, *Unmanageable Revolutionaries*, pp. 196–7.

68   The fatalities were Denis Barry and Andrew Sullivan. For details see Sweeney, 'Irish hunger strikes and the cult of self sacrifice', p. 430.

homes throughout Ireland.[69] She worked periodically at 6 Harcourt Street, the
headquarters of the Women's Reception Committee set up to look after the
needs of released prisoners. She recorded the clothing requirements of released
prisoners or travelled to Roebuck, the County Dublin home of Gonne and
Despard, to take statements from ex-prisoners. In true character Jacob took
pleasure in the sight of any attractive men who passed through the office
commenting, in particular, on 'a lovely, tall bright looking, handsome boy',
Nicholas O'Brien. Indeed, Jacob noted how he 'was so masculinely attractive
that I was shy to ask him if he wanted underclothes, which I'd have no
hesitation in doing with most of them'.[70] Even before she met Ryan, Jacob was
attuned to attractive men. She once wrote of travelling on the outside seat of a
Dublin tram and how she froze 'because there was such a handsome young
man in sight, just inside, whom I could not have seen properly from anywhere
else – dark, with an honest, rather square, serious face, and a beautiful mouth'.[71]
Her friend Helen objected to Jacob's 'interest in male nudity'.[72] Helen felt that
there 'was too much about boys' looks' in *The Troubled House* for the 'ordinary
reader'.[73] In *Callaghan* also Jacob spent a degree of time describing Andy
Callaghan's physical appearance. At the hurling match Callaghan 'was so well
made that he looked graceful even in his ugly costume'.[74]

At the end of 1923, family commitments in Waterford once again forced
Jacob to leave Dublin; she remained in Waterford until 18 February 1924. This
time her Aunt Hannah was ill, and a letter from her brother Tom informed her
that she would have to travel.[75] While this letter, no longer extant, must have
been dictated by a concern that Hannah might die, there was clearly also a sense
that Jacob, as a single woman, had a duty to care for the elderly members of her
family. This commitment was ongoing. In September 1927 she attended Dr
Ahern in Waterford with Tom to discuss her aunt's health. Jacob commented:
'Looks like I'd have to be in Waterford a good deal in the winter'.[76]

In the first decade of independence Jacob stood firmly behind de Valera. In
the 1923 General Election she cast her vote for Countess Markievicz but with
adulation declared 'If only one had a vote in Clare in it would be grand'.[77] She

69   See, for example, 2 Nov., 7–8 Nov. 1923, RJD Ms (44).
70   27 Nov. 1923; 20 Apr. 1924; 27 Apr. 1924, RJD Ms (45).
71   30 Aug. 1925, RJD Ms (49).
72   22 Sept. 1932, RJD Ms (71).
73   20 July 1936, RJD Ms (79).
74   F. Winthrop, *Callaghan* (Dublin: Martin Lester, n.d. [1920]), p. 13.
75   10 Dec. 1923, RJD Ms (45).
76   8 Sept. 1927, RJD Ms (58).
77   27 Aug. 1923, RJD Ms (44).

described de Valera as 'practical' and 'level headed' during his election work in February 1925.[78] Her absences from Dublin due to her Waterford commit- ments clearly played a part in her less than central role in the political and welfare activities of republican Dublin, her involvement mostly consisted in routine election work. She canvassed for Sinn Féin during the run up to the November 1924 by-election, a form of work, as noted, she detested but felt it was her duty to perform. Working in the area around Molesworth Street she noted the lack of political concern in the area, commenting that those she spoke to, mostly caretakers, 'were surprised to hear there was an election on'.[79] During the June 1925 elections Jacob presented herself at the Sinn Féin offices headed by Oscar Traynor[80] in Gardiner's Row and was relieved to be allowed fold leaflets instead of the usual round of canvassing. However, Sheehy Skeffington's attempt to secure election in 1925 did give Jacob an added incentive; she wrote enthusiastically when the possibility of Hanna standing emerged in late 1924: 'that *wd* give one some interest in canvassing'.[81] As on so many other occasions Jacob enjoyed the camaraderie of election work. 'I do like a place like that', she wrote of Gardiner's Row in the lead up to the March 1925 by-election, '& the talk that goes on in it'.[82] The election results she described as 'miserable', Sinn Féin gaining only 11 per cent of the poll despite the fact that Cumann na nGaed- heal did not run a party ticket. However, Jacob was glad Traynor 'is in & O'Mullane not'.[83] She was full of praise for de Valera's speech at Bodenstown in that year. She commented on how he did not yield to the temptation to abuse the Free State government and supporters and compared him favour- ably to Tone in that respect – her ultimate label of praise: 'Tone himself, in de V's position that day, wd certainly have yielded to the temptation'.[84]

---

78   25 Feb. 1925, RJD Ms (47).

79   6 Nov. 1925; 11 Nov. 1925, RJD Ms (46).

80   Oscar Traynor (1886–1963). Traynor was a republican activist involved in 1916 and to the fore in the guerrilla warfare of the Anglo-Irish War in Dublin. Traynor was elected a TD for Sinn Féin in 1925. He lost his seat in 1927 and became a Fianna Fáil TD in 1932. http://www.oxforddnb.com/ view/article/65861, accessed 13 Aug. 2008.

81   14 Dec. 1924, RJD Ms (47).

82   2–4 Mar. 1925, RJD Ms (48).

83   13 Mar. 1925, RJD Ms (48); Richard Dunphy, *The Making of Fianna Fáil Power in Ireland 1923–1948* (Oxford: Clarendon Press, 1995), p. 65.

84   21 June 1925, RJD Ms (48).

THE ADVENTURE OF REPUBLICANISM

Very quickly a tone of nostalgia rather than optimism pervaded Jacob's descriptions of the politics post independence. Attending the Sinn Féin Árd Fheis in the Mansion House in October 1923 she noted how 'it was grand to see it all again all the same, in the round room just like old times, & as many delegates as there used to be'. The escape of 19 republican prisoners from Mountjoy in November 1925[85] caused Jacob to inhale a large breath of the excitement of past times:

> Wonderful. Like old times again only better. D. [Macardle] found they wanted places for them, so we had one that evening, a cheerful buxom county boy named Murphy, very nice as a guest and full of interesting information about the escape & how it was done.

Her description of the escapee as a cheerful buxom country boy indicates the almost naïve sense of adventure she experienced. She escorted one escapee to a safe house and enjoyed the sense of subterfuge as the adornment of a pair of glasses 'changed him greatly'. [86] The manner in which republican campaigns of the 1920s and 1930s were designed, not to achieve concrete and far-reaching results but to keep membership busy, is documented by those who have written on the IRA during the period, and Jacob's activities in many respects fall into this category. The Boycott British Goods campaign of the autumn of 1932, for example, provided 'excitement and activity for its members'. The consequent arrest of IRA personnel allowed for 'protest marches, postering, wall painting and another round of activity. In the longer term this would achieve nothing concrete but would keep the membership busy and maintain the façade that they were preparing for war'.[87] Jacob's attraction to Ryan could also be seen in this context of a desire to construct her life in terms of adventure. McGarry correctly notes how much of the attraction for her was Ryan's 'gunman image'. [88] His wild stories of war allowed Jacob to transcend, for brief periods, the ordinary and the domestic sphere.

Despite her own nostalgia at the first Sinn Féin Árd Fheis following the Civil War Truce, Jacob shrewdly noted how Mary MacSwiney, in the chair due to the imprisonment of de Valera since 14 August 1923, betrayed the nationalist tendency to dwell on the politics of the past. What Jacob touched

---

85 This escape was orchestrated in part by George Gilmore. Hanley, *The IRA*, p. 192.

86 28 Nov. 1925; 9 Dec. 1925, RJD Ms (50).

87 Hanley, *The IRA*, p. 187.

88 McGarry, *Frank Ryan*, p. 5.

upon here was the manner in which the Party became sidelined due to its failure to recognise, and thereby engage with, the institutions of the State.[89] The past-orientated focus resulted in Sinn Féin's lack of a constructive future policy, disappointing Jacob even at this early stage in Free State politics.[90] This in turn made her a ready and willing candidate to join Fianna Fáil in 1926. Sinn Féin's lack of constructive policies for the future direction of Ireland, of course, evinced much criticism from the supporters of Cumann na nGaedheal. George Russell, for example, devoted much time as editor of the *Irish Statesman*[91] from 1923 to 1930 on the need for Sinn Féin and later Fianna Fáil to formulate an alternative set of social and economic policies to those of the Cosgrave governments: 'they must have clear imagination of a culture, a social order, a civilisation, an economic life attainable and of a higher quality than that possible under the existing constitution'.[92]

Sinn Féin tended to blame all the ills of the country on England; their policy was a vague amalgamation of Griffith's ideas of self sufficiency and principles drawn from the Democratic Programme of the first Dáil, radical sounding but lacking in substance.[93] Such criticism of the lack of clear policies amongst the republican opposition should be viewed in the context of what Tom Garvin refers to as the republican 'intellectual tradition' in Ireland. Garvin argues that Irish 'insurrectional republicanism is commonly pre-political in character, representing a somewhat unstructured wish for independence, freedom and change from an uncongenial present to a hazily imagined future rather than a highly organised political blueprint.'[94] It is noteworthy that Jacob's criticism was one which emanated from within the ranks of the republican opposition itself. However, this is not to suggest that Jacob had any highly developed political insight. Such perceptive criticisms from Jacob must be countered or juxtaposed with her naïve glee, for example, when Seán MacBride and other republican prisoners escaped from the ambulance that was taking them to Kilmainham in the same month as the 1923 Sinn Féin Árd Fheis: 'How nice', she wrote, 'to get a pleasant piece of news sometimes'.[95] Jacob, critical of speech making, was desirous of the evolution of republican politics

89 Dunphy, *The Making of Fianna Fáil Power in Ireland*, p. 64.

90 15–17 Oct. 1923, RJD Ms (44).

91 The *Irish Statesman* was financed by a group of Irish Americans and was designed to promote a reasonable trial for the Treaty settlement as Russell himself described it in the last edition of the paper. *Irish Statesman*, 12 Apr. 1930.

92 'The Free State and Fianna Fail', *Irish Statesman*, 4 Dec. 1926.

93 Dunphy, *The Making of Fianna Fáil Power in Ireland*, p. 65.

94 Tom Garvin, *1922: The Birth of Irish Democracy* (Dublin: Gill & Macmillan, 1996), pp. 11–12.

95 22 Oct. 1923, RJD Ms (44).

towards a 32-county republican-led Ireland. Events manifesting intrigue, subterfuge and a sense of adventure, all encapsulated in MacBride's escape from Mountjoy, often constituted republican advancement for Jacob, lacking as she did fully developed political acumen and knowledge. At the same time it is clear from her diary that within the anti-Treaty side there was, on the part of a few, recognition of the need to move beyond vague aspirations towards the construction of policies that had tangible possibilities for potential interest groups aligned to the republican opposition. Jacob recorded details of a lecture by Macardle on Mitchel delivered in Gonne's Roebuck House noting how 'she & I & Joan [Hanna] & Mrs Despard & Mrs MacBride were arguing that the Republican movement shd come out squarely as Labour – anti the capitalist economic system, if its to do any good really, all of us against Dorothy'.[96] Jacob recorded her presence at a debate in May 1925 on the topic of whether Sinn Féin should adopt a fighting policy. She talked of the sense of seriousness at this meeting and recorded the nascent move towards republican socialist ideals, noting enthusiasm on the idea of the 'Republican movement coming out definitely for the workers' republic if not for socialism. One man actually condemned the private ownership of means of production'.[97]

Despite her draw towards the adventure of republicanism, Jacob did have an organic perception of the political, believing that politics was more than party politics and that political involvement necessitated a commitment to a radical reorganisation of society at a socio-economic level and at the level of gender. Historians assessing the lack of commitment by the Cumann na nGaedheal governments to relieving the high levels of Irish poverty have commented on the manner in which the Irish revolution was 'more political than social', a fact that was not lost on contemporaries such as Jacob.[98] She criticised a Miss Cranwell: 'neither of them [herself and Miss Scarlett] seemed to have any conception of politics except *party* politics'. [99] Jacob, despite her dislike of Markievicz, agreed with her that politics should be about 'issues of food, clothing and housing' and was interested in debate and discussion which focused on the alleviation of socio-economic problems. During the period 1922–33 Dublin Corporation failed to sufficiently focus on the provision of local authority housing, the average annual output being only 483; in 1929 the Department of Local Government and Public Health estimated the total housing need for the entire 26 counties at 43,656.[100] Recalling her husband's

96   26 Apr. 1925, RJD Ms (48).

97   7 May 1925, RJD Ms (48).

98   Diarmaid Ferriter, *The Transformation of Ireland: 1900–2000* (London: Profile Books, 2004), p. 298.

99   13 Jan. 1925, RJD Ms (47).

100 Ferriter, *The Transformation of Ireland*, pp. 318–19.

Labour Party involvement with the Pearse Street Council of Action which investigated complaints of inadequate housing and rack renting in the late 1930s and early 1940s, Andrée Sheehy Skeffington remarked how the 1941 Dublin slum photographs resembled those of 1912.[101] Yet an emphasis on slum clearance was not evident until the early 1930s. On 16 December 1930 Jacob recorded her presence at the inaugural session of the Law Students' Debating Society at King's Inns and was critical of what would in later decades become the problem of mass housing estates outside Dublin without sufficient attention to infrastructural provision:

> Dillon lecturing on slums – his cure is to build lots of little cheap houses on outskirts of Dublin & give free bus rides to work . . . Gavan Duffy rather good – he wanted to build decent houses *in* towns instead of slums, but was clear nothing *would* be done till some leader arose with a raging storm of public opinion behind him. No one mentioned birth control, of course, or even making it illegal (to landlord) for more than so many people to live in one room.[102]

Jacob's reference to how the lack of reproductive rights and information impacted on levels of poverty and the disastrously inadequate levels of housing for the urban poor indicates a different, but equally relevant, gender perspective on the socio-economic realities of the period. The effects of the lack of even basic knowledge of birth control was something which poor women bore the brunt of as they struggled to create a domestic sphere on a day-to-day basis with growing families and insufficient resources or living space.

FIANNA FÁIL: FOUNDATIONS

De Valera's move towards re-entry into the field of parliamentary politics was mooted at the Árd Fheis held in Rathmines Town Hall in 1925. Sheehy Skeffington informed Jacob of the proceedings of a secret session, in particular of the opposition de Valera encountered to his amendment 'about going into the Dáil if the oath was gone'. At an open session the following day Jacob described de Valera as 'talking great sense, how the people have a right to take

101 Andrée Sheehy Skeffington, *Skeff: A Life of Owen Sheehy Skeffington 1909–1970* (Dublin: Lilliput, 1991), p. 114.
102 16 Dec. 1930, RJD Ms (65). George Gavan Duffy was the brother of Louise Gavan Duffy. He was one of de Valera's plenipotentiaries during the Anglo-Irish Treaty negotiations in 1921. Gavan Duffy was appointed a judge of the High Court in 1936.

less than independence if they like'.[103] At the next Árd Fheis in March 1926 de Valera unveiled his proposals to the Sinn Féin Party, making clear the manner in which he felt stymied and constricted by party members who refused to adapt principles to a changing political context:

> De V. very eager at one point, in saying he wanted the question of principle cleared up, how he's been gasping for breath for a year in the rarefied atmosphere Mary Mac & others keep up & can't stand it any more – won't go into the monastery as they want, even if it is the higher life.

According to Jacob's account of the debate on the oath at the 1926 Árd Fheis de Valera played the role of pragmatist to the idealist Mary MacSwiney. MacSwiney parried principle against de Valera's stress on the need for the party to advance, the latter claiming that the 2nd Dáil was not fundamental to the Republic and that the Irish nation transcended the Republic.[104] Sheehy Skeffington had earlier noted the increasing rigidity of MacSwiney's political stance. In 1921 Jacob described MacSwiney as having become 'painfully official since she was in USA, & conforms to the official refusal to help or speak for any good cause obnoxious to the USA government, for fear of displeasing it, which depresses H. in a person who used to be so good'.[105] During the period of de Valera's imprisonment in 1923–4 MacSwiney had elevated parliamentary abstention and the non-recognition of the institutions of the State to the level of core principles of the Party; de Valera, by contrast, saw abstentionism as a tactical tool.[106] Jacob's account of the 1926 Árd Fheis presents de Valera as the fulcrum, holding together a party of irreconcilables. Meeting Ryan in the middle of Stephen's Green during a tea break from proceedings on 10 March, Jacob noted how he 'disapproves of the proposals but knows we couldn't get on without de Valera'. Ryan informed her how he got as far as the door and 'thought it looked as if only de V.'s influence as chairman kept us from open war'. While the events of the Árd Fheis, initiating de Valera's trajectory out of the political wilderness towards parliamentary politics, made Ryan state 'something very disreputable about wanting to go out with a gun again', Jacob herself was supportive.[107]

103 17–18 Sept. 1925, RJD Ms (49).

104 9–11 Mar. 1926, RJD Ms (51).

105 30 Aug. 1921, RJD Ms (40). Mary and Muriel MacSwiney were invited to America by the commission to examine conditions in Ireland sponsored by the nationalist Irish-American newspaper, *The Nation*. They left Ireland on 26 November 1920. Muriel returned to Ireland in early 1921 with Mary remaining until the summer. For details of this tour see Fallon, *Soul of Fire*, pp. 66–74.

106 Dunphy, *The Making of Fianna Fáil Power*, pp. 63–4.

107 9–11 Mar. 1926, RJD Ms (51).

At the March 1926 Árd Fheis the Sinn Féin Party narrowly rejected by 223 votes to 218 de Valera's motion that the removal of the oath of allegiance changed the issue of parliamentary representation from one of principle to one of policy; de Valera resigned as President the following day.[108] Jacob herself 'spoke heretically' during the debate for de Valera's proposals and was flattered to find that 'he knows my name now, anyhow'. Describing de Valera's resignation from Sinn Féin and noting his parting speech, Jacob again laid stress on his pragmatism, on his belief that the 'Free State administration [was] solidifying itself as an institution & the people not prepared to go back on what they done of late'.[109] On 8 April 1926 Jacob formally resigned from Sinn Féin to join Fianna Fáil as officially named on 2 April. Beyond speaking in favour of de Valera's proposals in 1926, she did not, as has been suggested, help to found the Fianna Fáil Party.[110] She had, however, joined Fianna Fáil before the notice appeared in *An Phoblacht* on 16 April giving details of the formation of a provisional organisation committee and requesting all Sinn Féin officers and branches to make contact.[111]

Much of Jacob's anti-Treaty activity in the 1920s continued to be in the capacity of an extra, someone who could be despatched to run errands and fill in during periods of personnel shortages. On 6 December 1923 she recorded with a degree of irascibility 'how she had been forced 'to go to the ends of the earth ... with a bicycle' to deliver letters from the USA to Mrs Boland & Mrs Mellows.[112] Jacob continued to fill in for Hanna in caring for Owen; they both attended a performance of *Juno and the Paycock* in the Abbey on 7 March 1924. She stayed with him while Hanna travelled to Limerick on political work and minded him during a bout of flu in March 1925, during which time Hanna was in Roscommon with de Valera in the run up to the election of that year. In looking after Owen, Jacob put her attendance at art school to one side.[113] While rewriting *The Troubled House*, the first draft of which was finished in June 1924, she did research for Macardle in the National Library.[114] This was work she continued to do as Macardle worked on *The Irish Republic*. She spent the morning of the 23 June 1925 making a précis of the Army mutiny and recording

108 Dunphy, *The Making of Fianna Fáil Power*, pp. 70–1.

109 9–11 Mar. 1926, RJD Ms (51).

110 Nadia Smith contends that Jacob and Macardle helped to found the Fianna Fáil party in 1926. However, as far as Jacob is concerned there is no evidence to support this contention. Nadia Smith, 'A "manly study"? Irish women historians as public intellectuals, 1868–1949', unpublished PhD dissertation, Boston College, 2003, p. 203.

111 Dunphy, *The Making of Fianna Fáil Power*, p. 71.

112 6 Dec. 1923, RJD Ms (45).

113 6 Dec. 1924, RJD Ms (46).

114 1 July 1924; 9 July 1924, RJD Ms (46); 5–7 Mar. 1925, RJD Ms (47).

other information from the *Weekly Times* in the *Irish Times* office – 'standing all the time'. Such errand girl work for Macardle also necessitated borrowing books from Hanna and typing for her while on holidays in Glenmalure, County Wicklow, in August 1925. Indeed, Jacob recorded Macardle's comment on her versatility during that holiday: 'cook, scullery maid, book of reference, critic, typist, nurse & story teller'.[115] And a further comment shows both that Macardle was no easy person to work for and that she took Jacob for granted: 'D. wrote the preface & I typed it and cooked, but washing up and cleaning saucepans was a great part of my work, and D. is not a tidy person to wash up after, she *always* leaves something'.[116] Six days later Macardle gave 'her the morning off'![117] When the two moved into a flat together in later 1925 Jacob recorded how on 20 November she was 'working & doing things for her'.[118] Clearly, many of Jacob's contemporaries perceived her as someone who could be requested to perform menial tasks in the service of the careers and activism of others. It is unclear whether Jacob was paid for such work for Macardle. What is noteworthy, however, is that Jacob received no mention in the acknowledgements of the first edition of *The Irish Republic* published in 1937. Indeed, Jacob's friends clearly had some reservations about her treatment. She records how Sheehy Skeffington was 'anxious' when she agreed to share a flat with Macardle 'lest she play on me or keep me attending on her too much'.[119]

In early 1926 Jacob continued her low-key political activism, undertaking prison visits, leaving parcels and working to elicit information on the treatment of republican prisoners who continued to be held in Free State prisons.[120] The advent of Fianna Fáil into the political arena proved to be unworthy of Jacob's initial enthusiasm. The first party Árd Fheis in November 1926 saw a boycott of women for officer positions on the first executive. Indeed, the presence of six women on the first executive was the highpoint of visible female support for the party.[121] Jacob recorded a 'tiresome lot of virtuous discussions re what we wd like to do, all the afternoon', and criticised Seán T. O'Kelly[122] who, she

115 23 June 1925; 30 June 1925, RJD Ms (48); 5–13 Aug. 1925, Ms RJD (49).

116 5 Aug. 1925, RJD Ms (49).

117 11 Aug. 1925, RJD Ms (49).

118 20 Nov. 1925, RJD Ms (50).

119 5 Sept. 1925, RJD Ms (49).

120 2–3 Jan. 1926; 12 Jan. 1926, RJD Ms (51).

121 The six women were Constance Markievicz, Margaret Pearse, Kathleen Clarke, Dorothy Macardle, Linda Kearns and Hanna Sheehy Skeffington. See Margaret Ward, *Hanna Sheehy Skeffington* (Cork: Attic Press, 1997), pp. 208–81.

122 Later Fianna Fáil TD and Vice President of the Executive Council and Minister for Public Health and Local Government in the first Fianna Fáil government.

believed, reneged on his responsibility as chair and 'never stopped anyone for talking too long'; Father Kelly, in particular, 'had the time of his infernal life'. From Jacob's perspective, from the outset, Fianna Fáil was male orientated, full of obfuscation and with a high input from members of the Catholic clergy. Yet at this early stage in the party's trajectory Jacob still had faith in its leader. De Valera's once again received her praise for his comments 'about drink, and the language, & self-denial for the cause'. Indeed, in words rarely applied to the man, she declared he was 'delicious'.[123] That Christmas she received a de Valera penny as a present from Swik, the husband of Lucy Kingston.[124]

In August 1927 Sheehy Skeffington resigned from the Fianna Fáil executive in anger at de Valera's declaration of the oath as an empty formality in the context of the Electoral Amendment Act, 1927.[125] In September that year Jacob described Sheehy Skeffington as 'rather disgusted with de Valera'. [126] By August, Jacob was clearly herself disillusioned although she continued to work for the party in the lead up to the election: 'Went to Miss Butler Burkes – Mrs de Valera & others were there anxious to do canvassing. I spoke my mind about F. F. treatment of women – no one seemed to see it that way at all.'[127] As late as May 1928, over two years after de Valera founded Fianna Fáil, Jacob describes his need to talk about the oath of allegiance and 'justify F. F.' as 'a canker in his mind & he can't get off it'.[128] The 'delicious' man of 1926 was clearly failing to provide the decisive leadership so desired by women such as Jacob and Sheehy Skeffington. For Jacob it was the party's failure to advance the role of women in Irish society and its attitude towards the IRA in the 1930s that led to her disillusionment. Yet she still supported the party to election success in 1932, working at the offices in Terenure in February of that year folding leaflets and canvassing in Greenmount Road which she described as 'Horrible. Nothing but maids & non committal worldly people'. By contrast the poor cottages of Harold's Cross Road brought forth people favourable to the party and 'interested & nice, such a heavenly contrast to the richer people'. The attitude to poverty amongst middle-class women such as Jacob was ambivalent at times and betrayed the class-based nature of political activism in Irish society. On election day of 18 November 1924 she commented in her diary: 'Madame Markievicz came in & told of her efforts in collecting the female dregs of the Coombe and taking them to the poll in a lorry, shouting

123 24–25 Nov. 1926, RJD Ms (54).
124 15 Dec. 1926, RJD Ms (55).
125 Ward, *Hanna Sheehy Skeffington*, pp. 288–9.
126 1 Sept. 1927, RJD Ms (58).
127 30 Aug. 1927, RJD Ms (57).
128 4 May 1928, RJD Ms (60).

and cheering'.[129] Of course, the reference to 'female dregs' could reflect Markievicz's tone but if so it drew no criticism from Jacob.

The issues to the fore in the run up to the 1932 election were, from Jacob's perspective, those around the incarceration of republican prisoners and police powers, the election being fought 'against the background of an anti-communist witch-hunt'.[130] However, for Cumann na nGaedheal the real target was Fianna Fáil, the communist crackdown a convenient mask with which to pose as the party of law and order.[131] A perception of Cumann na nGaedheal as increasingly repressive was to the fore in Jacob's diary by this date. In August of the previous year she had noted the provisions of a new Coercion Bill in the *Independent* commenting on the 'special tribunal without juries, for political cases, & power to inflict death – internment on suspicion'. She noted with admiration the 'lovely pictures' in *An Phoblacht* later that month to 'illustrate the new police bill – evidently from medieval pictures of hell'.[132] Under the terms of the October 1931 Public Safety Act 12 societies were declared illegal, the IRA and the Friends of Soviet Russia, of which Jacob was a member, amongst them. The Act established military tribunals with power of execution and there were hundreds of arrests.[133] Visiting Hanna on 22 October 1931 Jacob found a meeting in progress on the Act which she described as 'very pleasant – stuff to be dug up re police atrocities in the past 3 years'. She herself spent the morning of 24 October in Hanna's 'getting up that list of public bodies who protested against the Act'.[134] It was with this perception of police atrocity and the coercive tendencies of Cumann na nGaedheal in mind that people like Jacob approached the February 1932 election. On 16 February, the day of the election, Jacob held a poster in support of Fianna Fáil outside the Terenure polling station, conducted register work and 'watched the life of the booth for 2 hours'. While her role was that of a foot solider in the cause, she clearly felt part of a vibrant movement, something she set much store to.[135] The success of Fianna Fáil she heralded as the approach of a new dawn in Irish

---

129 18 Nov. 1924, RJD Ms (46).
130 8 Feb. 1932; 10–12 Feb. 1932, 14 Feb. 1932, RJD Ms (69).
131 Dunphy, *The Making of Fianna Fáil Power*, p. 141, p. 143.
132 10 Aug. 1931; 22 Aug. 1931, RJD Ms (67).
133 Dunphy, *The Making of Fianna Fáil Power*, p. 142.
134 19 Oct. 1931; 22 Oct. 1931; 24 Oct. 1931, RJD Ms (68).
135 16 Feb. 1932, RJD Ms (69).

politics; the language in the following diary extract indicates the still huge faith she had in the party to deliver what had been stymied by the Treaty debacle of 1922. 'Great atmosphere of rejoicing and relief, like getting out of the daylight after years in the dark – some fresh recollection of trouble that will now stop turning up continually.'[136] The release of republican prisoners which quickly followed the Fianna Fáil victory was the zenith of Jacob's commitment to the party: 'Frank Aiken[137] & Geoghegan's[138] visit to Arbour Hill in the papers along with the formation of de V's government. A charming bit of proper action'. Ryan was among those released and Jacob records how she 'ran round to the crowd escorting P. . . and got a smile and a shake of hands and he is thinner, and his face looked fragile & transparent in texture'. He spoke words of 'thanks and determination' at a meeting at College Green. The next day Jacob attended a céilidhe at the Rotunda to welcome the released prisoners.[139]

Two days later Jacob attended a large prisoners' meeting where Ryan highlighted the ambivalent relationship of the IRA to the newly victorious Fianna Fáil Party. Although Seán Lemass described Fianna Fáil as a 'slightly constitutional party' this image was increasingly jettisoned as the party moved closer to the centre stage of Irish politics throughout the 1930s.[140] At the meeting on 13 March 1932 Ryan spoke last, following speeches by Peadar O'Donnell, Gonne and Sheehy Skeffington. Ryan was, Jacob stated, 'better than any', thanking those who kept the movement going when the prisoners were in jail and singling out Sheehy Skeffington for particular thanks for filling his role as editor of *An Phoblacht*. Ryan noted how the released prisoners were 'going to have a soft easy time for a while to come' and crucially highlighted the looming clash between the IRA and Fianna Fáil: '*maybe too soft & too easy*' – people are asking themselves what will the attitude of IRA be to F. F. – no *national* govment [*sic*] would prevent arming & drilling for recovery of the Republic'.[141] Ryan's words proved to be prophetic. During 1934 and 1935 the IRA came increasingly into conflict with Fianna Fáil and a large number of its members, including Ryan, found themselves arrested. By June 1936 Fianna Fáil had declared the IRA an illegal organisation.[142] But as Ryan predicted for a time

---

136 23 Feb. 1932, RJD Ms (69).

137 Frank Aiken, later Fianna Fáil TD and Minister for Defence in the first Fianna Fáil government. Aiken was appointed as Minister of Finance in June 1945.

138 James Geoghegan, later Fianna Fáil TD and Minister for Justice in the first Fianna Fáil government.

139 10–11 Mar. 1932, RJD Ms (69).

140 Quoted in Ferriter, *The Transformation of Ireland*, p. 364.

141 13 Mar. 1932, RJD Ms (69).

142 Hanley, *The IRA*, pp. 17–18.

things were 'easy' for the organisation. Throughout 1932 the IRA, as a result of their support for Fianna Fáil in the election, were able to recruit openly and exhibited a new found confidence following the declining membership figures of the post-Civil War period.[143] At the prisoners' meeting Jacob recorded in her diary how 'handsome' Ryan looked; 'and stately & country boy and earnest & simply and unconscious & altogether lovely'.[144] This focus on physical description betrays Jacob's sexual attraction to Ryan. By this date their affair had been going on for nearly five years

A LEFT-WING SUPPORTER AND A FIANNA FÁIL VOTER!

In the years following the election success of Fianna Fáil in 1932 the IRA maintained a profile as a very public organisation, parading openly at local commemorations and at the annual Easter and Bodenstown pilgrimages. The rise of the Blueshirts further increased recruitment to the IRA. Conversely the perceptions of the close links between the IRA and Fianna Fáil motivated membership of the Blueshirts.[145] Jacob very much participated in this culture of commemoration and public spectacle. Her diary testifies to the manner in which Irish politics was at a transitional point before and immediately after the election victory of Fianna Fáil in 1932. A shifting balance of forces prevailed within republicanism. In the run up to the 1932 election the IRA lifted General Order No 28 which prohibited members voting for election candidates; the organisation threw its weight behind Fianna Fáil's bid to oust Cumann na nGaedheal, and assumed a new direction in Free State parliamentary politics. Following the election success of the party, a period of uncertainty prevailed as to the relationship of the IRA and Fianna Fáil with men like Frank Aiken calling for a reunification of the party and the organisation. There are examples of crossover in membership in the period immediately after 1932, while a sense prevailed that Fianna Fáil would provide for those republicans who had been discriminated against under the Cosgrave regime. During 1932 and 1933 Fianna Fáil TDs and councillors were visible at IRA sponsored events. Fianna Fáil members could agitate for political clemency for jailed IRA members because the organisation was initially prepared to offer support for the party in the context of a challenge on British authority; a

143 Ibid., p. 14.

144 13 Mar. 1932, RJD Ms (69).

145 Hanley, *The IRA*, pp. 15–16; Mike Cronin, *The Blueshirts and Irish Politics* (Dublin: Four Courts, 1997), p. 130.

common Imperialist enemy allowed a degree of cultural and political interaction.[146] Jacob's political affiliations offer an individual example of the fluid and complex nature of political allegiances in the period. It was possible to hold what may appear, in retrospect, as conflicting political loyalties. What is noteworthy is that Jacob was, as will be discussed, immersed in the left-wing political and cultural scene of the late 1920s and early 1930s and yet continued to place trust in de Valera and Fianna Fáil to fulfil the promises of the period 1916–22. Indeed, Ferriter discusses the need to move away from a perception of '1930s oppression' and to consider the 'diversity in the ranks of de Valera's team' and the layers of 'ambiguities and contradictions' which become manifest on close analysis. Ferriter notes how in the lead up to the 1932 election different Fianna Fáil members 'had been apt to sing from different hymn sheets depending on audience'.[147] Jacob then was not alone in this balancing act. She noted how Linda Kearns McWhinney 'would stick on to FF till they got in, anyway, just to see *would* they abolish the oath, & if they didn't do that promptly she wd quit'.[148] A fluid situation existed where republicans who placed their hope in de Valera after 1926 left both Sinn Féin and an IRA who forbade its members standing for election under General Order No. 28. These republicans, however, reserved the right to retract this political shift and rejoin their former comrades. IRA member Patrick Smith from Cavan, who stood for election in 1927, stated that he hoped his 'action will not prevent me in future taking a line of action in which I have not lost faith'. During the period after 1927 in which the IRA consolidated its organisation and moved towards the left in terms of social policy, it was supported on many levels by Fianna Fáil who were particularly vocal in regard to republican prisoners. *The Nation*, the Fianna Fáil organ prior to the establishment of the *Irish Press*, carried Maud Gonne's weekly 'Prisoners' notes' and published details of republicans detained in Free State jails. Repeatedly Fianna Fáil Dáil deputies stated how when their party came to power retaliation would be enacted against the CID for attacks on republicans. This support for IRA prisoners allowed Fianna Fáil to retain the support of republicans who had not made the shift to the party in 1926.[149] It explains the manner in which someone like Jacob could simultaneously believe that change would be initiated under a Fianna Fáil government and continue to be active in republican politics outside the official

146 Brian Hanley, 'Moss Twomey, radicalism, and the IRA, 1931–33: a reassessment', *Saothar* 28 (2001), pp. 53–4; Hanley, *The IRA*, pp. 133–5, p. 137.

147 Ferriter, *The Transformation of Ireland*, p. 360, p. 362, p. 363.

148 14 Nov. 1931, RJD Ms (68).

149 Hanley, *The IRA*, p. 114, p. 118–20.

auspices of the Party. Furthermore, the existence of a left wing of the party was referred to by the Special Branch in 1930.[150]

LEFT-WING ACTIVISM

As Jacob became emotionally and physically involved with Ryan her political trajectory began to mirror his, particularly as he involved himself in the republican socialism of the first half of the 1930s. This, of course, was more than Jacob merely aping Ryan's views and political affiliations but was, in part, a reflection of the close-knit nature of Republican Dublin in the period. Within this small clique politics and social life were closely interlinked and like first-wave feminism in Ireland many of the same individuals could be found on the membership lists and attending the meetings of the various republican and left-wing movements of the period. In participating in the left-wing politics of the early 1930s Jacob moved once again within a counter-cultural political environment; her political experiences were, as they had been in the revolutionary and civil war periods, conducted within a paradigm of resistance to perceived oppression and the hegemony of Church and State.

In 1929 Ryan replaced Peadar O'Donnell as editor of *An Phoblacht*, at the point when the politics of the IRA moved perceptively to the left; Ryan was to the fore in establishing the socialist platform Saor Éire in 1931. Concerned to exploit the discontent generated by the economic crisis fuelled by the Great Depression after 1929, Saor Éire demanded communal ownership of key resources. In considering the economic climate Saor Éire noted the inability or unwillingness of people to pay the land annuities owing to the British government, coupled with the constriction of emigration outlets.[151] Focus was placed on workers, small farmers and traders in a short-lived attempt by a section within the IRA to marry republicanism with the politics of social justice and create a mass popular movement geared to revolutionary action.[152] One of the features of the politics of the IRA during the early 1930s was its close links with organisations such as the Irish Friends of Soviet Russia and the Irish Labour Defence League, leading to a Government concern about an IRA/communist alliance.[153] During the late 1920s and early 1930s the Department of Justice kept detailed files on the various and often interlinked left-wing organisations that existed in Ireland. A report by the Department on the position in August 1931 stated:

---

150 Ibid., p. 120.
151 Ibid., p. 14; Ó Drisceoil, *Peadar O'Donnell*, p. 50; McGarry, *Frank Ryan*, p. 24.
152 Hanley, *The IRA*, p. 31.
153 Ibid., pp. 12–13.

There are a number of Associations, many members of which are also members of the IRA, whose object is the bringing about in this country of a revolution along the lines of the Russian Revolution . . . a 'working class republic'. These Associations include the 'Friends of Soviet Russia', the 'Workers Union of Ireland, the 'Irish Working Farmers' Committee', the 'Workers' Revolutionary Party in Ireland'. The leading spirits are well known to the police. Visits to Russia have been organised both by these Associations and by the IRA, by the former for training in revolutionary techniques, by the latter for military training and the purchase of arms.[154]

Many government files from the period indicate a large degree of hysteria concerning the breakdown of law and order. Of course it should be noted that while the police and government did exaggerate the communist element of the scare their concerns relating to the impact of the IRA's assault on law and order were very real. The Chief Superintendent of the Garda Síochána in County Kerry declared in 1931: 'If the Soviet comrades are not dealt with more determinedly at once the State will perish'.[155] This tone of threat is reflected in a letter from the President of the Executive Council to the Cardinal, Edward Byrne, on 13 August 1931.

I refrained as long as possible from adding to the many anxieties of your exalted position until the facts made it imperative that the Head of the Church in this country should be given the fullest information about a situation which threatens the whole fabric of both Church and State.[156]

This letter gave rise to the Government introduction of a Public Safety Act to permit trial by military tribunal and the use of the death penalty with no right of appeal. In this the government was aided by the Catholic Church's denunciation of Saor Éire as an attempt to impose materialistic ideals of Soviet Russia on Ireland. The Catholic Church were committed to an offensive against communism in Ireland by 1931, reflective of the fixation of Pope Pius

154 Report by the Department of Justice 'on the present position (Aug. 1931) as regards the activities of unlawful and dangerous Associations in the Saorstat with a summary of similar activities in recent years', Department of Taoiseach (DT) Files, s 5864B 'Anti-State Activities, Joint Pastoral of Hierarchy and events leading up to its issue', NAI.

155 Included in Report sent by Eoin O'Duffy, Commissioner of the Garda Síochána, to the Secretary, Department of Justice, 27 July 1931, relating to illegal drilling and republican meetings, incidents of which have been obtained from the Garda Síochána in the different counties. DT, s 5864B. 'Anti-State Activities'.

156 Letter, 13 Aug. 1931, DT, s 5864B 'Anti-State activities'.

XI with Russia, particularly following the repression of Catholics in that country at the end of the 1920s.[157] Eleven organisations were banned and the republican and left-wing press suppressed.

To a degree the government crackdown was effective. At this point tensions had emerged within the IRA about the perceived link between the organisation, communism and irreligion.[158] Within the organisation the move towards social radicalism created fissures and at the 1934 General Army Convention, a number of key officers seceded to form the Republican Congress. The Congress was intended as 'an organising centre for anti-imperialist activities' and aimed at 'the full realisation of Fianna Fáil's original policies'. For someone like Peadar O'Donnell this meant a re-focus on small-farmer and labour issues.[159] George Gilmore described the Congress as 'another attempt to do what Lalor and Davitt and Connolly had tried to do' while also viewing it as the response of the 'republican population, irrespective of organisational loyalties . . . [to] the Blueshirt movement as a dangerous regrouping of the enemies of the Republic'.[160]

During the first half of the 1930s Jacob was regularly involved with *An Phoblacht*. To a point Jacob's involvement reflected the subservient streak in her nature; an earlier established pattern of political activism can once again be identified in this context. As already noted Jacob was not a leader by nature and, thus, was willing to offer her services to those she admired and craved respect from. As she had earlier run errands and performed perfunctory tasks for the more prominent women in the politics of the pre-independent period and during the Civil War, as she had filled a maternal role in the place of Hanna on so many occasions, so now from the late 1920s and into the early 1930s she acted as a hidden helpmate to Ryan, and later Peadar O'Donnell and Michael Price. This led to her work being undervalued or to her wasting time on tasks that failed to come to fruition. Even before Ryan took over as editor in 1929, Jacob assisted him. On 28 November 1926 she noted how she went to Sheehy Skeffington 'on a message from P [Ryan], looking for stuff for the Poblacht'. The next day she spent 'the morning in the service of the Poblacht – copying leading articles out of old Indepts in the Library . . . & waiting for Árd Fheis reports at 33 – de V's speeches'.[161] While clearly this was work that someone had to do in the wider interests of the cause and while *The Rise of the United Irishmen*

157 Emmet O'Connor, *Reds and the Green: Ireland, Russia and the Communist Internationals 1919–43* (Dublin: UCD Press, 2004), pp. 166–7.

158 Hanley, *The IRA*, pp. 16–17, p. 39.

159 Dunphy, *The Making of Fianna Fáil Power in Ireland*, pp. 187–8.

160 George Gilmore, *1934 Republican Congress* (Dublin: Dochas Co-Op Society, n.d.), p. 4, p. 12.

161 28–29 Nov. 1926, RJD Ms (54).

was serialised in the paper in 1928–9, still there is a sense that Jacob was fulfiling a menial role for Ryan and Sheehy Skeffington as she had earlier done for Macardle. This pattern was to continue in the 1930s. On 16 January 1933, for example, she spent time in the library 'to finish some calendar stuff for the paper, which P. did not use'. Later that day she chaired the Vegetarian Society meeting at the Mansion House, filling in for the imprisoned Hanna. The next day she received a phone call from Ryan asking her to go up to Armagh to visit Hanna who had been arrested while speaking at a banned meeting in contravention of the Exclusion Order by the Six County Government placed on her; Jacob was to ensure that she wasn't followed.[162] The *Irish Press* of 25 January noted how Jacob, described as the 'Dublin writer' accompanied Sheehy Skeffington at her trial.[163] Jacob worked for the Republican Congress, mainly typing material relating to housing problems for Michael Price, selling copies of the *Republican Congress* and stamping delegate cards.[164] When George Gilmore was concerned to ensure that the Communists would put up candidates in the corporation elections during 1936 she noted how he wants 'me to work of course. Thinks canvassing *is* useful, damn him'.[165] In these elections Ryan stood as a Congress candidate. A theme of the Congress was the capture of local government offices in a bid to remodel them into workers' and peasants' councils, a feature earlier of O'Donnell's anti-annuities campaign.[166] Jacob spent 22 June 1936 'writing election stuff' and 'offered to canvass next night, a terrible effort'. In the event, when no one would accompany her, she switched to printing posters. Despite her sense of being involved in unrewarding work, she referred to 'splendid company' and enjoyed 'election stories'. Two days later she 'went off to leave round George's leaflets . . . behind Hardwicke St. – slum tenements that took ages to get round'. What is noteworthy in the reference to 'George's leaflets' is Jacob's sense of doing someone else's work.[167] However, her personality again prevented her from assuming a leadership role. While Jacob was clearly capable of assuming a forceful position on the debates of the day within the diary, she was less able to assert a dominant presence in the campaigns in which she participated.

In the 1920s and early 1930s *An Phoblacht* offered a paper commitment to social revolution and to equality of gender rights and as such appealed to Jacob; this probably allowed her to accept her helper status in its service. In

162 16–17 Jan. 1933, RJD Ms (72). The Exclusion order had been placed on 4 Apr. 1926.

163 *Irish Press*, 25 Jan. 1933 in DT, s 2280, 'Arrest of Mrs Sheehy Skeffington in Northern Ireland'.

164 19 June 1934; 29 June 1934, Ms RJD (75); 23 June 1935, RJD Ms (77); 29 Sept. 1934, RJD Ms (76).

165 26 May 1936, RJD Ms (78).

166 Ó Drisceoil, *Peadar O'Donnell*, p. 60.

167 22–23 June 1936; 25 June 1936, RJD Ms (79).

addition, the paper's discussion of developments in the Middle East, China, India and Russia spoke to her international outlook.[168] Moreover, the Irish-Ireland ethos adopted by the paper with its 'An Saoghal Gaedhlach' ('Irish-Ireland News') column accorded with Jacob's continuing commitment to language revival; in theory the IRA was committed to the establishment of the Irish language as the first language of the country.[169] Under the editorship of Peadar O'Donnell and later Ryan, as noted, *An Phoblacht* became more left wing. A Department of Justice memorandum of 27 March 1930 stated: 'It will be remembered that Peadar O'Donnell is no longer interested in *An Phoblacht* but the tone of that paper indicates some understanding with the Communist Movement.'[170] From this period the paper began focusing on international as well as national issues of social justice and, crucially for Jacob, carried fewer religious articles while maintaining its cultural commitment to the Gaelicisation.[171] On 2 February 1936 she recorded how she spent a part of the day writing an article on schools for what she describes as George Gilmore's new paper, the *Irish People*, the all but moribund successor to the *Republican Congress* which had ceased publication due to a lack of funds in that month.[172] Again, it is likely that the fusion of culture and politics in this paper attracted Jacob: the *Irish People* blended politics, history and the arts in one production.[173] Ferriter, writing of republicanism in this period, notes how some in the movement 'saw themselves as embodying the broad inclusive nationalism of 1798, while others championed a more ethnocentric Catholic outlook.'[174] A tension existed between what has been described as 'the civic nationalist rhetoric of republicanism, which dated back to Wolfe Tone and the United Irishmen, and its ethnic nationalist reality'.[175] Jacob clearly saw republicanism in the context of the former. The serialisation of *The Rise of the United Irishmen* in *An Phoblacht* saw her work published side-by-side with other articles and comments on Tone and the men of 1798. On 16 June 1928, the day before the annual republican pilgrimage to Bodenstown, her article 'Matilda Tone: A noble Irishwoman' was published in an edition of the paper which devoted much space to Tone.[176]

168 Ferriter, *The Transformation of Ireland*, p. 311.

169 Hanley, *The IRA*, p. 61.

170 Department of Justice memorandum, 27 Mar. 1930, DT, s 5074A 'Communist Activities 1929–1930', Saorstat Éireann.

171 Ó Drisceoil, *Peadar O'Donnell*, p. 44.

172 2 Feb. 1936, RJD Ms (78); Richard English, *Radicals and the Republic: Socialist Republicanism in the Irish Free State 1925–1937* (Oxford: Clarendon Press, 1994), p. 237.

173 Adrian Hoar, *In Green and Red: The Lives of Frank Ryan* (Dingle: Brandon, 2004), p. 134.

174 Ferriter, *The Transformation of Ireland*, p. 311.

175 Fearghal McGarry, *Eoin O'Duffy: A Self-Made Hero* (Oxford: Oxford University Press, 2005), p. 56.

176 *An Phoblacht*, 16 June 1928.

GENDER EQUALITY IN THE 1930S

While Jacob knew and worked with many of the republican socialists of the period, her involvement was outside of IRA-organised participation in the field. Mick Fitzpatrick and Charlotte Despard founded the Irish Friends of Soviet Russia in April 1930 to offer details of life in Russia and to promote the ideals of the soviet system.[177] Jacob was involved from the outset when the organisation was in its protean stage. Her diary entry for 8 January 1930 reads:

> Russian meeting in evg, big attendance. Helena Molony awfully good – Russia seems the one sane decent country in the world, where justice & good feeling rule – but where they get all the money for the crèches & sanatoria & well run factories, & holidays & pensions at 50 & 55 beats me. *And* an increasing population. . . . Women so level in Russia that it is taken for granted.[178]

Jacob was thus drawn to the Irish Friends of Soviet Russia to a large part because of this perceived equality of women in Russian society, something she contrasted with the situation that pertained in Ireland. During this period she worked on a series of lectures for the United Irishwomen, noting how her beliefs were not in accordance with the conservative views of many of the women she met. The United Irishwomen, established in 1910 under the auspices of the Irish Agricultural Organisation Society, reflected the ideology of separate spheres. Working to create an Ireland from which no female would willingly emigrate, they saw the solution in securing women within a domestic role.[179] Speaking in Gorey, County Wicklow, on 14 February 1930 Jacob wrote: 'I think Miss Brickenden disapproved of my attitude, for in her speech of thanks she said their objects were not the same as the UI [United Irish] men's, & they didn't want to raise a rebellion'.[180] Jacob, by contrast, believed in the necessity for feminist societies and kept herself up to date with all discrimination against women in the Irish Free State. She was present at an infanticide trial at Green Street on 27 November 1928 and noted the lack of women on the jury.[181]

Jacob officially joined the Irish Women's Citizens and Local Government Association on 30 October 1934, following the publication of the Criminal Law Amendment Bill although she had earlier attended meetings in an

177   O'Connor, *Reds and the Green*, p. 132.

178   8 Jan. 1930, RJD Ms (63).

179   Leeann Lane, 'Female emigration and the cooperative movement in the writings of George Russell', *New Hibernia Review* 8: 4 (2004), pp. 84–100.

180   14 Feb. 1930, RJD Ms (63).

181   17 Oct. 1928, Ms (60); 27 Nov. 1928, RJD Ms (61).

unofficial capacity. As a member of the IWCA, Jacob was present at the inaugural meeting of the Joint Committee of Women's Societies on 12 March 1935. The Joint Committee was formed to bring together women's organisations to secure amendments to the Criminal Law Amendment Act, notably to raise the age of consent to 17 in order to protect girls, to ensure equal treatment of men and women under the solicitation laws, to agitate for the establishment of a permanent women police force, to increase in the number of probation officers for the better protection of women and children and to restore full and equal jury service rights to women.[182] After 1935 the Joint Committee repeatedly declared women police to be 'an essential service in every progressive country today', and claimed that the demand in Ireland was supported by 40 public bodies and the public press.[183] A perusal of the membership books shows that although individual women joined the Joint Committee of Women's Societies many of the subscriptions were in the form of society membership.[184] A Criminal Law Amendment Conference was held in 9 Ely Place on 7 November 1935.[185] The organisation extended its focus to examine other issues affecting the interests of women when it became clear that the Minister for Justice, Ruttledge, had 'no immediate intention of bringing in the suggested amendments'.[186] In particular, there was an emphasis on the problems of underprivileged women and children. The Joint Committee acted as a pressure group studying social legislation and recommending fundamental reforms.[187]At meetings of the society Jacob partook in discussions relating to the proposed new constitution, the representation of women in the 2nd Chamber of the Oireachtas and the continued agitation relating to women police.

At a meeting on 29 October 1936 Jacob noted how de Valera could receive no deputation from the Joint Committee of Women's Societies but 'he cd receive the German footballers alright'. Although de Valera finally received a women's deputation on 29 January 1937, nothing positive resulted.[188] By 1937, the man whom Jacob revered in the 1920s became the man who 'badly needs

182 Report on the history of the Joint Committee of Women's Societies and Social Workers, 1983, Papers of the Joint Committee of Women's Societies and Social Workers, 98/14/6/1, NAI.

183 Committee minutes, 5 Feb. 1940, Committee Minute Book, 1939–47, Papers of the Joint Committee, 98/14/5/2, NAI.

184 See, for example, Cash book, 1950–9, Papers of the Joint Committee, 98/14/3/1, NAI.

185 Planning for this conference was discussed at the meeting of the Joint Committee on 30 Aug. 1935. Committee minutes, 30 Aug. 1935, Committee Minute Book, 1935–9, Papers of the Joint Committee, 98/14/5/1, NAI.

186 Committee minutes, 30 Jan. 1936, 98/14/5/1, NAI.

187 Paper by Nora F. Browne on History of Joint Committee 1935–67, 9 June 1967, Papers of the Joint Committee of Women's Societies and Social Workers, 98/14/7/1, NAI.

188 Ward, *Hanna Sheehy Skeffington*, p. 324.

to be taught a lesson, if there were only enough women with the guts to do it'. She noted how de Valera saw difficulties in everything the deputation suggested, arguing that they had no public opinion behind them and 'showed ignorance of the article 3 in the 1922 constitution guaranteeing sex equality'.[189] As member of the Women Writers' Club she was among the 20 signatures on a letter to de Valera on 25 May 1937 regarding the status of women under the new constitution: 'We regard with utmost dismay the clauses in Articles 40, 41 and 45 of the Draft Constitution which provide for legislation to discriminate among certain classes of citizens and especially against women.'[190]

The Joint Committee throughout the late 1930s and into the 1940s acted as watchdog determined to monitor and realign the priorities of Government. When the Enforcement of Court Orders Bill was before the Dáil in March 1940 the Committee convened a special meeting on 12 April to discuss the question. One of the key features of the Bill was to make it easier for women to proceed against men in arrears in payment of maintenance and affiliation orders.[191] Members previously met with the Chief Clerk of the District Court and employees of the National Society for the Prevention of Cruelty for Children.[192] Government Ministers also utilised the Society as a source of information on issues with a female dimension. On 26 June 1941, for example, the Society received an enquiry from the Minister for Defence, Oscar Traynor, relating to the 'localities where soldiers were subjected to the undesirable attentions of young women'; the Committee, in response, mentioned Ballsbridge and Collins Barracks.[193] Issues relating to the treatment of prostitutes and inmates in reformatory schools were introduced at various stages, members visiting a number of these institutions. In the context of the treatment of prostitutes and women found guilty of crime, some members expressed the view that what was needed was a 'home' to teach girls an occupation to enable them to provide for themselves. It was decided to liaise with existing homes such as the one in Henrietta Street and Gloucester Street.[194] While the resulting report

189 25 Feb. 1937, RJD Ms (81).

190 Letter to de Valera, 25 May 1937, DT, s 9880, 'Women, position under Constitution 1937'. For details on the articles of the constitution referred to see Maria Luddy, 'A "sinister and retrogressive" proposal: Irish women's opposition to the 1937 draft constitution', *Transactions of the Royal Historical Society* xv (2005); Catriona Beaumont, 'Women, citizenship and Catholicism in the Irish Free State, 1922–1948', *Women's History Review* 6: 4 (1997).

191 See http://historical-debates.oireachtas.ie/D/0079/D.0079.194003190012.html, accessed 4 July 2008.

192 Committee minutes, 12 Apr. 1940, 98/14/5/2, NAI.

193 Committee minutes, 26 June 1941, 98/14/5/2, NAI.

194 See, for example, Committee minutes 5 June 1951, 98/14/5/2, NAI.

suggested various interesting concerns relating to the treatment of women in these institutions, little comment was made by members. It was noted that the girls in Henrietta Street did laundry work and the lack of training for subsequent work was recorded. The Joint Committee Minutes reported that the girls 'are well treated' and members seemed to find nothing strange in the fact that many women in both institutions remained there for the duration of their lives. It was noted, indeed, that permission had to be sought by women who wanted to become lifetime inmates, suggesting that this was a favour rather than an act of incarceration. The report concluded with the interesting but unanalysed comment: 'Many of the girls come from the country & the nuns report that a large number are sub-normal'. At the same meeting it was reported that most girls' reformatory schools 'seem to be run in a satisfactory manner'. At a later meeting on 23 October representatives of various institutions housing prostitutes and unmarried mothers were present: Lr Gloucester Street, Magdalen Asylum, Lower Leeson Street.[195]

Jacob spoke at few of the meetings of the Joint Committee maintaining her role as onlooker and recorder of events. However, there does appear to be some real discourse between the establishment and the Joint Committee; this mattered to Jacob and gave her a sense of the purposefulness of membership.[196] At the meeting on 25 September 1941 a letter was read from Mr Justice Hanna on the subject of prostitution. He suggested, in connection with the Committee's earlier comments on the housing of such women, that members 'might explore the possibility of the organisation of a group of such institutions in both city & county' to facilitate 'a segregation of the girls as to moral character, suitable training & age'.[197] It is noteworthy that such ideas around moral character and deserving and undeserving poor, integral to nineteenth-century thinking on the issues, were still prevalent in twentieth-century discourse. In the same letter Justice Hanna asked the Committee for information on women police in other countries, again indicating the role of the organisation in terms of providing the government and other pillars of the establishment with information; in that way the organisation was able to further the issues it considered relevant. Mr Justice McCarthy supported the notion of women police as useful in patrolling the streets to deal with prostitution at the level of arrest and immediate detention. However, he did not 'agree that their work would be invaluable in connection with the after care of prostitution as to keep the subject in her former environment would be disastrous'. Containment and

---

195 Committee minutes 26 June 1941; 23 October 1941, 98/14/5/2, NAI.

196 Jacob continued membership until 1941. On 21 November 1941 a letter was received from her resigning owing to inability to attend meetings. Committee minutes, 27 Nov. 1941, 98/14/5/2, NAI.

197 Committee minutes 25 Sept. 1941, 98/14/5/2, NAI.

confinement were still the response to issues of prostitution as in the nineteenth century: 'suitable homes would provide the only solution for the remedying of this evil'. The concern to segregate first-time offenders from hardened women was also still to the fore. These homes, the Justice argued, should 'be able to provide the treatment necessary for women showing signs of mental weakness or abnormality'. Mrs Clarke from the National Society for the Prevention of Cruelty to Children, however, stated at the meeting how the economic causes of prostitution had to be regarded as primary.[198]

At the founding meeting of the Joint Committee it was decided to 'organise a rota of women who could attend the Children's Court and trials for solicitation and gather facts connected with the workings of the [Criminal Law Amendment] Act'.[199] Throughout the next number of years minutes regularly recorded the request for members to attend court hearings pertaining to women's issues.[200] Jacob attended relevant trials in Green Street under the auspices of the 'Women's Societies' even before the establishment of the Joint Committee. On 31 January 1929 she was present at the trial of a black man for abortion and five days later heard details of an indecent assault case.[201] Jacob carried out this work, monitoring the treatment of women under the legal system, at various points in the late 1920s and during the next decade. She noted the discrepancy in sentences meted out to men and women, a reflection of the manner in which nineteenth-century attitudes to women still prevailed in the Free State. At the District Court on 3 February 1936 she observed how a woman received one month for being drunk and begging while a man received half that sentence for the same crime. On the same day three women were given six months for soliciting 'on the inaudible evidence of a policeman without one question asked of them or the chance given to say a word'.[202] In such entries Jacob recorded how the roles of power and powerless at the level of gender were entrenched in the Free State justice system, and at the most fundamental level in the wider Irish society, something she believed had been eradicated in the brave new world that was the USSR. In May 1924, at a meeting at 5 Leinster Street about the position of unmarried mothers and the state of homes provided to these women, Jacob shocked a number of those in attendance. Commenting on a proposed bill to make men responsible for the maintenance of their illegitimate children – which would ultimately become the 1930 Illegitimate Children (Affiliation Orders) Act – she stated: 'that as

198 Committee minutes, 23 Oct. 1941, 98/14/5/2, NAI.
199 Committee minutes 12 Mar. 1935, 98/14/5/1, NAI.
200 Committee minutes, 28 Sept. 1939, 98/14/5/2, NAI.
201 31 Jan. 1929; 5 Feb. 1929, RJD Ms (61).
202 30 Jan. 1936; 3 Feb. 1936, RJD Ms (78).

long as the girls thought it such a fearful disgrace, it wd be impossible to get justice done – that is, make the fathers pay'.[203] Under the 1930 Act a woman could take action against the father in her own right (previous to this action could only be taken by the local Board of Guardians or the woman's parents or guardian). But as Jacob rightly pointed out this was a process fraught with intimidation given the shame of illegitimacy and the need for corroboration in a hostile court environment in a period long before DNA testing.[204]

By contrast with her perception of the innate equality of women in the Soviet Union, a sense that the position of Irish women had regressed since independence was a theme of many of the talks and feminist meetings Jacob attended during the 1920s and 1930s. As will be discussed, Jacob's view of women in the Soviet Union was naïve, based as it was on little other than the anodyne perspective she was treated to as a visiting delegate of the Irish Friends of Soviet Russia in 1931. Indeed, her insistence on the equality of women in the Soviet Union says much more about her perception of the lack of such in Ireland. On 26 November 1935 Sheehy Skeffington gave a talk on the topic of 'have women advanced' concluding that 'things are going back in most countries & will go on doing so here if women don't resist'. Crucially the lack of commitment to feminist advancement amongst young Irish women during the period was remarked on.[205] Jacob continued to express concern at the manner in which women in various organisations refused to participate and make their voices heard. This concern was still particularly, she believed, the case with women in the Gaelic League. At a lecture on how to impose the Gaelic movement in January 1926 she noted how a woman 'actually spoke'. She castigated Mrs Dix in the context of a céilidhe committee, remarking, 'the confounded woman wd publicly give C. O'L. [Colm O'Lochlainn] the program to arrange – she always wants to put a man in charge of everything'.[206] Jacob perceived discrimination at even the most mundane levels, noting on a visit to the Jacob's Factory in 1933 how women were not permitted to smoke anywhere while a small garden served as smoking space for men.[207]

When a similar lecture on how far women had advanced due to be given by Sheehy Skeffington to the Rotary Club in January 1936 was cancelled, she discussed with Jacob that, aside from a religious motivation for the cancellation,

203 23 May 1924, RJD Ms (45).

204 Sandra McAvoy, 'The regulation of sexuality in the Irish Free State, 1929–1935' in Greta Jones and Elizabeth Malcolm (eds), *Medicine, Disease and the State in Ireland, 1650–1940* (Cork: Cork University Press, 1999), p. 260.

205 26 Nov. 1935, RJD Ms (78).

206 20 Jan. 1926, RJD Ms (51); 21 June 1926, RJD Ms (52).

207 25 May 1933, RJD Ms (72).

she believed that 'they feared she might say something on women in industry which wd annoy Lemass'. This, of course, was in the context of the Conditions of Employment Act, 1936, the most serious assault on women working outside the home in the period 1922–37. Under Section 16 of this Act the Minister for Industry and Commerce could control and restrict the numbers of women in all industries. This was passed in the context of a desire to alleviate male unemployment. The concern was to safeguard the right of the male citizen to work; the right of the female citizen to work 'not thought to be so great'.[208] Jacob had attended meetings of the Irish Women Workers' Union against the Bill, notably that of 20 November in the company of 'hosts of young women' – an interesting observation given the concern voiced above at the lack of young female activism – and men such as Peadar O'Donnell and George Gilmore.[209] The interest of men such as O'Donnell and Gilmore in women's right to work explains the attraction of republican socialism for Jacob. Moreover, the avowed aim of Saor Éire to 'restore and foster the Irish Language, culture and games' accorded with her continued support for the programme of Gaelicisation.[210]

THE SOVIET UNION

Jacob viewed her visit to the Soviet Union in 1931 as a delegate of the Irish Friends of Soviet Russia as a prism through which to reflect light on the deficiencies in Irish society, particularly the lack of gender equality and full independence. Already in possession of passports Jacob and Meg Connery were the only delegates able to travel of the seven selected to attend the annual May Day celebrations by the Central Trade Union Congress of the Soviet. The Irish government refused to issue passports to the remaining five.[211] Jacob commented on the attitudes to religion and the state of the workers in Soviet Russia but one of her key concerns was to note the position and status of women, and to establish a comparison with the situation in Ireland. Although she was dismayed to discover no woman in the government group at Lenin's

208 Beaumont, 'Women, citizenship and Catholicism', p. 573.

209 9 Jan. 1936; 20 Nov. 1935, RJD Ms (78). For Jacob's attendance at meetings against the Conditions of Employment Bill see also 3 Sept. 1935, RJD Ms (77).

210 Constitution and Rules of Saor Eire (Organisation of Workers and Working Farmers) adopted by the First National Congress held in Dublin, 26 and 27 September 1931, included in DT, S 5864B 'Anti-state activities, Joint Pastoral of Hierarchy and events leading up to its issue'.

211 O'Connor, *Reds and the Green*, p. 150.

tomb at the May Day celebrations, she noted a female head of the Education Department and the presence of women chairpersons of the Union of Medical Health & Sanitary Workers and of the Textile Union.[212]

Despite her perception of the equality of women in Soviet society relative to women in Ireland, Jacob was no willing dupe, eager to listen uncritically to a Soviet propaganda machine targeted at western visitors. With irony she noted how the western delegates 'dutifully worshipped at the shrine of the tractor' at the soviet farm to which they were brought outside Stalingrad.[213] Her hostility to the influence of the Catholic Church in Ireland notwithstanding, she was critical of the attempt in the Soviet Union to eradicate religion without educating people to understand the superiority of secular society.[214] '"We overthrew the Czar, we overthrew God along with him". Worrall[215] & I commenting on the one sideness & cocksureness of it, against all the other British.'[216] She recorded details of her discussions with a Russian woman who spoke English, notably the problems women had relating to queuing for foodstuffs and concerns relating to marriage arrangements.[217] Seán Murray, a student at the Lenin School established in 1926 to train foreign communists, was shocked by the position of women in the largely Muslim region of Daghestan in 1929. Yet it appears as if Irish left-wing supporters did not really see the harsher side of communist life in the USSR. While those who had been students of the Lenin School, like Murray, and those frequent visitors to the country like Jim Larkin, were in some position to understand the reality of Soviet life, 'a combination of Soviet secrecy, mistrust of anti-Soviet propaganda, and defensiveness about "the first workers' state" obscured the grim realities of famine, poverty and terror'. Moreover, the Catholic Church-led red scare of 1931 made left-wing supporters in Ireland sceptical of anti-Soviet discourse.[218]

Jacob's republican sympathies also influenced her perspectives. She responded eagerly to a talk at the Palace of Labour in Moscow on, amongst other matters, the communist duty of freeing Ireland, India and Egypt.[219] From the

212   23 May 1931, RJD Ms (66).

213   14 May 1931, RJD Ms (66).

214   23 May 1931, RJD Ms (66).

215   This was probably Ryan Worrall, an Australian doctor who came to London in 1927; he was a member of the Communist Party of Great Britain for a brief period at the end of the 1920s. See John McIlroy, 'The establishment of intellectual orthodoxy and the Stalinization of British Communism 1928–1933', *Past and Present* 192 (2006), p. 193.

216   22 May 1931, RJD Ms (66).

217   14 May 1931, RJD Ms (66).

218   O'Connor, *Reds and the Green*, pp. 168–9.

219   1 May 1931; 6 May 1931; 20 May 1931, RJD Ms (66).

outset the Irish delegation had trouble distinguishing themselves from the British.[220] Her report to the Irish Friends of Soviet Russia when she returned was entitled 'It's ours', Jacob clearly making a comparison on a number of levels between the situation in Ireland and the Soviet Union. While the title related to the class revolution which had occurred in Russia and was eagerly, if naively, awaited by the Irish republican socialists with whom she interacted, the title could also be viewed through a nationalist and feminist lens.[221]

CULTURAL COMMUNISM

For a number of years after 1930 Jacob's diaries abound with evidence of the vogue for all things Russian that existed amongst a small section of Dublin society. The official files kept on left-wing organisations in this period testify to the shared personnel of the various associations. On 17 September 1931 W. T. Cosgrave wrote to Cardinal Edward Byrne stating:

> It has become increasingly evident within the last two years that there is in existence, in defiance of the law, a conspiracy which has for its object the overthrow by violence of State Institutions. The persons engaged in this conspiracy are banded together in a number of organisations whose directing personnel has much in common but whose titles and avowed objects and methods provide sufficient variations to attract every type of element subversive of public order.[222]

Possibly as a result of the state concern about the subversive tendencies of communistic organisations, the left-wing activities of the late 1920s and early 1930s have been interpreted within a political framework at the expense of a full understanding of how much of the interest was manifested at a cultural level. Never a strong activist in the political sense of visible party membership, Jacob's political commitments were played out for the most part on a cultural and intellectual level. In the early 1930s things Russian and communistic were culturally fashionable amongst the small circles of intellectuals with whom Jacob interacted. The *Workers' Voice* under the editorship of republican socialist, Seán Murray, included articles of Russian culture and social organisation, as well as information on the first Soviet Union five-year plan and industrialisation

---

220 See, for example, 9 May 1931, RJD Ms (66).

221 12 June 1931, RJD Ms (67).

222 Draft Memorandum to Cardinal Edward Byrne from W. T. Cosgrave, 17 Sept. 1931, DT, s 5864B, 'Anti-state activities, Joint Pastoral of Hierarchy and events leading up to its issue'.

in the country.[223] On 16 May 1930 Jacob gave details in her diary of an Irish Friends of Soviet Russia meeting and noted how she was to review a pamphlet relating to the position of women in Russia for Hanna.[224] The Government memorandum to Cardinal Byrne in September 1931 represented large sections of the membership of the various left-wing organisations as 'dupes' – 'persons who in joining these organisations were not necessarily activated by evil motives but whose judgement can be swayed and whose conscience is being blunted by their more unscrupulous leaders'.[225] Yet according to Jacob's testimony, many of the events hosted by the Friends of Soviet Russia were simultaneously social occasions and opportunities for middle-class activists to promote issues of social justice as much as political events to undermine the fabric of the state. The meetings and social events also provided a forum for politically active women to come together and many of the women involved in the feminist-orientated campaigns for the relief of poverty are recorded in Jacob's diary as prominent in the Irish Friends of Soviet Russia, evident in the following account of the organisation's fair held in Roebuck in 1931:

> lots of poor people with children, Emer, John B. [Brennan], Madame M'B, Dorothy . . . and a young man who was a month in the Crimea in May . . . Songs & exhibition dances – I spoke off a chair, about leisure pursuits, palaces of culture, games, theatres, picture galleries.[226]

Of course, this, as Andrée Sheehy Skeffington has remarked in her memoir of Owen Sheehy Skeffington, was the period before the Moscow trials and executions, and consequently before the true authoritarianism of Soviet Union was evident.[227] The lack of real knowledge of the reality of life and politics in the Soviet Union facilitated a community of interests amongst those at various points on the continuum of left-wing politics in Ireland. During the period 1933–7 Owen Sheehy Skeffington, describing himself as a socialist, was willing to listen to other left-wing perspectives. The need for left-wing unity and co-operation was intensified by the spread of fascism in Europe and by the perception in Ireland of a fascist threat in the form of the

223 O'Connor, *Reds and the Green*, p. 168.
224 16 May 1930, RJD Ms (64).
225 Draft Memorandum to Cardinal Byrne from Cosgrave, 17 Sept. 1931, DT, S 5864B.
226 9 July 1931, RJD Ms (67).
227 Sheehy Skeffington, *Skeff*, p. 72. In 1936 Stalin began an arrest of hundreds within the Comintern, declaring that it was a hotbed of Trotskyists and spies. In August 1936 the first of a series of show trials was carried out. Grigori Zinoviev, Lev Kamenev and 14 others were tried for subversive activities. O'Connor, *Reds and the Green*, p. 214.

Blueshirts.[228] As late as 23 December 1933 Jacob wore a Russian costume to a fancy dress party at the house of a Dr McC.[229] In so many entries of the period Jacob's diary reflects the manner in which communism existed at the level of culture, becoming topics for debate within intellectual circles in Dublin. A Quaker circle meeting on 6 March 1933 was concerned with 'investigating Communism, Swik explaining Karl Marx, very interestingly, and Seán Murray, talking, answering questions on communism, very good'.[230] Jacob recorded the manner in which parallels were established between society and economy in Ireland and Russia, noting, for example, Peadar O'Donnell's attempt to create an analogy between a kulak and a gombeen man.[231] A circular issued by the Friends of Soviet Russia in March 1930 stated:

> The vital question for Ireland is whether she is to be made party to a war in which she has no interest except such friendly interest as she must feel for a country which has recently emancipated her workers and farmers from a notoriously brutal oppression, and is now building up a social fabric similar in many respects to our ancient Gaelic civilisation, and which the best of our National leaders have struggled to restore.[232]

Although she did not formally join the Irish Communist Party, established in June 1933, Jacob attended their meetings. In part this was facilitated by the united front approach of Irish party members despite the fact that this deviated from the third period of the Executive Committee of the Communist International 1928–34 that called for a class against class approach and denounced co-operation with social reformist parties.[233] Jacob never defined what exactly she meant when she used the words communist or communism but it is clear from her accounts of Irish political culture that many with whom she interacted would have agreed with Bill Gannon, a member of the IRA's Dublin Brigade who declared in 1933 that his commitment to communism was on the basis that 'Communism stands for the smashing up of the Empire. Every good Irishman should be in an organisation which is out for the smashing up of the Empire'. The Comintern's chief aim in Ireland up to 1934 was to incite revolution and this necessitated sporadic interaction with the IRA.[234]

228 Sheehy Skeffington, *Skeff*, p. 79.
229 23 Dec. 1933, RJD Ms (76).
230 6 Mar. 1933, RJD Ms (72).
231 4 Apr. 1930, RJD Ms (64).
232 Included in DT, s 5074A 'Communist Activities 1929–30, Saorstat Éireann'.
233 O'Connor, *Reds and the Green*, p, 10, pp. 197–198, p. 238.
234 Quoted in Hanley, 'Moss Twomey, radicalism, and the IRA', p. 57; O'Connor, *Reds and the Green*, p. 238.

The Socialist Republican Workers' Party of Ireland, established in April 1926 by Roddy Connolly, included Mrs Despard as women's organiser and this feminist perspective to left-wing agitation appealed to Jacob. This party situated itself, like so many other left-wing bodies, in opposition to the Free State; in the year of its foundation the party called for the establishment of a council of trade unions to develop industrial struggles and for a united front of all 'progressive parties' against the Free State.[235]

Jacob's attendance at Communist Party meetings and her membership of the Irish Friends of Soviet Russia should be viewed in the context of her simultaneous membership of such organisations as the Indian-Irish Independence League and her presence at Anti-Imperialist League demonstrations and meetings. The latter was established as a communist front at the Congress of Oppressed Nationalities in Brussels in 1927 attended by Frank Ryan and Donal O'Donoghue, and has been described as an 'increasingly important strand in the republican-communist matrix' of the late 1920s.[236] Jacob was elected to the committee on 28 September 1932. Many of the prominent members of the League were those of republican socialism, Jacob recording the attendance of, for example, Ryan, Moss Twomey and George Gilmore. Due to the influence of men like Ryan the speeches and discussions related the perennial debates of Irish physical-force politics to the Indian context. Of course this reductive tendency to contextualise international issues and trends within narrow Irish concerns and preoccupations was also seen in the manner in which the fascism of the Blueshirts, in particular that of the ordinary member, was fundamentally a domestic concern with the manner in which the Economic War (1932–4) had impacted on the farming sections of society.[237] The trend was also, as noted, evident in Jacob's attempt at a comparative analysis of the state of women in Ireland and the Soviet Union. Similarly, the IRA tolerance of communism in the early 1930s was rendered more palatable as the ideology was imbued with allusions to historical republican heroes. Tone, Connolly, Pearse, were, according to Twomey, communists, committed as they were to undoing the British conquest and ending inequities in land and social structures.[238]

Jacob noted the attack on Connolly House, the headquarters of the Communist Party of Ireland, on 29 March 1933 presenting it as a battle between progressives and 'the religious crowd'.[239] Although the *Workers' Voice* claimed

235 O'Connor, *Reds and the Green*, p. 132.

236 Ibid., p. 128, p. 143.

237 Cronin, *The Blueshirts and Irish Politics*, pp. 13–14.

238 Ferriter, *The Transformation of Ireland*, p. 416; Hanley, *The IRA*, p. 179.

239 30 Mar. 1933, RJD Ms (72).

that the Blueshirts directed the attack, Jacob was not alone in her view.[240] Moss Twomey also believed that the anti-communist campaign was the result of clerical influence, citing the almost total emphasis on the evils of communism in the Lenten pastorals of that year. He laid emphasis in particular on a report by Nora Connolly O'Brien detailing sermons in inner-city Dublin that called for an attack on communists to forestall church burning.[241] Indeed, retrospectively a number of Blueshirt members expressed a belief that the Catholic Church was responsible for fanning the flames of anti-communism in the period.[242] In the weeks following the attacks on Connolly House the Catholic Young Men's Society publicly burned copies of the *Workers' Voice* and conducted a campaign of intimidation to dissuade newsagents from stocking copies. St Patrick's Anti-Communist League held parades in April and June, and attempts were made to break up communist meetings in Dublin in June and July.[243]

On 7 May 1933 Jacob attended a meeting at 41 Parnell Square to prepare for a commemoration of Connolly with the intention of marking his birthday and selling cheap editions of his works. As usual she took likes and dislikes to the members of the committee, approving of Seán Murray but not of Roddy Connolly. Later that month she typed a pamphlet relating to Connolly House while she spoke on schools at the Connolly memorial meeting in the Mansion House on 4 June.[244] At Bodenstown in June 1933 Jacob sold 'Connolly stuff' from the Cumann na mBan stall. In her account of the day she castigated Moss Twomey, the IRA Chief-of-Staff between 1926 and 1936, for his denial of any connection between the IRA, communism and irreligion; 'It was a great blot on his speech being such a large part of it'. Throughout 1933 the IRA, particularly in its socialist guise, attempted to counter criticisms that the organisation was opposed to religion. Hanley argues that the decline in recruitment to the organisation as a result of criticism by the Catholic Church of its communistic doctrines influenced Twomey's 1933 Bodendstown speech.[245] Jacob's account of the 1933 Pilgrimage highlights these internal fissures within the IRA:

---

240 O'Connor, *Reds and the Green*, p. 185.

241 Hanley, *The IRA*, p. 66. Nora Connolly O'Brien was the daughter of James Connolly and the founder of the Belfast branch of Cumann na mBan. She and her husband, Seamus O'Brien, worked to build up the Labour Party established by her father and she tried in vain to re-establish the ICA. McCoole, *No Ordinary Women*, p. 153.

242 Cronin, *The Blueshirts and Irish Politics*, p. 134.

243 O'Connor, *Reds and the Green*, p. 186.

244 7 May 1933; 10 May 1933; 20 May 1933; 4 June 1933, RJD Ms (72).

245 Hanley, *The IRA*, p. 65.

Lil & Peader and Nora C. etc selling on the road, also Communists selling quite
good stuff on the road till, as I heard, they were confiscated by the order of Mick
P. [Price] which I wd call highway robbery, even if he did return the stuff later.

The irony of Price's confiscation of communist literature at Bodenstown in
the light of his key role in the establishment of the Republican Congress in
1934 must be noted.[246] Jacob herself bought *Marx, Lenin & Ireland* from the
Communists at Connolly House on the 20 June, and heard from them all
about Price's actions at Bodenstown.[247]

Jacob described how a 'communist banner', which had a red flag with
Connolly's portrait on it but not their name, was torn in two by a detachment
of IRA men at Bodenstown the following year. What Jacob described was, in
fact, the tension between the Republican Congress and the IRA and not, as
she mistakenly suggested, between the IRA and the Communist Party who
were not involved in the event.[248] Of course, Jacob's use of terminology reflects
the close connection between Congress and the Communist Party after the
former organisation split in September 1934.[249] Jacob's description of the 1934
Bodenstown event also highlighted the manner in which conservative attitudes
to gender roles were still entrenched within republicanism: 'finally we were
marshalled in order . . . all the women put at the back – for safety reasons
according to George – till Cora H. [Hughes][250] came along & protested, after
which we were put in the middle'.[251] Nearly a year later, in April 1935, Jacob
noted the accounts in the papers of the anti-Communist riots during the
procession to Glasnevin 'when George had his face cut & Cora was attacked,
& of hymn-singing riots at the College Green meeting on Monday when
Gallagher the Communist MP was to speak, when Peader was hit with a
brick'.[252] She attended the meeting on 8 May to discuss these attacks, clearly
accepting O'Donnell's speech 'on the anti-clerical tack, representing the
attacks as engineered thro religious bigotry working on the crowd' but also
noting George Gilmore's contention that 'it was purely political, worked by
the small clique that holds economic rule here, to disunite the workers'.[253]

246 Ibid., p. 105.
247 18 June 1933; 20 June 1933, RJD Ms (72). Lil O'Donnell, wife of Peadar O'Donnell.
248 McGarry, *Frank Ryan*, p. 43; Hanley, *The IRA*, p. 107.
249 Hanley, *The IRA*, p. 109.
250 Hughes was a Cumann na mBan activist and at an earlier period commander of the UCD branch.
Hanley, *The IRA*, p. 103.
251 23 June 1934, RJD Ms (77).
252 14 Apr. 1935, RJD Ms (78). Gallagher was probably Willie Gallacher a communist organiser from
Scotland. See O'Connor, *Reds and the Green*, p. 33.
253 8 May 1935, RJD Ms (78).

During 1935 Jacob continued to participate in what was becoming an increasingly defensive republican-socialist movement, collecting for the prisoners' meeting and selling flags, for example, to crowds waiting for a Connolly procession in May, commenting on how there was 'complete apathy. But no peeler interfered with me so I began to feel safe'.[254] The use of the word 'peeler', a word associated with the earlier period of British law and policing in Ireland is interesting here. The IRA and those, like Jacob, who refused to recognise the authority of the Free State, viewed the gardaí as the symbol of Free State authority and, as such, as the upholders of British rule in Ireland.[255]

NEGOTIATING PACIFISM AND REPUBLICANISM

The political, cultural and social milieu in which Jacob operated in the 1920s and 1930s led to certain tensions and inconsistencies in her beliefs. One needs to note her gleeful comments on Frank Ryan's destructive forays against the flying of Union Jacks on Remembrance days during the 1920s. To an extent her joy in the theatre of these attacks contradicted her pacifist tendencies. Remembrance Day rallies were occasions of large-scale disorder and even violence. She herself wrote in 1926 how she 'went down town looking for trouble ... & only found crowds engaged in the same search and an occasional screech and bustle with no visible baton charge to show for it'.[256] Moreover, the imagery invoked by the IRA, with its concern to target unionist businesses and students of Trinity College, could be construed, despite their avowals to the contrary, as sectarian, and hardly likely to appeal to Jacob.[257] Indeed, this dichotomy in her allegiances is shown when on the day following her participation in the poppy day 'trouble' of 1926 she attended a lecture at the Young Friends in Rathmines where the speaker talked about his conversion to pacifism.[258] Jacob recorded how at a 'packed' meeting in the Mansion House on 29 September 1932 Ryan was

> bloody (there was a hint of disapproval of the non-violent movement throughout, & the 2 Indians had an air of apologising for it that made me angry) ... Gandhi's policy only negative; prevents Britain succeeding but doesn't bring success to India.[259]

254 15 Apr. 1935; 11–12 May 1935, RJD Ms (77).
255 Hanley, *The IRA*, pp. 78–9.
256 11 Nov. 1926, RJD Ms (54).
257 Hanley, *The IRA*, pp. 71–2.
258 12 Nov. 1926, RJD Ms (54).
259 29 Sept. 1932, RJD Ms (71).

Jacob had attempted to negotiate this tension between pacifism and republican violence before she met Ryan. Interestingly, aspects of the relationship
between Frances Morrin and Andy Callaghan in *Callaghan* foreshadowed
what she experienced with Ryan. Frances is horrified and even afraid of
Callaghan when he shows no remorse at killing a police officer during an arms
run.[260] The refusal of men to consider how their political activism impacted on
women and family is also a theme of *The Rebel's Wife*; Tone is depicted as
selfish, although understandably so, in deserting his family in the service of
the United Irishmen.[261] Andy Callaghan, like Frank Ryan, acted instinctually,
hitting the English recruiting officer when he referred to England as the
mother country.[262] Andy Callaghan refuses to accept the legality of the British
legal system and remains mute during his trial for assaulting a recruiting officer,
a stance taken by Ryan during many of his court cases in the 1920s and 1930s.

In a sense Jacob had written her ideal man in Callaghan before she had met
his real life image in Ryan. Her issues with political violence notwithstanding
she was drawn to men who stood apart; a follower herself she courted the
society of charismatic leaders such as Ryan. Yet this was more complex than
blind devotion to a lover. She was able to describe Ryan as 'bloody' but she was
not a rigid doctrinarian and was sufficiently flexible politically to attempt to
negotiate her own conflicting allegiances to republicanism and pacifism, as
during an earlier period she had attempted to marry her nationalist commitment to her commitment to suffrage.

In 1929, at the request of Ryan, Jacob formed a Protection Committee
whose function was to 'investigate the arrest and continual re-arrest of certain
republicans' and to aid republicans who lost their jobs.[263] It should be noted
firstly that this concern over the employment problems faced by republicans
was one that had garnered Jacob's attention before she met Ryan. On 31 July
she recorded a conversation held with Lasairfhíona Somers who 'talked fearfully about the good men that are being sacked by the local bodies (teachers &
doctors) because the government won't give grants if they are kept. . . . These
things shd be made far more public – they are allowed to be all muffled up &
forgotten.'[264] One reading of Jacob's involvement in setting up the Protection

---

260 Winthrop, *Callaghan*, pp. 191–2.

261 Danae O'Regan, 'Representations and attitudes of republican women in the novels of Annie M.
P. Smithson (1873–1948) and Rosamond Jacob (1888–1960)' in Louise Ryan and Margaret Ward (eds),
Irish Women and Nationalism: Soldiers, New Women and Wicked Hags (Dublin: Irish Academic Press,
2004), p. 93.

262 Winthrop, *Callaghan*, p. 204.

263 Doyle, 'A bio-critical study of Rosamond Jacob', p. 53.

264 31 July 1925, RJD Ms (25).

Committee was that this was a commitment to political violence by affiliation or from a one-degree remove; she was involved in an organisation designed to help those whose adherence to a campaign premised on the threat of anti-state violence that had impacted negatively on their economic and personal lives. And despite the tensions it created in relation to her avowed pacifism, Jacob participated actively in the street culture, pageantry and gossip of republican and left-wing Dublin, motivated arguably by a desire for inclusion and participation. She attended the Bodenstown annual pilgrimage to the grave of Wolfe Tone which must be recognised as not just participation in political commemoration but in a social event, comprising bands and hospitality in tents provided by the Nás na Ríogh Hotel, Naas; a céilidhe in the Mansion House usually concluded the day.[265]

In particular, Jacob's republicanism at times jarred with her membership of the IIL. The question of the use of legitimate force was one which split the IIL on many occasions during the 1920s. Jacob was critical of Louie Bennett's belief in the 'courage and self-sacrifice shown by the soldiers in the Great War' while Bennett simultaneously denounced the Irish Civil War as 'utterly despicable – what could anyone be proud of in shooting from behind a hedge or in a house?'[266] Similarly Jacob was horrified at Lucy Kingston's comments at an IIL meeting as civil war became inevitable in July 1922: 'Lucy perfectly awful; sneering condemnation of the country altogether – how we have become stage Irish at last'.[267] Women such as Sheehy Skeffington believed that imperialistic wars such as the First World War were barbarous but accepted the right to use force to free subject nations from colonial rule. She interpreted the words Peace and Freedom in the nomenclature of the international organisation through the lens of Pearse's phrase: Ireland unfree can never be at peace. Indeed, at the 1926 Congress of the WILPF held in Ireland, issues of Irish freedom dominated the attitudes of many of the Irish delegates.[268] The case of Jacob suggests that an interpretation of the tensions within the IIL along clearly demarcated binary lines is too simplistic. The division tends to be viewed as that between those like Louie Bennett who believed that all resistance to violence was wrong and those who agreed with Hanna Sheehy Skeffington.[269] In other words, the point of analysis is the period leading up to

---

265 Hanley, *The IRA*, p. 51.

266 28 June 1925, RJD Ms (48); 15 Sept. 1926, RJD Ms (54).

267 12 July 1922, RJD Ms (41).

268 Margaret Ward, 'Nationalism, pacifism and internationalism: Louie Bennett, Hanna Sheehy Skeffington, and the problems of "defining feminism"' in Anthony Bradley and Maryann Valiulis (eds), *Gender and Sexuality in Modern Ireland* (Amherst: University of Massachusetts Press, 1997), p. 79.

269 Ibid., pp. 64–5.

Irish independence. Little is written on how alleged pacifists such as Jacob, discontented with limited political independence and a lack of gender equality, were willing to turn a blind eye to the politics of violence engaged in by the organisations which sought to effect change in Irish society in the 1920s and 1930s. Jacob was willing to tolerate IRA violence against Cumann na nGaedheal supporters. When the findings of the Boundary Commission were published in 1925, Bennett and fellow member, Mrs Dix, desired the Committee of the IIL to write a 'peace and good will issue' on the subject to which other members including Jacob objected strongly. Jacob was consequently told that she was 'no pacifist'.[270] Again in 1926 Jacob refused to sign a letter given to her by fellow IIL members, Lucy Kingston and Mrs Johnston, proposing that Armistice Day be made an international Peace Day. In Jacob's words, 'nothing was done to disgrace us'.[271] Jacob was alone in objecting to Bennett's proposal to adopt a 'resolution of horror and sympathy' with Kevin O'Higgins's wife following his assassination in 1927. Jacob did admit that it was logical for the section to 'express disapproval, & the words they finally put together were comparatively harmless'.[272] Despite such recognition and her avowed pacifism, Jacob's republican sympathies revolted against the expression of sympathy with the family of such a man as O'Higgins.

INTERNATIONAL PERSPECTIVES

The tensions Jacob's republican beliefs created for her within the IIL notwithstanding, the organisation still acted for her as a safety valve, insulated, as she perceived it to be, from the restrictive and repressive values of the Free State. Jacob acted as joint secretary with Lucy Kingston from 30 October 1925 to 7 September 1927 when she resigned to become official secretary to the Gaelic League. The IIL took an active part in agitating against much of the legislative measures to which Jacob was opposed. The organisation, for example, was opposed to the Censorship of Literature Bill and worked at committee level to draft amendments to it. The IIL on many occasions joined forces with other women's groups to agitate against gender discrimination in legislative measures. The group was part of a joint deputation with, amongst other feminist groups, the Women Workers' Union, to O'Higgins on the Jury issue in February 1927.[273]

270 4 Dec. 1925; 18 Dec. 1925, RJD Ms (50).
271 24 Sept. 1926; 1 Oct. 1926, RJD Ms (54).
272 15 July 1927, RJD Ms (57).
273 18 Feb. 1927, RJD Ms (55).

The IIL also allowed Jacob to partake in a culture of internationalism during a period in which she believed Irish society to have become increasingly introspective and conservative. Jacob travelled to Prague in 1929 as one of the Irish delegates to the Annual Congress of the WILPF. Earlier in 1924 she was delegate to the congress in Switzerland. The culture of internationalism within which Jacob participated was one suited to her holistic approach to discrimination. Chapter 6 of her history of the rise of the United Irishmen, entitled 'International brotherhood', concentrates exclusively on the links the organisation made with reform and democratic societies throughout Europe and America. She lauded the United Irishmen as a society that combined 'the principles of national independence and international brotherhood'. Similarly, she praised the United Scotsmen's commitment to principles of nationality and democracy, and their simultaneous determination to 'found on the ruins of the established government, three distinct republics of England, Scotland and Ireland'.[274] In focusing on the international links made by the United Irishmen Jacob would have been very much aware of the contemporary context in which disaffected republican activists, often leaning to the left, operated. Frank Ryan argued, for example, that the Irishmen who joined the International Brigade to fight Franco went not just to counter Eoin O'Duffy's Christian Front but also to 'restore a historical connection with the international struggle that existed in the time of the United Irishmen'.[275]

Jacob's diary indicates the manner in which those alienated from Irish society in the 1920s and 1930s adopted an internationalist approach. On 25 February 1925 a man from Montenegro talked of the treatment of his country by Serbia,[276] and the Committee of the IIL sent a condemnatory resolution to all branches of the WILPF. She noted that same month discussion at a gathering in Mia Cranwill's of an international organisation to help Irish republican prisoners.[277] In 1928 she led an IIL study circle on an unidentified book on Russia.[278] Richard English discusses the manner in which Frank Ryan viewed the Irish people's struggle for full independence as interlinked with the struggle of subject people all over the world. English, of course, critically analyses the inherent contradiction in this paradigm as Ryan became involved

---

274 Jacob, *The Rise of the United Irishmen*, p. 199, p. 202.

275 McGarry, *Frank Ryan*, p. 61.

276 Montenegro and Serbia were unified in 1918.

277 20 Feb. 1925, RJD Ms (47); 3 Apr. 1925, RJD Ms (48); 11 Feb. 1925, RJD Ms (47). Mia Cranwill (1880–1972) was a metalwork artist and illustrator. Nicola Gordon Bowe and Elizabeth Cumming, *The Arts and Crafts Movements in Dublin and Edinburgh: 1885–1925* (Dublin: Irish Academic Press, 1998), pp. 111–12.

278 13 Jan. 1928, RJD Ms (59).

with Seán Russell in a bid to act as an intermediary between de Valera and German fascists.[279] Jacob's participation in the culture of internationalism during the 1920s and 1930s has to be viewed as offering an alternative or extra layer to the discussion. Although Jacob's diary recorded her participation in, for example, the activities of the Republican Congress and Friends of Soviet Russia, her critique of such movements was not at the level of class conflict and socialist brotherhood but at the level of feminist advancement in Irish society and international feminist activism as was evident from her account of her visit to the Soviet Union in 1931 discussed above.

To live as a radical woman like Rosamond Jacob in Ireland in the 1920s and 1930s was at once exhilarating and disillusioning. Jacob's participation in the counter culture surrounding men such as Frank Ryan, George Gilmore and Peadar O'Donnell allowed her to feel a sense of participating on a certain edge. On the other hand, her life became increasingly a round of committees and political meetings which bore no fruit on the level of gender equality. Her existence as a single woman suffused her life with a large element of marginality and at times she struggled like her heroine Constance Moore, 'questioning the value of life', a situation which would become more pronounced in the last two decades in which she lived.[280] Certainly, however, Jacob's continued activism, her participation in a culture of internationalism, gives the lie to the allegation that Irish female politicisation was moribund between the end of the Civil War and the establishment of second-wave feminism in the 1970s. Her international perspective, as that of so many radical women in the period, forces a reconsideration of the concept of Ireland's insularity during the decades following independence. Furthermore, Jacob's gravitation towards left-wing republicanism during the late 1920s and early 1930s as a movement through which a synergistic republican and feminist programme might be fashioned adds a layer of complexity to the treatment of Irish republican socialism in the period.

279 English, *Radicals and the Republic*, p. 248.
280 Jacob, 'Third person singular', p. 2.

SEVEN

DECLINE AND NOSTALGIA
1937–60

—

Although one can no longer see the period after the ratification of the 1937 Constitution and before the advent of second-wave feminism as a moribund time for feminist activism in Ireland, historians of Irish women have until very recently ignored these decades. Indeed, on a wider societal level a recent book has dubbed Ireland in the 1950s 'the lost decade'.[1] While further historiography on the position of women in the period after 1937 will no doubt work to change perceptions of the 1930s and 1940s as fallow years in the history of Irish female activism, for Jacob these were difficult decades as she entered middle and old age. This stage in her life cycle and the fact that the political campaigns of the period had none of the overt romance and excitement of those of the revolutionary and first-wave feminist period conspire, from the evidence of her diary, to enhance perceptions of an insular Ireland shielded from foreign influences by rigid censorship laws, a country from which it seemed the young and vibrant were increasingly fleeing.

Following the ratification of the 1937 Constitution by the Irish public, the position of women as domestic and child-centred was enshrined as a fundamental tenet of the Irish state. For female activists such as Jacob the constitution reflected the 'Catholic dislike of liberty for anyone'.[2] This 'bigoted' notion of 'everyone-must obey-Catholic-rules point of view' was fundamental to Jacob's growing vocalism on the issue of birth control rights and her concern, even agitation, at the mixed marriages of her niece and nephews.[3] In the remaining two decades of her life Jacob continued to agitate for female advancement in society. She was galvanised in this period by the failure of women to secure adequate representation in the Seanad and full amendments to the status of

1   Dermot Keogh, Finbarr O'Shea and Carmel Quinlan (eds), *The Lost Decade: Ireland in the 1950s* (Cork: Mercier Press, 2004).
2   27 May 1937, RJD Ms (81).
3   7 May 1939, RJD Ms (87).

women under the Constitution.[4] The Joint Committee of Women's Societies
increasingly saw that an organisation was necessary to deal effectively with the
political discrimination of women. In this context the Women's Social and
Progressive League was formed.[5] Initially the Joint Committee discussed putting
up an independent female candidate for the Dáil elections. By March 1937 the
prohibitive cost of this had shelved the plan.[6] Jacob instead worked on various
elections campaigns to secure female representation in local government in the
late 1930s and early 1940s. Importantly, such female-centred organisations as
the WSPL were much more than vehicles to secure political change. These
organisations fulfiled a strong social need for Jacob, offering her social interaction and an outlet in a public space that was very limited for single women.
As Jacob moved into old age she struggled even further with feelings of loneliness, depression and a lack of purpose. These feelings were exacerbated by
the death of old friends and acquaintances made during her earlier service in
the suffrage campaign and the struggle for independence. One very interesting
feature of her later life was her interaction with women who had been involved
in the campaign for independence or who had lost family members in the
struggle. Jacob's diary indicates the manner in which many of these women
considered themselves forgotten by the state. Jacob recorded instances of
individuals reduced to penury and trapped by what was, in the 1940s and 1950s,
a jaded discourse of sacrifice that the state refused to recognise by granting
pension rights. Jacob's account of visits to women such as Mrs Mellows, the
mother of Liam Mellows, offers an indication of the price the national
struggle extracted in later decades from those who were involved. Describing
the final days of Mrs Mellows, Meg Connery and others, Jacob recorded
poverty and alcoholism; her account indicates that these women were unable
to leave the past behind and had become a hidden section of the population.
Jacob worked to attempt to secure financial aid for such women but in a sense
she too felt an elided individual in Irish society. Surrounded by established
families and families in the making as her niece and nephews married, she felt
increasingly on the fringes and without a core identity of her own.

4   The Irish Senate established in 1922 was abolished by de Valera in 1936. A new Senate was
established in 1937 with election on the basis of vocational panels. Female activists lobbied the
government throughout 1936 and into 1937 on the issue of the adequate representation of women in
the new Senate. See DT, s 8973, 'Second Chamber, Committee of Enquiry, 1936, miscellaneous
correspondence'; s 9278, 'Women, constitutional and economic position in Dáil Éireann'.
5   Report on the history of the Joint Committee of Women's Societies and Social Workers, 1983,
Papers of the Joint Committee of Women's Societies and Social Workers, 98/14/6/1 NAI.
6   18 Mar. 1937; 22 Mar. 1937, RJD Ms (81).

Jacob continued to attend Gaelic League meetings and participated in the hated yearly collections although she was able to breath a sigh of relief in September 1937 not to be Secretary any longer.[7] Throughout the 1940s her involvement lessened and by the early 1950s her attendance at the League was reduced to the annual meeting of the Craobh, where she noted in 1950 that it was 'nice to hear a bit of Irish again' but also commented on how there was 'hardly anyone I know'.[8] She noted that over the years gender issues around collections had not changed, and she welcomed the comment by a man outside Haddington Road Church: 'I'm watching this game now for 30 years, and 'tis always the same – they send the poor women out early in the cold, but the *gentlemen* don't come alone with their boxes till 11 o'clock. Sound view point . . . Home very glad it was over'.[9] She did, however, continue to attend céilidhe and the classes taught by Cú Uladh and Máirtín Ó Cadhain.[10] By the late 1930s the Gaelic League was exciting none of the enthusiasm from Jacob that she experienced in the early 1900s. Indeed, she attended a talk on the need for a united front among the different Gaelic societies, indicating how the Irish language movement had become fissiparous and lacked a solid core.[11] Her local branch in February 1939 had a working balance of £317 with a larger amount due in rates, rent and teachers' fees.[12] On a personal level money was still an issue for Jacob. Visiting Ryan's family she noted how she came home by tram as it was cheaper than the bus.[13]

THE DEATH OF FRANK RYAN

By 1937 the affair with Ryan had been over for some time and Jacob regarded him at this point as a friend. When he returned in March 1937 from his first involvement in Spain she talked with him and he was able to tell her how her letter in Irish so confused the censor that he himself had to read it for him.[14] Ryan had been wounded at the Battle of Jamura in February 1937 and his time

7   24 Sept. 1937, RJD Ms (82).

8   3 Nov. 1950, RJD Ms (139).

9   24 Mar. 1939, RJD Ms (86).

10   14 Nov. 1937; 29 Oct. 1937, RJD Ms (83); 19 Oct. 1938, RJD Ms (85). The novelist and later Trinity lecturer in Modern Irish, Mairtin Uí Cadhain (1906–70). Cú Uladh was the pseudonym of the language activist, Peadar T. Mag Fhionnlaoigh, from Ulster.

11   12 Nov. 1937, RJD Ms (83).

12   3 Feb. 1939, RJD Ms (86).

13   4 Feb. 1939, RJD Ms (86).

14   23 Mar. 1937, RJD Ms (81).

in Ireland was short, merely designed to convalesce. When he left again for Spain Jacob began a pattern of visiting his mother and father and became very friendly with his sister Eilís.[15] The Ryans in this way almost became a surrogate family for Jacob. On 3 April 1938 she noted the rumour in the *Sunday Independent* of Ryan's capture in Spain.[16] Like all of Ryan's friends she was reliant on rumour and hearsay as to his well being and whereabouts. On 18 May 1938 she learned from Cora Gallagher of his location in a concentration camp in Burgos; by the end of the year she wondered if she would ever see him again.[17] At a céilidhe she spent some time answering 'anxious questions' from a Nora Ní C about Ryan, she having heard that 'he went to fight for the wicked anti-religious Reds & she didn't' believe it in its fullness, & I was trying to set it before her. She thinks he is really religious'.[18] Jacob signed the Gaelic League petition to de Valera to encourage him to agitate for the release of Ryan in April 1939 and noted how other people seemed glad to sign it. The Women's Aid Committee, formed to act as a forum for news emanating from Spain and to aid the families of Irish volunteers in the International Brigade, largely organised the Release Frank Ryan Committee.[19] In May 1939 Jacob was to the fore in writing a leaflet on Ryan, again noting that it was well received when handed out to people on Sackville Place, 'nice to have something to hand out that people are almost eager for – hands sticking out from several points at once'.[20] On 25 September 1940 she received a note from civil servant, S. Nolan, to say that Ryan had been released, however, the lack of news thereafter was considered sinister.[21]

On 22 November 1944 Eilís Ryan told her of a letter from GOR[22] who still believed that Ryan was alive.[23] However, on 23 February 1945 she read a report in the *Irish Press* that he had died the previous June in a sanatorium near Dresden. 'No explanation, either of why he was there or of why it was not

15   15 Jan. 1938, RJD Ms (83).

16   3 Apr. 1938, RJD Ms (83).

17   18 May 1938, RJD Ms (84); summation of 1938, RJD Ms (85).

18   16 Oct. 1938, RJD Ms (85).

19   3 Apr. 1939; 10 Apr. 1939, RJD Ms (86); Andrée Sheehy Skeffington, *A Life of Owen Sheehy Skeffington 1909–1970* (Dublin: Lilliput, 1991), p. 83.

20   28 May 1939, RJD Ms (87).

21   25 Sept. 1940; 16 Nov. 1940, RJD Ms (93). In July Ryan had been permitted to 'escape' with the help of the Admiral Canaris, head of German intelligence, who hoped to forge a link between the IRA and Germany in the context of the Second World War. http://www.oxforddnb.com/view/article/65859, accessed 13 Aug. 2008.

22   Gerald O'Reilly with whom Ryan corresponded in New York. Ryan asked O'Reilly at various points to inform people that he was well.

23   22 Nov. 1944, RJD Ms (111).

known long ago'. Two days later she heard through Peadar O'Donnell that Ryan had been trying to get to America but was held in Germany.[24] On 7 March Jacob participated in the march to the Ormonde Hotel where a meeting was held to discuss the commemoration of Ryan. A sub-committee was formed to publish a commemorative pamphlet and Jacob was involved in its writing. From this date rumours of Ryan's collaboration with the Nazis circulated.[25] George Gilmore warned Jacob that T. Lynch[26] and B. Mulcahy[27] would represent him as friendly to the Nazis. Mulcahy and Clissman[28] wished to use Ryan's alleged collaboration as leverage to win the IRA over to help the Third Reich. Other friends of Ryan, such as George Gilmore, believed that the pamphlet should not be brought out if evidence was produced to corroborate the rumours.[29] Gilmore believed that Jacob had a misconception of Ryan: 'Thinks he was a big figure, but very different from my conception (sure he knows it, of course).'[30] Clearly her relationship with Ryan was still to the fore in her mind. Visiting Eilís she noted how beautiful Ryan was in a photograph with Ernest Hemingway, 'such a contrast. P. in uniform, tall & very fine looking'.[31]

BACKWARD GLANCES

By the late 1930s the excitement of first-wave feminism had become history and the subject of radio talks.[32] Indeed, commemoration was a feature of the Jacob's life more than activism from this point; her earlier activism had become historical precedent used to explain and extrapolate on present day issues and attitudes. In January 1939 she attended a meeting called in relation to a hostile

24   23 Feb. 1945; 25 Feb. 1945, RJD Ms (113). Ryan died in June 1944 after a stroke in January 1943. http://www.oxforddnb.com/view/article/65859, accessed 13 Aug. 2008.

25   For details o f Ryan's involvement with the Nazis see http://www.oxforddnb.com/view/article/ 65859, accessed 13 Aug. 2008.

26   Possibly Tadgh Lynch, editor of *An Phoblacht* from the summer of 1937 until its suppression later that year.

27   Budge Mulcahy moved in the same republican circles as Ryan. Adrian Hoar, *In Green and Red: The Lives of Frank Ryan* (Dingle: Brandon, 2004), p. 35.

28   Jacob misspells the surname as Helmut Klissman who was the husband of Budge Mulcahy. Clissman was part of German intelligence operations designed to foment trouble within enemy territory. Ibid., p. 238.

29   7 Mar. 1945; 8 Apr. 1945; 14 Mar. 1945, RJD Ms (113); 28 Sept. 1945; 8 Oct. 1945, RJD Ms (116).

30   29 June 1945, RJD Ms (115).

31   26 Oct. 1945, RJD Ms (116). Ryan met and spent time with Hemmingway in Madrid in 1937. Hoar, *In Green and Red*, p. 209.

32   17 Aug. 1937, RJD Ms (82).

letter complaining of the attitude of Mary Hayden and Lucy Kingston in the newspapers to the appointment of only one woman on a committee for refugees. 'He took it as hostility to refugees. Just as men 25 years ago took claim for the vote as an attack on Redmond's party'.[33] In November 1939 the WSPU listened to Gonne lecture on Irishwomen in the Irish-Ireland movement at the turn of the century culminating in an account of the formation of Inghinidhe na h-Éireann.[34] The election campaign in support of Hanna Sheehy Skeffington in 1943 was described by Molony as reminiscent of '30 yrs ago'.[35] Commemoration and remembrance was all pervasive. In February 1938 Jacob was asked to join a committee being established to commemorate 1798 and considered with George Gilmore a list of other potential members – 'any Republicans who are not thoroughly sectarian and wdn't be thought Communists'.[36] The Civil War split loomed large in this committee. By 22 May 1938 P. T. Daly[37] and Máire Comerford were named as secretaries; Maura Laverty, originally approached, could not fulfil the role because Cumann na mBan would not let its name appear as constituent society in conjunction with other societies which accept 'the FS parliament'.[38] In this committee Jacob was assigned her usual roles. She typed the pamphlet issued and recorded how she went to Croke Park in September 1938 trying to make sales before the match.[39]

Despite the backward glance, Jacob did embrace many aspects of a modernising Ireland, in particular the development of radio broadcasting and its impact on the Gaelic League mission. She regularly reported listening to Gaelic music broadcasts on the radio and participated in Irish language quizzes; listening to Gaelic games on the radio she noted how Michael O Hehir had a trace of an American accent which 'rather spoils him'.[40] On 1 October 1938 she gave a broadcast on Dublin in 1798. Two years later she and Lucy Kingston spoke on the subject of female education.[41] The development of air travel allowed her to fly to London to visit her publisher and to consult a medium. She left from Baldonnell in a 'long thin silvery aeroplane, 2 blasé business men & myself'. The plane had some trouble taking off but didn't appear to go as fast or

33   20 Jan. 1939, RJD Ms (86).

34   9 Nov. 1939, RJD Ms (90).

35   22 June 1943, RJD Ms (104).

36   13 Feb. 1938, RJD Ms (83).

37   Possibly Peter Daly who served with Ryan in Spain. See Hoar, *In Green and Red*, p. 205.

38   22 May 1938, RJD Ms (84).

39   21 Aug. 1938; 25 Sept. 1938, RJD Ms (85).

40   3 July 1938, RJD Ms (84); 31 May 1939, RJD Ms (87); 6 Aug. 1939, RJD Ms (89).

41   1 Oct. 1938, RJD Ms (85); 27 Mar. 1941, RJD Ms (95).

be making as much noise as she had feared.[42] Jacob by this time had jettisoned therapy in favour of consulting a medium. Mrs Nash in Queensbury Street, London, essentially repeated much of Mrs Hartley's commentary on Jacob's outlook on life, in particular her perception of the importance of her father and her belief that his death had robbed her of his necessary support, hindering her development. Jacob's failure to establish a family of her own was remarked on, an indication of how central this was to her sense of herself in the period:

> she went into trance . . . very quick, & talked in a childish voice (Sadie) of seeing a tall man . . . who belonged to me – loves me very much – kinder & more sympathetic than my mother, who said other people on earth weren't fair to me, he had seen me hurt & annoyed. I have been up against a barrier & pitched all my strength against it & am tired . . . Louis. My sister with him . . . also got Tom as someone fond of me in brotherly way on earth plane. I was a father's girl & his favourite . . . I've always had to sacrifice myself for others all my life – my individuality been [*sic*] consumed by other people . . . I put myself in little ice boxes – shut myself away from outside world because I can't help it – have had inferiority complex, that's why I've gone into ice box – shrink into corner . . . I ought to have been a mother, child of my upbringing wd have flourished – can help to mould Louis's destiny . . .[43]

There are a few references to children at this point in time which suggest that maybe the attitudes Jacob expressed regarding the undesirability of children were not so clear cut or without contradiction, or, indeed, perhaps changed over time. In July 1938 twin babies were born to an unmarried mother in the Rotunda and Annalies, who lived with Lucy Kingston's family, suggested that Jacob might adopt them.[44] Possibly Jacob's dismissive language towards children masked her own ambivalence on the issue. The following account highlighted this ambivalence:

> I went to see Mrs Cook who had written she was laid up with a cold. Found her better, but the baby (Theresa) missing her outings very much, so I took the brat in the pram for an airing . . . I was wishing to meet people I know and see their surprise . . . I visited Cora. She was highly amused to hear what I'd been at.[45]

42   24 May 1938, RJD Ms (84).
43   25 May 1938, RJD Ms (84).
44   5 July 1938, RJD Ms (84).
45   10 Nov. 1939, RJD Ms (90).

Cora Gallagher's amazement at Jacob's willingness to spend time with a child, coupled with her own use of the word brat, is noteworthy. Jacob fostered this anti-child attitude, possibly intentionally. Yet this aggressively dismissive stance towards children must be countered by Jacob's desire to be seen by people while pushing the pram – to be viewed in a maternal or caring role. Jacob did view children as over demanding of adults, 'a curse, interrupting and wanting . . . attention', as she described a meal with a mother and daughter in September 1945.[46] Yet, it is noteworthy that Jacob like so many other women writers of the period, such as Patricia Lynch and Macardle, wrote for children.[47] In 1960 Jacob finally found a publisher for *The Raven's Glen*, the story of a group of children who discover the last descendant of a matriarchal line of priestesses who 'worshipped' the Cailleach from pre-historic times.[48] Both Jacob and Lynch were childless but by writing for children subscribed to the dominant ideology of woman as child-orientated.

PHILANTHROPY AND THE SINGLE WOMAN

Jacob began concerted philanthropic work in the late 1930s, visiting the South Dublin Union inmates.[49] This type of work became central to her existence from this point in time. Although she had from an early age in Waterford been involved in activities of a charitable nature, her heavy involvement in philanthropic work at this point in her life represented in some way a reversal of the roles normally associated with the female life cycle. Oonagh Walsh notes how 'philanthropy gave meaning to life, especially if that life was single'. Philanthropy acted as a form of 'training' for young single women, designed to equip them 'for their presumed position in society as adults'.[50] For Jacob, by contrast, philanthropy and her membership of the various organisations of female activism, provided a scaffold, a series of touchstones to structure her adult life around. On 9 August 1938 she recorded how she was approached by Dr McCormick to visit a semi-paralysed woman in the Union; she wished to give the nun in charge the sense that people were aware of this woman's neglect.[51]

---

46 14 Sept. 1945, RJD Ms (116).

47 Gerardine Meaney, 'Identity and opposition: women's writing, 1890–1960', in Angela Bourke et al. (eds), *The Field Day Anthology of Irish Writing*, vol. v (Cork: Cork University Press, 2002), p. 980.

48 Rosamond Jacob, *The Raven's Glen* (Dublin: Alan Figgis, 1960), p. 147.

49 18 Nov. 1937, RJD Ms (82).

50 Oonagh Walsh, *Anglican Women in Dublin: Philanthropy, Politics and Education in the Early Twentieth Century* (Dublin: UCD Press, 2005), p. 90, p. 91.

51 9 Aug. 1938, RJD Ms (85).

The maternalistic focus of Irish feminist politics in the 1930s and 1940s was problematic for Jacob. Jacob's involvement as a single, childless, woman in the Joint Committee and her attendance at meetings of the IHA set up by Hilda Tweedy in 1942 involved her in many discussions and concerns of little imme-diate relevance to her own position in life, although integral to her wider com-mitment to female issues and equality. In giving evidence to the Commission on Vocational Organisation, which issued its report in 1943, the words home-maker and woman were used interchangeably.[52] This was problematic for single women such as Jacob. Making out the programme for the IWCA in early 1939 Jacob was regarded as extreme by fellow member Mrs Ditchburn for wanting women speakers.[53] When Mrs Dix suggested that it was not natural for women to take an interest in public life, Jacob retorted that children's futures depended on public affairs.[54] She railed against the prevailing tendency to attribute rising illegitimacy rates to the immorality of girls, stating that 'they cdn't do it alone'.[55] She noted how she had to take the chair at a conference on food and fuel at the Country Shop convened by the IWCA which she believed to be 'very unsuitable as I knew less about matters than anyone there'.[56] The IWCA on 28 January 1941 comprised various speeches on how to lighten household work. On 20 October that year the topic was 'The future we desire for our children'. An earlier Joint Committee on 25 April 1940 was mostly about 'midwives'.[57] On 1 May 1942 she met a fellow member of the IWCA, Mrs Manning, at the Country Shop and they talked of her idea that the organisation should ask Archbishop McQuaid to open Merrion Square to facilitate children's play, particularly since trains to the sea were to be restricted under the emergency conditions of the Second World War. While Jacob recommended on Hanna's advice that Saor an Leanbh (Irish Save the Children Fund) should approach the Archbishop as the Citizens were 'mostly non-Catholic', the child-centred focus of female activism clearly was an irritant at some level to her: '*Children*, of course, nothing else counts'.[58] Jacob described a talk by Helen Chenevix on school meals to the IWCA in

---

52   Caitríona Clear, "'The women can not be blamed": The commission on vocation organisation, feminism and "home-makers" in independent Ireland in the 1930s and '40s' in Mary O'Dowd and Sabine Wichert (eds), *Chattel, Servant or Citizen: Women's Status in Church, State and Society* (Belfast: Institute of Irish Studies, 1995), pp. 183–4.

53   11 Jan. 1939, RJD Ms (86).

54   30 Apr. 1940, RJD Ms (92).

55   1 May 1940, RJD Ms (92).

56   9 May 1941, RJD Ms (95). The Country Shop was on Stephen's Green and comprised a restaurant and a craft shop.

57   28 Jan. 1941, RJD Ms (94); 20 Oct. 1941, RJD Ms (97); 25 Apr. 1940, RJD Ms (92).

58   1 May 1942, RJD Ms (98).

February 1944 as 'not very interesting'.[59] This pattern continued throughout the 1940s. The Commission on Vocational Organisation took evidence from the various women's organisations on the status of 'home-makers'; the necessity that they be granted a public voice and be provided with a range of support services in areas such as childcare was discussed. Suggestion was also made that the government recognise women who engaged in voluntary social service work and who did not have an independent income. Of course the IHA's range of campaigns were Catholic and diverse, the organisation discussing topics such as recycling, which interested Jacob. She was also supportive of any discussion relating to the needs of poorer women. She applauded the talk of Mrs Redmond on issues of TB among the poor given to the IWCA on 24 February 1942 as 'very good work & interesting'.[60] Yet she described the work of Hilda Tweedy and Andrée Sheehy Skeffington on bringing food shortage issues to the attention of the Ministry of Supplies as 'not really interesting, only *practical*'.[61]

Domestic concerns and children were still a feature of many of the talks Jacob attended into the later years of the decade. Mrs Manning opened a discussion at the Citizens on 29 January of 1946 'on the subject of mistress & maid'. Talk revolved around the provision of hostels where girls could live while working as maids and learn domestic skills. Focus was placed on the need for good pay and conditions when compared with the higher wages to be had in England.[62] At the WSPL on 7 October 1948 Miss Blake was indicted to be a bad chairman as a discussion on what the League should do next was dominated by teachers on school meals, despite Jacob's suggestion about fuller integration with the other women's societies. Later that month W. Edwards spoke on parents and education: 'it was long, & very true I'm sure, but with Blake & Bergin afterwards, I'm sick of primary schools'.[63] A number of the literary discussions and events of the period became suffused with the prevalent maternalistic, domestic approach to female activism, a reflection of shared membership. The Women Writers' Club meeting held in the home of Maura Laverty on 6 February 1945 focused on seventeenth-century female writers. While the night was 'quite interesting' Jacob felt that Aphra Behn[64] 'seemed to write more about housekeeping troubles than wd be quite

59 15 Feb. 1944, RJD Ms (107).
60 Clear, 'The women can not be blamed', p. 185; 24 Feb. 1942, RJD Ms (98).
61 11 Nov. 1943, RJD Ms (105).
62 29 Jan. 1946, RJD Ms (117).
63 7 Oct. 1948; 14 Oct. 1948, RJD Ms (131).
64 Alpra Behn (1640?–89) was a playwright and prose writer.

interesting'. The homemade supper that Jacob was expecting from Laverty as the author of a number of popular cookbooks did not appear, with only one sandwich spread that was not shop bought![65]

Membership of IWCA and other female organisations undoubtedly gave Jacob a sense of community, and for her the chance for such social interaction was vital. The low numbers at the IWCA meeting on 10 February 1942 allowed those in attendance to gather around the fire and tell of recently read books.[66] Jacob's issues as a single woman in a society predicated on marriage and the family were still to the fore in the 1940s. Even going on a holiday alone highlighted the different social expectations and roles accorded to men and women. She wrote to Helen from Ballyvourney that if she were a man she would be able to spend at least part of each evening in the pub with some of the local men. Instead, as a woman, she was reduced to sitting alone in the sitting room of the hotel with only books for company.[67] Jacob's living arrangements were still problematic. On her brother's denunciation of her inadequate living conditions in 1941 Hanna suggested that she take her top floor flat. Jacob agreed to this contingent on her finances being in order. At the end of 1941 she noted the increasing expense of living due to the war. Early in March of that year she agreed to share this flat with Helen McGinley despite the endemic tensions between the two, noting that the arrangement would lessen expenses. Furthermore she was desirous of the company.[68] When Helen was hospitalised with diphtheria in April 1942 Jacob was told not to go among friends for ten days, a period she found 'very lonely & solitary'.[69] Immediately on moving into the flat tensions rose to the surface. Jacob noted a sense of respite when Helen went to the McGinley family home, writing how it was 'rather a relief getting dinner alone, free, not having to do things just as H. wants. She always washes up before she begins, & again in the middle'. In rows Helen continued to goad Jacob with why men didn't like her.[70] One of the issues that continually emerged was Jacob's lack of household skills – her 'alleged dirtiness'.[71]

65   6 Feb. 1945, RJD Ms (113). See, for example, Maura Laverty, *Maura Laverty's Cookbook* (London: Longmans, Green 1946); Maura Laverty, *Full and Plenty* (Irish Flour Millers Assoc., 1960).

66   10 Feb. 1942, RJD Ms (98).

67   Jacob to Hele 24 Aug. [1940], included in RJD Ms (92).

68   8 Mar. 1941; 13 Mar. 1941; 26 Mar. 1941, RJD Ms (95). Helen McGinley appears, from the evidence of Jacob's diary, to have had an unconventional and unhappy marriage to Douglas McGinley. The two never appear to have established a home of their own and while Douglas was on the legal circuit Helen either lived with Jacob or resided at the home of her parents-in-law.

69   25 Apr. 1942, RJD Ms (98).

70   13 May 1941, RJD Ms (95); 1 Nov. 1941, RJD Ms (97).

71   31 July 1942, RJD Ms (99).

Jacob found it very difficult to do any writing when Helen was around, 'she either talks or tells me to do something, and then there's visiting the blind, & the Union, & shopping, & committees, & God knows how many things'.[72] Yet, as has been already noted, Jacob needed such philanthropic work and committee activities to forge social interactions.

A FORGOTTEN PEOPLE

The early 1940s also saw the first death of Jacob's friends and acquaintances of the pre-independence campaigns. On 2 July 1942 the Gaelic League activist Cú Uladh died suddenly. Ten days later she received news of Mary Hayden's[73] death. On 27 May 1944 Madeline ffrench Mullen passed away, Jacob attending her funeral mass at Whitefriars three days later.[74] The emphasis on ensuring that the relatives of dead nationalist activists were provided for testifies to the backward-looking focus of much of Jacob's life in the 1940s. In the context of her growing philanthropic work she visited Mrs Mellows and attempted to improve her material circumstances, agitating for her to receive a state pension. This was a long and protracted business testifying to the manner in which, for so many, the legacy of the national struggle was not state remembrance of service or of dead relatives but the bitterness of poverty and the indignity of supplication. The state had its pantheon of heroes; beneath that layer there existed a hidden people who had been scarred by the campaigns. Eve Morrison states that Arthur Griffith's wife was 'a lonely figure in the Free State, embittered that the country for whose independence her husband had given his life had forgotten him'.[75] Anne Dolan discusses the provision made by the Government for Maud Griffith and her children; Mrs Griffith was incensed that she was taxed on the monies she received. Dolan discusses how to 'silence her the tax was reduced' and continues: 'Her grief was too brutal and too human for men who seemed to begrudge paying her their miserly estimation of her husband's worth'.[76] Mrs Griffith was able to emphasise, as Dolan

---

72   Summation for 1942, RJD Ms (101).

73   Mary Hayden (1862–1942) was active in the language movement and in the constitutional campaign for suffrage. She was appointed lecturer in modern Irish history in UCD in 1909. See http://www.oxforddnb.com/view/article/50995, accessed 13 Aug. 2008.

74   2–3 July 1942; 12 July 1942, RJD Ms (99); 27 May 1944; 30 May 1944, RJD Ms (108).

75   Eve Morrison, 'The Bureau of Military History and female republican activism, 1913–23' in Maryann Valiulis (ed.), *Gender and Power in Irish History* (Dublin: Irish Academic Press, 2009), p. 77.

76   Anne Dolan, *Commemorating the Irish Civil War: History and Memory, 1923–2000* (Cambridge: Cambridge University Press, 2003), pp. 114–16.

discusses, that she was no ordinary widow; she was a President's wife.[77] Mrs Mellows had no such leverage. In 1936 the Minister for Finance Lemass proposed, following representations, the introduction of civil list pensions, 'in respect of a certain limited number of persons who had rendered service to the State'. In his proposal he listed four individuals to whom such pensions might be awarded, including Mrs O'Callaghan, widow of Michael O'Callaghan who was murdered by crown forces.[78] A further memorandum stated that the cases of Mrs Mellows and Mrs O'Connor, mother of the late Rory O'Connor,[79] had been brought to the attention of the Minister for Finance as meritorious of a pension. However, the Department of Finance noted that if Mrs Mellows 'were wholly or partially dependent on her son she might be granted an allowance or a gratuity respectively' under the 1932 Army Pensions Act. This would preclude her, 'unless destitution is present', from receiving in addition a civil list pension.[80]

In September 1931 Mrs Mellows had received a grant of £25 from the Dáil Special Fund. The cheque was requested by W. T. Cosgrave and made payable to Colonel Joseph O'Reilly.[81] However, this was a one off payment and Mrs Mellows's circumstances declined over the next decade, and it is clear that she was not informed as to her possible rights. A memorandum from the Department of Finance in December 1936 noted that Mrs Mellows had made no application under the 1932 Army Pensions Act.[82] In March 1941 Jacob received a letter from Seán Norton stating that Oscar Traynor had promised that Mrs Mellows's case would be dealt with quickly. However, on 27 March Mrs Mellows received a letter denying her compensation claim.[83] On 14

77 Ibid., p. 115.

78 Memorandum on Civil List Pensions for the Executive Council from the Department of Finance, 5 December 1936. The other three individuals named were Mr Carl Hardeback, involved in service to the state in the area of Irish music, Mrs E. Duggan, widow of Mr E. Duggan, Parliamentary Secretary under Cumann na nGaedheal and Mr Joseph Crofts who composed prayer music including for a number of those translated into Irish by Thomas Ashe. DT, s 9422A, 'Civil List pensions, legislation, 1936–44'.

79 Rory O'Connor (1883–1922) was executed on 8 December 1922 for his part in the Four Courts siege. R. F. Foster, *Modern Ireland, 1600–1972* (London: Penguin, 1989), p. 511.

80 Memorandum on Civil List Pensions for the Executive Council from the Department of Finance, 10 Dec. 1936, DT, S 9422A, 'Civil List pensions, legislation, 1936–44'.

81 Letter to D. O'Hegarty from Liam Cosgair, 4 Sept. 1931; Statement from Sarah Mellows indicating receipt of £25 from Colonel Joseph O'Reilly, 4 Sept. 1931, 'Mrs Sarah Mellowes [*sic*], DT, s 7658, 'Grant from Dáil Special Fund'.

82 Memorandum on Civil List Pensions for the Executive Council from the Department of Finance, 10 Dec. 1936, DT, s 9422A, 'Civil List Pensions, Legislation, 1936–44'.

83 4 Mar. 1941; 27 Mar. 1941, RJD Ms (95).

February 1942 Jacob received a phone call, from de Valera's Secretary, Kathleen O'Connell, asking her to call at Government Buildings. De Valera gave her £100 to give to Mrs Mellows in weekly instalments of £2: 'Said he was surprised she wasn't getting a pension, & so was Aiken – they apparently don't know the latest pension legislation. He seemed concerned about her, but why in hell he can't send her cash weekly himself I don't know – it's a queer way to do it, & he must have great trust in me'. This comment once again testifies to a lifelong trait in Jacob. She desired to be recognised and appreciated and, simultaneously, perceived herself as someone whom people took advantage of. At the meeting in Government Buildings de Valera informed her of his intention to have something permanent done in the matter of Mrs Mellows but wanted her to say nothing of this beyond the room.[84] However, nothing came of de Valera's promises and three years later she recorded how de Valera had still not behaved with 'any sign of decency' towards Mrs Mellows.[85] Jacob did not let the matter rest and discovered that de Valera's lack of action was based on a misunderstanding, he believing that she had £40 a year from the Army pension, Jacob informing him that it was only £13. He agreed to arrange £1 a week for Mrs Mellows to be paid in kind to ensure that she maintained her entitlement to the old age pension. In typical fashion, Jacob noted on this meeting in 1946 his 'lovely hands'.[86] Eamonn Martin of the Irish Sweepstakes had also intervened earlier on Mrs Mellows behalf. He was critical of the notion of giving her £2 a week believing that this would exacerbate her drink problem. In response Jacob agreed to pay the rent herself from the weekly instalment while he looked after Barney's insurance and medical expenses.[87]

Jacob's account of Mrs Mellows offers an interesting example of the manner in which lives in Ireland were in many ways negatively dominated by earlier nationalist activism. Mrs Mellows loved to gossip with Jacob, telling her of Lemass's racing debts and his public denunciation by a bookie at the Phoenix Park races for failure to pay.[88] She repeatedly told her of taking food parcels to Mountjoy before breakfast although agreed with Jacob that if the women were

84   14 Feb. 1942, RJD Ms (98).

85   13 Dec. 1945, RJD Ms (116).

86   7 Feb. 1946, RJD Ms (117). On 12 July 1946 Mrs Mellows was stated to be receiving a Special Allowance of £13 17s 6d per annum under section 37 of the Army Pensions Act, 1937. She also received an Old Age Pension of 10s per week. Note, 12 July 1946. 'Mrs Sarah Mellowes [sic], DT, s 7658, Grant from Dáil Special Fund'.

87   10 Mar. 1942, RJD Ms (98). Christened Herbert Charles, Barney Mellows was the younger brother of Liam Mellows. See C. Desmond Greaves, *Liam Mellows and the Irish Revolution* (London: Lawrence & Wishart, 1971).

88   2 Oct. 1941, RJD Ms (97).

in jail the men would not have worked so hard to feed them.[89] Trapped in the past, the loss of her son had clearly impacted on her life. Jacob regularly recorded her drinking problem. On 26 March she noted how Mrs Mellows was 'pretty drunk'. Her loneliness was transparent and manifested itself in her need to re-live her past as the mother of a national hero: 'Stories of Fred and the drive to Bodenstown in the Trap in 1914'.[90] She enjoyed the renaming of the bridge in May 1942 and gloated at Mulcahy's election defeat in 1943.[91] In 1949 a committee of Republican women organised a presentation to Mrs Mellows, asking Jacob what she needed.[92] Indeed, Mrs Mellows was not the only person dealing with addiction at this point. A visit to Roebuck allowed Maud Gonne to discuss Helena Molony's 'drinking fits' and 'her own addiction to drugs & uncanny power of telling where they were hidden, & how she stopped herself when told it was like a drunkard knowing where pubs were'.[93] This comment offers an interesting insight into perceptions of drink and drugs, a drink addiction being accorded a far worse profile than one based on drugs.

As Jacob became increasing involved in overseeing financial aid and in caring for Mrs Mellows in the 1940s, Helen's health deteriorated; despite the tensions between the two women, Jacob worried greatly about the situation. In part this worry was the result of feeling almost completely responsible for Helen, her husband, Douglas, having abdicated any share in her care. At the end of 1942, before she became ill, Jacob noted the problems in Helen's life and the manner in which she filled the void left by Douglas's absence:

> D hardly ever writing, & spending money wrong. I feel she hasn't much satis-
> faction in her life, & its very hard on her not having a place all her own, & her temper
> is partly caused by blood pressure, but its awful.[94]

Jacob's proposal to spend Christmas 1943 in Waterford was stymied by Helen's declaration that she 'wd cut her throat if I did'. When she tried to visit in February 1944 she again had to shelve her plans as Helen 'seemed to hate so

---

89 30 May 1946, RJD Ms (118).

90 26 Feb. 1942; 23 Apr. 1942; 2 Apr. 1942, RJD Ms (98). Fred may be a reference either to Liam's paternal uncle or brother, both named Frederick.

91 28 May 1942, RJD Ms (98); 24 June 1943, RJD Ms (104). Mrs Mellows would have viewed Richard Mulcahy as Minister for Defence as one of those responsible for the execution of her son. In 1942 Queen's Bridge over the River Liffey linking Queen Street with Arran Quay was renamed Mellows Bridge.

92 19 May 1949, RJD Ms (134).

93 29 Aug. 1944, RJD Ms (110).

94 Summation for 1942, RJD Ms (101).

being left alone, & got so frightfully depressed, that as there was no necessity, it didn't seem right to go'. Throughout all of 1944 Jacob did not feel free to be away long from Helen. However, although this curtailed her movements her diary entries suggest she seems to have enjoyed being valued.[95] There is a sense that Jacob, like the menial political work she performed in the service of others, courted the role of martyr in Helen's illness, enjoying the attention it brought her. After Sheehy Skeffington died in 1946 she heard from Sybil Le Brocquy that Hanna had felt Jacob sacrificed herself to Helen.[96]

In 1944 Helen suffered from a series of fits, causing her to lose the power to remember words. Dr Lynn, whom Jacob talked to about the situation in June 1944, declared her to be suffering from anaemia of the brain. During this period Helen worried about the lack of money from Douglas.[97] On 1 October 1944 Douglas left the army to go back on the legal circuit. Helen received no money from him from the time he left the army until late December of 1944.[98] Jacob believed that if Douglas 'behaved more as he ought – wrote to her, & saved some money', Helen's health would improve. The situation continued throughout 1945 and 1946, Jacob receiving respite when other friends took responsibility of having Helen to visit. Had Jacob been a married woman with the responsibilities of a family it is unlikely that she would have found herself in the role of prime carer to Helen, friendship notwithstanding. In July 1946 Helen stayed with George Gilmore's sister, Dorrie, in Howth but returned 'queerer mentally than she was, more irritable, and with less hold on words. Frightened me'. Jacob suffered nightmares worrying about Helen. At this point Jacob's other philanthropic activities were taking their toll on her. A Mrs Mellone, whom she regularly visited, wished to stay with her while her carer had a week's holiday but Jacob admitted to not feeling 'equal to it'. She believed that she was not sufficiently nice to Mrs Mellone, worried as she was about Helen, 'tired & on edge'.[99] On 18 August 1946 Helen was hospitalised but returned home four days later. Doctors were concerned about her blood pressure and her weak heart. During her absence Jacob found the flat lonely, especially at night; what she needed, she believed, was someone to help her care for Helen, particularly since she was very 'depressing company' and 'liable to fierce ill temper'.[100] Mrs Mellows's drink problem weighed heavily with her also, drunk and 'gloomy, just the way I don't like her'. Yet Jacob continued to

---

95 19 Dec. 1943, RJD Ms (106); 7 Feb. 1944, RJD Ms (107); summation of 1944, RJD Ms (112).

96 10 Feb. 1947, RJD Ms (121).

97 17 June 1944; 13 July 1944, RJD Ms (109).

98 6 Sept. 1944, RJD Ms (110); summation of 1944, RJD Ms (112).

99 12 July 1946; 19 July 1946; 27 July 1946; 9 Aug. 1946, RJD Ms (119).

100 18 Aug. 1946; 20 Aug. 1946, RJD Ms (119); summation of 1946, RJD Ms (121).

help her, collecting £13 for her food and medical needs from Kathleen O'Connell on 7 September 1946.[101]

Helen's health continued to weigh largely on Jacob's life and impact freedom of movement in the later 1940s. Jacob referred increasingly to Helen's silence and gloomy nature.[102] Increasingly Jacob felt unable to leave Helen behind when she visited friends and acquaintances.[103] In October 1948 R. Mills offered the loan of a cottage in Creagh, County Fermanagh, for a week. The two travelled, Helen wanting to go despite her ill health. Within two days Helen was 'in a shocking state of dottiness, speech nearly gone, & she entirely useless to herself'. Jacob had to make the decision to 'get her home quick'. By this date Jacob described Helen as 'like a child'. Mrs Mellows, whom she visited the next day, had fallen and unable to get up was forced to knock on the wall to attract her neighour's attention.[104] Visiting her friends, the Doyles in Portroe, County Tipperary, at the end of October 1948 she had to pay Dorrie Gilmore to mind Helen.[105] At the end of November she booked the Padua Nursing Home at 87 Waterloo Road for a week. The question of putting Helen in long-term care was to the fore in her mind at this point. She considered St Mary's in Pembroke Park but it was full and not considered suitable. Diagnosed with a stroke, a bed was found for Helen in Baggot Street Hospital in mid December 1948 but the responsibility of getting her there rested with Jacob.[106] When Douglas arrived back to Dublin in late December they discussed money, he believing that he could not afford the cost of her care.[107] In early 1949 a home for semi-invalids was found in Delgany, County Dublin; by 6 January Douglas had left Dublin again and that night there was a message for Jacob from the hospital that Helen was worse. By 21 December she was unconscious and died that night at eight o'clock. Jacob described herself as lonely in the flat after Helen's death, more so than when she had been in hospital.[108] Helen left Jacob all she owned which amounted to £33-5.[109]

After Helen's death Jacob moved to share a house in Charleville Road with Lucy Kingston, newly widowed. The two shared this house with Lucy's recently married daughter, Daisy. This living arrangement clearly suited Jacob

101 22 Aug. 1946; 7 Sept. 1946, RJD Ms (119).
102 5 Aug. 1948, RJD Ms (130).
103 9 Oct. 1948, RJD Ms (131). This was in the context of a visit to Owen and Andrée.
104 20–21 Oct. 1948, RJD Ms (131).
105 5 Nov. 1948, RJD Ms (131).
106 27 Nov. 1948; 6 Dec. 1948; 11 Dec. 1948, RJD Ms (132).
107 20 Dec. 1948, RJD Ms (132).
108 1 Jan. 1949, RJD Ms (132); 6 Jan. 1949; 21 Jan. 1949; 24 Jan. 1949, RJD Ms (132).
109 4 July 1949, RJD Ms (134).

better than her previous situation with Helen. She enjoyed the sense of being part of a family; 'she living with me suits me *well*, and Daisy & Ralph coming in adds family effect & I like them more & more'; Jacob also noted in her resume of 1949 the release of Helen's death. She missed Lucy when the latter spent part of 1949 and early 1950 in India. Yet many of the same issues of house sharing as a single and, now ageing, woman were still to be dealt with. The move itself in June 1949 was traumatic for her and she worried about the high rent.[110] Her lack of privacy and personal space were concerns. She was 'angered' to have her room swept out by Lucy and things moved to prepare for a visitor, but 'was very quiet about it'. Not voicing her anger suggests that the house share was not equal; Jacob was not part of the extended Kingston family and, thus, had a lesser voice in the house. A friend commented how she and Lucy 'appeared on each other's nerves when she met us last'.[111] Of course, many of the disagreements were commonplace tensions which arise in any household but Jacob took them to heart, arguably a reflection of her own sense of not being part of the family. When Jacob used the house as a venue for an anti-war talk, Lucy was 'chilly and sarcastic for 2 days or more – it was awful'.[112] Yet when Lucy attended a Quaker conference in Wicklow in October 1950 Jacob wrote how she was lonely without her.[113] However, many of the same tensions she experienced in sharing a flat with Helen resurfaced in her new living arrangements. Returning home on a snowy night in December 1950 she protested at the lack of coal in the scuttle to Lucy's fury 'at being found fault with, & I now feel she will go on like that if I ever say anything like complaint or protest – she seems slightly mad that way, the way she spurned the idea that she cd complain of me just as much'.[114] Although Jacob reiterated much of the nature of this complaint in her summation of 1950 she did add 'It's a good thing we agree on some important things'.[115]

It must be noted that Lucy reiterated the same criticisms made earlier of Jacob by Helen and more venomously by her sister-in-law Dorothea. Clearly, Jacob was unique in her unwillingness to compromise on her beliefs and viewpoints leading to tensions. In 1951 Lucy talked to her of 'her peculiarities – better if I tried to be more like other people – when a majority is against you, you're probably wrong.' Her nephew, Louis, remarked that 'I argue so as to set anyone against me'.[116] As Helen had complained of the problems associated

110 Summation for 1949, RJD Ms (136).
111 17 Sept. 1950; 24 Sept. 1950, RJD Ms (139).
112 18 Feb. 1952, RJD Ms (144).
113 8 Oct. 1950, RJD Ms (139).
114 6 Dec. 1950, RJD Ms (139).
115 Summation of 1950, RJD Ms (139).
116 18 Mar. 1956, RJD Ms (155).

with Jacob's cat in the house, Lucy contended that 'one wrong thing' about her was 'my being so absurdly fond of animals'.[117] Kingston was 'raging' when a window left open by Jacob to allow access to her cat, Riabhach, attracted a neighbouring cat into the house who 'made a smell'.[118]

POLITICS AND THE WIDER WORLD

Jacob's diary from the late 1930s does not have any of the sense of political excitement and expectation recorded by her in earlier decades. This was both a reflection of her declining years and the wider political climate. The rise of Nazi Germany features in small incidents, almost asides. Hitler's speech at Nuremberg in 1938 she described as 'not conclusive, but bad enough'.[119] Earlier in June she described a report at the City Committee of the Gaelic League of a visit by fellow member, Giolla, to Hamburg. Giolla gave details of his attendance at a physical culture gala at which Irish children were photographed in the procession giving the Nazi salute. She notes how she complained of this to the surprise of the speaker who stated that they didn't know what they were doing.[120]

As she recorded so often, many Irish dissidents interpreted the rise of dictatorship in Germany through the lens of Irish political preoccupations. In September 1938 Jacob expressed a widely felt belief in the imminence of war following Hitler's invasion of the Sudetenland. On 27 of September she attended a meeting in Hatch Street Hall 'where the Left . . . talked about . . . Ireland & the crisis . . . rather bad in tone – anti-British & nothing else matters – making out that we & England have just as little democratic rule as Germany'. Hanna chaired the meeting and the speakers included Roddy Connolly, Helena Molony and Seán Murray who called for a series of public meetings for peace and neutrality on left-wing lines.[121] Jacob objected to Irish republicans such as Joe Kelly and Joe Dowling who could not see beyond anti-English propaganda and refused on those lines to decry the actions of Hitler.[122] It should be noted that this was a much more nuanced approach to wider international politics than she had adopted during the First World War. Yet she objected at the

---

117 31 July 1951, RJD Ms (140).

118 17 Feb. 1954, RJD Ms (150).

119 13 Sept. 1938, RJD Ms (85). The Nuremberg Rally of 1938 took place in September before the first mass expulsion of Jews from Germany on Kristallnacht, the Night of the Broken Glass, 9 November 1938.

120 28 June 1938, RJD Ms (84).

121 27 Sept. 1938, RJD Ms (85).

122 16 Oct. 1938, RJD Ms (85).

Left Book Club meeting in honour of the returning Spanish Civil War volunteers on 13 December 1938 to contributing food for Spain through England. When she suggested making the Irish contribution a separate one from the English one she was rebuked by Mr Tweedy as offering 'a shocking example of "sectarianism"'.[123]

When England and France capitulated to Hitler's demands Jacob described the event as 'probably a turning point towards hell in European history'.[124] In December 1939 she noted the difficulty of looking ahead 'without miserable fear' and believed that the neutrality was the best option for Ireland.[125] Early in 1941 she noted the prevalent fear, disseminated through the papers, of Nazi attacks on England and Ireland. She attended an emergency committee at 32 Batchelor's Walk, relating to issues around the creation of communal feeding stations in the event of an invasion, and commented how there was 'nothing but talk of evacuation these days'.[126] She recorded on 31 May 1941 the bombing of the North Strand and areas of the North Circular Road and the Phoenix Park by the German Air Force the previous night.[127] She described Mussolini's death in a plane crash as 'too easy'.[128] Macardle and herself discussed what they would 'want done' in the event of a German invasion, Macardle believing that England and the USA should be asked to help.[129] Many diary entries in this period were frequently mundane in content documenting how rationing personally impacted on them: Jacob's was no different. Jacob recorded how the calls to use less gas and the introduction of gas rationing on 3 March 1942 impacted on her, noting that she had to be home early at night to be sure of hot water. Dinners in Woolworths, she noted in 1942, 'are very bad since the gas got short. Jam was not available for purchase unless you got tea and bread in the same shop'. Visiting Lucy Pim for supper in March 1944 Jacob moaned how she 'cheated me out of a pinch of tea'. By mid 1946 there was no margarine to be had and frying was problematic. To compound irritation around

123 13 Dec. 1938, RJD Ms (85). The English publisher, Victor Gollancz established the Left Book Club in 1936. He aimed to publish monthly, at a reduced price, a book with a social message that would be read at local centres. Owen Sheehy Skeffington convened the Left Book Club Centre in Dublin. The Club met at 5 Leinster Street, splitting up into sub-groups for detailed study. Sheehy Skeffington, *Skeff*, pp. 83–4. Robert Tweedy, husband of Hilda Tweedy.

124 30 Sept. 1938, RJD Ms (85). With the Munich Agreement of 30 September 1938 England and France agreed to the occupation of the Sudetenland by the German Army.

125 Summation 1939, RJD Ms (90).

126 12–13 Feb. 1941; 18 Feb. 1941, RJD Ms (95).

127 Possibly a navigational error. See Clair Wills, *That Neutral Island: A History of Ireland During the Second World War* (London: Faber and Faber, 2007), p. 212.

128 8 Aug. 1941, RJD Ms (96).

129 26 Aug. 1942, RJD Ms (100).

rationing, rumours circulated in November 1946 about a 'load of coal seen going in Dr [*sic*] de Valera's yard'.[130] Rationing continued to feature heavily in Jacob's life after the war; bread rationing was introduced in January 1947. A sugar strike in late 1946 meant that she was unable to bring the usual sweets to the Union inmates until 15 January 1947.[131]

FAMILY MATTERS

Much of Jacob's life in the 1940s and 1950s revolved around visiting her niece and nephews and participating in their family life. In the late 1930s the deteriorating nature of Tom and Dorothea's relationship reforged the bond between sister and brother. Although Jacob's version of events must be considered in the light of her antipathy to her sister-in-law, it does appear there were some issues. Jacob commented on a number of occasions in the diary on Dorothea's very close and open relationship with Willie Glen.[132] However, she fails to go into clear details as to whether this was a sexual relationship. Certainly Jacob presented Dorothea as failing to consider Tom's feeling in all her dealings. Tom's plan to spend time with Jacob in Bunmahon in August 1939 was upset by Dorothea's invitation to her nieces and nephews leaving no room for her in the holiday home.[133] Jacob did not go to Waterford for Christmas in 1939 or in 1941. Whatever the nature of Dorothea's relationship with Tom it is clear that the couple had become hostile towards each other. Yet as his wife Dorothea felt a socially ordained duty towards Tom; this could only be absolved if he were to find someone else to look after his household needs. By 1945 Dorothea was dreaming that Tom was coming in to kill her and requesting that Jacob save her from living with him: 'she wants to take a job and go off to it, if I wd go and live with him instead of her.' Dorothea complained of his tightness with money. Dorothea claimed that since Jacob was the only person living 'to whom Tom has shown himself consistently' she ought to be responsible for him, drawing the retort: 'She has a mad streak about women being responsible for men'.[134]

130 15 Jan. 1942; 3–4 Mar. 1942, RJD Ms (98); 31 Aug. 1942 RJD Ms (100); 15 Mar. 1943, RJD Ms (102); 22 Mar. 1944, RJD Ms (107); 27 July 1946, RJD Ms (119); 8 Nov. 1946, RJD Ms (120).

131 4 Jan. 1947; 15 Jan 1947, RJD Ms (121).

132 This may have been William Glynn who was headmaster of Newtown School in the period 1949–61. Earlier he had been, with Tom and Dorothea, one of the key supporters of the Waterford art exhibitions held in the gym at Newtown. Maurice Wigham, *Newtown School Waterford 1798–1998: A History* (Waterford: Newtown School, 1998), p. 142.

133 24 Aug. 1939, RJD Ms (89).

134 17 Feb. 1945; 22 Feb. 1945; 26 Feb. 1945, RJD Ms (113).

Jacob's niece and two nephews were married in the early 1940s. Her comments on these mixed marriages reveal how Jacob's anti-Catholicism grew
ever more strident. In the summer of 1940 she received a letter from Tom
suggesting that Margaret and the youngest boy, Christy, were in danger of
being influenced in the direction of Catholicism by Catholic friends. Louis,
the oldest, Tom believed was 'safe owing to his naturally cynical mind'.[135] In
1943 Margie was involved in a relationship with Billy Shanahan, a Catholic,
whom she would marry the next year. Margie's feeling that she could not
marry him without converting to Catholicism appalled Jacob. The issue, in
particular, was that a Catholic Church wedding could not take place with one
party not being baptised:

> found Tom awaiting Billy S . . . when he had gone I came back & heard he had
> great hopes of converting Margie, wdn't marry her if he thought the conversion
> was not genuine, & when the possibility of her being baptised in Protestant church
> was mentioned, said it was very hard to get a dispensation where the woman was
> the Protestant. Tom seemed to have been surprised that a P. baptism counted with
> them – he has an exaggerated view of R Cism – doesn't realise all the holes in it . . .
> I feel it will probably end with her turning Catholic.[136]

It is interesting to note that when Dermot Webb of Whitebeam Road
married his Catholic wife in a Catholic church in 1946 without being baptised
Jacob confrontationally described it as a 'very interesting and praiseworthy
feat'.[137] In early June 1943 Louis visited Jacob for dinner, offering the news that
his father believed Christy was 'in danger of the Catholic church'. Jacob
response was 'Thank God Louis anyhow is sound'. When Christy's move
towards Catholicism became overt with his engagement to Billy Shanahan's
sister, Maisie, Jacob described him as 'losing the use of his mind & heart'.[138]
In late 1943 Christy was received into the Catholic faith, to scathing diary
comment from Jacob: 'in spite of Tom asking him to wait; he apparently really
believed if he died suddenly it wd affect his chances in the next world! The
priest evidently thought non-Catholic parents had no rights'.[139] When Louis
got a new job as assistant works manager in the Talbot Press in early 1944,
Jacob declared that it 'made up a little for the delinquencies of Margaret &

135 Letter from Jacob to Helen McGinley, 24 Aug. 1940, included in RJD Ms (92). The letter from
Tom to Jacob is not extant but she gave details of his concerns in this letter to Helen McGinley.
136 12 May 1943; 20–21 May 1943, RJD Ms (103).
137 24 Sept. 1946, RJD Ms (119).
138 6 June 1943, RJD Ms (103); 9 Nov. 1943, RJD Ms (105).
139 30 Dec. 1943, RJD Ms (105).

Chris'.[140] Yet Louis did not escape her ire when he declared that he would be willing to have a church marriage believing that the words could be viewed as a 'social convenience' and need not be taken seriously, a 'revolting' idea in Jacob's view.[141]

The conversion of Margaret and Christy to Catholicism brought Jacob closer to Tom as they bonded over their lack of religion: 'Had a grand walk with Tom . . . agreeing that irreligious people like us take religion more seriously than most religious people do'.[142] In late May and early June 1944 they took a biking holiday together and talked over such concerns as Catholics and the way their minds worked.[143] Tom during this period was engaged on work on a religion and ethics.[144] Religion was one of Jacob's favourite topics during this decade: she described a discussion of 'religion, the universe, the soul, etc, that lasted hours and I cd have gone on with it until midnight'.[145] Margie married Billy Shanahan on 14 June in Haddington Road Church, drawing ironic commentary from Jacob who portrayed herself above such ritual, almost as one from a civilised country viewing the backward natives. The minority position of non-Catholics in the Free State is evident in her depiction of the hoards at the public mass:

> Margie & Billy knelt at the altar, & stayed so long on their knees, getting 'the sacraments' and during 8 o'clock mass lengthened out by others getting communion (hordes) and nuptial mass & God knows what, you'd think they wd stiffen & never be able to rise again. I heard nothing from them in the way of answers, & only mutterings from the 2 priests. But I did see that the acolyte who pressed up against the priest's shoulder as he went along the row of God-eaters with his bowl, was engaged in holding a little brass shovel under the wafer, lest it might fall . . . the whole thing was frightful.[146]

When Chris was married on 4 March 1946 Jacob did not attend the church ceremony, minding Margie's baby; however, she did attend the social gathering which followed the ceremony held at the newly married couple's flat at 22 Elgin Road.[147]

140 21 Jan. 1944, RJD Ms (106).
141 3 Feb. 1946, RJD Ms (117).
142 12 Mar. 1944, RJD Ms (107).
143 3 June 1944, RJD Ms (109).
144 2 Dec. 1948, RJD Ms (132).
145 8 Oct. 1948, RJD Ms (131).
146 14 June 1944, RJD Ms (109).
147 4 Mar. 1946, RJD Ms (117).

Jacob's hostility to Catholicism did not end with the marriage of Christy and Margie. Jacob was shocked to hear a number of months after the former's marriage that McQuaid had 'the right to forbid those in his diocese to read the bible if he thinks their doing so wd for any reason encourage heresy'. Frank, Louis's friend, conjectured that McQuaid's hostility to Trinity College might be connected with the fact that Trinity students were at this time associated with abortion cases. Jacob believed that this was quite likely as 'R.C. clergy are capable of anything'.[148] George Gilmore described her in October 1944 as a 'bigot towards the Catholic Church', thinking too ill of it.[149] Jacob advocated the adoption of ethics without religion and noted how this was an alien concept to most Catholics who believed that 'ethics don't exist except as God's commands'.[150] A sense of superiority pervaded Jacob's attitudes in this context. She denounced people who believed that morals depended on religion as those who '*won't* use their brains, just go by shibboleths'.[151] Visiting friends in London in September 1948 discussion ranged around whether Catholicism was preferable to the growing 'unmoral materialism', Jacob believing that people who adhered to the latter 'were at least free to use their minds'.[152]

When Daisy Kingston intended to marry the Catholic, Billy Swanton, in 1948 Jacob was morbidly interested to hear details of her dealings with the Catholic clergy. She listened to Daisy's accounts of the interviews she had with relevant priests. The two discussed 'the "canonical causes" for a Catholic being let marry a Protestant, one of which seems to be, if they have passed a night together. The priest seemed rather to be hinting at this'.[153] In this decade Jacob's diary is full of such accounts; they indicate her sense of being a member of a minority on the defensive taking refuge in feelings of superiority. While this issue of mixed marriage had occupied Jacob in earlier decades it was not as pressing as it became in the 1940s. In 1908 she recorded her sense of standing apart from the local Quaker community on the subject of Catholics and mixed marriages.

> went down to the meeting house a.d. to help Dolly & Bessie get the monthly meeting tea . . . The tone of the company towards Catholics was pretty vicious and it culminated in Dolly's short speech about the poor house, & how we ought to see after the Protestants there, & protect them against Catholics, & how the priests

148 20 Aug. 1944, RJD Ms (110).
149 24 Oct. 1944, RJD Ms (111).
150 4 Feb. 1945, RJD Ms (113).
151 9 Aug. 1948, RJD Ms (130).
152 16 Sept. 1948, RJD Ms (130).
153 1 Dec. 1948, RJD Ms (132).

tried to pervert a Protestant woman there, but she being a Christian remained firm. Also how dreadful is the quantity of mixed marriages in which the Prot. turns Catholic. So then I said the meeting seemed to think it a dreadful thing to be a Catholic, & that according to the last speaker a Catholic couldn't be a Christian, and were the mixed marriages any worse after they turned Catholic than before?[154]

A similar entry in December 1909 suggests her antipathy towards any manifestation of anti-Catholicism within the Friends with whom she worked in the area of poor relief in Waterford.

I went to tea at Albert Bell's who was having a small gathering to discuss social reforms needed in this city. After tea different people brought forward their concerns. E. Bell the gambling that goes on in the street and W. Hill gambling on races and several people drink. . . . Different people were appointed to interview priests and peelers about different things, and I God help me was appointed secretary. There is a horrible little journal . . . the Catholic, but really Protestant & anti-Catholic, that they seem attached to, with [sic] had a temperance article in it that they want to get published in the local papers.[155]

Jacob's less than hostile attitude to mixed marriage during the first two decades of the twentieth century was also evident in the manner in which she refers to the issue in *Callaghan*: in fiction, as least, she seems able to quickly resolve her concerns. In the novel Andy Callaghan's marriage to the Protestant Frances Morrin is viewed as problematic by the latter's sister-in-law conscious of status amongst her fellow Protestant neighbours. Of course fictionally it was easy to resolve the issue by having the unorthodox Callaghan reject his religion. Andy Callaghan notes how the English could not have held Ireland for three centuries without the help of the Catholic Church, adding 'Whatever reasonable thing you want to do, the Church hinders you'.[156] Jacob viewpoint on the matter even in the early twentieth century did at times border on patronising. In 1912 she recorded the following account of a conversation with acquaintances in Dublin regarding the Ne Temere decree which came into effect on 19 April 1908 according to which children of mixed marriages were to be brought up Catholics and the Catholic spouse would attempt to bring the non-Catholic partner to a knowledge of the true religion:

154 4 Nov. 1908, RJD Ms (18). 'a. d.' meaning after dinner.
155 22 Nov. 1909, RJD Ms (19).
156 F. Winthrop, *Callaghan* (Dublin: Martin Lester, n.d. [1920]), pp. 163–5.

M. & L. were telling me to-day that it is now impossible for a Protestant to marry a Catholic, according to the laws of the Catholic church, but I thought differently, and I asked L[asirfhiona] to-day, who told me it is quite possible, if you get a dispensation and agree to have all the children baptised Catholics. It is certainly incomprehensible to me how any sane person of any intelligence can be a Catholic.[157]

By the 1940s the reality of family marriages and the Catholic ethos of the Free State further exacerbated Jacob's antipathy towards Catholicism. Visiting Louis and his wife, Amy, in December 1948 she told them of the religious issues relating to Daisy's proposed marriage. Amy countered with a story of her own 'about the R. C.s in the railway office & how they boasted to her & the other Prot. there of the mixed marriages where the Prot turned C., & Amy was pleased once to have a marriage to tell them of, where the C. turned'.[158] Amy was 'sorry to hear' from Jacob as the two discussed conscience and scruples that Chris's wife, Maisie believed that she ought to go to Mass.[159]

Jacob was still sensitive to what she viewed as the omnipresence of the Catholic clergy in national politics. In particular she noted their presence during the late 1940s at the commemorative events of milestones in the national struggle. On 7 November 1948 she gave a speech at Kilcullen on Tone and the Catholic Committee commenting:

> Damn these dead-killed-in-a-battle commemorations, they give the clergy such opportunities. The monument was a cross, and though the chairman was Ó Modrain, the local priest came in all his robes & blessed the cross in Latin . . . to start off with, and made a speech . . . I . . . talked of the Church's reprobation of the rising & UI, how they would have been called 'subversive' if the word had been invented.[160]

Jacob's ire was not confined to male clerics; in a reductive fashion she took Noel Browne's view on the nursing issue of the later 1940s 'because the Church wants all new hospitals bossed by nuns, and he wants to make nursing attractive to Irish girls, wh can't be done unless the higher posts are open to them. Saw proof of this in press . . . Some damned bigoted layman in Co. Council wanting nuns in hospitals'.[161] Jacob indulged very much in the notion

---

157 19 May 1912, RJD Ms (23).

158 5 Dec. 1948, RJD Ms (132).

159 8 Dec. 1948, RJD Ms (132).

160 7 Nov. 1948, RJD Ms (131).

161 12 Nov. 1948, RJD Ms (131). In October 1948 Browne addressed the Irish Matrons' Association and connected the shortage of nurses with the conditions of employment experienced in Ireland. See Gerard M. Feely, *A History of Apprenticeship Nurse Training in Ireland* (London: Routledge, 2005), p. 116.

of a 'Church-state clash', which Ferriter describes as a misleading label in assessing 'the complex distribution of power in Ireland'. Ferriter notes how lay groups often brought the Church on board if they were determined to oppose change, a notable example being the Irish Medical Association during the 'mother and child' controversy of 1951.[162]

As the 1940s closed Jacob's chief concerns were her family links and her lack of publishing success; both were to be even greater worries in the final decade of her life. In November 1948 Jacob received a letter from Tom; he had digestive trouble and the doctor wanted to do tests. He had anaemia and low blood pressure but was unable to take time from work to rest. The results of an X-ray indicated that there was nothing seriously wrong with him but this was to change in the next decade, causing Jacob much personal heartache.[163] During the 1940s Jacob's literary work failed to progress and she could not help comparing herself to disadvantage with the women at the Women Writers' Club as the following account of the meeting at Mrs Le Brocquy's on 1 December 1948 reveals:

> very nice, till they started the program[*sic*] which was each one telling about her literary doings. I had to leave before it came to me, & was full of envy & jealously at all the plays taken & acted – asked for on the radio, & prizes won, and books published.[164]

Patricia Lynch tried to encourage her; she took *The Raven's Glen* to read and comment on and encouraged her to keep trying publishers, telling her that 'one may some day take it'.[165]

By 1950 Jacob was entering her later years and her health began to decline. In December 1950 she attended a clinic for rheumatism in Mount Street. Although her knuckle pain was not diagnosed as rheumatism it was clear that she had entered late middle age, the doctor describing her as 'doing very well for my age'.[166] In April 1951 she wrote how she had a 'queer pain in my chest, like a blow, the last week or more. She attended the Raghnallach Health Institute where the pain was diagnosed as potential pleurisy 'coming from toxins'. She was advised to eat only fruit and to drink carrot juice and she underwent 'electrical works' and massage. In June 1951 she suffered a bout of

162 Diarmaid Ferriter, *Occasions of Sin: Sex and Society in Modern Ireland* (London: Profile Books, 2009), p. 7.
163 4 Nov. 1948; 9 Nov. 1948; 11 Nov. 1948, RJD Ms (131); 7 Dec. 1948, RJD Ms (132).
164 1 Dec. 1948, RJD Ms (132).
165 8 Dec. 1948, RJD Ms (132).
166 15 Dec. 1950, RJD Ms (139).

shingles.[167] In 1953 she suffered three falls and as the 1950s progressed she recorded many days or half days spent in bed with colds and other ailments.[168] In October 1955 she suffered much with a pain in her hip, diagnosed as neuralgia.[169] In 1959 she was advised by her doctor to take some hours in bed one morning a week. Diagnosed with anaemia she had to have injections.[170] In many ways Jacob accepted below par health as a fact of life and did not record any overt sense of entering into old age. Indeed, her constant round of visitations to the sick and elderly probably reinforced her own relative mobility and energy. Jacob's diet must have contributed to her many colds and sore throats. Although a vegetarian in later life, Jacob did not appear to eat much fruit or vegetables. Bread, jam, cake were all her stock foods although it is difficult to get a full picture in this regard as the diary only records what she ate sporadically. Meat appeared to be substituted in many cases by eggs. Present day dietary and health standards differ greatly; thus, one must, of course, beware of projecting contemporary health and diet concerns onto the past.

FEMALE ACTIVISM AND THE POLITICS OF PEACE

Peace campaigns galvanised Jacob in the last decade of her life, in particular the concern at the growth of nuclear power and nuclear weapons. On 15 December 1950 she attended the meeting at the Society of Friends premises at Eustace Street to hear Revd Armstrong on the Warsaw Congress, attending a similar gathering on 21 December at the Abbey Theatre Lecture Hall.[171] The international situation, particularly perceptions of American aggression in Korea and concern over nuclear testing in the Pacific, was a source of concern. The paradigm central to the establishment of the Women's International League for Peace and Freedom in 1915 was still central to the debate in the 1950s. In particular the link between female political involvement and peace was stressed as was evident in Jacob's account of a meeting at the Women Workers' Union on 23 April 1954:

167 3 Apr. 1951; 12 May 1951; 16 May 1951; 22 June 1951, RJD Ms (140); 27 Feb. 1954, RJD Ms (150).

168 Summation of 1953, RJD Ms (149).

169 13 Oct. 1955, RJD Ms (153).

170 22 June 1959, RJD Ms (166); summation of 1959, RJD Ms (168).

171 15 Dec. 1950; 21 Dec. 1950, RJD Ms (139). International Peace Congress held in Warsaw in November 1950.

Yates said women cd save the world, which men had got in a bad way – some
American women working for peace wonderfully – women are strong against
MacCarthy [*sic*] – readier to speak out & less frightened than men.[172]

Jacob attended a meeting at the Engineer's Hall in October 1954 to protest
against the Hydrogen Bomb; speakers included some of the same activists as
early years – Helen Chenevix, Kathleen Lynn and Peadar O'Donnell.[173] A
similar meeting was held at the Royal Hibernian Hotel in December 1958
attracting 'a couple of hundred'. Jacob listened to speeches by scientists, some
of whom expressed their lack of foreknowledge that splitting the atom would
have military implications. At the same gathering Donal Nevin spoke on how
Irish trade unions could oppose nuclear weaponry.[174] In January 1959 a nuclear
disarmament organisation was established at a meeting at the Court Laundry
Hall.[175] Members were issued with the task of posting information leaflets and
following up with house-to-house calls.[176] Two women whom Jacob called on
in Charleville Road 'said they wdn't live long & didn't care what happened
to the world.[177]

Jacob's involvement in the Irish Housewives Association (IHA) during
the 1950s was in the area of the international politics, with a particular focus
on international peace; she acted as a member of the International Sub-
Committee, a role that allowed her to circumvent her frustration at the
domestic and maternalistic impulses of the Association. The International
Sub-Committee was affiliated to the International Alliance of Women and
united by statute to the United Nations and one of its chief aims was to see
more women in 'politics and public office'.[178] Committee members were also
concerned with the growth of nuclear power. In March 1955 the committee
resolved to send delegates to the Ceylon Conference against atomic bombs.[179]

172 23 Apr. 1954, RJD Ms (150). Senator Joseph McCarthy is the man most associated with the anti-
communist suspicion which permeated American society for nearly a decade from the late 1940s and
resulted in the investigation of government officials and entertainers amongst others.

173 26 Oct. 1954, RJD Ms (151).

174 15 Dec. 1958, RJD Ms (164). Donal Nevin would be a future general secretary of the Irish Congress
of Trade Unions. A labour historian, publishing for example: *James Connolly – A Full Life* (Dublin: Gill
and Macmillan in association with SIPTU, 2005).

175 30 Jan. 1959, RJD Ms (165).

176 15 July 1959, RJD Ms (166).

177 7 Sept. 1959, RJD Ms (167).

178 Minutes of General Meeting, 16 Sept. 1959, Minutes of General Meeting of Drogheda Branch, 29
July 1959, report on International sub-committee, Tweedy papers, 98/17/2/1/8, NAI.

179 14 Mar. 1955, RJD Ms (152).

Yet tensions arose out of a fear which permeated the discourse that peace activists were linked with communists, much to Jacob's disgust. On 27 March 1958 a proposal was made at the International Sub-Committee of the IHA that a congratulatory letter be sent to those marching from London to Aldermaston protesting against nuclear testing and weaponry. Jacob wrote how 'a lot of them opposed it for fear there were Communists behind it . . . It was awful – an international committee to behave so.'[180]

This concern – not to be associated with communism – featured in the minutes of the IHA from the late 1940s. In 1953, the IHA discussed sending delegates to the Naples Congress of the International Alliance of Women. Mrs O'Connell from the Cork branch drew attention to 'rumours' that the Alliance was 'suspect'. A letter from the Minister for External Affairs was read out confirming that the Alliance 'has no connection with Communist sponsored organisations'. A resolution not to send delegates was thus defeated.[181] The context for this concern with communism was the trouble that arose following resolution by the Association to send a message to the Paris Peace Conference in support of international peace in 1949.[182] Many of the sponsors of this Conference were perceived as communist. The Bray branch resigned from the IHA as a result of the resolution; the Mount Merrion and New Ross branches also voiced their concern. Members felt that to issue a statement of support to the Paris Conference was not within the remit of a non-political Association. Members such as Hilda Tweedy responded by asserting that what was proposed was purely a peace message.[183] However, the spectre of communism continued to shroud the organisation. The *Roscommon Herald* issued a statement on 12 April 1952 to the effect that while the membership of the IHA was 'largely made up of people who have no Red sympathies' the Association 'has always been used as a medium of expression by others whose ideological allegiance is not in doubt'. The paper expressed the allegation after violence had broken out in Dublin the previous Sunday following the recent budget cuts. The paper claimed that 'every organisation that has ever been associated with Marxian activities in Dublin has been articulately posing as a friend of the people during the last ten days'. The IHA, it claimed, 'has been

180 27 Mar. 1958, RJD Ms (162). This was the first in a series of Aldermaston marches and was associated with the newly formed Campaign for Nuclear Disarmament.
181 Irish Housewives, Minutes of Extraordinary General Meeting of members, 25 June 1953, Tweedy papers, 98/17/1/4, NAI.
182 The World Peace Council in support of international peace and nuclear disarmament was formed in 1949.
183 Typescript minutes of the extraordinary general meeting, 18 May 1949, Tweedy papers, 98/17/5/2/3, NAI.

very much to the fore in voicing "popular indignation" during the past week'. The paper claimed that relying on food subsidies created a false sense of security in the consumer.[184] On behalf of the IHA, Mrs Coote, Betty Morrissey, Andrée Sheehy Skeffington, Kathleen Mills and Maud Rooney took the *Roscommon Herald* to court for libel in 1953, generating some discord as other members, including Tweedy, believed that their action was not representative. Jacob's name does not appear in this controversy or in any matter relating to the allegation of communism. However, it is clear from her chagrin over the later controversy generated by the proposal to send IHA delegates to the Ceylon conference that she believed such allegations to be parochial and bigoted. The *Roscommon Herald* retracted the allegation against the IHA on 15 August 1953 and the issue was settled out of court, the paper paying a token £50 in damages.[185] In the context of this controversy the newspaper questioned how far the Association and other similar organisations – notably the WSPL and the IWCA – were representative of Irish women. The article noted the proliferation of associations and societies in Irish society and commented on the presence of the same personnel in these societies. The IHA in this regard was linked with, amongst other organisations, the Irish Friends of Soviet Russia, the WSPL and the Left Book Club, all associations Jacob held membership of.[186]

Jacob's concern at threats to international peace in the 1950s exacerbated her irritation at censorship laws in Ireland, as is clear from her diary précis of the year 1950:

> The public trouble of the year was the Korean war and all the determined madness of the USA govt., pulling UNO after it. The peace committee here was able to do very little, as newspapers & ruling elements are determined to keep it unknown or slandered. I can't see much hope for it, but its better than nothing, & it was very worth while getting a couple of delegates to the Congress of Warsaw.[187]

---

184 'Dangerous trends in Ireland', typescript copy of article in *Roscommon Herald*, 12 Apr. 1952, Tweedy papers, 98/17/5/2/3. The 1952 budget removed food subsidies. The government, the Minister for Finance MacEntee stated, 'are satisfied that, as incomes generally have already advanced more than the cost of living and as essential foodstuffs are no longer scarce, there is now no economic or social justification for a policy of subsidising food for everybody'. *Dáil Debates*, vol. 130, 2 Apr. 1952.

185 Typescript copy of writ in the High Court between IHA and *Roscommon Herald*; *Roscommon Herald*, 15 Aug. 1952, Tweedy papers, 98/17/5/2/3, NAI; IHA Twelfth Annual Report, 1953–4, Tweedy papers, 98/17/1/2/2, NAI.

186 'Social thought in Ireland', *Roscommon Herald*, Tweedy papers, 98/17/5/2/3, NAI.

187 Summation of 1950, RJD Ms (139).

Many of the various meetings in support of world peace that Jacob attended in Dublin were deficient in numbers, a reflection of the multiplicity of small activist groups targeting the same membership base in the period.[188] Jacob's diary recorded her day-to-day work as a peace activist. She hated being involved in selling tickets for raffle to raise funds for G. Jeffares's travel to the Berlin Council but, as always, did her duty.[189] She recorded the opposition of Maria Duce to the Dublin Peace Campaign; noting the report in June 1951 of how Maria Duce 'thugs went to pubs & billiard rooms looking for men to help them attack our meeting but cd find none.'[190] In November 1951 she attended, at the urging of Louie Bennett and Lucy Kingston, a talk by the Honorary President, Michael MacWhite, at the International Affairs Association, formed in 1936–7 as a non-political study group, on the question of Ireland joining the Atlantic Pact which she described as 'awful beyond words'.[191] In October 1951 the Peace Committee received notice to quit their premises, the landlady alleging receipt of 'abusive letters for having us, & did not know we were connected with "people abroad"'.[192]

The WSPL mirrored the concerns of some members of the IHA at the alleged link between the International Peace Campaign and communist proclivities. The WSPL refused to accept the Peace Campaign's proposal to provide speakers for its meetings, not even answering the letter of offer in June 1951.[193] A more specific offer to provide a talk on the Berlin Youth Rally held the auspices of the World Peace Council in February was made to the WSPL when the organisation was fixing its winter programme for 1951: 'Mrs H. wdn't soil her fingers by answering, apparently so, I took it'. Not alone were the members of the WSPL suspicious of the tenor of international politics but, according to Jacob's testimony, the League had become a less than radical force in feminist and social activism. 'Spiteful remarks of women if you show any

188 13 Feb. 1951; 2 Apr. 195, RJD Ms (140).

189 19 Feb. 1951, RJD Ms (140). The Berlin Council was held under the auspices of the World Peace Council in February 1951.

190 4 June 1951, RJD Ms (140). Maria Duce was a lay Catholic organisation formed in 1942 by Father Denis Fahey, C. S. Sp. The group agitated for the recognition of the Catholic Church as the one true Church in the Irish Constitution. See Enda Delaney, 'Political Catholicism in post-war Ireland: The Revd Denis Fahey and Maria Duce 1945–54', *Journal of Ecclesiastical History* 52: 3 (2001), pp. 487–511.

191 27 Nov. 1951, RJD Ms (143); Sheehy Skeffington, *Skeff*, p. 257, n. 22. Michael MacWhite (1883–1958) was an Irish diplomat who served as representative of the Free State on the League of Nations, in the United States and in Rome. The Atlantic Pact was signed on 4 April 1949 establishing NATO as a defensive alliance of member states pledged to take collective action in response to an attack by an outside aggressor.

192 22 Oct. 1951, RJD Ms (142).

193 18 June 1951, RJD Ms (140).

interest in social politics.'[194] Useful proposals were discussed at meetings, notably the need to provide aid to impoverished lonely and ageing women, and to alleviate the problems of working mothers. Such discussions notwithstanding, the League was in many respects a spent force at this point. While discussion was generated at meetings, there appeared to be little attempt at follow through. At best the League, through its contributions to the press, created some public awareness of issues such as the omission of domestic servants and female agricultural workers from the Social Insurance Bill, 1952.[195] The failure to transform aspirations into action and result by the WSPL appears to be in sharp contrast to the experiences of the Irish Countrywomen's Association (ICA). This is somewhat ironic, given that the latter are retrospectively viewed as highly conservative in their focus on women in the home. Despite such perception, the 1950s saw the ICA reach an understanding that 'their role was to articulate not just the transformations they wished to see in rural Ireland, but the means by which changes could occur'.[196] By contrast the WSPL appeared at many meetings to act as a mere talking shop with the same issues being debated repeatedly with no tangible result. Meetings often took the form of intellectual debate rather than impetus to practical activity. In September 1952, for example, the discussion was on the question of 'whether Irishmen's anti-feminism [was] due to their upbringing', some members suggesting that mothers inculcate such attitudes, Jacob to herself adding, 'Of course one mustn't suggest their Church has a hand in it'.[197]

As secretary, Jacob continued to attend meetings of the WSPL as the organisation moved into a period of decline in the 1950s. In July 1951 long-time member, Mrs Kettle, resigned believing that there was a 'need to shake up old members, League can't go on unless they do something'.[198] In September of that year Mrs Kettle discussed with Andrée Sheehy Skeffington the possibility of the Association joining with the IHA.[199] Mrs Kettle, of course, may have had private reasons for needing to resign, her daughter suffering a nervous breakdown at this time.[200] Only 14 attended the meeting on the League's future in October, Lucy Kingston opting to attend a bridge night instead. The chair of the meeting was 'all for giving up in despair' but others, including

194 19 Sept. 1951, RJD Ms (141).

195 21 Feb. 1952; 6 Mar. 1952; 21 Mar. 1952, RJD Ms (144).

196 Diarmaid Ferriter, *The Transformation of Ireland: 1900–2000* (London: Profile Books, 2004), p. 496.

197 11 Sept. 1952, RJD Ms (144).

198 31 July 1951, RJD Ms (140)

199 18 Sept. 1951, RJD Ms (141).

200 Sheehy Skeffington, *Skeff*, p. 159.

Jacob, were for 'keeping on'. No resolution was achieved.[201] In November the question was again posed whether members should vote to disband the League; most were against the proposal.[202] However, the issue of terminating the League was brought up at various later meetings.[203] In October 1952 the group was given notice to quit because the landlady had no domestic help and 'we leave the room in a shocking state'. An alternative room was found at the Alpha restaurant. At this point the League owed £15 in back rent and some members began to indicate concern at the lack of financial records. In November 1952 it was decided to restore the weekly collection, the first of these new financial drives yielding 8/- from the 17 members present.[204] By the close of 1953 meetings were confined to every second week to save room fees.[205] In April 1954 it was suggested holding bridge evenings with a 5/- admission fee which appeared popular but Jacob refused to help organise them.[206] At a meeting on 14 October 1955 she 'cried for a treasurer, saying we had only £3 7[s] cdn't go on without a treasurer'.[207] Petty tensions and squabbles dominated many meetings as the following account shows:

> Letter from Ursula, how she won't come to Thursday meetings any more (except M. Cumberland's) for sake of peace, because of Mrs O'Reilly being so rude & Miss Blake not letting her answer her. Seems to think she can go on being joint sec. without attending, which is absurd.[208]

It was decided to 'warn members against personalities' in a bid to stymie such dissension.[209] But such problems were endemic; in April 1953 Mrs Fitzsimons resigned, Jacob concluding that 'people are frightful, the way they'll penalise a whole society for the fault of one'.[210] Occasionally discussions were held on means of attracting young members but to little avail, although new members did join for a brief period as a result of the controversy over the Mother and Child Scheme. Plans were put forward to co-operate with the ICA in an attempt to get women onto local councils as a first step to

201 4 Oct. 1951, RJD Ms (142); 2 Apr. 1954, RJD Ms (150).
202 15 Nov. 1951; 22 Nov. 1951, RJD Ms (143).
203 9 Oct. 1954, RJD Ms (149).
204 4 Oct. 1952, RJD Ms (144); 5 Nov. 1952; 6 Nov. 1952; 13 Nov. 1952, RJD Ms (145).
205 4 Dec. 1953, RJD Ms (149).
206 2 Apr. 1954, RJD Ms (150).
207 14 Oct. 1955, RJD Ms (155).
208 19 Nov. 1952, RJD Ms (145).
209 15 Dec. 1952, RJD Ms (145).
210 15 Apr. 1953, RJD Ms (147).

inaugurating change in the position of women in Irish life and politics.[211] The 1952 Adoption Bill which permitted limited legal adoption in Ireland, drew discussion and it was decided to ask questions of the Adoption Society, particularly about the short birth certificates 'which apparently is very much left to illegitimates so doesn't disguise them as much as it might'.[212] The 15 January 1954 meeting was devoted to the question of women police but only six members were present.[213] Perennial issues such as the link between feminist politics and pacifism continued to be touched on. In February 1954 Jacob read a paper on 'Women on armaments' and it was decided to write to Oscar Traynor and to the papers against his praise of conscription in the Seanad. It is noteworthy that Jacob felt it worthy of comment that no one called her a communist for objecting to armaments. At this meeting she sold five Neutrality booklets and distributed 'several copies of *Peace News*'.[214]

Women police was also the subject of discussion in January 1955 both at the WSPL and at the Contemporary Club, with a feeling that 'it might be coming'.[215] A certain contradiction appears in Jacob's view on the need for women police. As did so many female activists, she advanced the belief that women police were essential in dealing with cases that pertained particularly to women and children. Parents who left children alone during the evening could be dealt with, she believed, by women police.[216] However, Jacob was critical of the allocation of separate societal roles for men and women. As always she was sensitive about the double standard of sexual morality. At the Contemporary Club meeting she noted how none of the men were really against the provision of women police

211   20 Nov. 1952, RJD Ms (145). The Mother and Child Scheme brought the First Inter Party Government (18 Feb. 1948–13 June 1951), in particular Minister for Health Noel Browne, into opposition with the Catholic Church and the Irish Medical Council with its plan to provide free maternity care to mothers and health care to children up to the age of 16 regardless of means.

212   9 Oct. 1953, RJD Ms (149); Ferriter, *Transformation of Ireland*, p. 516.

213   15 Jan. 1954, RJD Ms (149).

214   26 Feb. 1954, RJD Ms (150). Traynor's remarks were made in the context of the Defence Forces (Temporary Provisions) Bill, 1954. Traynor distinguished between conscription and military training. Conscription was 'something foreign to this nation'. Military training, however, 'would be of outstanding benefit to the youth of this nation if ever any Government had the courage to face the situation and ensure that every young man at some period of his life would devote some portion of those years to training himself to be fit to defend the nation'. *Senate Debates*, vol. 43, 25 Feb. 1954.

215   28–29 Jan. 1955, RJD Ms (152). These were probably issued by the Booklet Group established in 1952.

216   28 Oct. 1955, RJD Ms (153).

but some of the men got going about whores & harlots, talking as if they did it all
by themselves – I had to ask what shd we call the men who employ them – lechers?
& why did Mrs Watson speak as if it was a law of nature that all surgeons be male?
The men thought of course they were – no women surgeons, but 2 women spoke
up & told of women surgeons they had experienced. Mrs W.'s word for prostitutes
was 'bad women'.[217]

As a matter of course, Jacob voted for the only women candidate, Mrs Stobie,
in her constituency in the municipal election in June 1955.[218] Much of the work
of the WSPL was at this point in time single-issue discussions with no
sustained campaign that would galvanise public attention. This may have been
down to the older age of many of members such as Jacob, most of them having
cut their political teeth in earlier campaigns of the first-wave feminist and early
Free State periods. On behalf of the WSPL she wrote a letter a few weeks later
protesting against the Castleblayney Urban District Council's objection to the
appointment of a postmistress on the basis of the inferiority of women.[219] The
issue of flats for single women was mentioned as a topic to be discussed in
October 1954.[220] There was a lot of discussion but very little sustained action on
behalf of members. Indeed, talks drew only small groups. Ten turned up to
hear Miss Blake on equal pay for women teachers in November 1955.[221] Jacob's
writing reveals that she hated the work involved as secretary, typing programmes, reports and press releases.[222] She found this work particularly onerous
given her secretaryship also of the Irish Anti-Vivisection Association and her
committee work for the International section of the Irish Housewives.[223]
Moreover, there was none of the excitement of the anti-Treaty or left-wing
socialist period – the compensation for her errand girl status in earlier times. By
September 1956 she described the WSPL as 'in abeyance'.[224]

217 29 Jan. 1955, RJD Ms (152).
218 23 June 1955, RJD Ms (152).
219 6 July 1955, RJD Ms (152).
220 22 Oct. 1954, RJD Ms (151).
221 25 Nov. 1955, RJD Ms (154).
222 23 Sept. 1953, RJD Ms (148); 2 Oct. 1953, RJD Ms (149).
223 30 Nov. 1954, RJD Ms (152).
224 5 Sept. 1956, RJD Ms (157).

CIVIL LIBERTIES

As in earlier decades Jacob's feminist concerns in the 1950s were threaded through her involvement in a wide range of organisations. She attended meetings of the Civil Liberty Association throughout the period. Set up on 22 March 1948 and dedicated to 'guarding jealously the rights of the individual', the Association was non-sectarian and non-party political and modelled itself on the Council of Civil Liberty in France, England and the USA.[225] The Association also aimed to broaden the democratic outlook in Ireland by establishing 'further civil liberties which should, but do not, exist, or which could exist if we were capable of using them wisely'.[226] Jacob was elected onto the Provisional Committee to draw up the rules of the Association.[227] The Council discussed various issues such as desired amendments to the Criminal Justice Bill, 1949 and the 1953 Health Bill. Jacob was concerned that in inviting speakers women would be included.[228] In May 1955 she suggested that the organisation promote equal jury service for women.[229] The WSPL also dealt with the latter issue, proposing a letter to the Press in October 1955 to end the property qualification.[230] In 1956 the Council for Civil Liberties, 'while not questioning the necessity of some form of censorship', called for an investigation into the 1946 Censorship Act in the light of the 'undesirable banning of publications of widely recognised literary merit'; a petition was prepared and sent to the Taoiseach. The Council's aim in preparing such a petition was to 'reconcile the protection of morals with the reading habits and interests of the educated public in Irish society'. The Council members stressed that the censors were morally obliged to 'read and carefully consider what they may be obliged to censor' instead of flicking through the volume in question.[231] A

---

225 'Civil Liberty Association', *Irish Independent*, 10 Mar. 1948, DT Private Office File 97/9/825, 'Irish Association of Civil Liberties',

226 C. Gore Grimes, Acting Secretary, Preliminary Organising Committee, Irish Association of Civil Liberties, 'Irish Association of Civil Liberty', Letter to the Editor, *Irish Independent*, 22 Mar. 1948, DT Private Office File 97/9/825 'Irish Association of Civil Liberties'.

227 'New body aims to end bureaucracy', *Irish Independent*, 23 Mar. 1948, DT Private Office File 97/9/825, 'Irish Association of Civil Liberties'.

228 On the Association's proposals relating to the amendment of the Criminal Justice Bill, 1949 see Thomas Coyne to Gore Grimes, 27 Oct. 1949, DT Private Office File 97/9/825, 'Irish Association of Civil Liberties'; 6 July 1954, RJD Ms (151).

229 24 May 1955, RJD Ms (152).

230 14 Oct. 1955, RJD Ms (153).

231 Circular letter enclosing petition from Irish Association of Civil Liberty, Mar. 1956; 'Indecent literature: Demands for police action to minister', *Irish Independent*, 7 Dec. 1957, DT, s 2321A, 'Censorship of publications, miscellaneous resolutions and representations'.

memorandum from the Department of Justice in September 1956 concluded
that the Association did not reflect public opinion on the matter of censorship.[232] Indeed, it should be noted that many of the representations to the
Taoiseach endorsing censorship and calling for greater restrictions came from
those who identified themselves clearly as Catholics. In 1957 Aileen Killen
from Malahide, County Dublin, wrote to the Taoiseach as 'a Catholic parent'
referring to the 'terrible dangers that threaten the youth today by the unres-
tricted sale in our shops and paper stalls of indecent books and magazines'.
Similar letters were received from St Philomena's Girls' Club and the Past
Pupils' Union of the Dominican Convent in Cabra.[233] Despite these examples
members of the Association believed that the Censorship Board did not reflect
the minority view, and hoped that of the two new appointments pending in 1956
at least one would be a member of the minority religion.[234]

THE FINALITY OF DEATH

Jacob's old friends and acquaintances began to die in increasing numbers or
suffer ill health in the 1950s. In January 1951 she noted that she was 'sorry to
have him gone' in response to Aodh de Blácam's death.[235] Her philanthropic
activities continued in this period; she took residents from the Home for the
Blind in Gardiner's Place to visit friends across Dublin. [236] Despite her advancing years she gave up her bed when Barbara Walsh from the Home visited in
January 1954, spending a 'poor night in the narrow bed'.[237] Barbara continued
to visit and it is clear that Jacob increasingly found her stamina taxed. A typical
day with Barbara in 1958 included a visit to the League for the Blind in
Gardiner's Place, from there to 21 New Street where they walked part of the
way home, Jacob commenting 'I do get tired'.[238] Visits to elderly individuals
were increasingly difficult as she herself struggled with the pains of increasing

232 Thomas Coyne, Department of Justice Memorandum on the request by the Association of Civil
Liberty to amend the Censorship Act, 1946, 3 Sept. 1956, DT, s 2321A 'Censorship of publications'.
233 Letter to De Valera from Aileen Killen, 12 Dec. 1957; letter to the Secretary Department of Justice
from Private Secretary, Department of the Taoiseach, 16 Dec. 1957, DT, s 2321A, 'Censorship of
publications'.
234 'Minority view needed on Censorship Board', *Irish Times*, 7 Nov. 1956, DT, s 2321A 'Censorship of
publications'.
235 15 Jan. 1951, RJD Ms (139).
236 22 July 1952, RJD Ms (144).
237 17 Jan. 1954, RJD Ms (149).
238 22 Apr. 1958, RJD Ms (162).

years. Struggling with sciatica in her hip she remarked how 'It was a sort of hell walking from the bus to the old women's place in St Kevin's in sheets of rain with the 2 loads of papers, etc, & the umbrella to try & hold up.'[239] As she did for Mrs Mellows, Jacob arranged items relating to rent for a Mrs Purcell, visiting the Sick and Indigent Room Keepers and St Vincent de Paul to seek advice on her possible eviction for arrears; much of the 27 July 1953 was spent on this task although she managed also to visit Meg Connery, one of her key philanthropic concerns in the 1950s.[240]

Meg Connery became bedridden in 1950 at the same time as the death of her husband. Visiting her in July 1951 Jacob noted how she had got 'very stout' as a consequence. By March 1952 Connery was in St Monica's Old People's Home near Mountjoy Square and, by Jacob's account, 'miserable & lonely'. Connery spent her final years in such institutions, moving from St Monica's Home to St Kevin's.[241] Attempts by Alfie Byrne to organise a pension for her came to nothing. Despite this failure she wanted Jacob to inquire from Máire Comerford about 'the pension she connects with C. na mBan'.[242] Connery, like Mrs Mellows in the 1940s, offers an example of the latter years of individuals active in or touched by the politics of independence who believed that the State owed them recognition and fiscal compensation. At the end of the 1930s Old Cumann na mBan noted the problem of restricting the pension claims of members to those who saw service in Easter Week. They wrote how there were 'claimants who are practically destitute and whose cases call for immediate attention. We regret to say that some of these claimants have since died and others are living in dire privation'.[243]

Women like Connery and Mrs Mellows, who believed that they had contributed either personally or through family members to the process of state formation, experienced a sense of disillusionment in latter life as they failed to have that contribution underscored by monetary recognition. There was a gap between what the state believed they had done and how they themselves measured their contribution. The state was locked into carefully constructed rules surrounding pensions and compensation and was unable to consider any claims outside such a bureaucratic edifice that could not register and regulate

239 22 Mar. 1955; 28 Mar. 1955, RJD Ms (155).

240 27 July 1953, RJD Ms (148).

241 14 July 1951, RJD Ms (140); 28 Mar. 1952; 30 May 1952, RJD Ms (144).

242 14 Apr. 1953, RJD Ms (147); 9 Nov. 1953, RJD Ms (149). Alfie Byrne (1882–1956) was Lord Mayor of Dublin.

243 Old Cumann na mBan Statement on Pension Restrictions *c*.1938–9 in Angela Bourke et al. (eds), *The Field Day Anthology of Irish Writing*, vol. v (Cork: Cork University Press, 2002), p. 151. Cumann na mBan split in 1933, the group which became Old Cumann na mBan recognising the Free State.

for emotional toll. Jacob continued to visit Mrs Mellows who by 1952 had become somewhat delusional, increasingly difficult and was 'as incontinent as blazes'. Jacob's responsibility for paying her rent from the monies available to Mrs Mellows continued.[244] The latter's death at the end of 1952 'removed all but 1 of the 5 old women I used visit, but I have 3 more in Mrs Connery, Aunt Gertie and Mrs Purcell'.[245] The Government was represented in some numbers at the funeral of Mrs Mellows on 3 December 1952. The *Irish Press* listed ten members of Cabinet as well as a number of parliamentary deputies in attendance.[246] The state visibly participated in honouring this mother who had given her son for the Irish cause. What was hidden was the manner in which the day-to-day care of this old and troubled woman, whose life was shaped by her loss, was left to such ordinary individuals as Jacob who received no mention in the account of the funeral proceedings. The same pattern manifested itself in relation to Meg Connery.

Máire Comerford informed Jacob that in relation to Connery's claim 'there were no grounds for any kind of pension & she had been to see her over & over.'[247] Yet in December 1953 Comerford sent Connery a letter 'hopeful of some pension for her in Oct.'.[248] By May 1956 Connery was in Grangegorman Mental Hospital and Jacob perceptively remarked on the lack of dignity accorded to her as a patient: '*no* place to keep anything. She has not even her handbag'.[249] In Janet Frame's fictionalised account of her mental hospital experience she describes the importance of holding onto a small bag as a symbol of her unwillingness to become institutionalised. When Jacob next visited her Connery had still not received her bag and she attempted to intervene by leaving a note for the doctor.[250] It later emerged that patients were not allowed to 'keep anything. All locked away till they leave, if ever. Not conducive to recovery'.[251] Connery declined quickly as the following account by Jacob suggested: 'found M. C. pretty bad – full accounts of the awful things done to her, & how *she* sent her sister to a convent in England because a bad man was pursuing her. A pity for insanity to take forms that hurt a person

244 31 July 1952; 2 Aug. 1952; 14 Aug. 1952, Ms (144).

245 Summation of 1952, RJD Ms (145).

246 'Funeral of Mrs Mellows' *Irish Press,* 4 Dec. 1952, DT, s 14426A, 'Deaths of persons other than heads of state & church dignitaries. Messages of sympathy & representations at funerals, 1932–1952'.

247 14 Nov. 1953, RJD Ms (149).

248 1 Dec. 1953, RJD Ms (149).

249 6 May 1956, RJD Ms (155); Janet Frame, *Faces in the Water* (London: Women's Press, 1980), pp. 105–6.

250 20 May 1956, RJD Ms (156).

251 3 June 1956, RJD Ms (156).

so.'[252] Of course, this concern by Connery on what had happened to her sister may not have been as delusional as Jacob imagined. Work by James Smith and Diarmaid Ferriter considers the manner in which female victims of sexual abuse were themselves punished. As Smith states in his study of the Magdalen laundries, after 1922 even when a 'young girl was the victim of a crime, the various authorities initially regarded her as a threatening embodiment of sexual deviancy'.[253] Throughout 1957 Jacob repeatedly attempted to talk to the medical authorities on Connery's behalf, and finally a letter from Dr Donne allowed Connery to receive some of her clothes and be helped out of bed.[254] Visiting her in the height of a 'hellish cold' January in 1958 Jacob found Connery without a bed jacket, it having gone to the wash. Jacob organised an alternative but was forced to repeat the procedure on a later visit.[255] When Connery died in December 1958 Jacob response was interesting in showing her utilitarian approach: 'Good for her. So I didn't have to go to Grangegorman.'[256] Connery's death did not end Jacob's responsibilities in the area of visitation. She visited Miss Colston and Maeve Cavanagh, both earlier political activists and, by the 1950s, elderly and immobile.[257]

Connery's death in 1958 had been preceded by the deaths of closer friends and colleagues in activism. In November 1953 Mrs Jean Coote, former member of the Joint Committee of Women's Societies and Chairwoman of the IHA since 1949, died. News came in August 1955 that Kathleen Lynn was very ill; she was to die the following month.[258] The IHA launched the Jean Coote Memorial Fund 'for some non-denominational social service'. Jacob took over in a temporary capacity as chairwoman of the IHA International Sub-Committee, remaining in this position until the annual meeting for the year 1957–8.[259] In November 1956 Louie Bennett died. This elicited no emotional response from Jacob other than a cursory entry in her diary relating to the funeral.[260] She attended a meeting in February 1957 at the Mansion House to start a memorial to

252 2 Aug. 1956, RJD Ms (156).

253 James M. Smith, *Ireland's Magdalen Laundries and the Nation's Architecture of Containment* (Manchester: Manchester University Press, 2007), p. 20. See also Ferriter, *Occasions of Sin*, p. 329.

254 8 Sept. 1957, RJD Ms (160).

255 19 Jan. 1958, RJD Ms (160); 27 Apr. 1958, RJD Ms (162).

256 21 Dec. 1958, RJD Ms (164).

257 11 Oct. 1958, RJD Ms (164); 25 Mar. 1960, RJD Ms (169).

258 23 Nov. 1953, RJD Ms (149); 2 Aug. 1955; 15 Sept. 1955, RJD Ms (152).

259 IHA Twelfth Annual Report, 1953–4, Tweedy papers, 98/17/1/2/2, NAI. The money collected for the Coote memorial fund was handed over to the Civics Institute of Ireland. IHA Thirteenth Annual Report, 1954–1955, Tweedy papers, 98/17/1/2/2 NAI; IHA Sixteenth Annual Report, 1957–8, Tweedy papers, 98/17/1/2/2 NAI.

260 25–26 Nov. 1956, RJD Ms (157).

Lynn; the plan was to establish a surgical unit for St Ultan's.[261] She attended the unveiling of the seat to Louie Bennett in September 1958 but was disappointed that, despite good speeches by Helen Chenevix, no mention was made of Bennett's connection with international pacifism or her work for the WILPF.[262]

The 1950s saw Jacob increasingly worried about Tom.[263] In Waterford in April 1951 she noted how he couldn't eat and had slept badly the previous night. The perennial tension between herself and Dorothea was still in existence; she did not stay at 'The Limes' unless the latter was away from home. A verbal exchange over the building of 40 new houses in the Grange Park area of Waterford drew the wrath of her sister-in-law on Jacob as Dorothea screamed that 'she cdn't stand Tom & me'. Jacob blamed the atmosphere in the house for much of Tom's ill health. Indeed, her nephew Chris believed that his parents should separate.[264] In July 1951 Tom was admitted to the Adelaide Hospital in Dublin, diagnosed with an obstruction between the stomach and the bowels. She was, she wrote, 'frightfully anxious about him . . . feeling it's all selfish to want him to get over it, as he'd probably be so much happier in the next world'. On 24 July Tom was operated on and four days later Jacob received a call to say that, despite earlier reports of his progress, his condition was bad and that Dorothea should be alerted. Visiting him two days later, he 'seemed hardly alive & terrified me', although a student doctor informed her that he had improved. By the end of July he was declared much better.[265] In her yearly summary for 1951 she expressed her fear that his death 'wd cut me off from all my early life – no one left that could remember me'.[266] By mid 1953 Tom was again complaining of 'discomfort' and Jacob was worried.[267] Visiting him in June 1954 in the absence of Dorothea she again found him 'not too well, tires easily & has some indigestion symptoms'.[268] In May 1955 he was diagnosed with anaemia.[269] Two years later a call came that he was 'very ill' in London, suffering from a form of exhaustion. She describes how she 'came home in terror'.[270] In the event it was Dorothea who was ill in the summer of 1957:

261 1 Feb. 1957, RJD Ms (158).
262 24 Sept. 1958, RJD Ms (164).
263 5 Apr. 1951, RJD Ms (140).
264 5 July 1952, RJD Ms (144); 16 Apr. 1951; 18 Apr. 1951, RJD Ms (140).
265 6 July 1951; 12 July 1951; 23–24 July 1951; 28 July 1951; 30 July 1951, RJD Ms (140).
266 Summation of 1951, RJD Ms (143).
267 14 May 1953, RJD Ms (147).
268 20 June 1954, RJD Ms (150).
269 21 May 1955, RJD Ms (152).
270 14 May 1957, RJD Ms (159).

diagnosed with heart trouble, she died in late November.[271] Jacob questioned whether she should now live with Tom but decided that she couldn't 'break off everything here'.[272] She travelled to Waterford at the end of January 1958, 'learning' from the housekeeper, Miss O'Neill, the order and routine of the house. She kept house for Tom prior to his move to his son Chris's residence. She quite successfully made her first dinner but the 'pudding' was somewhat burned as she was not accustomed to the temperature of the stove.[273] When Chris and Maisie went on holidays Jacob travelled to Waterford to fill in. She looked after Tom in June 1958 and again at the end of August. Waterford and more particularly closeness to Tom were important to her. She 'hated', she wrote in September 1958 'the thought of leaving'.[274] Shortly after she returned from this visit news arrived that Tom was ill and was being brought to Richmond Hospital to have a brain operation, having had a seizure. Nothing was found during the operation.[275] In December 1958 he became ill with his ulcer. Again in early February news came that he was 'very weak', diagnosed with pernicious anaemia and that she had 'better come quick'. Although he improved he had to see a surgeon at the Burlington Clinic and was moved from there to the Adelaide.[276] While he recovered somewhat, in late November 1959 he was taken to Maypark Hospital and 'not expected to live'. On 3 December news reached her that Tom was dead. She herself was sick and unable to attend the funeral. Interestingly, despite declaring it a 'hellish happening, miserable', she held an anti-vivisection meeting on the day of the funeral.[277] Her summation for 1959 was incomplete, discussing how the first half of the year was dominated by concerns over Tom's health with no mention of his death or her feelings.[278]

What is clear is that Jacob resented the sense that she, as a single woman, was always available and could always be called to help; 'Letter from Lucy Pim wanting me to go & help her for a *fortnight* in June when she'd be alone!'[279] Indeed, Jacob's diary offers a number of examples of single women whose lives were subordinated to family duties to ageing parents and other relatives. She tried to persuade fellow anti-vivisectionist, Moira Henry, to take a rest 'while her father is away' and noted how a Gladys Peard 'seems to sacrifice herself too

271 31 Aug. 1957, RJD Ms (159); 26 Nov. 1957, RJD Ms (160).
272 Summation of 1957, RJD Ms (160).
273 31 Jan. 1958; 2 Feb. 1958, RJD Ms (161).
274 4 Sept. 1958, RJD Ms (164).
275 16–17 Sept. 1958, RJD Ms (164).
276 7 Feb. 1959; 9–10 Feb. 1959; 4 Mar. 1959, RJD Ms (165).
277 30 Nov. 1959; 2–4 Dec. 1959, RJD Ms (168).
278 Summation of 1959, RJD Ms (168).
279 24 Apr. 1951, RJD Ms (140).

much to her father'.[280] She herself did much babysitting for her nephews and niece and for Daisy Swanton. On 2 March 1955 she spent the afternoon babysitting for Daisy and the evening for Margie.[281] However, she did not appear to mind such a duty and when Daisy was absent for a few days she found her 'lack' greater than the benefit of the quietness consequent on the absence of her daughter, Sylvia.[282] When Sylvia began school in 1955 Jacob often collected her.[283] She still struggled with loneliness, suggesting that as Jacob became older it became harder to deal with her.[284] She continued to be viewed by those more successful or more involved in the activism of the period as a useful individual to perform menial or commonplace tasks, a fact she was not unaware of as the following extract shows: 'Met the Deevys at the Hibernian ... they had asked me to the PEN court case about restraining writers from abusing publishers – partly, I think to write the points for Tessa'. Jacob did secretarial type work for Teresa Deevy and others on a number of occasions.[285] In late September 1952 she was brought by George [Gilmore?] to act as temporary secretary to a group, including Louie Bennett, Helen Chenevix, Armstrong and Peadar O'Donnell, 'trying to get strong Unions to declare for peace & neutrality'; she agreed to go to a later meeting at 48 Fleet Street to 'write letters for them'.[286] This group became known as the 'Booklet Group' and produced a pamphlet in defence of neutrality.

Despite her sense of always being available to perform mundane tasks Jacob needed to stay involved in the campaigns of the period on some level, as much for personal as for ideological reasons. There is a sense that Jacob's round of visits to older women and her need to stay in contact with old friends and acquaintances such as Owen and Andrée Sheehy Skeffington, the McGinleys and the Coffeys, betrayed a certain need. She lacked a family of her own; despite her home with the Kingston/Swanton family and despite her closeness to her nephews and niece it was only really Tom who made her feel accepted. Her relationship with Owen Sheehy Skeffington was still important to her but she did not see much of him outside meetings of the Civil Liberties Committee.

280 26 July 1952; 30 July 1952, RJD Ms (144).

281 2 Mar. 1955, RJD Ms (152).

282 See, for example, 22 Feb. 1954; 20 Mar. 1954, RJD Ms (150).

283 22 Nov. 1955, RJD Ms (154).

284 19 June 1955, RJD Ms (152).

285 17 Nov. 1951, RJD Ms (143); 23 Nov. 1952; 14 Jan. 1953, RJD Ms (145). Teresa Deevy (1894–1963) was active in Cumann na mBan in Waterford, although Jacob does not indicate any earlier connection between them. Deevy was a playwright who wrote for the stage and for radio. Bourke et al. (eds), *Field Day Anthology*, vol. v, pp. 1,043–4.

286 30 Sept. 1952; 7 Oct. 1952, RJD Ms (144).

Lucy Kingston touched on this when she remarked in September 1958: 'Lucy thought me very funny to go around so much – to be so restless – when she found I was going out to the Coffeys in the evening. I should stay in more'.[287] When Jacob left for Bristol in May 1960 she noted 'No one minding about my departure – L. not home, & Daisy away upstairs when I started'.[288] When the Coffeys left for London in June 1960 she described it as a 'great loss'.[289]

PUBLISHING

Jacob agonised at her lack of publishing success. Advised to take poems she was writing in the early 1950s to Duffy and the Metropolitan, she bemoaned the fact that, such a suggestion aside, she received no 'hard criticism' from her acquaintances.[290] In early March 1951 she finally received a letter from Browne and Nolan stating that printing problems and commitments meant they could not take any new material for three years; she received as similar response from Duffy's in relation to her poetry. [291] Later that year, in September, she received *The Raven's Glen* back from H. Bourne 'as "scruffy" in look, too short, & writing "not good enough" to make up for that'. However, he did request to see her manuscript on Matilda Tone.[292] Nothing appeared to come of this and in February 1952 she left two chapters of the manuscript to be viewed by Peadar O'Donnell to see if he could serialise it in *The Bell*, and in August left a bound copy at Gills and the Talbot Press. The latter press responded with 'a letter talking of her [Matilda Tone] life being ruined by politics, & that they doubted wd the public be interested in her story'.[293] By September Jacob had decided to write a novel version of Matilda's life thinking it might be more attractive to publishers than a biography. George Gilmore advised her to 'put in plenty of heart-throbs and informers'.[294] As she worked on this novel she continued to search for a publisher for the biography, taking a manuscript in November to Moynihans in Capel Street.[295] At a meeting of the Women Writers earlier in July she was hopeful to discover a Dublin Authors' Guild to

287 21 Sept. 1958, RJD Ms (164).
288 17 May 1960, RJD Ms (169).
289 19 June 1960, RJD Ms (170).
290 16 Feb. 1951, RJD Ms (140).
291 3 Mar. 1951; 14 Mar. 1951, RJD Ms (140).
292 9 Sept. 1951, RJD Ms (141).
293 27 Feb. 1952; 12 Aug. 1952; 29 Aug. 1952; 11 Sept. 1952, RJD Ms (144).
294 21 Sept. 1952; 30 Sept. 1952, RJD Ms (144).
295 11 Nov. 1952, RJD Ms (145).

whom she might right to secure an agent.[296] Overtures to an agent in New York drew a blank; there was no interest in the United States in her work on Tone's wife.[297]

Refusal followed refusal; the rejection of an article on Thomas Russell by the *Irish Press* in October 1953 caused her to wonder if the paper had 'taken a vow against me. Very depressing'.[298] At the end of 1953 she had received rejections for her Tone manuscript from an English University firm, Cork University Press and the *Kerryman*. By this time she had nearly finished the novel version of the life and she continued to present extracts at work in progress evenings at the Women Writers Club.[299] She was still hoping to find a publisher in 1954 taking it to Cahill's on the advice of Sybil Le Brocquy.[300] In July 1955 Methuen declined *The Rebel's Wife* on the grounds that it 'wd not interest people "here"'.[301] Jacob's interest in Tone became quite obsessive, maybe a later-life manifestation of her earlier crushes on heroes of the revolutionary period. On 20 June 1955 she 'decided to keep Tone's birthday' and travelled to Bodenstown.[302] On 19 August that year she noted that this was the day of Matilda Tone's wedding to Wilson.[303] What Jacob designated as a good experience was to meet and talk to someone working in the same area of 1798 and the United Irishmen. In October 1955 she met Máire McNeill who was writing on Mary Ann McCracken, describing how they 'had a grand talk, I showed her the 12 yr portrait of Tone – she thinks he was a bit of an adventurer. Neilson – Russell, & his writing – showed her T.'s letter from USA. She is great value'.[304] Meeting the academic, Maureen Wall, at a historical meeting in UCD in March 1955 she described her as:

296 2 July 1952, RJD Ms (144).

297 16 Feb. 1953, RJD Ms (145).

298 3 Oct. 1953, RJD Ms (149). Thomas Russell 1767–1803 was involved in the United Irishmen and was executed after involvement in the Emmet Rebellion of 1803.

299 Summation of 1953, RJD Ms (149); 24 Mar. 1954, RJD Ms (150).

300 27 Mar. 1954, RJD Ms (150).

301 16 July 1955, RJD Ms (152).

302 20 June 1955, RJD Ms (152).

303 19 Aug. 1955, RJD Ms (152).

304 2 Oct. 1955, RJD Ms (153). Mary Ann McCracken (1770–1886) was the sister of United Irishman Henry Joy McCracken (1767–98). United Irishman, Samuel Neilson (1761–1803). Mary McNeill, *The Life and Times of Mary Ann McCracken 1770–1866: A Belfast Panorama* (Dublin: Allen Figgis, 1960)

[a] very worthwhile woman, knows nearly as much about '98 as I do – really knows Tone's diary & is writing something on the Catholic Committee – asking what was I writing, & seemed to think the USA wd eagerly grab at a book on M. Tone![305]

Wall visited her at the end of May while in October she enjoyed a visit from Máire McNeill who 'knows a lot about the M'Crackens & Russell'. Yet Jacob was disappointed when the McNeill did not enjoy the fictional account of Matilda Tone's life believing it would be better as a biography.[306] In April 1958 she went to Queen's University to hear the psychiatrist, O'Malley, lecture on suicide in general and with reference to Tone. At Queen's she meet McNeill again and participated in the discussion, telling 'some of Matilda's evidence of what Tone said to her'.[307] Wall believed that what was wrong with her work in this area from a publisher's point of view was that she 'expected readers to know too much'.[308] Earlier, in May of that year the historian Owen Dudley Edwards suggested that she try Hodges & Figgis as they were to begin publishing again.[309] In July she tried Clonmore & Reynolds.[310] Summing up 1956 she noted her difficulty in writing anything new until she had something published.[311] Early in January 1957 she brought a play, 'The plain truth' to the Globe office in the Gas Company 'but the man there said they got so many scripts they'd rather people didn't bring them, & it wd be a long time before I'd hear anything. It is an awful world for writers'.[312] This play was returned 'without a word' by the middle of February.[313]

In March 1957 a possibility to have *The Rebel's Wife* published at her expense emerged; this she described 'as a real gleam of hope'.[314] The *Kerryman* agreed to print for about £380.[315] Despite all the rejections Jacob's sense of herself as a writer did not waver or, one might conjecture, that she could not allow it to waver as it defined her place in the world in terms of occupation and

---

305 13 Mar. 1956, RJD Ms (155). Maureen Wall (1918–72). Tom Dunne, 'Maureen Wall (*née* McGeehin) 1918–1972: a memoir' in Gerard O'Brien and Tom Dunne (eds), *Catholic Ireland in the Eighteenth Century: Collected Essays of Maureen Wall* (Dublin: Geography Publications, 1989).

306 28 May 1956, RJD Ms (156); 18 Oct. 1956; 22 Oct. 1956, RJD Ms (157).

307 23 Apr. 1958, RJD Ms (162).

308 23 Oct. 1956, RJD Ms (157).

309 15 May 1956, RJD Ms (156).

310 10 July 1956, RJD Ms (156).

311 Summation of 1956, RJD Ms (158).

312 9 Jan. 1957, RJD Ms (158).

313 16 Feb. 1957, RJD Ms (158).

314 11 Mar. 1957; 19 Mar. 1957 RJD Ms (158).

315 4 June 1957, RJD Ms (159).

purpose. Indeed she was in no way awed by the academic historians with whom she began to mix in the later 1950s at *Irish Historical Studies* meetings, although it should be noted that Robin Dudley Edwards's 1938 review of *The Rise of the United Irishmen* criticised Jacob's lack of 'proper historical perspective' arguing that her own political beliefs obscured her vision of the eighteenth century.

> The principle of equality, and the rights of man (and of woman) were so far from being standards of excellence at that time that those who favoured such notions were regarded with no more toleration than is nowadays afforded to anarchists.

Edwards commented that there was much manuscript material not utilised by Jacob and stated: 'Nowadays investigation of manuscript material is usually left to professional historians, as the examination of unedited material demands a scientific training.'[316] The year of 1938 was, of course, the year in which Moody and Edwards established *Irish Historical Studies* 'exclusively devoted to the scientific study of Irish history'.[317]

Throughout the later 1950s Jacob continued to interact with historians such as Maureen Wall. She listened to Wall's Thomas Davis lecture on Keogh in October 1958 and commented that it was 'fairly good, but nothing about him being in the UI and sending messages to Tone in USA'.[318] Indeed, there was a note of derision in her account of Wall's refusal to speak at the Women Writers' Club banquet in honour of *The Rebel's Wife* when finally published in 1958: 'terrified of speaking in public – and she a university lecturer'.[319] Jacob was delighted with the publication. Summing up 1957 and considering the year ahead she hoped for good reviews and was 'furious' with one by 'F. T.' in the *Independent* that described the dialogue as 'for the most part stilted, artificial & over-sentimental'. This was, she claimed, the 'one fault I know it hasn't got'. At this point there were no reviews in the *Irish Press* or the *Irish Times*.[320] On 18 January a review appeared in the latter written by old friend Robert Brennan

316 R. D. Edwards, review of *The Rise of the United Irishmen, 1791–94* in *Dublin Magazine* XIII: 3 (July–Sept. 1938), pp. 70–1.
317 T. W. Moody and R. D. Edwards, 'Preface to *Irish Historical Studies*' in Ciaran Brady (ed.), *Interpreting Irish History: The Debate on Historical Revisionism 1938–1994* (Dublin: Irish Academic Press, 1994), p. 36.
318 5 Oct. 1958, RJD Ms (164). John Keogh (1740–1817) was a leading Catholic rights activist in late eighteenth-century Ireland.
319 10 Nov. 1958, RJD Ms (164).
320 4 Jan. 1958, RJD Ms (160).

which she described as 'quite nice'.[321] In February 1958 she wrote to Dr Dickson who had favourably reviewed the book in the *Irish Times* with George Gilmore's suggestion that the Tone memorial be used to fund a cheap edition of the *Life*. Although he agreed to approach T. W. Moody on the issue he was not hopeful. Nevertheless, Jacob enjoyed an afternoon with him in the Hibernian Hotel conversing on Tone matters.[322] In October 1958 she received, as noted above, the Women's Writers' Club Award for the best book published by a member in 1958.[323] She attempted to organise that booksellers would display the book with notice on it of the award, and was delighted too with the interviews by Ina Foley of the *Irish Press* and Department of External Affairs.[324] Discussing the pending award banquet with George Gilmore they agreed that she would refer to the lack of a Tone monument and 'then letters cd be written, if the reference cd be got into the press report'.[325] The banquet went well although she felt that Lorna Reynolds made too much of 'Tone's other flirtations'.[326] The *Irish Times* the next day reported on her comment that 'this country basically owed its freedom to Tone – and it owed a great debt also to his wife, Mathilda [*sic*] – and yet it had no monument to his memory in the capital city – his own town'.[327] She wrote to the *Irish Press* and *Irish Times* in February 1959 suggesting a potential site for the monument.[328] Jacob attended a meeting in Middle Abbey Street to mark the beginning of Wolfe Tone Week, 1959, the procession laying a wreath at Tone's birthplace, the late Stafford Street. The speeches, she noted, were mostly about contemporary politics from a Sinn Féin perspective.[329]

Jacob's perception that family and close friends were little interested in her doings also irked her from time to time:

> To Margie's later – Tom there, & Billy. Telling about the PEN – no one there, nor Lucy, a bit interested in my being called to speak. Not one 'My!' or 'why?' Depressing.[330]

321 18 Jan. 1958, RJD Ms (160).
322 19 Feb. 1958, RJD Ms (161); 18 Mar. 1958, RJD Ms (162).
323 2 Oct. 1958, RJD Ms (164).
324 2 Nov. 1958; 2 Dec. 1958, RJD Ms (164).
325 11 Nov. 1958, RJD Ms (164).
326 9 Dec. 1958, Ms (164). Lorna Reynolds (1911–2003), literary critic and lecturer in English literature in UCD 1940–66. Bourke et al. (eds), *Field Day Anthology*, vol. v, p. 1,070.
327 'No monument yet to "Greatest Dubliner"', *Irish Times*, 10 Dec. 1958.
328 22 Feb. 1959, RJD Ms (165).
329 15 June 1959, RJD Ms (166).
330 11 Mar. 1951, RJD Ms (140).

In late March she typed for the playwright, Teresa Deevy.[331] She was paid for this work but most of all she enjoyed the interest Deevy took in her work. Deevy read 'French help' and 'was very interested & noticed things. A lovely experience. . . . how it wd help to have someone showing interest in one's stuff.'[332] When *The Rebel's Wife* was published Jacob noted repeatedly how those close to her had not yet read it.[333] Her niece Margie 'seemed to find it interesting but I don't recall any definite comment'.[334] When definite comment was forthcoming it highlighted the family sense of Jacob as someone apart. In a letter to her father Margie wrote 'I find it impossible to realise that Aunt Rose, who is so unusual in all her ideas about *everything*, can write quite a normal book about more or less ordinary people in such a human way'.[335] Praise and affirmation from family mattered much to Jacob and she was 'depressed' when her nephew Louis thought 'poorly of it – no wonder publishers wdn't take it – can't think why some reviews are so favouring – Matilda is dull & he doesn't see why she shd be written about, and Tone was "ineffective". He admitted it was "well-written"'.[336] Louis, she believed, found her 'very annoying, not in the *way* I say things, but in the kind of things I say'.[337] He believed that her house-to-house calls for the Campaign for Nuclear Disarmament 'was the way to make people thoroughly dislike me'.[338] Frank Coffey similarly didn't like the work believing that Tone was sidelined it in, Matilda taking 'the importance'. This was in contrast to others who believed 'that Tone steals the show from her'.[339] Although she was happy with the reviews she noted despondently how there were not even 400 copies sold; in February 1959 she received a cheque for £30.[340] Again lack of affirmation from her family depressed her: 'Various people praised the book, my own relatives not among them, especially Louis'.[341]

Certain days, notably Valentine's Day, caused Jacob to remember Frank Ryan, the defining relationship of her life, fondly. Dead cats also featured in her musings: 'I hope Val is happy somewhere' she wrote in 1952.[342] Jacob's commitment to animal welfare carried through her to this period. Her

331 19 Mar. 1951, RJD Ms (140).
332 10 May 1954, RJD Ms (150).
333 26 Jan. 1958, RJD Ms (161).
334 27 Jan. 1958, RJD Ms (161).
335 7 Feb. 1958, RJD Ms (161).
336 13 Apr. 1958, RJD Ms (162).
337 15 Mar. 1959, RJD Ms (165).
338 8 Sept. 1959, RJD Ms (167).
339 27 Apr. 1958, RJD Ms (162).
340 Summation 1958, RJD Ms (164); 9 Feb. 1959, RJD Ms (165).
341 Summation 1958, RJD Ms (164).
342 14 Feb. 1951, RJD Ms (144).

membership of the Vegetarian Society coalesced with her membership of the Anti-Vivisection Society. She was interested in alternative forms of medical treatment and dietary advice. In April 1953 she attended a Vegetarian Society lecture at the Country Shop by G. Rudd on the excessive consumption of meat and protein by British people, stressing the need to eat raw food and blaming the increase in tonsil trouble among English children on the introduction of free school milk.[343] In November 1959 the Irish Vegetarian Society hosted Gordon Latto who spoke on the 'healthy life'. Attendees were encouraged to walk, smell more, chew their food carefully, deep breathe and paddle in cold water.[344] Jacob continued to pay her Gaelic League subscription and attended the annual meeting of the branch and a few musical evenings.[345] At one such in February 1954 she recited Mise Éire to the accompaniment of a recorder.[346] Her complaint about the lack of female involvement in the League's activities was still voiced. At the Feis Átha Cliath in March 1956 she noted how all the speakers were male.[347]

Religious issues continued to galvanise Jacob and she lost no opportunity to discuss her perceptions of sectarianism. On 22 October 1955 she attended the Contemporary Club discussion on 'the political role of religious spokesmen in Ireland'. She castigated Peadar O'Donnell for adopting a 'middle of the road as usual' approach. Other speakers discussed the lack of a progressive party in Ireland. Jacob complained of the segregation of Catholics and Protestants and claimed 'P. O'D. lumped all Prots together too much'.[348]

In February 1957 Lucy, the Swantons and Jacob moved to Wynnefield House. In October 1957 her beloved Riabhach was put down. The vet told her 'he wdn't get better, so I let her kill him . . . It was awful. . . . it was awful without R. in the house – black lonely. Daisy was civil'.[349] Jacob's new cat, Tibby, caused tension between herself and Lucy to the point where she worried that she might have to find alternative accommodation. Lucy, she

---

343 30 Apr. 1953, RJD Ms (147). Geoffrey L. Rudd, a member of the English Vegetarian Society. Carolyn Steedman offers her perception of the benefits of state intervention in children's lives in Britain in the 1950s in the form of free milk and school dinners. 'It was a considerable achievement for a society to pour so much milk and so much orange juice, so many vitamins down the throats of its children, and for the height and weight of those children to outstrip the measurements of only a decade before.' Carolyn Steedman, *Landscape For a Good Woman* (London: Virago, 2000), p. 122.

344 15 Nov. 1959, RJD Ms (168). Mistakenly listed by Jacob as 16 November. Dr Gordon Latto (1911–98) member of the British Vegetarian Society.

345 3 Dec. 1953; 2 Jan. 1954, RJD Ms (149).

346 20 Feb. 1954, RJD Ms (150).

347 10 Mar. 1956, RJD Ms (155).

348 22 Oct. 1955, RJD Ms (153).

349 22 Oct. 1957, RJD Ms (160).

wrote in November 1959, was 'rather ferocious about Tibby at tea'. Kingston
wanted a cat-free house on account of Daisy's asthma.[350]

Jacob was killed crossing the road in October 1960. Members of the Central
Committee of the IHA 'stood in tribute' as Hilda Tweedy told how she had
'always taken a tremendous interest in our Association'.[351] In the months before
she died Jacob had been involved in planning for the International Congress of
the IAW to be held in Dublin in 1961. In June 1960 two delegates from the
IAW, Madame Deranyagala of Ceylon, President, and Mrs Halsey, from
America, Secretary, came to Dublin to help with organisation, meeting members of the IHA on 28 June 1960 at the Institute of Catholic Sociology.[352] In the
decades after her death Jacob faded from the historical record. Fortuitously, the
gift of her daily diary to the National Library has allowed the voice of a less
prominent figure to shed complexity and diversity on the history of Irish
nationalist and feminist activism in revolutionary and Free State periods.

Oliver MacDonagh wrote 'every concept of reality is unique, and may be
burning glass upon the past if angled correctly'. This statement underscores
the merits in moving the practice of biography outside the traditional focus on
leaders and pioneers in movements for political and social change. The
importance of a biography of Rosamond Jacob lies in the contrast it offers to
such biographies. Certainly Jacob was no Hanna Sheehy Skeffington or Frank
Ryan, dominant in the campaigns of the period and to the fore in the public
consciousness in agitating for societal and political change. Nonetheless, by
seeing how such demands and their consequences were interpreted,
negotiated and understood by foot soldiers in the cause, the canvas of activism
is rendered more nuanced and complex. Jacob's diary offers a first-hand
account of an ordinary, but no less important life in the changing Ireland of
the first half of the twentieth century. At all times she added her own personal
interpretation to the events of the broad political, cultural and social spectrum
of the period and thereby offered an important alternative angle on what it
meant to be a woman, a republican supporter and a human being in Ireland in
the period.

350 14 Nov. 1959, RJD Ms (168).

351 Minutes of general meeting, 19 Oct. 1960, Tweedy papers, 98/17/2/1/8, NAI.

352 Minutes of meeting with delegates from International Alliance of Women, 28 June 1960, Tweedy
papers, 98/17/2/1/8, NAI.

Bibliography

—

PRIMARY SOURCES

PUBLIC RECORDS

NATIONAL LIBRARY OF IRELAND
Gaelic League Papers (Ms 11,538)
Rosamond Jacob Papers
Mary Leadbeater Diaries
Sheehy Skeffington Papers
Diary of Celia Shaw (Ms 23, 409)

NATIONAL ARCHIVES OF IRELAND
Bureau of Military History Witness Statements
Department of the Taoiseach Files
Hilda Tweedy Papers
Joint Committee of Women's Societies and Social Workers Papers

SOCIETY OF FRIENDS LIBRARY, DUBLIN
Harvey Pedigree.
Jacob Pedigree.

NEWSPAPERS AND MAGAZINES

An Phoblacht
Irish Book Lover
Irish Statesman
Waterford Standard
Waterford News
Worker's Republic

BOOKS, PAMPHLETS AND ARTICLES

Corkery, Daniel, *Synge and Anglo-Irish Literature* (Cork: Cork University Press, 1913).
Downey, Edmund, *Waterford: An Illustrated Guide and Tourists' Handbook* (Waterford: Waterford News, n.d. [*c*.1931]).
Fianna Handbook (Dublin: Patrick Mahon, 1914).

Gilmore, George, *1934 Republican Congress* (Dublin: Dochas Co-Op Society, n.d.).
Macardle, Dorothy, *The Irish Republic* (London: Victor Gollancz, 1937).
O'Kane, Rev. Michael, *Women's Place in the World* (Dublin: Gill & Son, 1913).
Wollstonecraft, *A Vindication of the Rights of Women* (London: Longman, 2006).

MEMOIRS, NOVELS AND PLAYS

Braddon, Mary Elizabeth, *The Doctor's Wife* (Oxford: Oxford University Press, 2008).
Brennan, Robert, *Allegiance* (Dublin: Browne & Nolan, 1950).
Clarke, Kathleeen, *Revolutionary Woman* (Dublin: O'Brien, 1991).
Colum, Mary, *Life and the Dream*, (New York: Doubleday, 1947).
Cousins, J. H. and M. E. Cousins, *We Two Together* (India: Ganesh, 1950).
Frame, Janet, *Faces in the Water* (London: Women's Press, 1980).
Gaughan, J. A., (ed.), *Memoirs of Senator James G. Douglas, 1887–1954: Concerned Citizen* (Dublin: UCD Press, 1998).
Harrington, John P., (ed.), *Modern Irish Drama* (New York: W. W. Norton, 1991).
Jacob, Rosamond, *The Raven's Glen* (Dublin: Alan Figgis, 1960).
Jacob, Rosamond, *The Rebel's Wife* (Tralee: The Kerryman, 1957).
Jacob, Rosamond, *The Troubled House: A Novel of Dublin in the 'Twenties* (Dublin: Browne & Nolan, 1938).
Jacob, Rosamond, *The Rise of the United Irishmen 1791-94* (London: George G. Harrap, 1937).
Laverty, Maura, *Full and Plenty* (Irish Flour Millers Assoc. 1960).
Laverty, Maura, *Maura Laverty's Cookbook* (London: Longmans, Green, 1946).
Lawrenson Swanton, Daisy, *Emerging from the Shadow: The Lives of Sarah Anne Lawrenson and Lucy Olive Kingston: Based on Personal Diaries, 1883–1969* (Dublin: Attic, 1994).
Moore, George, *A Drama in Muslin* (Gerrards Cross: Colin Smythe, 1981).
Sheehy Skeffington, Andrée, *Skeff: A Life of Owen Sheehy Skeffington 1909–1970* (Dublin: Lilliput, 1991).
Skinnider, Margaret, *Doing My Bit For Ireland* (New York: The Century Co., 1917).
Steedman, Carolyn, *Landscape For a Good Woman* (London: Virago, 2000).
Wilde, Oscar, *The Importance of Being Earnest* (London: A & C Black, 2004).
Winthrop, F., *Callaghan* (Dublin: Martin Lester, n.d [1920]).
Woolf, Virginia, *A Room of One's Own* (New York: Harcourt Brace Jovanovich, 1991).
Young, Ella, *Flowering Dusk. Things Remembered Accurately and Inaccurately* (New York: Longmans, Green, 1945).

SECONDARY SOURCES

Adams, Michael, *Censorship: The Irish Experience* (Alabama: University of Alabama Press, 1968).
Allen, Nicolas, *Modernism, Ireland and Civil War* (Cambridge: Cambridge University Press, 2009).
Allen, Nicolas, *George Russell (AE) and the New Ireland, 1905-30* (Dublin: Four Courts, 1993).
Anderson, Benedict, *Imagined Communities. Reflections on the Origin and Spread of Nationalism*, rev. edn (London: Verso, 1991).

Beaumont, Catriona, 'Women, citizenship and Catholicism in the Irish Free State, 1922–1948', *Women's History Review* 6: 4 (1997), pp. 563–85.

Biletz, Frank A., 'Women and Irish-Ireland: the domestic nationalism of Mary Butler', *New Hibernia Review* 6: 1 (2002), pp. 59–72.

Bloom, Lynn, Z., '"I write for myself and strangers": private diaries as public documents', in Suzanne L. Bunkers and Cynthia A. Huff (eds), *Inscribing the Daily: Critical Essays on Women's Diaries* (Amherst: University of Massachusetts Press, 1996), pp. 23–37.

Bourke, Angela, *Maeve Brennan: Homesick at the New Yorker* (London: Jonathan Cape, 2004).

Bourke, Angela et al. (eds), *The Field Day Anthology of Irish Writing*, vols iv–v (Cork: Cork University Press, 2002).

Bowe, Nicola Gordon and Elizabeth Cumming, *The Arts and Crafts Movements in Dublin and Edinburgh: 1885–1925* (Dublin: Irish Academic Press, 1998).

Brady, Ciaran, '"Constructive and instrumental": the dilemma of Ireland's first "new historians"', in Ciaran Brady (ed.), *Interpreting Irish History: The Debate on Historical Revisionism 1938–1994* (Dublin: Irish Academic Press, 1994), pp. 3–31.

Brennan, Helen, *The Story of Irish Dance* (Dingle: Brandon, 1999).

Brown, Terence, *Ireland: A Social and Cultural History 1922–79* (Glasgow: Fontana, 1981).

Brunton, Deborah, 'The problems of implementation: the failure and success of public vaccination against smallpox in Ireland, 1840-1873' in Greta Jones and Elizabeth Malcolm (eds), *Medicine, Disease and the State in Ireland, 1650–1940* (Cork: Cork University Press, 1999), pp. 138–57.

Butler, Hubert, *The Sub-Prefect Should Have Held His Tongue, and Other Essays* (London: Allen Lane, 1990).

Callanan, Frank, *T. M. Healy* (Cork: Cork University Press, 1996).

Clear, Caitríona, '"I can talk about it, can't I?": The Ireland Maura Laverty desired, 1942–46', *Women's Studies* 30: 6 (2001), pp. 819–35.

Clear, Caitríona, '"The women can not be blamed": the commission on vocational organisation, feminism and "home-makers' in independent Ireland in the 1930s and '40s' in Mary O'Dowd and Sabine Wichert (eds), *Chattel, Servant or Citizen: Women's Status in Church State and Society* (Belfast: Institute of Irish Studies, 1995), pp. 179–86.

Clyde, Tom, *Irish Literary Magazines: An Outline History and Descriptive Bibliography* (Dublin: Irish Academic Press, 2003).

Coleman, Marie, 'The origins of the Irish hospitals' sweepstake', *Irish Economic and Social History* 29 (2002), pp. 40–55.

Coleman Marie, *The Irish Sweep: A History of the Irish Hospitals Sweepstake, 1930–87* (Dublin: UCD Press, 2009).

Corbin, Alain, *The Life of an Unknown: The Rediscovered World of a Clog Maker in Nineteenth-Century France* (New York: Columbia University Press, 2001).

Costello, Francis J., *Enduring The Most: The Life and Death of Terence MacSwiney* (Dingle: Brandon, 1995).

Crawford, Elizabeth, *The Women's Suffrage Movement: A Reference Guide 1866–1928* (London: UCL Press, 1999).

Cronin, Mike, *The Blueshirts and Irish Politics* (Dublin: Four Courts, 1997).

Cullen Owens, Rosemary, 'Women and pacifism in Ireland, 1915–1932' in Maryann Valiulis and Mary O'Dowd (eds), *Women and Irish History* (Dublin: Wolfhound, 1997), pp. 220–39.

Cullen Owens, Rosemary, *Smashing Times: A History of the Irish Women's Suffrage Movement 1899–1922* (Dublin: Attic Press, 1984).

Daly, Mary, "'Oh, Kathleen Ni Houlihan, your way's a thorny way!" The condition of women in twentieth-century Ireland', in Anthony Bradley and Maryann Valiulis (eds), *Gender and Sexuality in Modern Ireland* (Amherst: University of Massachusetts Press, 1997), pp. 102–26.

Deane, Seamus, (ed.), *The Field Day Anthology of Irish Writing*, vols I–III (Derry: Field Day, 1991).

Delaney, Enda, 'Political Catholicism in post-war Ireland: The Revd Denis Fahey and Maria Duce 1945–54', *Journal of Ecclesiastical History* 52: 3 (July, 2001), pp. 487–551.

Diner, Hasia, *Erin's Daughters in America: Irish Immigrant Women in the Nineteenth Century* (Baltimore: Johns Hopkins University Press, 1983).

Dolan, Anne, 'Killing and Bloody Sunday, November 1920', *Historical Journal* 49: 3 (2006), 789–810.

Dolan, Anne, *Commemorating the Irish Civil War: History and Memory, 1923–2000* (Cambridge: Cambridge University Press, 2003).

Doyle, Damian, 'A bio-critical study of Rosamond Jacob and her contemporaries', unpublished PhD thesis, University of Colorado, 2000.

Duby, Georges and Michelle Perrot (eds), *A History of Women: Emerging Feminism from Revolution to World War* (London: Belknap, 1993).

Dudley Edwards, Ruth, *Patrick Pearse. The Triumph of Failure* (Dublin: Irish Academic Press, 2006).

Dunphy, Richard, *The Making of Fianna Fáil Power in Ireland 1923–1948* (Oxford: Clarendon Press, 1995).

Elliott, Malcolm, 'Opposition to the First World War: the fate of conscientious objectors in Leicester', *Transactions of the Leicestershire Archaeological and Historical Society* 77 (2003), pp. 82–92.

English, Richard, *Ernie O'Malley IRA Intellectual* (Oxford: Oxford University Press, 1998).

English, Richard, *Radicals and the Republic: Socialist Republicanism in the Irish Free State 1925–1937* (Oxford: Clarendon Press, 1994).

Fallon, Charlotte, *Soul of Fire: A Biography of Mary MacSwiney* (Cork: Mercier, 1986).

Feely, Gerard M., *A History of Apprenticeship Nurse Training in Ireland* (London: Routledge, 2005).

Ferriter, Diarmaid, *Occasions of Sin: Sex and Society in Modern Ireland* (London: Profile, 2009).

Ferriter, Diarmaid, *The Transformation of Ireland, 1900–2000* (London: Profile, 2004).

Fitzpatrick, David, 'Divorce and separation in Modern Irish History', *Past and Present* 114 (Feb. 1987), pp. 172–96.

Fitzpatrick, David, 'The geography of Irish nationalism, 1910–1921' in C. H. E. Philpin (ed.), *Nationalism and Popular Protest in Ireland* (Cambridge: Cambridge University Press, 1987), pp. 113–44.

Foster, R. F., *Modern Ireland 1600–1972* (London: Penguin 1989).

Fothergill, Robert, A., *Private Chronicles: A Study of English Diaries* (London: Oxford University Press, 1974).

Garvin, Tom, *1922: The Birth of Irish Democracy* (Dublin: Gill & Macmillan, 1996).

Gaughan, J. Anthony, *Scouting in Ireland* (Dublin: Kingdom Books, 2006).

Gordon Bowe, Nicola and Elizabeth Cummings, *The Arts and Crafts Movements in Dublin & Edinburgh 1885–1925* (Dublin: Irish Academic Press, 1998).

Greaves, C. Desmond, *Liam Mellows and the Irish Revolution* (London: Lawrence & Wishart, 1971).

Hanley, Brian, *The IRA, 1926–1936* (Dublin: Four Courts, 2002).

Hanley, Brian, 'Moss Twomey, radicalism, and the IRA, 1931–33: a reassessment', *Saothar* 28 (2001), pp. 53–61.

Hart, Peter, *The IRA and Its Enemies: Violence and Community in Cork 1916–1923* (Oxford: Clarendon Press, 1998).

Hay, Marnie, 'The foundation and development of Na Fianna Éireann, 1909–16', *Irish Historical Studies* XXXVI: 141 (May 2008), pp. 53–71.

Helland, Janice, 'Embroidered spectacle: Celtic Revival as aristocratic display', in Betsey Taylor Fitzpatrick and James H. Murphy (eds), *The Irish Revival Reappraised* (Dublin: Four Courts, 2004), pp. 94–105.

Hill, Myrtle, *Women in Ireland: A Century of Change* (Belfast: Blackstaff, 2003).

Hoar, Adrian, *In Green and Red: The Lives of Frank Ryan* (Dingle: Brandon, 2004).

Hogan, Robert and Richard Burnham, *The Years of O'Casey, 1921–1926: A Documentary History* (Gerrards Cross: Colin Smythe, 1992).

Holden, Katherine, *The Shadow of Marriage: Singleness in England 1914–60* (Manchester: Manchester University Press, 2007).

Huff, Cynthia Anne, 'Reading as re-vision: approaches to reading manuscript diaries', *Biography* 23: 3 (2000), pp. 504–23.

Hufton, Olwen, 'Women in revolution 1789–1796', *Past and Present* 53 (1971), pp. 90–108.

Jacob, W. J., 'The Dublin family of Jacob', *Dublin Historical Record* 11: 4, (June–Aug. 1940), pp. 134–40.

Joannou, Maroula, 'Suffragette fiction and the fictions of suffrage', in Maroula Joannou and June Purvis (eds), *The Women's Suffrage Movement: New Feminist Perspectives* (Manchster: Manchester University Press, 1998), pp. 106–16.

Keogh, Dermot, Finbarr O'Shea and Carmel Quinlan (eds), *The Lost Decade: Ireland in the 1950s* (Cork: Mercier, 2004).

Laffan, Michael, *The Resurrection of Ireland: The Sinn Féin Party 1916–1923* (Cambridge: Cambridge University Press, 1999).

Lane, Leeann, '"In my mind I build a house": the quest for family in the children's fiction of Patricia Lynch', *Éire-Ireland* 44: 1 & 2 (Spring–Summer 2009), pp. 169–93.

Lane, Leeann, 'Rosamond Jacob: nationalism and suffrage', in Louise Ryan and Margaret Ward (eds), *Irish Women and the Vote. Becoming Citizens* (Dublin: Irish Academic Press, 2007), pp. 171–88.

Lane, Leeann, 'Female emigration and the cooperative movement in the writings of George Russell', *New Hibernia Review* 8: 4 (2004), pp. 84–100.

Lane, Leeann, '"It is in the cottages and farmers' houses that the nation is born": AE's *Irish Homestead* and the cultural revival', *Irish University Review* 33: 1 (Spring–Summer, 2003), pp. 165–81.

Lee, J. J., *Ireland 1912–1985* (Cambridge: Cambridge University Press, 1989).

Leerssen, Joep, *Mere Irish and Fíor-Ghael: Studies in the Idea of Irish Nationality, Its Development, and Literary Expression Prior to the Nineteenth Century*, 2nd edn (Cork: Cork University Press in association with Field Day, 1996).

Lejeune, Philippe, 'How do diaries end?', *Biography* 24: 1 (2001), pp. 99–112.

Levine, Philippa, *Feminist Lives in Victorian England* (Oxford: Blackwell 1990).

Luddy, Maria, *Prostitution and Irish Society 1800–1940* (Cambridge: Cambridge University Press, 2007).

Luddy, Maria, 'A "sinister and retrogressive" proposal: Irish women's opposition to the 1937 draft constitution', *Transactions of the Royal Historical Society* xv (2005), pp. 175–95.

Luddy, Maria, (ed.), *Women in Ireland 1800–1918: A Documentary History* (Cork: Cork University Press, 1995).

Luddy, Maria, *Hanna Sheehy Skeffington* (Dundalk: Historical Association of Ireland, 1995).

Lyons, F. S. L., 'The minority problem in the 26 counties' in Francis MacManus (ed.), *The Years of the Great Test* (Dublin: Mercier, 1967), pp. 92–103.

Mac Aodha, Breandán S., 'Was this a social revolution?' in Seán Ó Tuama (ed.), *The Gaelic League Idea* (Cork: Mercier, 1972), pp. 20–30.

MacDonagh, Oliver, *Jane Austen: Real and Imagined Worlds* (New Haven: Yale University Press, 1991).

MacDonagh, Oliver, *The Nineteenth Century Novel and Irish Social History: Some Aspects.* (Dublin: National University of Ireland, 1970).

Marreco, Anne, *The Rebel Countess* (London: Weidenfeld & Nicolson,1967).

Martin, Peter, *Censorship in the Two Irelands 1922–1939* (Dublin: Irish Academic Press, 2006).

Maume, Patrick, *The Long Gestation: Irish Nationalist Life 1891–1918* (Dublin: Gill & Macmillan, 1999).

McAvoy, Sandra, 'The regulation of sexuality in the Irish Free State, 1929–1935' in Greta Jones and Elizabeth Malcolm (eds), *Medicine, Disease and the State in Ireland, 1650–1940* (Cork: Cork University Press, 1999), pp. 253–66.

McAvoy, Sandra, 'Sex and the single girl: Ireland 1922–1949' in Chichi Aniagolu (ed.), *In From the Shadows: the UL Women's Studies Collection*, vol. III (Limerick: Women's Studies and Department of Government and Society, University of Limerick, 1997), pp. 55–67.

McCarthy, Pat, 'The Irish Volunteers in Waterford, Part I, 1913–1916', *Decies* 60 (2004), pp. 197–220.

McCarthy, Pat, 'The Irish Volunteers in Waterford, Part II', *Decies* 61 (2005), pp. 245–66.

McCoole, Sinead, *No Ordinary Women: Irish Female Activists in the Revolutionary Years* (Dublin: O'Brien, 2004).

McCormack, W. J., 'The intellectual revival (1830–50)', in Seamus Deane (ed.), *The Field Day Anthology of Irish Literature* (Derry: Field Day, 1991), 1, pp. 1, 173–7.

McGarry, Fearghal, *Eoin O'Duffy: A Self-Made Hero* (Oxford: Oxford University Press, 2005).

McGarry, Fearghal, *Frank Ryan* (Dundalk: Historical Association of Ireland, 2002).

McGarry, Fearghal, *Frank Ryan*, 2nd edn (Dublin: UCD Press, 2010).

McIlroy, John, 'The establishment of intellectual orthodoxy and the Stalinization of British Communism 1928–1933', *Past and Present* 192 (2006), pp. 187–230.

McMahon, *Grand Opportunity The Gaelic Revival and Irish Society, 1893-1910* (Syracuse: Syracuse University Press, 2008).

McMahon, Timothy G., '"To mould an important body of shepherds": the Gaelic summer colleges and the teaching of Irish history', in Lawrence W. McBride (ed.), *Reading Irish Histories: Texts, Contexts and Memory in Modern Ireland* (Dublin: Four Courts, 2003), pp. 118–39.

McMahon, Timothy G., '"All creeds and all classes"? Just who made up the Gaelic League?', *Éire-Ireland* Fall–Winter (2002), pp. 118–68.

Meaney, Gerardine, 'Regendering modernism: the woman artist in Irish women's fiction', *Women: A Cultural Review* 15: 1 (2004), pp. 67–82.

Morrison, Eve, 'The Bureau of Military History and female republican activism, 1913–23' in Maryann Valiulis (ed.), *Gender and Power in Irish History* (Dublin: Irish Academic Press, 2009), pp. 118–68.

Mulvilhill, Margaret, *Charlotte Despard* (London: Pandora, 1989).

Murphy, Cliona, *The Women's Suffrage Movement and Irish Society in the Early Twentieth Century* (New York: Harvester, 1989).

Murphy, William, 'Suffragettes and the transformation of political imprisonment in Ireland, 1912–1914', in Louise Ryan and Margaret Ward (eds), *Irish Women and the Vote. Becoming Citizens* (Dublin: Irish Academic Press, 2007), pp. 114–35.

Moran, Sean Farrell, *Patrick Pearse and the Politics of Redemption: The Mind of the Easter Rising, 1916* (Washington, DC: Catholic University of America Press, 1994).

Norquay, Glenda, *Voices and Votes: A Literary Anthology of the Women's Suffrage Campaign* (Manchester: Manchester University Press, 1995).

O'Brien Gerard and Tom Dunne (eds), *Catholic Ireland in the Eighteenth Century: Collected Essays of Maureen Wall* (Dublin: Geography Publications, 1989).

O Casey, Seán, *The Story of the Irish Citizen Army* (Dublin: Maunsel, 1919

O'Connor, Emmet, *Reds and the Green: Ireland, Russia and the Communist Internationals 1919–43* (Dublin: UCD Press, 2004).

Ó Drisceoil, Donal, *Peadar O'Donnell* (Cork: Cork University Press, 2001).

O'Faolain, Seán, *Countess Markievicz*, 3rd edn (London: Cresset Library, 1967).

O'Leary, Philip, *The Prose Literature of the Gaelic Revival, 1881–1921: Ideology and Innovation* (Pennsylvania: Pennsylvania State University Press, 1994).

O'Neill, Kevin, 'Mary Shackleton Leadbeater: Peaceful rebel' in Dáire Keogh and Nicholas Furlong (eds), *The Women of 1798* (Dublin: Four Courts, 1998), pp. 137–62.

O'Regan, Danae, 'Representations and attitudes of republican women in the novels of Annie M.P. Smithson (1873–1948) and Rosamond Jacob (1888–1960)' in Louise Ryan and Margaret Ward, (eds), *Irish Women and Nationalism: Soldiers, New Women and Wicked Hags* (Dublin: Irish Academic Press, 2004), pp. 80–95.

Pašeta, Senia, 'Censorship and its critics in the Irish Free State, 1922–1932', *Past and Present* (2003), pp. 193–218.

Preece, Rod, 'Darwinism, Christianity and the great vivisection debate', *Journal of the History of Ideas* 64: 3 (July 2003), pp. 399–419.

Pugh, Patricia, *Educate, Agitate, Organize: 100 Years of Fabian Socialism* (London: Methuen, 1984).

Purvis, June, *Emmeline Pankhurst* (London: Routledge, 2002).

Quinn, Antoinette, (ed.), 'Ireland/Herland: women and literary nationalism, 1845–1916' in Bourke et al. (eds), *The Field Day Anthology of Irish Writing*, v, pp. 895–900.

Rafter, Kevin, *Sinn Féin 1905–2005: In the Shadow of Gunmen* (Dublin: Gill & Macmillan, 2005).

Rapp, Dean, 'The early discovery of Freud by the British General Educated Public, 1912–1919', *Social History of Medicine* 3: 2 (Aug. 1990), pp. 217–44.

Reynolds, Paige, 'Modernist martydom: the funerals of Terence MacSwiney', *Modernism/Modernity* 9: 4 (2002), pp. 535–59.

Ryan, Louise, "'Drunken tans": representations of sex and violence in the Anglo-Irish War (1919–21), *Feminist Review* 66 (Autumn 2000), pp. 73–94.

Shannon, Richard, *The Age of Disraeli 1868–1881: The Rise of Tory Democracy* (London: Longman, 1992).

Smith, Angela, K., *Suffrage Discourse in Britain during the First World War* (Aldershot: Ashgate, 2005).

Smith, James M. *Ireland's Magdalen Laundries and the Nation's Architecture of Containment* (Manchester: Manchester University Press, 2007).

Smith, Nadia Clare, *Dorothy Macardle: A Life* (Dublin: Woodfield Press, 2007).

Smith, Nadia Clare, 'A "manly study"? Irish women historians as public intellectuals, 1868–1949', unpublished PhD dissertation, Boston College, 2003.

Sweeney, George, 'Irish hunger strikes and the cult of self-sacrifice', *Journal of Contemporary History* 28: 3 (July 1993), pp. 421–37.

Tweedy, Hilda, *A Link in the Chain: The Story of the Irish Housewives Association, 1942–1992* (Dublin: Attic Press, 1992).

Urquhart, Diane (ed.), *The Minutes of the Ulster Women's Unionist Council and Executive Committee 1911–1940* (Dublin: Irish Manuscripts Commission, 2001).

Urquhart, Diane, *Women in Ulster Politics, 1890–1940: A History Not Yet Told* (Dublin: Irish Academic Press, 2000).

Valiulis, Maryann 'Engendering citizenship: women's relationship to the state in Ireland and the United States in the post-suffrage period', in Maryann Valiulis and Mary O'Dowd (eds), *Women and Irish History* (Dublin: Wolfhound Press, 1997), pp. 159–72.

Valiulis, Maryann, 'Nether feminist nor flapper: the ecclesiastical construction of the ideal Irish woman', in Mary O'Dowd and Sabine Wichert (eds), *Chattel, Servant or Citizen. Women's Status in Church State and Society* (Belfast: Institute of Irish Studies, 1995), pp. 168–78.

Walker, Brian, (ed.), *Parliamentary Election Results in Ireland, 1801–1922* (Dublin: Royal Irish Academy, 1978).

Walker, Graham, "'The Irish Dr Goebbels": Frank Gallagher and Irish Republican propaganda', *Journal of Contemporary History* 27: 1 (Jan. 1992), pp. 149–65.

Walsh, Oonagh, *Anglican Women in Dublin: Philanthropy, Politics and Education in the Early Twentieth Century* (Dublin: UCD Press, 2005).

Walsh, Oonagh, 'Testimony from imprisoned women', in David Fitzpatrick (ed.), *Revolution? Ireland 1917–1923* (Dublin: Trinity History Workshop, 1990), pp. 69–87.

Walshe, Eibhear, *Kate O'Brien: A Writing Life* (Dublin: Irish Academic Press, 2006).

Ward, Margaret, *Hanna Sheehy Skeffington: A Life* (Cork: Attic Press, 1997).

Ward, Margaret, 'Nationalism, pacifism and internationalism, Louie Bennett, Hanna Sheehy Skeffington, and the problems of "defining feminism"', in Anthony Bradley and Maryann Valiulis (eds), *Gender and Sexuality in Modern Ireland* (Amherst: University of Massachusetts Press, 1997), pp. 60–84.

Ward, Margaret, 'The League of Women Delegates and Sinn Féin', *History Ireland* 4: 3 (Autumn 1996), pp. 37–41.

Ward, Margaret, *Unmanageable Revolutionaries: Women and Irish Nationalism* (London: Pluto Press, 1995).

Weihman, Lisa, 'Doing my bit for Ireland: transgressing gender in the Easter Rising', *Éire-Ireland* 39: 3–4 (2004), pp. 228–49.

Wigham, Maurice, *Newtown School Waterford 1798–1998: A History* (Waterford: Newtown School, 1998).

Wigham, Maurice, J., *The Irish Quakers: A Short History of the Religious Society of Friends in Ireland* (Dublin: Historical Committee of the Religious Society of Friends in Ireland, 1992).

Wills, Clair, *That Neutral Island: A History of Ireland during the Second World War* (London: Faber and Faber, 2007).

Wills, Clair, 'Women writers and the death of rural Ireland: realism and nostalgia in the 1940s', *Éire-Ireland* 41: 1 (2006), pp. 192–212.

Young, Phil, *Patricia Lynch, Storyteller* (Dublin: Liberties Press, 2005).

Index

—

Saor an Leanbh, 263
Second World War, 263
   bombing of Dublin, 274
   imminent, 273
   rationing, 274–5
sexuality, constructions of, 183–6
Sheehy Skeffington, Andrée, 141–2, 221,
   244, 264, 287
Sheehy Skeffington, Francis, 54, 64, 72,
   74, 76, 98–9
Sheehy Skeffington, Hanna, 27–8, 44,
   53–4, 64, 72–3, 78, 82, 84, 102, 110,
   130, 139, 181, 206, 212, 217, 222,
   240–1, 251, 260
   arrest of, 233
   encourages Jacob, 105
   views on Jacob, 107–8, 171
   visits America, 142–3
Sheehy Skeffington, Owen, 110, 181, 212,
   244
Sinn Féin, 25, 29–30, 91, 128, 218–19
   growth of, 125–6
   pro-German sympathies, 75
   relations with Labour Party, 131–2
   role of women in, 118, 127–30
   support for, 134
   Waterford branch, 29–30, 91, 125,
      130
Skeffington, Joseph, 141
Skinnider, Margaret, 90
Smith, James, 295
Smith, Nadia, 2–3
Socialist Republican Workers' Party of
   Ireland, 246
Society for the Prevention of Cruelty to
   Animals, 90
Society for the Prevention of Cruelty to
   Children, 237, 239
Solomons, Estella, 114
Somers, Charlie, 102
Somers, Lasairfhíona, 35, 65, 69, 104,
   250
   arrest of, 102
   encouragement of Jacob, 105
Somerville, Edith, 76
Spark, 96
Stephens, James, 56
Stephens, Ned, 106, 115, 188–9

Strangman, Mary, 55, 57, 83–4
Strike and Lock Out (1913), 66
suffrage
   campaign, 25–8, 36, 44–5, 49–50, 53–5,
      57, 62–3, 72, 76, 82–4
   fiction, 77–8, 81–2, 86
   violence, 111
Swanton (née Kingston), Daisy, 278, 298
Swanton, Billy, 278
Swik, 225, 245

Tod, Isabella, 16, 20, 170
Tone, Wolfe, 161, 208
trade unions, 153
Traynor, Oscar, 217, 237
Trench, Margot, 109
Tweedy, Hilda, 22, 263, 264, 284, 306

United Irishwomen, 235
Upton, J., 60, 90

voter impersonation, 133

Wall, Maureen, 300–1
Walsh, Annie, 72
Walsh, Liam, 88
Walsh, Oonagh, 32–3, 262
Walshe, Eibhear, 10
War of Independence, 91, 101, 130, 146–50,
   215
Ward, Margaret, 107–8, 194, 206
Waterford City
   barracks in, 93
   by-elections (1918), 93–4
   politics in: 91–2, 112–16; and class, 95
Waterford News, 45, 58, 62, 76, 93, 116
Waterford Standard, 58
Watson, Seton, 89
Webb, Josephine, 180
Wheeler, 130, 131
White, Vincent, 94, 112, 125, 133–4
White Cross, 147, 150
Whittle, Nicholas, 62, 92, 93–4, 95–6, 125,
   133
WILPF (Women's International League
   for Peace and Freedom), 15, 150,
   208, 251, 282
Winthrop, F. (Jacob's pseudonym), 145